C000161302

Perspectives in Male Psychology

BPS Textbooks in Psychology

BPS Wiley presents a comprehensive and authoritative series covering everything a student needs in order to complete an undergraduate degree in psychology. Refreshingly written to consider more than North American research, this series is the first to give a truly international perspective. Written by the very best names in the field, the series offers an extensive range of titles from introductory level through to final year optional modules, and every text fully complies with the BPS syllabus in the topic. No other series bears the BPS seal of approval!

Many of the books are supported by a companion website, featuring additional resource materials for both instructors and students, designed to encourage critical thinking and providing for all your course lecturing and testing needs.

For other titles in this series, please go to **http://psychsource.bps.org.uk**

Perspectives in Male Psychology

AN INTRODUCTION

LOUISE LIDDON & JOHN A. BARRY

The British
Psychological Society **WILEY** Blackwell

Registered Office(s)
John Wiley & Sons, Inc., 111 River Street, Hoboken, NJ 07030, USA
John Wiley & Sons Ltd, The Atrium, Southern Gate, Chichester, West Sussex, PO19 8SQ, UK

Editorial Office
The Atrium, Southern Gate, Chichester, West Sussex, PO19 8SQ, UK
For details of our global editorial offices, customer services, and more information about Wiley products visit us at www.wiley.com.

Wiley also publishes its books in a variety of electronic formats and by print-on-demand. Some content that appears in standard print versions of this book may not be available in other formats.

Library of Congress Cataloging-in-Publication Data
Names: Liddon, Louise, author. | Barry, John A. (Honorary lecturer in
   psychology), author. | John Wiley & Sons, publisher.
Title: Perspectives in male psychology : a scientific and humanistic
   approach / Louise Liddon, John A.Barry.
Description: Hoboken, NJ : John Wiley & Sons, [2021] | Series: BPS
   textbooks in psychology | Includes bibliographical references and index.
Identifiers: LCCN 2020043051 (print) | LCCN 2020043052 (ebook) | ISBN
   9781119685357 (paperback) | ISBN 9781119685364 (pdf) | ISBN
   9781119684930 (epub) | ISBN 9781119685340 (ebook)
Subjects: LCSH: Men--Psychology. | Masculinity.
Classification: LCC BF692.5 .L54 2021 (print) | LCC BF692.5 (ebook) | DDC
   155.3/32--dc23
LC record available at https://lccn.loc.gov/2020043051
LC ebook record available at https://lccn.loc.gov/2020043052

Cover image: Courtesy of John Barry
Cover design by Wiley

Set in 11/12.5pt Dante MT Std by Integra Software Services Pvt. Ltd, Pondicherry, India
Printed and bound by CPI Group (UK) Ltd, Croydon, CR0 4YY

C106539_050421

For our baby son Thomas, and to everyone who has wanted more for men and boys than has been available from the field of psychology in recent decades.

Brief Contents

Contents

List of Figures and Tables

List of Abbreviations

ABGT	Action-Based Group Therapy
ACEs	Adverse Childhood Experiences
ACS	Acute Coronary Syndrome
ACT	Acceptance and Commitment Therapy
ADHD	Attention Deficit Hyperactivity Disorder
ADT	Androgen Deprivation Therapy
AFVBC	Armed Forces and Veterans' Breakfast Clubs
AHSSBL	Arts, Humanities, Social Science, Business and Law
APA	American Psychological Society
APD	Auditory Processing Disorder
APS	Australian Psychological Society
AS	Asperger Syndrome
ASD	Autism Spectrum Disorder
ASPD	Antisocial Personality Disorder
ASRM	American Society for Reproductive Medicine
ASVAB	Armed Services Vocational Aptitude Battery
ATPF	All to Play for Football
BBC	British Broadcasting Corporation
BCT	Behaviour Change Technique
BDI	Beck Depression Inventory
BIGI	Basic Indicator of Gender Inequality
BMA	British Medical Association
BPA	Bisphenol A
BPS	British Psychological Society
BSRI	BEM Sex Role Inventory
CALM	Campaign Against Living Miserably

CAT	Cognitive Analytic Therapy
CBT	Cognitive Behavioural Therapy
CCTV	Closed-Circuit Television
CFT	Compassion Focused Therapy
CJS	Criminal Justice System
CMD	Common Mental Disorders
CMI	Chartered Management Institute
CPT	Cognitive Processing Therapy
CSA	Child Support Agency
CVD	Cardiovascular Disease
DCMH	Departments of Community *Mental Health*
DMS	Defence Medical Services
DoD	Department of Defense
DOE	Department for Education
DSM	Diagnostic and Statistical Manual of Mental Disorders
DV	Domestic Violence
EAP	Employee Assistance Programmes
ED	Erectile Dysfunction
EMDR	Eye Movement Desensitisation and Reprocessing
EPDS	Edinburgh Postnatal Depression Scale
ET	Existential Perspective
EUPD	Emotionally Unstable Personality Disorder
FASO	False Allegations Support Organisation
FDA	Food and Drug Administration
FIFA	Fédération Internationale de Football Association (International Federation of Association Football)
FSH	Follicle Stimulating Hormone
GGGI	Global Gender Gap Index
GIGO	'Garbage In, Garbage Out'
GS	Gender Studies
HEED	Healthcare, Early Education and Domestic Jobs
HESA	Higher Education Statistics Agency

HIV	Human Immunodeficiency Virus
HRQOL	Health-Related Quality Of Life
HSE	Health and Safety Executive
IAT	Implicit Association Test
ICD	International Classification of Disease
IPA	Interpretive Phenomenological Analysis
IPV	Intimate Partner Violence
IPVA	Interpersonal Violence and Abuse
IT	Information Technology
LTC	Long-Term Condition
MACE	Major Adverse Cardiac Events
MDRS	Male Depression Risk Scale
MOD	Ministry of Defence
MPN	Male Psychology Network
MRA	Men's Rights Activist
MRI	*Magnetic Resonance Imaging*
MRNI	Male Role Norms Inventory
NHS	National Health Service
NICHD	National Institute of Child Health and Human Development
NIMH	National Institute of Mental Health
ONS	Office for National Statistics
PCB	Polychlorinated biphenyls 15
PCOS	Polycystic Ovary Syndrome
PE	Prolonged Exposure Therapy
PhD	Doctor of Philosophy
PHE	Public Health England
PHQ-2	Patient Health Questionnaire-2
PMI	Positive Mindset Index
PND	Postnatal Depression
PPPM	Positive Psychology / Positive Masculinity
PSA	*Prostate-Specific Antigen*
PSYOPS	Psychological Operations

PTMF	Power Threat Meaning Framework
PTSD	Post-Traumatic Stress Disorder
RAF	Royal Air Force
RCT	Randomised Controlled Trial
REBT	Rational Emotive Behaviour Therapy
SAHD	Stay-At-Home Dads
SARS	Severe Acute Respiratory Syndrome
SD	Standard Deviation
SEM	Structural Equation Modelling
SEN	Special Educational Needs
STE	Science, Technology and Engineering
STEM	Science, Technology, Engineering and Mathematics
TBI	Traumatic Brain Injury
TIMSS	Trends in International Mathematics and Science Study
TMGS	Traditional Male Gender Script
TPB	Theory of Planned Behaviour
TV	Television
UAV	Unmanned Aerial Vehicles
UEFA	Union of European Football Associations
UK	United Kingdom
UN	United Nations
UNESCO	United Nations Educational, Scientific and Cultural Organization
US/USA	United States of America
VA	Veteran Affairs
VTP	Veterans' Transition Programme
WBEA	Wellbeing Benefits of Everyday Activities Scale
WHO	World Health Organization

Series Preface

Since the beginnings of psychology – the scientific study of the mind and behaviour – men, women and animals have been the subjects of theory, practice and research. It is only very recently that the psychology of men has become a formal branch of study.

Psychology is one of the most popular undergraduate degrees in many countries, e.g. the fourth most popular in the US and the second most popular in the UK. In other parts of the world psychology has become increasingly popular, e.g. in Turkey the number of psychology departments at universities increased from around 300 in 1986 to nearly 5000 by 2013 (Reddy et al., 2014).

An undergraduate degree in psychology not only reveals fascinating insights into why people behave the way we do, but also teaches students very transferable skills in numeracy, literacy and communication. Typically, most psychology students graduate into employment in a variety of areas. In most countries only a minority go on to train as professional psychologists, which involves further training at masters or doctoral degree level.

Psychology overlaps with other fields in the social sciences and humanities, as well as healthcare and statistics. There is even some overlap with the arts, e.g. poetry and literature (Kipling's poem *If—* in SPOTLIGHT box 12.4), television (*The Sopranos* in Section 11.5.4) and other aspects of popular culture (Section 12.5.2), making it a fascinating area of interest to so many people.

Male psychology is a dynamic and much needed new field focusing on the psychology of men and boys. It brings a more humanistic and scientific approach to the study of the psychology of men and boys than has been seen in recent decades when, for example, masculinity has been depicted, controversially, as homophobic and misogynistic.

Perspectives in Male Psychology: An Introduction is the first in a series of textbooks exploring the various facets of this complex field. These books will rely on the usual standards of psychology as a science to explore the key areas in which the uniqueness of men is discovered. Each book in the series will be written by one or more leading experts in the field, and include not only the latest in research in male psychology but also reassessments of previous research through a male psychology lens where required. The books are structured so they can be used as teaching and training resources, but they will also be stimulating for the layperson and undergraduate. The overall aim is to create a series of books that inform and stimulate further interest in this topic. Given the prominent interest in sex and gender as well as the growing interest in men's mental health in the modern world, I hope these are timely and helpful books.

Dr John Barry,
Honorary Lecturer in Psychology, University College London (UCL)
Series Editor, 2020

Preface

A lot has started happening in the world of male psychology in recent times. We are really pleased that you want to find out more and are joining us in exploring the psychology of men and boys from a fresh perspective.

This book came into being as the result of conversations with psychologists at conferences and public lectures. Although I (JB) initially saw male psychology as primarily a mental health topic, it soon became apparent that the core issues in male psychology were themes that recurred in several areas of psychology. For example, I was presenting research on the specific needs of men in therapy, and one of the findings was that men tended to want to just fix their problems, whereas women wanted to explore their feelings about the problem. A neurologist specialising in traumatic brain injury said this resonated exactly with what she saw in the sex difference in the recovery of her clients – all patients wanted to get their life back on track, but the female clients were more inclined to talk about their feelings during the process, whereas the men mostly wanted to get themselves fixed.

We soon found that other psychologists, specialising in sports, the military and education, identified with what we were saying about male psychology. Across different topic areas, male psychology was an 'aha' moment for many, and it became apparent that male psychology was the hub at the centre of a Venn diagram, connecting the various topic areas of psychology (not unlike the cover of this book). Drawing these connections together in a single book seemed like a sensible way to answer the questions people started asking us.

Because the topic was gaining as much interest outside of psychology as within, it made sense to make the book accessible to professionals outside psychology (e.g. counsellors, coaches) and people working in a variety of related fields (e.g. volunteers and workers in charities dealing with men). In fact, we were finding that many non-psychologists were more informed about men's psychology than were many psychologists, having gained insights from working in the various charities that support men's mental health, or in some cases being users of these services. Many of these non-professionals are volunteers with limited income, and the black-and-white illustrations in this book are part of the effort to ensure that cost was not too much of an obstacle to finding out about male psychology.

In researching this book we (JB and LL) realised that there was not only no existing book that tied the relevant topics together, but much less published literature on these topics than might be expected for such a wide-ranging field. The reason for this is possibly academic barriers to research and publication, which anecdotally have impacted many people interested in this field. For example, research can be delayed or prevented by ethics committees, or completed research can be rejected by journals, and remain unpublished or published in minor journals overlooked by most of academia. I (JB) have extensive experience with various ethics committees and journals, so have my own insights into this issue. However, I am very grateful to those ethics committees that have been supportive, and to those journals that have published our work. Although some of these publications have been relatively successful, some of the publications in more modest journals deserve equal success. For example, my paper with Sam Russ et al. was turned down by several mainstream psychology journals before being accepted by *New Male Studies*, and I am grateful to the editor, Professor Miles Groth, for giving this excellent paper a home (Russ et al., 2015).

My (JB) decision to move from women's health to male psychology means that I have gone from being published in internationally recognised journals to – usually – much less well recognised journals. This in part is a reflection on the relative value that academia – and society – places on women's issues compared to men's issues, something that Martin Seager has termed 'male gender blindness'. But on a more optimistic note, in only a few years we have gone from the academic hinterlands to having a handful of more prestigious publications, e.g. *BMC Ophthalmology* and *Infant and Child Development*, including one in the *British Journal of Clinical Psychology* which has remained one of their top downloads since publication in 2017 (Liddon et al., 2017). Also, we have been cited relatively widely in the press and social media, which reflects our experience of how the general public have been ahead of professional psychologists in awareness and understanding of male psychology issues.

The aim of this book is to encourage learning and reflection on what currently are some of the most important topics and issues of male psychology. Other topics could have been included (e.g. male circumcision) or dealt with at greater length (e.g. relationships) and our intention is to deliver to the reader the best information on key topics in future books in this series.

The intended readership is relatively wide. This is a new field, so even very experienced psychologists might not have come across information on this topic previously. With this in mind, the book has been written so as to connect with academics at every level, while also being accessible to the intelligent lay reader. Some concession has been made to the breadth of readership in terms of keeping technical language and information to a minimum. This has meant excluding some details of inferential statistics (*p* values etc) which some academics would have liked to have seen, though full references are included for all studies mentioned, so the interested reader can find details in the original publications. We have however included two widely recognised measures of effect size, Cohen's d and Pearson's r (see glossary), mostly because they are relatively easy to understand. The result is a book that is pitched somewhere down the middle of the readership, probably at about an undergraduate level.

This book is significant in several ways. Firstly, it deals with issues that are widespread, are serious in terms of their impact (e.g. crime, suicide) and have not been highlighted in quite the same way before. Secondly, issues around sex and gender appear to grow more complex day by day, and correspondingly the need for clarity on these issues has become more pressing. Thirdly, the way gender issues have been dealt with up to now has left room for improvement. When I (JB) started researching with Martin Seager and others in 2011, before I initiated the Male Psychology Network in Feb 2014, our starting point was the dominant model of masculinity: the deficit model. We published a paper (Seager et al., 2014a) that, in retrospect, suffered from many of the flaws in the deficit model that we discuss in this book (see Section 12.2) which we now recognise as beta bias (we combined men and women in the factor analysis sample for our gender scripts), the presumption that masculinity is harmful to mental health (the 'deficit model') and the 'schoolboy error' of tacitly presuming that correlation indicates causation. One of the aims of this book is to create a better informed starting point for researchers and others, so that the repetition of flaws of previous research can be avoided.

This book aims to give an overview of what we know about the different aspects of male psychology. It also highlights recurring themes that are woven through the different topic chapters, as well as evaluating – where necessary – the theory and research. Although the book is written at the level of the psychology undergraduate, it will be accessible to both the informed lay reader, and informative to experienced professional psychologists who want to familiarise themselves using a resource based on science and research evidence. The structure of the book is intended to make the subject easily accessible, and the companion website offers opportunities for learning and reflection, that will be especially useful for tutors who want ideas for seminars. This online material also encourage readers to think independently about the issues raised.

As well as being educational, many readers will find the content interesting. This is partly because much of it will be new, but also partly because it combines two topics that lots of people find fascinating: understanding the psychology of men, and understanding what makes men and women different. This is the first book to achieve this from the position of male psychology.

The process of writing this book has been a challenging but rewarding one. It has allowed us to explore in greater detail topics we are familiar with (e.g. health and mental health) and discover the connections with topics we were once less familiar with (e.g. sports and military psychology). This process was punctuated with 'aha!' moments, such as the realisation that the army – for all the good and bad that can be said about it – can be thought of as the original and ultimate Men's Shed. (We mean that with great respect to both the Armed Forces and the Men's Sheds movement!)

We look forward to working on the rest of the books in this series, and hope that this introductory book whets readers' appetite for more.

Louise Liddon
John Barry,
England, 2021

Acknowledgements

We owe our gratitude to so many people who have inspired, encouraged, supported and assisted us in making this book possible. Our thanks go especially to everyone who voted for a Male Psychology Section of the British Psychological Society (BPS), all those who have attended the Male Psychology Network (MPN) conferences at University College London (UCL) between 2014 and 2019 and given free and open lectures at UCL for the MPN, all of the authors of chapters for the *Handbook of Male Psychology and Mental Health*, and all of the academic journal editors that took the risk of disapproval from peers by publishing papers on male psychology, and in some cases having this rewarded with a much greater number of readers than any of us could have hoped for. We are especially thankful to the Wiley team for their support during the coronavirus pandemic of 2020, and to our wonderful illustrator, Aimee McLernon, who helped bring our ideas to life with such artistry. We extend our appreciation to all of the people who volunteer their time tirelessly to help educate the public on male psychology issues, and support the men and boys who need – often very desperately – their support. A special acknowledgement is needed for consultant clinical psychologist Martin Seager, who started the campaign for a BPS Section for male psychology, and whose seemingly endless energy, insight and knowledge have been invaluable resources for all of us.

About the Authors

John Barry

John Barry is a Chartered Psychologist and Associate Fellow of the British Psychological Society (BPS), Honorary Lecturer in Psychology at University College London, clinical hypnotherapist and author of around 70 peer-reviewed publications on a variety of topics in psychology and health, including many on male psychology. He has also co-authored letters to *The Psychologist* magazine to raise awareness of issues relevant to male psychology. John co-founded both the Male Psychology Network and the Male Psychology Section of the BPS, and has been lead organiser of the Male Psychology Conference (2014–present) and co-editor of the *Palgrave Handbook of Male Psychology and Mental Health* (2019). At time of writing John is Chair of the Male Psychology Section of the BPS and previously was the first Honorary Secretary of the Male Psychology Section. John's interest is not only in male psychology; his PhD was on the *Psychological Aspects of Polycystic Ovary Syndrome*, which is also the title of his book, published by Palgrave Macmillan (2019).

Louise Liddon

Louise is an independent researcher and author in the field of male psychology. In addition to *Perspectives in Male Psychology*, her work also includes a chapter in the seminal and successful *Palgrave Handbook of Male Psychology and Mental Health* called 'What are the factors that make a male-friendly therapy?' and a number of research papers such as 'Gender differences in preferences for psychological treatment, coping strategies, and triggers to help-seeking', published in the *British Journal of Clinical Psychology* (2017), which is one of this journal's top 20 downloads since publication. Louise has been a member of the BPS Male Psychology Section Committee since its creation and was elected secretary in 2019. Louise has previous work experience as a specialist mentor for students with mental health problems, has tutored for an online mental health course and has worked as a support worker in a secure mental health unit. Louise has an MSc in Health Psychology and BSc in Psychology. Previous to her psychology studies, Louise worked as a project manager for a multinational corporate company.

Part 1

An Introduction to Perspectives in Male Psychology

1 How to Use This Book Effectively

CHAPTER OUTLINE

LEARNING OUTCOMES

By the end of this chapter, you should be able to:

1. Understand how the chapters are structured so the book can be used effectively
2. Be aware of learning and reflective opportunities
3. Be aware of the potential usages of the material in this book and the responsibility attached to that usage
4. Recognise the role of self-care when reading about content that could potentially bring about challenging emotions

Perspectives in Male Psychology: An Introduction, First Edition.
Louise Liddon and John A. Barry.
© 2021 John Wiley & Sons, Ltd. Published 2021 by John Wiley & Sons, Ltd.

1.1 INTRODUCTION

To get the best out of this book it is worth taking a few minutes to read this chapter to learn a little more about its structure and content.

1.2 BOOK STRUCTURE AND CONTENT

1.2.1 *Book Structure*

As can be seen from the contents page, the book is split into four parts:

- *Part 1: An introduction to perspectives in male psychology*
  This part consists of one chapter, How to Use this Book Effectively, and provides some context to the book.
- *Part 2: An introduction to male psychology*
  This part consists of two chapters, Male Psychology: An Introduction and Studying Sex and Gender Differences: An Introduction, which provide context for Part 3.
- *Part 3: 'Male psychology and ...'*
  This part consists of nine different areas of focus: Child Development; Education; Sport and Exercise; The Workplace; Forensics and Crime; The Military; Mental Health, Therapy and Support Services; Health and Wellbeing; and Regarding Masculinity.
- *Part 4: Concluding remarks and final thoughts*
  The final part of this book consists of some concluding remarks based on the contents of the book, starting with a summary of the key themes uncovered in the course of writing this book, an outline of a systems approach to male psychology and a list of recommendations for research and further development of male psychology as a discipline.

1.2.2 *Book Content*

Writing an introductory book that explores the psychology of men and boys is a potentially enormous task, focusing primarily on roughly half of humanity, with implications for the whole of humanity, encompassing numerous areas of interest across the human condition. You may therefore be wondering why we have included one topic area and not another. Our choices were based on many considerations, such as what we thought would be most interesting, important, relevant to the field of psychology, and with at least a basic evidence base. Future books within the series will delve deeper into some topics addressed here, as well as exploring new areas not covered here. In the present book we have aimed to, where appropriate, incorporate information that shows where there is another point of view on a topic.

1.2.3 *Readability of Content*

Writing a book that translates psychological science into an accessible format is a challenge for any author. If a book is written only for specialists, it excludes others who may benefit from reading the book, but if it's too accessible, there is a concern that the material lacks precision. In this book we have tried to find a middle ground between writing for professional psychologists and writing for the intelligent layperson. In practice this means using as little technical language and statistical detail as possible, while maintaining accuracy. Where we haven't been able to avoid necessary technical terms, we have attempted to explain such terms in the glossary (see companion website).

1.3 CHAPTER STRUCTURE AND CONTENT

All chapters follow a similar structure in order to provide easy, clear presentation and access. Each chapter is broken down as follows:

Start of chapter

The beginning section of each chapter is structured to allow you to identify, at a glance, areas of interest to you:

- **Chapter title**
- *Chapter outline*
- *Learning outcomes*

Main body of chapter

The main body of each chapter contains description, analysis and evaluation of the specific area of focus. These have been broken down into different sections and subsections:

- *Introduction*
- *Sections and subsections*
- *Spotlight boxes*

- *Summary*
- *Concluding remarks*

Within each chapter some of the material is flagged up for special attention in three ways.

- Textboxes 'spotlight' material that is particularly relevant or interesting, as well as recurring themes found in male psychology.
- Themes are flagged in the body of text in each chapter. Themes are summarised in Figure 13.2. The themes are: unintended consequences (resulting from things like 'slow violence'), the nature/nurture debate (often resulting in reductionism), help-seeking (often resulting in victim-blaming), research and methodology (featuring flawed definitions and over-interpretation of findings, and overlooking the importance of sex differences – the difference that makes the difference, 'there are more similarities than differences', yin and yang), bias in research (gamma bias, delta bias, population bias, 'unknown unknowns').
- Information in one section that is relevant to another is flagged as, for example, '(Section 13.2)', indicating that you should see the second section of Chapter 13.

1.4 OPPORTUNITIES FOR REFLECTION AND LEARNING (ONLINE ONLY)

To develop a sound understanding of male psychology (and sex and gender issues in general) it is worth trying to be as objective as possible. This means basing your understanding on objective evidence as opposed to relying on your subjective views based on experiences, assumptions, emotions etc. While it is impossible to be truly objective, you should aim to be as aware as possible of your own perceptions, personal history and biases, and explore the impact these may have on your position. On the Wiley companion website we have provided a few questions to help you both self-reflect and discuss with others the chapter content. We have also provided some further reading and additional resources to enhance your learning experience. Below is an example of the types of content that appears on the Wiley website accompanying this book. Note that not all chapters will contain all possible types of the additional material.

Questions

- Reflection (questions suited to a person thinking on their own and referring specially to their own biases etc)
- Scenario-based questions (questions related to topic(s))
- Discussion points (questions suited to groups such as a class-room exercise)
- Essay questions (questions suited to a person writing an essay)

Further reading

- Books
- Journal articles
- Websites
- Reports

Types of resources

- Videos
- Films
- Books
- Book chapters
- Journal articles
- Reports
- Blogs
- Websites

1.5 RESPONSIBLE USE OF BOOK MATERIAL

As this book is presenting some ideas for the first time, readers will probably appreciate that – for the sake of brevity and clarity – most of the material will describe the male psychology perspective more than other perspectives (see Section 2.2) Readers are encouraged to read around any particular subject and make up their minds based on the balance of evidence available. There are other points of view and new research findings, and they should be given due consideration.

1.6 SELF-CARE

Discussions about sex and gender can be enlightening and beneficial, and also challenging, emotive and confusing, but that doesn't mean we should never talk about these matters. You may have bought this book out of general interest, or because you are struggling with a personal issue and are looking for answers. Although you will probably find this book useful, it is not in any way designed as a form of therapy or self-help, but rather as an introduction to some things we think are important to the field of male psychology. We therefore hope you enjoy this book, but if any of the information in these pages brings up difficult emotions for you, then please do engage in some self-care or seek professional help. It might be an idea before you read further to think about what you could do if negative emotions were to arise. This book covers many serious issues and, we hope, helps to develop the narratives around these topics in a positive way and create a new discourse, but readers might find some of the material challenging and should be prepared to take care of themselves while reading this book.

1.7 CONCLUDING REMARKS

You can familiarise yourself with the layout and structure of this book in order to use it more effectively. Remember to engage with the additional resources and opportunities for learning and reflection to enhance your experience of the book. This book may be utilised for a range of purposes, and readers should take responsibility for their particular usage. Try and be aware of any self-care needs that may occur when reading this book and think ahead to any challenging emotions that may arise.

Part 2

An Introduction to Male Psychology

2 Male Psychology: An Introduction

CHAPTER OUTLINE

LEARNING OUTCOMES

By the end of this chapter, you should be able to:

1. Offer a definition of male psychology

Perspectives in Male Psychology: An Introduction, First Edition.
Louise Liddon and John A. Barry.
© 2021 John Wiley & Sons, Ltd. Published 2021 by John Wiley & Sons, Ltd.

2. Gain some insight into the theoretical basis of male psychology
3. Understand how male psychology is different to other perspectives e.g. gender studies
4. Understand the benefits of studying male psychology
5. Appreciate the how male psychology values being practical, and seeks realistic solutions to real-world problems

2.1 INTRODUCTION

This chapter starts by providing a definition as to what male psychology is, looks briefly at the origins of male psychology as an academic field and highlights why it is a much needed area, and how it is different from other approaches to studying men and gender.

2.2 WHAT IS MALE PSYCHOLOGY?

Male psychology is a new field within the discipline of psychology, with a focus on men and boys. Below are some examples of what male psychology is about.

Studying men and boys:

- in different settings (e.g. school or university)
- using different services (e.g. health, legal)
- from different perspectives (e.g. evolutionary, social)
- in the light of different theories (e.g. gamma bias, social identity theory)
- as an essential group (e.g. biological statistical norms)
- as specific demographics (e.g. age groups, social class)

Areas of interest may include:

- issues that predominantly impact men and boys, e.g. suicide, rough sleeping
- issues that may impact women more than men, but where the impact on men is under-researched, e.g. male victims of sexual abuse
- understanding the strengths that men often have, and how these can potentially be harnessed to help solve men's problems e.g. wanting to take control of problems.

Questions someone coming from a male psychology perspective might have:

- What does existing research tell us about masculinity?
- How can we best help with the mental health of men?
- What are the causes of male criminality?
- What are the causes of boys' underperformance in school?

Activities in male psychology may include:

- Conducting research (e.g. testing hypotheses, designing therapies)
- Work in the community (e.g. with homeless men)
- Clinical practice (i.e. conducting therapy)
- Teaching male psychology
- Informing government policy
- Disseminating factual information in the media

2.3 ORIGINS OF MALE PSYCHOLOGY

Early ventures into the field of men's psychology in the US in the 1990s borrowed from concepts in sociology and feminism. They developed a 'deficit view' of masculinity, focusing on the ways in which masculinity might harm men and the people around them.

A new development has taken place in the past decade, which has brought a more recognisably psychological approach to understanding men, placing much less emphasis on sociocultural theories of masculinity and more emphasis on science and clinical practice. This began in the UK as the Men's Mental Health Research Team (MMHRT) in 2011, becoming in 2014 the Male Psychology Network (MPN), a focal point for therapists, researchers, lecturers and third sector workers and volunteers. 2014 saw the first annual Male Psychology Conference, bringing together academics and therapists from around the world, especially at that time the UK, US and Canada. The same year saw the first academic publications from the UK-based MPN research group, and 2018 saw the first professional male psychology body (the Male Psychology Section of the British Psychological Society (BPS)), which was first proposed in 2010 by consultant clinical psychologist Martin Seager. The year 2019 saw the first major book on the topic (the *Palgrave Handbook of Male Psychology and Mental Health*), which has been an international success, and 2020 saw the first undergraduate module on the subject (at the University of Sunderland, UK). Although a relative newcomer in academic terms, male psychology is a dynamic new field and – arguably – the leading edge today in understanding the psychology of men and boys.

2.4 FOUNDATIONS OF MALE PSYCHOLOGY

Male psychology aims to understand the psychology of men and boys. This involves various aspects, including:

- identifying patterns and themes relevant to males in key areas (mental health, education etc; Section 13.2)
- expanding knowledge and insights relating to the lives of men and boys, and consequently – given that we all share this world – improving the lives of women and girls
- gaining a broader understanding of men and boys and their interactions with their social environment

2.4.1 *Male Psychology Recognises that Sex and Gender Differences Exist to Varying Degrees*

Much of the study of one sex requires an understanding of the other sex, thus one aspect of male psychology is about understanding sex differences. For example, men seek psychological help less than women do, and understanding this is helped by an assessment of sex differences in the needs and preferences of men and women for therapy (Holloway et al., 2018; Liddon et al., 2017; Russ et al., 2015). In one respect, male psychology could be seen as one half of the study of sex differences research. However, it goes deeper than that, and can be considered the exploration of the complex, multifaceted experience of males. This has been overlooked in the academic literature, with research on 'gender' and 'inequality' being focused on women or sexual minorities.

2.4.2 *Male Psychology is Ethical and Respectful*

The BPS is the representative body for psychologists and psychology in the United Kingdom. The BPS Code of Ethics (Section 3.1) states that gender differences are to be respected: 'Respect for the dignity of persons and peoples is one of the most fundamental and universal ethical principles across geographical and cultural boundaries, and across professional disciplines. It provides the philosophical foundation for many of the other ethical principles. Respect for dignity recognises the inherent worth of all human beings, regardless of perceived or real differences in social status, ethnic origin, gender, capacities, or any other such group-based characteristics' (British Psychological Society et al., 2018, p. 5).

2.4.3 *Male Psychology Recognises the Complexity of the Human Condition and Takes a Holistic Approach*

Male psychology takes a holistic approach to the person, thus looking at men from different perspectives (e.g. biological, evolutionary, humanistic) and in different areas of life (e.g. school, sport, workplace, healthcare), and considers the role of the environment. It not only spans almost every topic in psychology, but also accepts that there are many ways to be a man, without always needing to put men into different demographic or other categories. It is also about understanding men in relation to women, as shown by the inclusion of women as researchers and participants in many of the studies in male psychology. It also relates to other fields, such as biology and sociology, and is more interested in relationships between disciplines than in reinforcing academic or philosophical silos.

Male psychology is about focusing not solely on differences or inequalities but on the broader cultural and historical context, considering variables which may enhance our understanding, such as the roles of the workplace in shaping behaviour, of evolutionary adaptations in shaping traits and of childhood trauma in influencing delinquency. Understanding the causes of antisocial behaviour is not equivalent to excusing that behaviour, but is about gaining a valid understanding of causes – and perhaps then the solutions – to social problems of this kind (see Chapter 8). Male psychology studies the male gender holistically, coming from as many perspectives as prove relevant and useful.

2.4.4 *Comment on Intersectionality*

The primary focus of male psychology is on men in general, rather than splitting the focus into subdivisions of men. Although sometimes it is important to focus on specific demographics, e.g. in study of homophobia (see Section 6.5.2), or ethnic differences in prostate cancer (see Section 10.2.5), as a general rule most of the issues facing men are faced by almost all men to a greater or lesser degree. For example, Black men are more likely than white men to suffer from prostate cancer. However, prostate cancer is an important issue for all men, so focusing on trying to improve prostate cancer outcomes for all men provides an opportunity to improve the situation for groups who are especially impacted by it. If specific extra help is needed for particular groups, that is to be investigated too.

An analogy is that medicine is a legitimate category of science. Medicine has subdivisions for older people, children, cancer etc. The subdivisions are vital, but an overarching meta-discipline is vital too. People who specialise in the subdivisions benefit greatly by learning about the general field first, and new information in one field can be shared with others.

2.4.5 *Comment on Identity Politics*

Male psychology is not about identity politics. Firstly, male psychology does not encourage men to completely define themselves as men as their primary identity, but rather to understand and value being a man. Secondly, male psychology is not concerned with politics either in terms of political parties or gender politics, gender power relations etc. Exceptions to this are instances where men's wellbeing is impacted by laws or policies, in which case it is important that those who are responsible for these laws or policies should make adjustments.

2.4.6 *Male Psychology is Evidence-Based*

Male psychology is a new field with the first shoots of an evidence base having emerged. The evidence so far suggests that a humanistic approach to men's mental health is needed, as well as a evolutionary/biopsychosocial understanding of the roots of male psychology. Although the sociocultural view is also important, the overreliance on that perspective in recent decades has not yielded impressive results (Section 5.5.1). If male psychology is successful it must be guided by theories that stand up to testing, and clinical practice that is evidence-based (see SPOTLIGHT box 12.2). Male psychology supports the view of testing and revising theories in the light of evidence.

2.5 WHY STUDY MALE PSYCHOLOGY?

Other fields have studied the psychology of men either as a specific aim of the research, or as a byproduct of other research. Section 2.5.1 will look at why male psychology is needed.

2.5.1 *Male Psychology Offers a New Way of Looking at Sex and Gender*

There are many possible viewpoints, and no doubt some will be more applicable to some issues more than others. Feminism has been very helpful in highlighting the importance of gender, but has focused mainly on women and explained phenomena mainly from a female and sociopolitical perspective, involving ideas of patriarchy, power and privilege (see SPOTLIGHT box 12.1).

Male psychology offers a more science-based view of the psychology of men, incorporating a range of perspectives (evolutionary, biological, sociocultural and humanistic) as an explanatory framework. It is hoped that findings from male psychology will be useful to women too. For example, our suggestions for male-friendly therapy (see Figure 11.3, Male-friendly therapies) may well be useful to any women who find the present standard model of therapy does not suit them.

In contrast to the scientific approach of male psychology, *men's studies* views masculinity as a social construct, with a postmodernist preoccupation with identity, power and subjectivity (Capraro, 2004). Men's studies has a lot in common with women's studies and feminism, and many men's studies scholars (e.g. Kimmel, 1987) are activists who regard themselves as engaged in the larger project of changing men away from traditional masculinity, which is seen as psychologically dysfunctional and causing sex role strain (Pleck, 1981). This is part of the *New Psychology of Men* that became popular in the US in the 1990s, taking a 'deficit approach' to men's psychology, viewing masculinity as a source of mental health problems (Levant & Pollack, 1995). This contrasts with male psychology, which takes a more psychological and scientific approach, and a more humanistic approach in being willing to see how we can harness the strengths in men and masculinity in a beneficial way.

2.5.2 *Male Psychology Values Practical Solutions*

As a general principle, male psychology is interested in building practical solutions. These are ideally theory-driven and based on evidence. This book gives several examples of where problems are identified or redefined and solutions suggested (see Section 13.4).

2.5.3 *Male Psychology is Relevant to a Range of Careers*

Because of the relevance of male psychology across the spectrum of topics in psychology, this subject might be useful in a range of occupations, for example:

1. Jobs related to child development, such as teaching or child psychology
2. Jobs in education, such as mentoring male students of all ages
3. Jobs involving sports and exercise
4. Human resources or workplace stress-management
5. Jobs related to crime, such as the police or social services
6. Working with military personnel

7. Working as a therapist or mental health support of any kind (e.g. with the homeless)
8. Jobs related to health or wellbeing
9. Lecturing on any of these topics, including on sex differences or masculinity
10. Working as a therapist in areas related to any of these topics

2.5.4 *Male Psychology Makes Common Sense*

It has been found that laypeople can predict which social science studies can be replicated, suggesting that a certain amount of common sense is relevant to judging the validity of psychological research (Hoogeveen et al., 2019). Some of the findings of research in male psychology – for example, findings that women cope with stress by talking about their feelings more than men do – have seemed novel to academics, but were often familiar to therapists and the general public (Holloway et al., 2018; Lemkey & Barry, 2015; Russ et al., 2015). This situation hints at the 'reality gap' between what is produced in gender studies and the everyday experiences of the average person (see Section 5.5.1). A famous example is that of feminist author Naomi Wolf, who claimed in her best-selling book *The Beauty Myth* that 150,000 women in the US were dying from anorexia-related eating disorders each year (Wolf, 1991), when in fact the true figure was in the region of 100–400 per year (Sommers, 1995).

2.5.5 *Male Psychology Brings a New Perspective*

Sometimes people – in science as in everyday life – get used to seeing things in a particular way, and don't notice that their thinking contains certain blind spots. Male psychology brings a fresh perspective and challenges outdated ways of thinking.

2.5.5.1 *Cognitive bias regarding gender: gamma bias*

It is normal for people to see their world in ways that are not perfectly rational. Since the 1960s a wide range of biases and errors in cognition have been identified, some of which can cause mental health problems (Beck, 1967). Common cognitive distortions are *magnification* – the tendency to exaggerate the importance of things – and *minimisation* – the tendency to reduce the importance of things. In relation to gender, *alpha bias* is the tendency to exaggerate or magnify gender differences, and *beta bias* is the tendency to overlook or minimise gender differences.

A cognitive distortion that combines alpha and beta bias is *gamma bias*, which is the tendency to magnify some gender differences while simultaneously minimising others (Seager & Barry, 2019). This is suggested to be a widespread distortion in modern Western culture, and can be conceptualised in a *gender distortion matrix* where agency (doing, or being done to) interacts with types of events (good events, bad events), resulting in four cells explaining *perpetration, victimhood, privilege* and *celebration*. Examples from each cell are:

When people **do harm** (perpetration)
Being male is magnified e.g. male criminality is 'toxic masculinity'
Being female is minimised e.g. women's crime is due to trauma, deprivation etc
When people **are harmed** (victimhood)
Being male is minimised e.g. male victims of domestic violence are overlooked
Being female is magnified e.g. female victims of domestic violence are highlighted
When people **are successful** (privilege)
Being male is magnified e.g. men's wealth is 'privilege' or due to 'sexist wage gap'
Being female is minimised e.g. unremarked that 13 girls go to university for every 10 boys
When people **do good things** (celebration)
Being female is magnified e.g. UN Days celebrate women more for their gender than their actions
Being male is minimised e.g. the fact that most dirty / dangerous but essential jobs are done by men is not celebrated

Gamma bias is related to concepts such as the *gender empathy gap*, which describes the phenomenon of people caring more about women's wellbeing than men's (Collins, 2019), and *male gender blindness*, where problems facing men are less visible than women's problems (Seager et al., 2014b). These inter-related phenomena probably explain the finding that – contrary to *Social Identity Theory* (Tajfel & Turner, 1979), which would predict that people favour others similar to themselves – both men and women tend to have more empathy for women than men (Rudman & Goodwin, 2004). Favouring women may have significant adaptive value in evolutionary terms, in that women are more necessary to population growth than are men (Warren Farrell, 2001).

2.5.5.2   Delta bias

Delta bias is another cognitive distortion, where traditional gender roles are applauded but only when the performer of an activity is not of the traditional gender for that activity (Seager & Barry, 2020). An example of this is encouraging women to take on the traditional male role (placing career over family) and simultaneously encouraging men to be less career-orientated and more focused on housework.

2.6 WHAT DO PSYCHOLOGISTS GENERALLY MEAN BY *PERSPECTIVES*

While broadly speaking a perspective is a particular way of looking at something, within the field of psychology it relates more specifically to certain ways in which we regard human behaviour.

There are several different perspectives in psychology. The main ones are the evolutionary, social, biological, humanistic, psychodynamic, behavioural and cognitive perspectives (Fernald, 2007). Other perspectives can be important, though are generally considered subsets, combinations or variations of the main perspectives.

It is possible to look at any example of human behaviour from different perspectives, and the explanation for their behaviour will be different from each perspective. This doesn't mean that one perspective is right and the others are wrong, or that all are equally right; it is usually the case that – given a specific type of behaviour – one explanation fits better than the others, or that two or three perspectives combine to give a satisfactory explanation ('triangulation').

For example, how might different perspectives in psychology explain one man shouting at another man in the street? The evolutionary perspective might suggest that in some way his behaviour is aiding his survival; the social approach might suggest it is part of assertion of his social group identity; the biological explanation might say low blood-sugar levels are causing an attack of hypoglycaemia-related aggression; the humanistic approach might say his behaviour is caused by a frustration of the ability to achieve basic human needs such as a sense of safety; the psychodynamic approach might suggest that he is displacing his feeling of anger towards his boss onto a passerby; the behavioural approach might say the man has found that when he shouts at others he gets what he wants.

As you can see, some of these explanations are more likely than others. In this book, we have chosen to focus mainly on the evolutionary, social, biological and humanistic approaches because these are the ones that tend to be the most relevant in assessing male psychology. This doesn't mean that other perspectives are not relevant. For example, the cognitive perspective is important in relation to social cognition (see Section 2.5.5.1) and psychodynamic and behavioural processes are crucial in some therapies discussed in this book (see Chapter 11).

Note that we use the term 'humanistic perspective' in a broad sense, which includes Maslow's hierarchy of needs (Maslow, 1943) and Rogers' emphasis on empathy (Rogers, 1975), but especially more recent developments such as the 'positive psychology' approach, which is an offshoot of humanistic psychology. An example of this is the strengths-based approach to therapy (see Section 9.6.2).

2.7 CONCLUDING REMARKS

This section has given some flavour of what male psychology is. The following chapters will further demonstrate what the subject is about, and why the new perspective on men and boys is a necessary addition to the field of psychology.

2.8 SUMMARY

- This chapter has given a basic explanation of what male psychology is.
- The origins of the male psychology perspective were outlined.
- Some of the ideas behind male psychology were explored.
- Some of the reasons to study male psychology were discussed.
- An explanation of perspectives in psychology was given.

3 Studying Sex and Gender Differences: An Introduction

CHAPTER OUTLINE

Perspectives in Male Psychology: An Introduction, First Edition.
Louise Liddon and John A. Barry.
© 2021 John Wiley & Sons, Ltd. Published 2021 by John Wiley & Sons, Ltd.

LEARNING OUTCOMES

By the end of this chapter, you should be able to:

1. Recognise ways in which sex and gender are defined, and the relationship between sex and gender
2. Acknowledge the evolutionary perspective on sex and gender differences
3. Appreciate some of the controversies around studying sex and gender differences
4. Recognise the benefits of understanding sex/gender for physical and mental health
5. Appreciate the complexity of the nature/nurture debate around sex and gender differences

3.1 INTRODUCTION

This chapter provides an introduction to key questions around sex, gender and sex/gender differences. It starts with definitions of sex and gender and the relationship between the two, and addresses the influence of evolution, biology, psychological differences between men and women, the influence of culture and controversies related to these topics.

Although some people are sensitive about these topics, they aren't inherently taboo or offensive. They are certainly important enough that we should understand them properly. As an introductory-level book covering a wide range of issues, it is impossible to delve into the complexities of every topic; this chapter aims to offer a sound basis from which further reading can be done if needed, either through following the forthcoming books in the Wiley male psychology series, or through reading around other authors and points of view.

For most of the population in everyday life, people don't tend to define themselves entirely by their sex or gender, because each individual's past, present and future are a diversity of experiences that don't really feel like they are bound by sex or gender. Some people will have similar life experiences and share common attitudes and opinions with others regardless of their sex or gender, and regardless of other demographics. At the same time, there will be patterns to people's lives. Some of these will be influenced by the time and place in which they were born. For example, some people's lives will be influenced by a childhood lived during wartime, or a childhood lived in a time of great economic prosperity. These shared experiences of people living through different times will impact everyone differently, because everyone is an individual. However, if we step back we might see certain common patterns in people who have had similar childhood experiences – perhaps a shared attitude to thrift, or a shared optimism about spending. Sometimes the patterns are so clear that people don't question their existence because so many have experienced them. Some patterns are physical (e.g. height) and we see them over and over again with our own eyes. Some patterns are less obvious, and even though they exist we might not notice them until we experience them. Sometimes patterns are subtle and go unnoticed unless epidemiologists point out statistically significant patterns that are real, but difficult to notice on an individual level.

3.2 DEFINING SEX AND GENDER

There is often confusion and debate over these terms, and depending on where you look they can be defined differently, as discussed below. The term 'normal' typically refers to the 'statistical norm', i.e. what is most common, and is not a judgement about what is morally right.

3.2.1 *What is Meant by a Person's Sex?*

Sex is a description at the level of the biology of a person, which is typically dichotomised as male or female. There are various definitions. For example, the World Health Organization (WHO) states that sex 'is biologically determined' (WHO, 2020). The UK government defines sex as: '1) referring to the biological aspects of an individual as determined by their anatomy, which is produced by their chromosomes, hormones and their interactions; 2) generally male or female; 3) something that is assigned at birth' (ONS, 2019d). However, for some authors the issue is more complex, and the line between biology and culture is not so categorical: 'Sex is based in a combination of anatomical, endocrinal and chromosomal features, and the selection among these criteria for sex assignment is based very much on cultural beliefs about what actually makes someone male or female' (Eckert & McConnell-Ginet, 2013, p. 2).

3.2.2 *What is Meant by a Person's Gender?*

Gender is a description at the social and cultural level of a person, and at a basic level can also be dichotomised as male and female. As with sex, there are various definitions. For example, the WHO says that '"Gender" describes those characteristics of women and men that are largely socially created' (WHO, 2020). The UK government defines gender as '1) a social construction relating to behaviours and attributes based on labels of masculinity and femininity; gender identity is a personal, internal perception of oneself and so the gender category someone identifies with may not match the sex they were assigned at birth; 2) where an individual may see themselves as a man, a woman, as having no gender, or as having a non-binary gender – where people identify as somewhere on a spectrum between man and woman' (ONS, 2019d). Other sources go further: 'Gender is not something we are born with, and not something we *have*, but something we *do*... something we *perform*' (Eckert & McConnell-Ginet, 2013, p. 10).

3.3 THE RELATIONSHIP BETWEEN SEX AND GENDER

Sex and gender can be understood as two separate, but related, concepts. 'Sex is a biological categorization based primarily on reproductive potential, whereas gender is the social elaboration of biological sex' (Eckert & McConnell-Ginet, 2013, p. 10). The UK government says that 'Sex and gender are terms that are often used interchangeably but they are in fact two different concepts, even though for many people their sex and gender are the same' (ONS, 2019d).

For some people these definitions are just technical issues but for others they impinge on core parts of their being that they feel are misunderstood, so discussions of these topics can be emotive. For others, it can be interesting or enjoyable to approach gender in a creative way by trying different fashions or wearing clothes that are gender-atypical for one's culture. Experimentation with gender is not at all unusual in the arts, and relatively common in the teenage years, when young people explore their identity and discover what feels comfortable for them (Barry, 2020).

3.3.1 *Embodiment: Biology Experiencing Culture*

The anthropological concept of embodiment creates an interesting link between biology and culture. The concept is interpreted by different scholars in different ways, but the general idea is that people perceive the world through the physical attributes of their bodies. One hypothesis is that the starting point for understanding culture is one's experience of being in a body (Csordas, 1994).

This means lived experience is related to the experience of one's body, its physical attributes (strength, weaknesses etc) and the cultural meanings attached to one's body (as attractive, useful etc). The experience of embodiment implies that men will understand themselves in relation to others in ways related to their physicality, e.g. being more or less strong etc. In relation to his partner and children a heterosexual man might experience his physicality as a means to be supportive and protective. In fact, women's embodiment as people who can gestate children impacts not only women but men, because then men experience the world as the one who does not carry a child but instead is the protector of the family, the 'breadwinner', needing to undertake certain jobs and act more stoically in order to protect and provide for women and children. In the modern world there is more flexibility around how men and women engage with their environment, though in many situations men and women will choose more gender-typical roles (see Section 7.2.2), and biology seems to influence lifestyle choices as shown in SPOTLIGHT box 3.1.

SPOTLIGHT BOX 3.1

TESTOSTERONE: 'THE MALE SEX HORMONE'

Testosterone is a sex steroid known as the 'male' sex hormone, because it has masculinising effects (e.g. muscle mass, penile and testicular development and hair growth) and is around ten times higher in men than in women (Barry & Owens, 2019).

Testosterone and health

Testosterone is vital to men's general health, and too little can lead to serious health problems such as type 2 diabetes, infertility and obesity (Ruth et al., 2020). Low testosterone is also associated with depression, and a meta-analysis of 27 randomised placebo-controlled studies with 1890 men found that testosterone therapy caused a significant improvement in depressive symptoms, even in men who did not have low testosterone levels pre-treatment (Walther et al., 2019). There has been some concern recently over a global trend of falling testosterone levels (see Section 10.2).

It is normal for men to have small amounts of oestrogen (the 'female' hormone), and a balance between the two is associated with good health and well-being (Barry, 2019). Similarly, it is normal for women to have a small amount of testosterone, but if it becomes too high this imbalance can cause health and psychological issues (Barry & Owens, 2019) similar to men with low testosterone (*theme: 'Yin and Yang'*, in Section 13.2.4).

Testosterone and masculinity

The physiological effects of testosterone seem to support traits that are said to be an evolved part of masculinity (Seager et al., 2014). For example, the provider role is enhanced by strength and visuospatial ability, which could help with hunting tasks. The protector role is helped by muscle mass and stronger bones, which help fight off predators (Morris et al., 2020). Even having control over emotions seems to be enhanced by testosterone, as some research suggests that it reduces tearfulness (Ng et al., 2012).

Testosterone and aggression

Men can be aggressive (see SPOTLIGHT box 3.2) and there is a popular belief this is caused by testosterone. This is understandable, because testosterone causes aggression in some species (e.g. rodents). However, the relationship between testosterone and aggression in humans is much more complex than in rodents. This is probably because humans have more highly evolved brains and have developed many ways to achieve dominance that do not require physical strength and violence (Barry & Owens, 2019). So although some research shows that testosterone is associated with winning and losing in competition (see Section 6.3.1), sometimes the competition in humans is about who can be the most altruistic or virtuous, a type of competition which can be beneficial to others (BliegeBird et al., 2005).

Nonetheless, the popular view that testosterone causes violence and aggression is so strong that it seems to cause a placebo effect (or nocebo effect) whereby people become more aggressive if they think they are taking a testosterone supplement (Eisenegger et al., 2010). So engrained is the idea that testosterone causes aggression that it has been used as a defence in a case of domestic violence in a lesbian couple, one of whom had a medical condition that elevated her testosterone levels (Dunphy, 2018). In reality there is little evidence that testosterone directly causes violence in humans, though some interesting research exists, e.g. the finding that testosterone is correlated to violence in female prisoners but not male (Assari et al., 2014).

Testosterone and fatherhood

Testosterone levels in men appear to map onto the life cycle needs of the typical man, in a way that fits evolutionary theory. For example, testosterone increases during adolescence, which is a life-stage when energy and dominance are an aid to gaining the resources needed to improve mating opportunities. At the age when men traditionally have achieved these goals (by around age 30), testosterone levels typically begin to decrease (Uchida et al., 2006). Lower testosterone levels reduce energy and inclination towards risk-taking and competition, and allow a more nurturing and bonding side to emerge with a partner and offspring. There is evidence that testosterone levels are different in men depending on their fatherhood status: men who are fathers in stable relationships have lower testosterone than men who are in stable relationships but are not fathers, who in turn have lower testosterone than single men who are not fathers (McIntyre et al., 2006).

3.3.2   Is it Nature or Nurture... or Both?

There is a popular view that any nature/nurture debate is always unresolvable. However, many authors agree that there is no need for a debate, because both sides are right: 'while we think of sex as biological and gender as social, this distinction is not clear-cut ... nature and nurture intertwine, and there is no obvious point at which sex leaves off and gender begins' (Eckert & McConnell-Ginet, 2013, p. 2).

The ratio of contribution of nature and nurture will vary from one phenomenon to another. For example, sex differences in the amount of body hair are mostly due to nature, but gender difference in hair style is largely about nurture. So although 'gender builds on biological sex', gender differences related to fashion are an example of where gender 'exaggerates biological difference, and it carries biological difference into domains in which it is completely irrelevant' (Eckert & McConnell-Ginet, 2013, p. 2).

Sex and gender can interact to influence health. For example, men are more inclined towards risk-taking, and this can lead to taking risks with health, e.g. smoking and drinking. Interestingly, these behaviours 'can modify biological factors and thereby health: exposure to stress, environmental toxins, poor nutrition or lifestyle choices can induce genomic and epigenetic modifications in adults, children and even the developing fetus' (Regitz-Zagrosek, 2012, p. 596). In other words, gender-typical behaviour can impact the biological health not only of the individual, but of their offspring.

Rather than things being either genetic or socially defined, it is often the case that genes contribute to some degree, and socialisation to another (see Section 8.3.4). In fact, the impact of genes can be influenced by the environment, so that genes can be 'turned on' or 'turned off' by experiences such as childhood nutritional deficiency, and this genetic alternation can be passed on to the next generation, in a phenomenon known as epigenetics (Gräff & Mansuy, 2008). Thus epigenetics represents a synthesis between the nature and nurture positions (Zhu et al., 2019).

3.3.3 *Masculine Females and Feminine Males*

Gender is relatively flexible compared to sex, and masculinity and femininity are aspects of gender that are not affixed to either men or women. The types of behaviours that we think of as typical of men or women can be seen in men or women. For example, there are masculine women (e.g. women who are large and aggressive), and feminine men (e.g. men who are small and passive). Variation in expression of gender is normal (*theme: 'Yin and Yang'*, in Section 13.2.4).

There are differences in secondary sexual characteristics (e.g. pubic hair, breast size, Adam's apple) due to normal variations in sex hormones (i.e. testosterone and oestrogen), so that some women have a lot of facial and body hair, and some men have less muscle and less facial and body hair than other men. Variations in sex hormone levels are healthy as long as they don't go beyond clinically normal ranges (see Section 10.2.2).

3.3.4 *Cultural and Historical Variations on Gender*

It is widely accepted that gender varies by culture and time. 'There are a number of cultures, for example, in which greater gender diversity exists and sex and gender are not always neatly divided along binary lines such as male and female' (WHO, 2020). Although this fact is sometimes taken to imply that gender differences are purely a product of culture (a 'social construct'), in reality there are relatively few cultures throughout history that didn't demonstrate pretty clear gender differences (see Section 3.5.3).

3.3.5 *A Complex Biopsychosocial Picture*

So far in this chapter we can see that sex and gender are more complex than a black and white view of the world will allow. To make things even more confusing, not only do sex hormones influence behaviour, but behaviour can influence sex hormones. There is evidence that in primates, including humans, moving up the social dominance hierarchy can cause an increase in testosterone (Eckert & McConnell-Ginet, 2013). This suggests that sex and gender exist within a complex dynamic system of culture, psychology and hormones (the *biopsychosocial* system), although this complexity is more recognised in psychology than in gender studies (see Section 6.3.1).

3.4 SEX/GENDER SIMILARITIES AND SEX/GENDER DIFFERENCES

Men and women are alike in so many ways, and indeed more similar to each other than they are different. However, men and women are not identical, and we should be open to the possibility that the differences are important to recognise and understand. This section will explore some of these differences, including the distinction between sex differences and gender differences.

When patterns occur that relate to sex and/or gender, either because we experience them ourselves or because we see them in other people or read about them, these are generally described as sex differences or gender differences. Identifying patterns relating to sex and/or gender can be very useful. For example, knowing that only men are at risk of penile cancer can help to design awareness programmes. It's also important to know there are exceptions to general rules, e.g. most people who develop breast cancer are women, but around 1% of cases are men (CRUK, 2020). For many people this is a surprisingly high figure, and it shows that although there are general patterns there are exceptions, and these patterns and the exceptions can have important consequences.

3.4.1 *Sex Differences Versus Gender Differences*

Sex differences in health are related to biological factors such as sex hormones and gene expression on the X and Y chromosomes, whereas gender differences in health are associated to behaviour, lifestyle and work patterns (Regitz-Zagrosek, 2012). It is important to recognise sex and gender as distinct factors in some contexts, because some diseases are caused more by sex than gender, and others more by gender than sex, and some are a mix of both (Cislaghi et al., 2020). For example, prostate cancer is influenced mostly by a person's sex, but lung cancer – when caused by smoking – is influenced relatively more by gendered behaviour, because men smoke more than women do (to varying degrees) internationally. Smoking is an example of a health issue that could be influenced by men's greater tendency towards risk-taking. (For more examples see Table 1 in Cislaghi et al., 2020.)

3.4.2 *Differences are Based on Averages*

Sex differences are about differences on average between men and women on specific traits, and shouldn't be taken to imply that men and women are different in every way or even most ways. It's important to realise that while the population of men differ – on average – from the population of women on some traits, not all men and women will be different on these traits. For example, some men will differ from women on all relevant traits, some men will differ from women on a few of those traits and some men will differ from women on none of those traits. On a personal level, a man might read that 'men are more likely than women to smoke cigarettes' but say to himself 'hang on, I don't smoke cigarettes – this idea of gender differences is rubbish'. It's important for that man to realise that these differences are on a population level, and they indicate that on average there is a difference. Just because that pattern doesn't exist for you doesn't mean that the pattern does not exist for others (see Section 4.4.3).

3.4.3 *Statistics are not Moral Judgements*

Some people find discussions of sex differences uncomfortable, often because they think that highlighting the differences between men and women is like saying that men and women are unequal, which sounds like sexism. However, the reality is that people can be different in various ways but still be of equal worth. People might have different strengths and weaknesses, but overall be able to contribute in equally important ways to society.

Just because some things are unequal doesn't mean they are unfair. Statistics are not political or moral statements, they are just factual information. The exception to this is where statistics are compiled or presented in a way that creates misunderstanding (see Section 2.5.5.1) or when people use facts to promote a selfish agenda.

3.4.4 Benefits of Studying Sex/Gender Differences

There are lots of good reasons for studying sex and gender differences. Firstly, lots of people find information about sex differences fascinating. On the level of basic human interest it is intriguing to know, e.g., that when distressed women are more likely than men to 'comfort eat' as a way of coping, and men are more likely to use sex or pornography (Liddon et al., 2017). Secondly, although information of this kind is immediately recognisable when it is pointed out, these things are not always immediately obvious until they have been formally identified through research. Thirdly, this information can have practical applications that can help people. For example, if a man starts to use pornography excessively, this could be a sign that he is distressed and might benefit from talking to a psychologist or other professional. Being aware of the potential for gender differences when doing research can help highlight issues that impact men and women differently, and inform as to areas in which help is needed (WHO, 2020).

3.4.5 Small but Significant Differences

Often, sex and gender differences are small enough or subtle enough that most people don't notice them unless they directly impact their daily life in a tangible way, or become noticeable due to being seen recurrently over years. However, the fact that a difference is subtle doesn't mean that it isn't significant. For example, at four weeks of gestational age the male and female foetus are identical except that one has a Y chromosome. Having the Y chromosome causes the foetus to become male rather than female, demonstrating that sometimes a small difference can lead to a big difference (see Section 13.2.4).

There are various ways in which the importance of small differences can be shown. For example, several small differences can create something that is 'more than the sum of the parts' – a recognisably different profile that suggests maleness or femaleness. This combined difference can be overlooked when research focuses on just one difference per study, or looks at several differences but without combining their effect. This is like identifying the various ordinary ingredients of a cake (milk, eggs, flour etc) without realising that they combine to make something unique (see SPOTLIGHT box 3.3).

Another phenomenon often overlooked is the way that sometimes a small difference between men and women on average for a trait can show up as large differences in men and women who are unusually high or low in that trait (Kaufman, 2019). This was demonstrated by the largest ever meta-analysis of sex differences in brain structure, which found that men show greater variability of brain structures, and are more likely to fall in the extremes of brain structure dimensions (Wierenga et al., 2020).

3.4.6 Danger of a 'One-Size-Fits-All' Approach to Research

There are a number of conditions in which the health of men and women is different. If a data set about health conditions doesn't show which patients are men and which are women, then important information about sex differences are obscured (*theme*: '*beta bias*', in Section 13.2.5). Therefore presenting data clearly by sex, rather than as an average for people overall, is important. This unmixing of data is known as 'sex disaggregation of data' and its importance is recognised in male psychology both in terms of health behaviours (Lemkey et al., 2016) and psychological therapy (Liddon et al., 2019). However, sex disaggregation of data typically does not happen in research on the outcomes of psychological therapy (e.g. Parker et al., 2011), nor always in health research e.g. a report on the global burden of tuberculosis neglected to mention that being male was a major risk factor for tuberculosis (Cornell et al., 2020). This is an interesting omission, seeing as the WHO's position for years has been that 'Sex and gender are both important determinants of health. Biological sex and socially-constructed gender interact to produce differential risks and vulnerability to ill health, and differences in health-seeking behaviour and health outcomes for women and men' (WHO, 2020; see Section 2.5.5.1).

3.5 EVOLUTIONARY AND SOCIOCULTURAL EXPLANATIONS FOR SEX/GENDER DIFFERENCES

Explanations for the differences between males and females tend to come from two main perspectives: that of evolution(nature), and that of socialisation (nurture). Although 'nature/nurture debates' are common, polarisation of opinions in this way is not usually productive, and it is hoped that this section helps demonstrate that both sides are important.

3.5.1 An Evolutionary Perspective on Male Psychology

The question arises of why biological sex differences that underpin behaviour exist, and evolutionary psychology often has plausible answers (Geary, 2021; Stewart-Williams, 2018). Human biology and behaviour today have been shaped by living for millennia in an environment that was stable enough to allow the adaptations recognisable today. Although today the environment is very different to how it was before the agricultural revolution 10,000 years ago, our biology and instincts remain more or less unchanged. Our evolution is constrained by the pace of our reproduction, which – unlike with fruit flies – is a slow process.

Although most people accept the impact of evolution on anatomy and physiology, it is easier to forget the corresponding impact on psychological and behavioural characteristics. For example, it would make little sense for a creature to evolve eyes but have no interest in seeing. Similarly, it would be strange for a herbivore to have evolved teeth and a digestive system suited to chewing vegetation if it didn't also develop a set of behaviours that influenced it to seek out nutritious plants rather than hunt animals. In the same way, we might consider the potential influence that sex differences in muscle mass, height and capacity to become pregnant have on the innate behaviours of humans. Communal living and civilisation depend upon learning to channel innate tendencies in controlled ways, and of course many of these innate tendencies and their modifications remain valuable today (e.g. pair-bonding, altruism, hunting, caring for children etc; Cummings-Knight, 2019).

Although the popular view today of psychological sex differences is that they are typically a product of socialisation, an alternative view – based on evolutionary theory – is that because sex differences in behaviour are pervasive in nearly every other species, it's difficult to imagine that sex differences in human behaviour would be totally unlike other species, in particular the different reproductive roles which are apparent across human evolutionary history (Kaufman, 2019). It could be argued that the sex differences in other species are caused only by socialisation, but this suggestion also seems implausible because animals don't – as far as we know – have gender stereotypes that might socialise sex differences in behaviour. Evolutionary psychologists propose that environmental influences don't operate on a 'blank slate'; they operate on minds that are already differentiated by sex to some degree (Geary, 2021; Stewart-Williams, 2018). It seems more likely that many of the psychological differences between men and women are due to sex-specific selection pressures in our evolutionary history. This is because the keys to successful reproduction (and therefore passing on genes) were different for men and women. This fundamental difference between men and women has profound implications for psychological sex differences, and it is plausible that masculinity and femininity have evolved as a result of evolutionary pressures to specialisation in behaviours in order to enhance reproductive success.

3.5.2 *Sex Differences are International*

Analysis of the *Big Five* personality traits (openness to experience, conscientiousness, extraversion, agreeableness and neuroticism) of 23,031 people in 26 countries found that although gender differences were small relative to individual variation within genders (i.e. there were more similarities than differences), the gender differences were broadly consistent with what are seen as 'gender stereotypes' across adults of all ages (Costa et al., 2001). Men scored higher in assertiveness and openness to ideas, whereas women scored higher in neuroticism, agreeableness, warmth and openness to feelings. Contrary to predictions from the social role model, gender differences appeared across nations, and were most pronounced in European and American cultures in which traditional sex roles are minimised (*Theme: 'don't make assumptions'*, Section 13.2.5). One evolutionary interpretation of these findings is that it would be a remarkable coincidence if sex differences were replicated across cultures that might have had little or no contact with each other throughout most of history.

3.5.3 *Sex Roles Influenced by Biology and Culture*

The prevailing view in the social sciences and popular culture is that gendered behaviour is due only to socialisation. For example, the popular paper 'Doing Gender' (West & Zimmerman, 1987) has been cited around 15,000 times and is an example of how biology is often minimised in gender studies. Cultural anthropologist Margaret Mead is best remembered for popularising the notion, early in her career in the 1920s and 1930s, that sex roles are a product of culture, but it is less remembered that later in her career (in her book *Male and Female*) she wrote that 'cultural variability in sex roles was founded on "primary sex differences" conditioned by the reproductive functions and anatomical differences between the sexes' (Mead, 1949, cited in Sanday, 1980, p. 340).

3.5.4 *Archetypes and Stereotypes*

Some sex differences are more obvious than others, e.g. men tend to be taller and physically stronger than women. Most people aren't very upset by such facts. However, the more subtle the difference, as with psychological traits (such as risk-taking, or being people-orientated), the more likely they are to be dismissed as stereotypes.

3.5.4.1 *Gender difference or stereotype?*

There are lots of examples of stereotyping being used in immoral ways, such as refusing to help someone because of their race. However, other examples show that stereotyping is a 'rule of thumb' based on experience, evolved as a method of quickly navigating the world and still existing today because it is accurate enough to be useful (Neuberg et al., 2020). For example, you probably wouldn't ask a toddler for help with a crossword puzzle, not because you dislike toddlers, but because your guess – or stereotype – is that they won't be able to help much. This example shows that stereotypes aren't necessarily moral judgements, just an assessment based on experience.

Sometimes gender differences are mistakenly dismissed as stereotypes. This dismissal may be well-intentioned, done because people think that making assumptions about people based on popular generalisations is factually and morally wrong. Part of the problem is that the word 'stereotype' has strong negative connotations, whereas the term 'schema' – which is a familiar concept in psychology – has fewer negative connotations. A schema is a 'social script' that helps people to know how to behave in social situations. Thus in the UK, if you walk into a room full of people dressed in black and looking tearful, you could make a reasonable guess that you have stumbled upon a funeral. (For an interesting discussion of this topic, see Shpancer, 2018.)

3.5.4.2   *The masculinity archetype*

Rather than stereotypes, psychological and behavioural sex differences are more accurately described as archetypes, because this puts them in the context of evolved traits as much as physiological traits. This recognises that phenomena such as masculinity and femininity are evolved patterns of behaviour, instincts that have benefited the human species for millennia. The masculinity archetype is to be a fighter and a winner, a provider and protector, and to have mastery and control of one's feelings (Seager, 2019). The fact that the basic blueprint for masculinity can be seen across all cultures – albeit in varying forms – suggests that it is evolved and adaptive (Ellis et al., 2008; see Section 3.7.2).

Even though there is a fashion these days to see masculinity in a negative light, it is easy to see how masculinity has adaptive value. For example, men's tendency to seek help less compared to women is viewed negatively (Courtenay, 2000), but masculinity can be adapted to encourage help-seeking. For example, instead of being given the message that seeking help is a sign of weakness, the message might be: '*By seeking help you are taking action, taking control and fighting your problems; It takes strength and courage to confront and master your problems; Looking after yourself means protecting your family*' (Seager, 2019, p. 241). This shows the importance of social forces in discouraging or encouraging behaviours, even behaviours rooted in archetypes, in a way analogous to epigenetic processes (see Section 3.3.2).

SURVIVAL OF THE 'BAD BOY'

There can be a dark side to masculinity. Men commit crime more often than women, especially violent crime (see Section 8.2). This gender gap in offending is sometimes explained by different historical selection pressures on males and females (Daly, 2014). The traits that promote sexual selection are the same traits that are associated with male-typical criminal behaviour. These traits are: greater risk-taking; sensation seeking; dominance and the pursuit of social status; physical aggression, particularly in same-sex competition; and greater size and strength (Durrant, 2019). In support of this notion, there is evidence that women today find the 'dark triad' of personality traits (narcissism, Machiavellianism and psychopathy) attractive in men (Carter et al., 2014). This explains to some degree the phenomenon of serial killers who have a large fan-base of women (Ogas & Gaddam, 2011). In contrast, women have much less to gain from having these traits, due to the risk of reducing their reproductive success; the reproductive rate for women is slower than for men, and injury could lead to miscarriage or reduced care for offspring.

Evolutionary theory explains why younger men, and men from lower socioeconomic classes, are more likely to engage in short-term rather than long-term relationships: harsh and unpredictable environments make longer-term strategies, such as parenting, less appealing than shorter-term goals, such as mating. Males in these harsh environments will take greater risks at a younger age to gain immediate reward, such as casual sex or criminality (Ellis et al., 2012). For example, in less harsh conditions putting effort into parenting will lead to better outcomes than putting effort into mating widely).

So it seems that environmental conditions can impact how likely it is that 'bad boys' will mate, with more harsh conditions favouring the more ruthless strategies and more affluent conditions favouring more co-operative strategies. These correspond with life history theory, which suggests that harsh environments produce a fast strategy of criminality and casual sex, while in more safe environments it is more adaptive to have a slower strategy (Kwiek et al., 2016). Thus it makes sense in evolutionary terms for men to be sensitive to environmental cues that signal the most appropriate mating strategies (Brown, 2019).

3.6 CONTROVERSIES IN SEX DIFFERENCES RESEARCH

3.6.1 *Reluctance to Recognise Sex/Gender Differences*

Although sex differences are obvious to many people, in some circles mentioning this topic is virtually taboo, even when the more accepted 'gender differences' is used instead. This appears to be in part due to the success of the spread of the maxim that 'there are more similarities than differences between the sexes', which has become axiomatic in the social sciences (Hyde, 2005). Although this maxim is undoubtedly true, like any valid idea it can be harmful if taken to be the whole truth. In the social sciences today discussion of sex differences is discouraged, almost as if acknowledgement of sex differences is itself sexist, or at least in poor taste in terms of gender politics.

'GENDER SIMILARITIES' VERSUS 'GENDER REALITIES'

The *gender similarities hypothesis* is summarised by the idea that there are more similarities than differences between men and women (Hyde, 2005). This was based on a review of 46 meta-analyses of sex differences, with a supposedly thorough list of behaviours and traits related to cognition, communication, personality, wellbeing, motor skills, and some miscellaneous variables that didn't fit into the other categories. The review concluded that although 'gender differences can vary substantially', 'overinflated claims of gender differences carry substantial costs in areas such as the workplace and relationships' (Hyde, 2005, p. 581).

The *gender similarities hypothesis* has been hugely influential both inside and outside the social sciences. However, some authors have pointed out that it somewhat deflects attention away from important sex differences (*Theme: 'beta bias'*, Section 13.2.5). For example, in psychologist Richard Lippa's letter (entitled 'the gender reality hypothesis') in *American Psychologist*, he pointed out:

Some striking omissions from Hyde's (2005) review are worth noting ... For example, there are large differences in women's and men's preferences for [practical] occupations (e.g., mechanic, carpenter; $d = 1.06$) and moderate differences in their preferences for social and artistic occupations ($d = 0.62$ and 0.63, respectively). Women and men also show large differences ($d = 1.29$) in their placement on the people–things (see Section 7.3.1) dimension of interests, with women being more people-orientated and men more thing-orientated (Lippa, 2006, p. 639).

Lippa goes on to list various mental illnesses and behavioural problems that show large sex differences (e.g. depression, antisocial behaviour, autism etc), as well as general behaviours (e.g. children's play styles), and points out that these 'undoubtedly have substantial societal consequences, affecting women's and men's behavior in the workplace and in close relationships. Minimizing these gender differences may carry more costs than acknowledging their existence and investigating their causes' (Lippa, 2006, p. 639).

Lippa also warns against relying on experiments that take one-off measures of behaviour under specific conditions rather than triangulating measures over time in different situations. As an example of better practice, he cites the study by Moffitt and Caspi (2001) of antisocial behaviour (see Section 4.4.2) in boys and girls, which found a small effect size ($d = 0.25$) when behaviour was assessed by looking at various outcomes separately. However, when the outcomes were pooled to reflect a more complete picture of behaviour, the effect size almost doubled to $d = 0.49$, giving a more realistic reflection of the sex difference in offending.

In conclusion, Lippa suggests: 'The task that confronts gender researchers is to explain the complex profile of psychological gender differences and to untangle the myriad social and biological factors that generate both gender differences and gender similarities' (Lippa, 2006, p. 639). This is a valid approach and reminds researchers and others to avoid the black and white mentality of alpha bias and beta bias.

3.6.2   If Men and Women are so Similar, do we Need Sex Differences Research?

There is some interesting history, spanning several decades, demonstrating the confusion that can be caused when mixing gender politics with science (*Theme: 'Unintended consequences'*, in Section 13.2.1).

3.6.2.1   The case that researching sex differences is bad for women

In the 1980s, authors such as feminist philosopher Alison Jaggar suggested that sex differences research 'helps to rationalize and justify the continuation of sex inequality' (Jaggar, 1987). Her reasoning was that 'in a society where the sexes are unequal, it is inevitable that scientists should be assigned to discover whether this inequality is grounded in some inherent difference between the sexes' and that 'the research context of sex inequality makes it more likely that research programmes that promise to confirm existing sex prejudice will be funded, that sex differences rather than sex similarities will be discovered, that those differences will be interpreted as female deficiencies' (Jaggar, 1987, p. 31).

In 1994, a special edition of the journal *Feminism & Psychology* edited by Professor Celia Kitzinger was published on the subject of researching sex differences. It featured papers authored by leaders in this field, such as Janet Hyde and Alice Eagly. Kitzinger gives an overview of the special edition in her paper entitled *Should Psychologists Study Sex Differences?* She begins: 'The feminist belief that there are serious social inequalities which work to discriminate against and to oppress women has implications for sex differences research. [Also] biological theories ... tend to have troubling implications for feminist political goals. ...The huge proliferation of "sex differences" research within "psychology of women" can be attributed to a range of pragmatic and political considerations' which might be viewed 'in the light of the frantic race for tenure' (Kitzinger, 1994, pp. 502–3). She cites feminist psychologist Professor Wendy Holloway, whose 'alternative epistemological tradition' suggests that sex differences research is more about gender power relations than science. Quoting sociologist and feminist Professor Christine Delphy, Kitzinger says: 'It is *oppression which creates gender* ... *Gender in its turn created anatomical sex*, in the sense that the hierarchical division of humanity into two transforms an anatomical difference (which in itself is devoid of all meaning, like all physical facts) into a category of thought' (emphasis in original; Kitzinger, 1994, p. 505).

Thus the views expressed in these papers challenge the standard scientific study of sex differences with radical notions such as that anatomical sex differences are a product of sociopolitical oppression. The idea that sex differences research might genuinely help men and women is not given serious consideration. Indeed concerns about sex differences research have been promoted in academia for several decades, using ideas such as the gender similarities hypothesis (Hyde, 2005) to claim that it is not needed and that it would erode gender equality. In 1995 Gloria Steinem called sex differences research 'anti-American crazy thinking' (cited in Charen, 2018, p. 56), resulting in a climate where sex differences research was 'career suicide' (Cahill, 2019, 2014). One researcher commented that 'for a number of years it was an act of courage for academic researchers to study sex differences at all' (Charen, 2018, p. 56).

3.6.2.2   The case that sex differences research is good for women

In a landmark break from the anti-research narrative, in 2001 the Institute of Medicine highlighted the benefits to health outcomes of researching sex differences in medicine (Pardue & Wizemann, 2001). It noted:

'To acknowledge and explore nonreproductive aspects of sex differences in health and illness requires a view of males and females as different but equally "legitimate" biological entities without respect to whether there is (or should be) equivalence or equality in all other domains. RECOMMENDATION 14: Reduce the potential for discrimination based on identified sex differences. The committee noted that, historically, studies on race, ethnicity, age, nationality, religion, and sex have sometimes led to discriminatory practices. The committee believes, therefore, that these historical practices should be taken into consideration so that they will not be repeated. The past should not limit the future of research but should serve as a guide to its use. Ethical research on the biology of sex differences is essential to the advancement of human health and should not be constrained' (Pardue & Wizemann, 2001, pp. 9–10).

This was welcome news, though the Institute for Medicine appeared to turn a blind eye to the true cause of the lack of sex differences research.

In 2016 the National Institute of Health (NIH) adopted a policy called *Sex as a Biological Variable*, requiring anyone using NIH funding to examine sex differences in order to better understand females (NIH, 2015). This was to correct the assumption that many neuroscientists had – allegedly – made up to that time, that sex differences were unimportant. Apparently the NIH was not aware of the culture of beta bias that had been forced on neuroscientists for decades (Cahill, 2019). Indeed, even recently, one neuroscientist suggested that 'perhaps we should just stop looking for [sex] differences altogether?' (Rippon, 2019).

3.6.2.3   Who is responsible for beta-bias in research?

The anti-sex differences research agenda had a chilling effect on sex differences research in academia, with researchers risking accusations of sexism. Sex and gender-related issues became increasingly the province of gender studies, and gender issues became part of the curriculum in academia, including medical schools (Risberg et al., 2011; Verdonk, 2007; see SPOTLIGHT box 5.2 and Section 10.5.2).

Equality programmes and gender and sex analysis (GSA) of data research have for several years been encouraged by both the European Commission and the NIH (Nielsen et al., 2017). Against this backdrop, one study found that women are more likely than men to be the most prominent authors (either first or last author position) on medical research that involves GSA (Nielsen et al., 2017). They interpreted this to show the benefit of women in medical science, and that 'expanding gender equality may have broader implications for knowledge and health outcomes than previously suspected' (Nielsen et al., 2017, p. 794). An alternative view is that campaigners for gender equality have for decades been discouraging sex differences research, so it is likely that researchers – especially men, who are more vulnerable than women to accusations of sexism – might be much less inclined than women to get involved in such research.

On the surface it appears that, with sex differences research now encouraged (mostly), the forces of common sense have prevailed, and science can continue to engage in sex differences research again. It is somewhat disingenuous, however, that a male-dominated research environment was blamed for both doing too much sex differences research and then doing too little gender differences research, when in fact it was people promoting a gender equality agenda who campaigned first to stop sex differences research and then campaigned to start it again. This is unfair to the researchers who were so strongly discouraged from conducting sex differences research that they felt it was career suicide to do so, only to be told a few years later that their failure to pay attention to sex differences had been harmful to women's health. This exasperating saga demonstrates the unintended negative consequences of mixing gender politics and science (see Sections 11.4.3 and 13.2.1).

3.6.3 'The Future of Sex and Gender in Psychology'?

Janet Hyde, whose work helped discourage sex differences research in the social sciences, has recently found additional reasons to avoid studying sex differences. In her 2019 paper 'The Future of Sex and Gender in Psychology', she suggests that the 'gender binary should be supplemented by additional categories (e.g., genderqueer)' (Hyde et al., 2019, p. 185). This seems reasonable, and indeed most researchers do some variation of this: e.g. *'What is your gender? Please select one of these options: male, female, other'*. Another of her suggestions is 'treating all gender/sex constructs as multidimensional and continuous, rather than unidimensional and dichotomous' (p. 186) e.g. *'In the past 12 months, have you thought of yourself as a woman?'*, with five response options from 'always' to 'never'. This suggestion is appropriate to studies of gender, but probably not studies of other topics, where many people might find this question unnecessary.

Hyde's general case in this paper is that that 'gender/sex should be ignored altogether' because it may not be 'scientifically useful', because 'intersectionality highlights that women and men are not homogeneous categories' (Hyde et al., 2019, p. 185). Many scientists, for example those who value the sex-dissagregation of data in healthcare, will recognise that this line of thinking represents a step backwards, away from the kind of science that has practical applications for the majority of people, and back into a nebulous mix of philosophy and gender politics from the 1990s which stifled sex differences research for so many years (see Section 3.6.2.1).

3.7 MEN AND MASCULINITY

Exasperated man, shouting at his stubborn horse: *'Call yourself a horse!?'*
From the film *The Seven Samurai* (Kurosawa, 1954).

3.7.1 *What is a Man?*

It's pretty obvious that even if a horse is stubborn, or very intelligent, or violent, or has three legs, or is as small as a dog, it is still a horse. In fact, no matter what it does, it is still a horse. Similarly, it is possible to take a biological (or 'essentialist') view of men: there might be lots of different ways to be a man, but all men are men of some kind. In most cases, the presence of a Y chromosome could be taken as being indicative of being a man. However, biology is complex, and identifying who is a man or woman becomes even more complex when people's feelings about their gender identity are taken into account.

3.7.1.1 *Genes and sex differences*
The general consensus of scientific opinion is that most women have an XX chromosome pairing and most men have an XY pairing. There are sometimes genetic variations on this theme, but in general people with a Y chromosome are genetically male.

Genes on the X and Y chromosomes influence a range of traits associated with gender, such as sex differences in aspects of social behaviour and language (Printzlau et al., 2017). The presence of a Y chromosome triggers male development at about week 13 of pregnancy. At this time, the foetal gonads produce a surge of testosterone, at levels similar to those seen in males at puberty. The presence of testosterone has a dramatic masculinising effect on foetal development, impacting all of the organs and especially those parts with more androgen receptors, including the sexual organs and the brain. This programmes the foetus for postnatal development throughout the lifespan, most clearly at puberty.

3.7.1.2   Genetic and biological variations on being a man

When variations on the typical XX or XY chromosome pairing occur, these are called *intersex* conditions. A few births per thousand will have a single sex chromosome (sex monosomies), three or more sex chromosomes (sex polysomies, see below) or mutations on regions of the Y chromosome (WHO, 2020). The two most common variations involve having extra X or Y chromosomes (sex polysomies). These examples provide evidence of how sometimes aspects of gender-typicality can be clearly attributed to genes and other innate factors.

3.7.1.3   Klinefelter syndrome and XYY syndrome

Men who have one or more extra X chromosome (called Klinefelter syndrome, occurring in around 1 in 600 men) tend to be slightly feminised, e.g. they produce low levels of testosterone, and are less hairy than typical men. They also tend to be relatively unassertive and have slightly impaired ability in reading, motor skills and verbal IQ (Leggett et al., 2010). Men who have an extra Y chromosome (XYY, around 1 in 1000 men) tend to be taller than average and have higher levels of testosterone, but are psychologically similar to other men (Leggett et al., 2010).

3.7.1.4   Complete androgen insensitivity syndrome (CAIS)

More rarely, other conditions occur which impact gender. For example, complete androgen insensitivity syndrome (CAIS) is seen in less than 1 in 10,000 male (XY) foetuses. They have cell receptors that don't recognise androgens (such as testosterone), so the foetus develops as a female, the child is raised as a girl and the condition is only detected on examination around puberty because of absence of menstruation (Hines et al., 2003). A milder version of CAIS is more common, though it is difficult to estimate the prevalence of this because it most likely goes undetected in many cases.

3.7.1.5   Transgender and intersex

Although this fascinating topic is too complex to be discussed in full here, some basic notes are presented as a beginner's guide. Prevalence of conditions varies according to definition, but intersex conditions in which the appearance of genitals is altered by the condition are rare (around 1 person in 1000). Intersex conditions that are very mild or indentifiable only by chromosomal analysis might – according to the most extreme estimate – impact up to 1 in 60 people (ISNA, 2008). A systematic review of studies suggests that around 4 people in 1000 self-identify as trans (Collin et al., 2016). Note that these figures are for men and women, not just men.

It is difficult to make generalisations about transgender people because this umbrella term covers so many different types, e.g. 'non-binary' (i.e. don't identify as masculine or feminine), and it is possible to be both intersex and transgender. In general, though, transgender people feel that their birth sex does not match their gender identity. Some people who are intersex or transgender might seek medical intervention in order to 'transition' from one sex to another. The social and legal aspects of transgender vary by country and are complex, though from a biological perspective, it is the procreative function of sex that confirms the binary nature of sex, regardless of intersex conditions or identities (Del Giudice, 2021).

3.7.1.6 Psychological aspects of transgender people

A Dutch study of transgender people found they were at three or four times higher risk of suicide than the general population, that trans women (genetic men identifying as women) were at increased risk of suicide compared to trans men (genetic women identifying as men), and that this risk appeared unrelated to stage of transition (hormones, surgery etc; Wiepjes et al., 2020).

A study of 5000 men in the US found that 14 participants identified as 'non-binary' and 10 as 'female to male transgender' (Barry, 2020). The mean mental positivity score for the participants who identified as male ($n = 4976$) was 3.72, which was significantly higher than non-binary participants (3.02) and transgender participants (2.63). The transgender group mean score suggests clinically low levels of mental positivity. The findings of this survey demonstrate two things. Firstly, surveys of the general population are usually much too small to recruit enough trans people to give the study enough 'statistical power' to include their results in the data analysis. Also, if too few people respond it will be difficult to 'generalise' their results to other trans people, because we don't know how representative the opinions of a small group of trans people might be of other trans people. Even in this very large survey ($N = 5000$), with a geographically representative sample of the general population, it can be difficult to generalise from only ten female-to-male transgender participants. Secondly, there is a need for sensitivity in discussions of trans issues. This is especially true of male-to-female transgender people, who tend to experience more distress than female-to-male transgender people (Wiepjes et al., 2020). There are many aspects of this issue that need more research e.g. people on the autism spectrum are more likely to have preoccupations about transgender feelings than are other people (van Wijngaarden, 2019).

3.7.2 Sex Differences are Found Internationally

For the majority of men (98% or more) who are not intersex or transgender, they are likely to fall along a spectrum of various degrees of being masculine. Although generalisation is a one-size-fits-all activity that inevitably fits virtually nobody perfectly, it is a useful way for gaining a broad understanding of most people.

A review of findings from more than 18,000 studies, mostly of cognitive or behavioural traits, across the seven world regions (Africa, Asia, Europe, Latin America, Middle East, North America and Oceania), identified 65 sex differences that were found internationally (Ellis, 2011; Ellis et al., 2008). The traits they found coalesced into seven domains.

1. Stratification and work: men were more work-orientated and in more male-typical jobs (see workplace in SPOTLIGHT box 3.3).
2. Substance use and criminal behaviour: men consumed more alcohol and engaged in more criminal behaviour (see Sections 8.2.3 and 11.2.2).
3. Social and play behaviour: men were more competitive and viewed women more sexually than women view men (see Section 6.2.1 and SPOTLIGHT box 3.2).
4. Personality and behaviour: men take greater risks, explore their environment, and are more aggressive to each other (see Section 7.3.1).
5. Attitudes and preferences: men were more interested in STEM, sports and women younger and shorter than themselves (see Section 7.2.3).
6. Mental health: men were more prone to alcoholism, learning disabilities, ADHD, psychoticism and ASD (see Section 11.2.2).
7. Emotions and perceptions: men were less stressed but more bored (see clinical in Section 8.2.3).

Other sex differences found were also recognisably gender-typical, e.g. boys were more interested in science but less interested in school (Ellis, 2011; Ellis et al., 2008). Overall, the findings of Ellis et al. (2008) echo much of the other research evidence in this book, and support the 'gender reality hypothesis' (Lippa, 2006) rather than the 'gender similarities hypothesis' (Hyde, 2005).

3.7.2.1   *Biological basis for masculinity*
It is interesting that many of the 65 gender differences (see Section 3.7.2) can easily be mapped onto masculinity. For example, the following traits (in italics) which were found to be higher in men by Ellis et al. (2008; 2011) correspond to the components of masculinity (the 'male gender script', shown in bold) described by Seager (2019) and Seager et al. (2014a):

- **Be a fighter and a winner**
  - *Competitiveness; physical aggression; interest in sports; criminality*
- **Be a provider and protector**
  - *Longer working hours; male-typical occupations; exploring environment; taking risks; interest in sex*

- **Mastery and control of emotions**
  - *Less fear; less crying; substance abuse* [possible self-medication for emotions]

Research such as Ellis et al. (2008) showing sex differences internationally, and studies of the influence of testosterone on psychology and behaviour (Barry & Owens, 2019), suggests that male-typical behaviour is influenced by biology. Biological differences map onto masculinity in interesting ways. For example, a review of evidence from psychology, criminology, archaeology, anthropology and physiology concluded there are 26 sex differences that indicate men that are adapted to combat to a greater degree than are women, e.g. men tend to be taller and have heavier bodies, faster reaction times, more accurate throwing, stronger bones, e.g. the jawbone, and greater tolerance of danger (Sell et al., 2012). Men's upper bodies have 75% more muscle mass and 90% more strength, and a study comparing 20 men and 19 women found that on average, men could punch 162% harder than females (Morris et al., 2020).

This evidence does not mean that cultural factors have no influence on masculinity, and it seems most likely that both nature and nurture work together to create what we see as sex differences. These facts make the question of whether something is a sex difference or a gender difference almost redundant, and in fact some experts in this field purposely use the terms 'sex' and 'gender' interchangeably (e.g. Maccoby, 1988; Hines, 2017).

3.8 CONCLUDING REMARKS

Understanding the influence of biological factors in creating sex differences is a fascinating and important topic, but discussions are often framed as a nature/nurture debate, which 'generates more heat than light'. Any systematic bias in research is unwelcome, and at present the view of gender – both in the social sciences and beyond – is prone to bias, especially beta bias. One example is that in the UK the national census in 2021 is planning to include a new question on gender identity, which will help highlight the true number of trans people in the UK. However, there is also concerns that the question on sex will also be changed so that it can be answered according to subjective gender identity (Sullivan, 2020). From the point of view of GSA research and for epidemiological and healthcare purposes, this is a retrograde step that will obscure sex difference data that is important to the healthcare needs of the population. These issues need more discussion, but the cancel culture of gender politics means that the usual process of academic debate is often avoided, because the view that biology can influence gender is often treated with hostility (Stewart-Williams, 2018).

3.9 SUMMARY

- This chapter has described how sex and gender are defined, how they are related to masculinity and behaviour and how this complex topic has impacted research.
- Differences between men and women are the result of a combination of biological and cultural influences.
- The chapter described how sex differences are measured, and why they are important.
- The chapter gave explanations for the existence of sex differences from the evolutionary and sociocultural perspectives.
- It set out the unintended consequences of gender politics in constraining our understanding of sex differences and ability to conduct research.
- It explained that intersex and transgender matters are complex issues with mental health implications.

Part 3
Male Psychology and …

4 Child Development

CHAPTER OUTLINE

Perspectives in Male Psychology: An Introduction, First Edition.
Louise Liddon and John A. Barry.
© 2021 John Wiley & Sons, Ltd. Published 2021 by John Wiley & Sons, Ltd.

LEARNING OUTCOMES

By the end of this chapter, you should be able to:

1. Understand some of the different explanations for boys' and girls' different toy and play preferences
2. Recognise some of the vulnerabilities experienced by boys during their development
3. Recognise the different influences of parents on delinquency and mental health
4. Appreciate the role good fathers may have
5. Understand the impact of negative masculinity discourse on development of masculine identity
6. Be able to identify different types of biases related to boys

4.1 INTRODUCTION

Give me a child until he is seven and I will show you the man
–attributed to St. Ignatius Loyola (founder of the
Jesuit order) and Aristotle

Childhood is seen by many as the time that shapes a person's future. For this reason, it's important that those formative years help bring out the best in the child, or at least aren't damaging. Developmental psychology is a vast and fascinating discipline, and what you will see in this chapter is just a quick tour of some of the interesting areas that are relevant to male psychology.

The topics here are intended to approximate a lifespan approach, beginning with exploring the factors that influence toy preference. This is an interesting – sometimes controversial – topic, and highlights the nature/nurture debate around gender. There follows a discussion of autism spectrum disorder (ASD) and attention deficit hyperactivity disorder (ADHD), both of which are more common in boys than girls. The causes of delinquency are examined, covering issues such as childhood attachment, adverse experiences, violent video games and father absence. The chapter closes with two under-researched issues: the importance of fathers to child development, and a question that seems to have occurred to few people: what is it like for boys growing up in a culture obsessed with 'toxic masculinity'?

4.2   BOYS' PLAY STYLES AND TOY PREFERENCES

Many Western middle-class parents promote gender-neutral play (Zosuls et al., 2009). Naturally they want to do what is right for their children, and are acting on the assumption that sex differences in play behaviour reinforce harmful gender stereotypes (see SPOTLIGHT box 4.1).

Although a child typically develops a sense of their own gender, and the gender of others, around 18–24 months old (Martin & Ruble, 2010), they can already distinguish between male and female faces and voices by six months of age (Martin & Ruble, 2010). The child's concept of gender develops in tandem with their experience of the people around them, and although the child's behaviour does not necessarily mirror the gendered behaviour they see around them (Signorella et al., 1993), gender-typed toy preference tends to increase with age (Davis & Hines, 2020; Todd et al., 2018).

Several factors influence the developmental trajectories of the play behaviour of boys and girls, which might explain why the trajectories sometimes vary between studies (Servin et al., 1999). However based on the findings of a large number of studies spanning almost 100 years, one finding is pretty constant: there are large sex differences in toy preference, with boys preferring what are seen as male-typical toys such as cars, and girls preferring what are seen as female-typical toys such as dolls (Davis & Hines, 2020; Todd et al., 2018). These sex differences are statistically large (Cohen's $d > 0.8$), so the question is not whether boys and girls in general prefer different toys, but what the cause of this sex difference is. The three main explanations are the environment, biology or some combination of both.

4.2.1   *Impact of The Environment on Toy Preference*

It seems plausible that toy preference in children is influenced by a range of environmental cues, such as cultural norms and the attitude of parents. However, the evidence for a cultural influence is not as strong as might be thought. For example, Sweden has been one of the most gender-equal countries in the world for decades (World Economic Forum, 2017), and a Swedish study found girls – and boys – both preferred female-typed toys less as age increased (Servin et al., 1999). This type of cultural influence is not commonly seen in the literature on toy preference, and Servin et al. suggest their finding may have been caused by Sweden's 'equal-roles' family model, which could have encouraged young girls away from the traditional family role and thus away from female-typed toys. However, a study in Sweden a few years later found that the toyboxes of children had the same mix of gender-typical toys as found in other Western countries, suggesting a cultural influence of the 'equal-roles' model is doubtful (Nelson, 2005).

4.2.1.1 Impact of societal changes over time on toy preference

Without a doubt, cultural attitudes to gender have changed in recent decades. Two meta-analyses of toy preference literature, one of studies from 1963 to 2013 (Davis & Hines, 2020), and another of studies from 1980 to 2016 (Todd et al., 2018), found no impact of historical time on the sex difference in toy preference. In other words, the sex difference in how much boys and girls liked to play with toys typical of their own sex remained roughly the same over the years. However, the latter study also took into account the actual duration of play (in seconds) of boys and girls with sex-typical toys, and found both boys and girls – but especially girls – spent less time playing with toys typical of their sex in studies published more recently (Barry & Todd, 2021; Todd et al., 2018). We can't be certain of the reason for this, but the authors speculated that perhaps the cause was increased social pressure for children to be less gender-typical, although – as noted by Davis & Hines (2020) – actual advertising aimed at children remains traditional.

In a German study of 208 boys and girls aged five to eight years old in 1977, and 168 children of the same age in 2015, it was found that drawings depicting female figures were significantly more feminine today than in the 1970s (Lamm et al., 2019). The researchers also found that drawings of men were less masculine over time, but this trend was statistically non-significant. The authors also found that girls were significantly more likely to draw females in 2015 (82%) than in 1977 (34%). As with the trend identified by Todd et al. (2018), the changes over time were seen mainly in the girls rather than the boys. Lamm et al. suggest that the changes might reflect changes in gender equality and increased self-esteem of girls, and male attributes becoming 'less valued or socially accepted' (Lamm et al., 2019, p. 123). However, this study had some methodological limitations, e.g. the authors noted that because the drawings were made at school, 'participants may have anticipated teachers' rejection of male attributes and thus omitted them', and that 'all drawings were coded and rated by female research assistants' rather than asking the child which sex their drawing was (Lamm et al., 2019, p. 123). These issues suggest social desirability bias (the children guessed what the study was about and changed their behaviour accordingly) and experimenter effects (the ratings were influenced by subjectivity), casting doubt over the validity of the findings (*Theme: 'research and methodology'*, in Section 13.2.4).

Other social factors that potentially impact children's toy preference appear to do so only weakly, if at all. The meta-analysis and meta-regression by Todd et al. (2018) found no significant effect on children's toy preference of the presence of an adult, whether the study took place at the child's home or at a research institute, or whether gender-neutral toys were available to the child in the study. Given that the large magnitude of sex differences in toy preference are not explained by environmental factors, it seems plausible that innate forces are a stronger explanatory factor.

4.2.2   Influence of Biology on Toy Preference

One way to try and distinguish between biological and social influences is to examine the behaviour of very young infants, for whom the duration of socialisation is minimal. In contrast to the relatively weak evidence for the impact of the environment on toy preference, there is a lot of evidence for a biological influence. There is even evidence that prenatal exposure to androgens (testosterone-like substances) is correlated with the gender-typicality of toy choice (Nordenström et al., 2002).

Overall, evidence appears to converge towards the hypotheses that boys prefer toys that move, and girls prefer toys with faces. These differences may have biological and evolutionary underpinnings because they seem to map onto cognitive and behavioural differences between boys and girls which are seen from an early age (see section 7.3.1). For example, toys that move or have a mechanical aspect might appeal more to boys because of boys' relative advantage in the mental rotation of objects (Moore & Johnson, 2008; Quinn & Liben, 2008, 2014), event mapping (Schweinle & Wilcox, 2004; Wilcox, 2003) and mechanical reasoning (Lemos et al., 2013). Conversely, girls' greater interest in toys with faces might be related to girls' greater tendency to mutual gaze (Lavelli & Fogel, 2002; Leeb & Rejskind, 2004) and processing of facial expressions (McClure, 2000).

4.2.3   Evidence from Evolution: Monkeys Show a Sex Difference in Play Behaviour

Some of the most intriguing evidence supporting the biological basis for sex differences in toy preferences comes, unexpectedly, from animals. There is a large body of evidence in animal research finding strong effects of prenatal and perinatal exposure to sex hormones on a range of sex-related behaviours, including juvenile play (Meyer-Bahlburg et al., 2004). Even more intriguingly, some research has found that male monkeys spend longer than females manipulating toys that move (wheeled toys or a ball), whereas female monkeys make more contact with a doll and cooking pot (Alexander & Hines, 2002; Hassett et al., 2008). Most intriguing of all is research that finds a sex difference in how primates play with objects: young females tend to play with objects as if they are nurturing an infant, and young males play with the same objects with more vigour, often as a weapon.

Compelling evidence for a biological basis for play behaviour comes from a 14-year study of 'stick-carrying' in Ugandan chimpanzees (Kahlenberg & Wrangham, 2010). These chimps tend to use sticks to signal aggression, to find food (e.g. taking honey from a hole), during play or as 'stick-carrying'. This latter behaviour accounted for about 40% of stick-related behaviour, and was initially puzzling for researchers. The behaviour was observed to be most common in juvenile females, compared to weapon use, which was most common in males. The researchers noted that stick-carrying sometimes involved cradling of the stick, and the behaviour always occurred prior to the female's first birth and ended when the female became a mother. The researchers concluded that stick-carrying is a form of play-mothering. The sex difference in stick-carrying appeared to be spontaneous and without any teaching by adult chimps, making social learning an unlikely explanation.

The overall explanation for the sex differences observed in these various human and non-human animal studies is that, in general, males are naturally predisposed to activities such as hunting and building, and females are naturally predisposed to nurturing the young (Hines, 2005). Extrapolating this evidence to humans, when boys are playing with cars this could be an expression of an innate tendency to track moving objects, as might be done in hunting, and when girls play with dolls this could be an expression of an innate tendency to nurturance and mothering.

SPOTLIGHT BOX 4.1

IS SANTA SEXIST?

Santa gives little boys things like toy soldiers and cars, and gives little girls baby dolls. That's very generous ... but isn't it also a little bit sexist? The accusation of sexism in this scenario is based on the presumption that boys and girls don't really have preferences for those toys, and the apparent preferences are imposed on them by culture, via Santa.

Children's toys have become the focus of heated controversy. On the one hand, toy manufacturers, advertisers and retailers are accused of exaggerating sex typing of toys, and on the other hand, feminist campaigners are accused of damaging children by forcing them to accept a gender-neutral lifestyle which oppresses the child's personal preferences (Theme: 'one-size-fits-all', Section 13.2.4).

On one side of the argument is the evidence that toy preference is largely biological. This side of the argument might be accused of being characterised by alpha bias, the tendency to focus on sex differences. On the other side of the argument is the belief that masculinity and femininity are merely social constructs, and gender-typicality is a dubious type of social conformity. The arguments on this side are supported by research characterised by beta-bias – the tendency to overlook sex differences – such as the review of meta-analyses of psychological sex differences (Hyde, 2005) that didn't take into account dozens of toy preference studies, or the hundreds of studies reviewed by Ellis (2011), that would have undermined her 'gender similarities hypothesis'.

So what kind of toys should Santa give to children? Probably he should give them the type of toys they like, regardless of gender norms. Differences in gendered preferences are part of the spectrum of human behaviour – most children will be gender-typical in their preferences, but it's normal for some children to be atypical in their preferences. What if Santa doesn't know the preferences of a particular child? Then it would make sense statistically to choose the gender-typical option, which is the option that on average is most likely to be preferred. This might be a safer option than a choice based on delta bias (Seager & Barry, 2020), where the gender-atypical choice is the one preferred for the child.

4.3 DEVELOPMENTAL DIFFERENCES AND VULNERABILITIES IN BOYS

It is normal for boys to be delayed in their development compared to girls. An important issue is how much this impacts their academic future, and if so, what can be done about it.

4.3.1 *Language and Memory*

Language is a prime example of the sex difference in cognitive development: at one year old the vocabulary of a girl raised by a mother with little education is larger than that of a boy raised by a highly educated mother (Zambrana et al., 2012). The reading and writing skills of boys continue to lag behind those of girls throughout education, and the percentage of girls who get a top grade in English is sometimes double that of boys (Stoet, 2019).

Memory is another major issue: the natural process of 'pruning' brain connections begins around age 10 in girls but age 15 in boys (Lim et al., 2015). Also, boys are 16 times more likely to be colour blind, which puts up a myriad of obstacles to their educational achievement, which often go unnoticed by schools (see also SPOTLIGHT box 5.1).

4.3.2 *Attention Deficit Hyperactivity Disorder (ADHD)*

Both ASD and ADHD are generally more highly represented in boys than in girls (Yang et al., 2018). Boys are more likely than girls to show difficult behaviour at school, and this can be a sign of underlying attentional problems such as ADHD (DuPaul & Stoner, 2014).

ADHD is characterised by hyperactivity, impulsivity and distractibility (Chheda-Varma, 2019). Brain imaging of children with ADHD often finds patterns of neuroanatomical abnormalities (Swanson & Castellanos, 2002), but the cause is far from clear. There is evidence that several factors increase vulnerability to developing ADHD. The list includes trauma (e.g. difficult birth), problems at home, anxiety and conflictual or difficult relationship with parents (Chheda-Varma, 2019), specifically father absence (Briggs, 2019).

Environmental factors may be important, e.g. endocrine disruptors such as BPA are associated with both ADHD and ASD (see Section 10.2.3). Maternal tobacco smoking and low iron during pregnancy are also risks for ADHD, though it's unclear why this impacts mainly male children (Chheda-Varma, 2019). Elevated prenatal testosterone levels might also be a risk factor: a large GP database found autism and ADHD are more common in women with PCOS, a condition associated with elevated testosterone (Berni et al., 2018). Genetic inheritance is also a possibility: there is a 60–90% greater risk of developing ADHD if a family member has ADHD (Gizer et al., 2009).

When their father is absent, children are more vulnerable to mental health-related outcomes, such as ADHD, self-harm and sexually inappropriate behaviour (Briggs, 2019). The link between an absent father and a patient with ADHD is through the impact of boundaries on emotional regulation. With the father at home the child grows up with a more developed sense of boundaries, learning that it is separate from the mother and the father, and that the parents have a relationship that the child is not part of. 'Internalising boundaries allows for emotional regulation. Internalising a father allows for emotions to be held in check that might otherwise run riot' (Briggs, 2019, p. 73). Without emotional regulation and development of executive functioning, the child is at risk of developing the symptoms recognised as ADHD.

There is some suggestion that ADHD is overdiagnosed and overmedicated, and the true cause of the problem is that schools today are feminised and are no longer ready to adequately channel the high energy normal among boys (Sax, 2009). High activity levels are often seen as problematic and 'naughty' or even pathological, although in careers that require energy and daring, high energy can be an asset (Chheda-Varma, 2019).

4.3.3 *Autism Spectrum Disorder (ASD)*

It is usually estimated that autism is four times more common in males and Asperger syndrome is nine times more common in males, though it is possible that ASD presents differently in girls, with less social deficit, meaning that autism is under-diagnosed in girls (van Wijngaarden-Cremers, 2019). People 'on the spectrum' may have a reduced 'theory of mind', i.e. less ability to understand others' feelings and points of view, as well as a greater tendency to be interested in numbers and facts rather than people, and because these two traits are usually seen more in men than women, it has been suggested that autism is an extreme version of the male brain, caused by exposure to elevations in testosterone prenatally (Baron-Cohen et al., 2011). There is compelling evidence for genetic influences, e.g. the concordance rate in twin studies of ASD is 90% (van Wijngaarden-Cremers, 2019). It is worth noting that some ASD traits (e.g. attention to detail) can be very useful.

4.4 FACTORS THAT INFLUENCE DELINQUENCY AND MENTAL HEALTH

Identifying the causes of crime is a means to help prevent crime, not an excuse for criminality. It is possible for many factors to influence criminality (see Chapter 8), and just the ones related to early life are listed in this section. The section covers attachment, adverse or difficult childhood environments, the influence of mothers and fathers and violence from parents.

4.4.1 *Sex Difference in Attachment*

Childhood attachment is an important and popular topic in psychology, exploring the emotional bond which forms from birth between an infant and their 'primary caregiver', who is traditionally the mother. The quality of attachment can have a profound and lasting impact across the child's lifespan, shaping the character of any significant relationships – for better if the attachment is 'secure', or for worse if the attachment is anxious or insecure in some other way (Seager, 2013).

It is generally accepted that there are no sex differences in attachment in young children (van IJzendoorn et al., 2000), but some research suggests that starting around seven years of age, sex differences emerge. For example, an Italian study of 122 seven-year-olds doing a story completion task found a prevalence of avoidant patterns (e.g. dealing with distress by oneself or by watching TV) in boys and a greater prevalence of ambivalent patterns (where distress was difficult to resolve) in girls (Del Giudice, 2008). The authors explain this sex difference as indicating normal developmental processes related to the onset of puberty in preparation for emotional bonding in later adult relationship formation. Much research suggests that early childhood attachment is predictive of behavioural outcomes in later life, but the findings of Del Giudice suggest that attachment is not completely stable over time, and changes during middle childhood.

Some studies suggest that attachment is the key predictor of delinquency, even more than economic factors, or other family factors. A nationally representative sample of 9636 adolescents and their mothers in the US found that maternal attachment was a stronger predictor of delinquency than family structure (intact, divorced, death of parent or never married) or economic resources, irrespective of the race and gender of the child (Mack et al., 2007). A weakness of this study is that attachment to the father was not measured, and there were not enough single-father families in the sample for meaningful statistical analyses to assess their effect.

A meta-analysis of 74 published studies (55,537 boys and girls in total) found that poor attachment to parents was significantly linked, to a similar degree, to delinquency in boys and girls (Hoeve et al., 2012). In terms of delinquency, 'attachment to mothers was more important for girls, while attachment to fathers was more important for boys', though this doesn't explain the gender gap in crime (Hoeve et al., 2012, p. 780). The influence of attachment on delinquency reduces as youngsters grow older, but nonetheless an interesting but unexplored question is the possibility that different types of attachment predict different types of criminal behaviours (Del Giudice, 2008).

An online survey of 551 women and 172 men, mean age of 25 years old, found that memories of insecure attachment are linked to suicidality in adulthood (Zortea et al., 2020). A meta-analysis of 52 studies (21,777 males and 24,689 females) found that secure attachment protects against suicide risk and insecure attachment increases suicide risk, especially for women, probably by impairing the ability to cope with relationship problems (Zortea et al., 2019). Unfortunately, the separate roles of the father and mother are not usually differentiated in these studies.

4.4.2   *Adverse or Difficult Childhood Environments*

Note that this section is mostly about the impact of adverse *environments* in childhood (such as poverty, violence between parents, lack of educational opportunities), rather than *adverse childhood experiences* (ACEs, discussed in Section 4.4.3), which place more emphasis on the person rather than their environment.

Adverse childhood environments negatively impact boys and girls, but whereas for girls this increases anxiety and depression (Ellis & Del Giudice, 2019), the effect on boys is to increase the likelihood of greater risk-taking, antisocial behaviour and intra-sexual aggression (i.e. aggression with other boys; Durrant, 2019).

Moffitt and Caspi (2001) found that childhood delinquency, in contrast to adolescent-onset delinquency, was predicted by inadequate parenting, neuro-cognitive problems and temperament and behaviour problems. They suggest that the triggers to delinquency were similar for males and females (child-hood-onset delinquency was linked to high-risk backgrounds), but males are more susceptible to childhood-onset delinquency. In fact, boys are ten times more likely than girls to have childhood-onset delinquency, though only slightly more likely (a ratio of 1.5:1) to have adolescent-onset delinquency.

Various studies have found that compared to adolescent-onset offenders, childhood-onset offenders show heightened impulsivity, structural brain abnormalities, neuropsychological deficits and temperamental deficits (Gesch, 2013b). Papalia et al. (2017) say although 'Moffitt's taxonomy' (child-hood-onset vs late-onset offending) has been very influential, some research suggests that only a minority of offenders who have neurocognitive diffi-culties and other problems fit this model (e.g. Jennings & Reingle, 2012; Mof-fitt, 2006b), and that other relevant predictors include familial fragmentation, early regulatory and mental health problems, drug abuse and disrupted schooling (e.g. Odgers et al., 2008).

Interestingly, the risk of psychopathology is more strongly associated with subjective measures rather than objective measures of childhood maltreat-ment (Danese & Widom, 2020). The next section discusses a measure that has become very popular in recent years: the *ACEs* measure.

4.4.3   *Adverse Childhood Experiences (ACEs)*

ACEs quantify the number of adverse experiences a person experiences as a child, such as emotional abuse, physical abuse or sexual abuse. One point is given for each event, and scores can range from zero to ten. A systematic review and meta-analysis of 37 studies (253,719 participants) found that com-pared to people with an ACE score of 0, those with a score of 4 or more were at increased risk across the full spectrum of health outcomes measured, from obesity to violence (Hughes et al., 2017). The risk related to an ACEs score was highest for sexual risk-taking, mental illness and alcohol abuse, and espe-cially strong for drug abuse, self-harm and violence.

The originator of the concept of ACEs, Robert Anda, has criticised the misapplication of the concept (Anda et al., 2020). He cautioned that although ACEs are strongly correlated with mental and physical health outcomes at a *population* level, thus useful for research and public health, it is a relatively crude measure on an *individual* level, thus difficult to apply ACEs scores to each per-son's life. Related to this issue, someone with an ACEs score of 1 might have experienced intense abuse over a long period, whereas another person with a score of 5 might have experienced five mild and very brief adverse experiences (Anda et al., 2020). These two examples are atypical but not unusual, but in theory differences of this kind should even themselves out on a population level, where they will be mixed in with a large number of other people's scores. Accordingly, Anda et al. suggest that programmes using ACEs scores for screening, diagnosis or other clinical purposes should be properly assessed to make sure that ACE scores are clinically useful in specific contexts.

Note that this issue of 'individual vs population' is relevant also to sex differences research, where the differences are seen in men on average, not necessarily in the individual man (*Theme: 'research and methodology'*, in Section 13.2.4).

4.4.4 *Family Environment and Delinquency*

There is a great deal of literature to suggest that the traditional family unit reduces the risk of delinquency (see e.g. the review by Mwangangi (2019)). Various theories have been developed over the years as to how the family might reduce delinquency. Hirschi's (1969) *social control theory* suggests that delinquency is seen in youngsters with poor attachment, and who have little faith in the benefits of conventional behaviour. Studies identify various mechanisms of encouraging conformity in children, e.g. through monitoring behaviour, applying consistent discipline and developing healthy attachments (Gottfredson & Hirschi, 1990). The *family crisis model* suggests that issues often seen in divorce (psychological distress, emotional resentment, social tension) cause children to seek attention by 'acting out' through antisocial behaviour (Felner et al., 1981). A meta-analysis by Wells and Rankin (1991) concluded that the death of a parent may have an impact on delinquency too, though not as strong as the impact of loss of a parent through divorce or family separation. Children of single parents are more likely than those from intact traditional families to show more delinquent behaviour (e.g. Juby & Farrington, 2001).

This pattern of findings from earlier studies regarding family structure and delinquency is particularly significant in studies that use official data compared to those that use self-report measures, and for certain types of juvenile conduct problems, such as 'status offending' (e.g. truancy, underage drinking etc; Mack et al., 2007). However, there are different types of single parent households, and generalisations don't hold across them. Also, many studies show that offenders tend to come from large-sized families, probably because of the difficulty of parents dividing attention simultaneously between several children at once (Farrington, 2010).

A longitudinal study of 411 boys in the UK found that parents can reduce the chance of antisocial tendencies by building a strong conscience in the child and helping them to value good behaviour, e.g. through rewarding good behaviour and encouraging respect for the law (Farrington, 1995). Delinquent behaviour was associated with harsh or erratic parental discipline; cruel, passive or neglecting parental attitudes; parental conflict; and poor supervision.

4.4.5   *Violence from Parents*

Data collected from child welfare agencies in the US found that of the 3,534,000 children who received a child protective services investigation, 53.5% of all child abuse and neglect was perpetrated by women (Pecora et al., 2018). In cases of maltreatment, 39.4% of victims are maltreated by the mother acting alone, and 21.5% of victims by the father acting alone. There were 25.5% more fatalities due to abuse of boys than girls (2.87 per 100,000 boys and 2.11 per 100,000 girls). Of fatalities, 78% involved a parent acting alone, 26.8% by the mother and 16.4% by the father. In cases of sex trafficking, 7% were by the mother and 4.5% by the father. Abuse and neglect was much more likely to come from biological parents than from stepparents, foster parents, legal guardians or others.

4.4.6   *Importance of Mothers*

A National Institute of Child Health and Human Development longitudinal study of 1364 families in the US found from the earliest assessments that more hours in child care and more centre-type care were related to higher levels of behavioural problems from early childhood to age 15 (Vandell et al., 2010). Of a sample of 1003 American parents, 51% said that children are better off if their mother is at home, and 34% said children are as well off with a working mother (Pew, 2013). Only 8% said that children are better off if their father stays at home and doesn't have a job, while 76% said children are just as well off if their father's job is outside the home.

A longitudinal study in the UK of 191 women and 148 men from the *Understanding Society* panel, from 2010 to 2013, found that when women became mothers for the first time their attitudes become more favourable to traditional parenting roles, with the mother staying more at home and the father taking on the bulk of earning the household income (Grinza et al., 2017). The shift in attitude happened gradually over a year or so after birth, and was largest for women who were more non-traditional in their views before becoming a mother. Men's attitudes to traditional family roles were largely unaffected by becoming a father. Anecdotally, people who become parents start to see gender-typical behaviour in their children, and are thereafter less inclined to think gender-typical behaviour is caused by socialisation. This under-researched topic is lent indirect support by a study of 1,041 adults, finding that mothers of two or more children were relatively accurate in estimating the heritability level of psychological traits, such as violence and personality (Willoughby et al., 2019).

4.4.7 *Importance of Fathers in Preventing Delinquency*

A report on youth crime England and Wales estimated that 76% of all men in prison had an absent father and 33% an absent mother (Jacobson & Prison Reform Trust (Great Britain), 2010). A large meta-analysis found that poor attachment to the father was linked to delinquency in boys (Hoeve et al., 2012). It has been suggested that 'dad deprivation' leaves boys more vulnerable to a life of crime, and prisons have been described as 'centres for dad-deprived young men' (Farrell & Gray, 2019, p. 327).

A high percentage of gang members come from father-absent homes (Davidson, 1990). Through gangs, sometimes youths can find a sense of community and acceptance, and the gang leader may fill in for the role of the father (Farrell & Gray, 2019). In contrast, data from a UK longitudinal study found that the children of active fathers were up to 28% less likely to suffer behavioural problems in their pre-teen years compared to children without a father figure at home (Opondo et al., 2016). Another longitudinal study in the UK found that having a father who rarely joined in the boy's leisure activities at age 12 predicted persistence in crime in adulthood, possibly due to the son compensating by 'showing off' to peers in displays of aggression (Farrington, 1995). Criminal fathers can influence sons into criminality, though it is said to be rare for criminal men to commit offences with their fathers (Farrington, 1995).

4.5 IMPORTANCE OF INCLUDING FATHERS

The child who is not embraced by the village will burn it down to feel its warmth
                                                                    –African proverb

4.5.1 *Importance of the Role of Fathers*

In traditional cultures, the men are crucial to initiating the boys into adulthood and making them productive members of the community (Brown, 2016). In the modern West, by contrast, fatherhood tends to be overlooked in the literature on parenting, and has been for decades. This lack has been described as a 'systemic pathology in our understanding of what being a man and being a father entail' (Laquer, 1992, p. 155). Despite this, there is evidence for the benefits of fathers (see Section 4.4.7).

A study of 2000 men in the British Isles found that the more a man aspires to be like his father, the better his mental health (Barry, 2020). This raises the question of how diminished the mental health is of boys who grow up without a father who they want to be like. Disturbed attachment to the father is a risk factor for delinquency, especially in boys (see Section 4.4.7), and there is evidence that interventions for delinquency are more effective when the father is involved (Hoeve et al., 2012; Lundahl et al., 2008). This all raises the further question of why the benefits of fatherhood are so relatively overlooked in research, and the wider modern Western culture.

4.5.2 *Sex Difference in Parenting Style, and Emotional Regulation*

Compared to women, men tend to have a 'generative' fathering style, which focuses on the child's positive social, emotional and intellectual growth, to help the next generation live a better life (Kiselica & Englar-Carlson, 2010). This is in contrast to mothering, which is more likely to involve meeting essential emotional and physical needs (Mitchell & Lashewicz, 2019). A meta-analysis of 78 studies, mostly in the US, found that rough and tumble play of the kind typically done more by fathers with their young children (up to three years old) can be beneficial for children's social, emotional and cognitive outcomes (Amodia-Bidakowska et al., 2020). Fathers engaged more than mothers in tickling, chasing and piggy-back rides, and the benefits come from the child learning to regulate their feelings during these interactions. During such play the child learns what behaviour is acceptable, e.g. not lashing out in anger if their father accidentally stands on their toe. This play provides a safe arena in which to 'road test' how to respond to situations with someone who can correct those responses in a caring way.

Involvement in home life and childcare is fundamental to many fathers' identity, especially younger men (Shirani et al., 2012). Becoming a father is associated with lower testosterone levels, which probably serves the adaptive purpose of keeping energies focused on bonding within the family (Barry & Owens, 2019). In recent times in the West the father role has been faced with the challenge of fathers needing to spend more time at home, or even becoming 'stay-at-home-dads'. However, the reality of 'involved fathering' is quite different from the theory, and pressures to be more intimate and involved have not reduced expectations to be a 'breadwinner' (Hadley, 2019). There are several factors that often prevent fathers from accomplishing their desired level of involvement, including 'societal attitudes, issues relating to the development of their baby, economic barriers, a lack of support from healthcare practitioners and government policies' (Machin, 2015, p. 36). It is sometimes said that men just aren't very interested in becoming fathers, and don't feel much pressure because they can have children at any time in their lives. Although this is true for some men, especially younger men, this narrative might have the consequence of influencing men to plan less for family life and more for personal independence (Fisher & Hammarberg, 2017). Furthermore, men's fertility is impacted by older age, and fertility problems for men can have a similar level of psychological impact as that associated with heart complaints or cancer (Saleh et al., 2003). Ultimately, men who are fathers are happier and less socially isolated than men who want children but don't have any (Hadley, 2019).

4.5.3   *Biological Fathers vs Stepfathers*

The question of whether there is any advantage to having a biological father while growing up is an interesting one, especially given evidence of the importance of father involvement (see Section 8.6.3). Despite an apparently high level of research interest in the impact of fathers on children, there has been surprisingly little research that focuses on the biological father as opposed to father figures. What research there is has found interesting results. A longitudinal study in the US of 2733 children concluded that the children of biological fathers who were highly involved in their upbringing had better outcomes than children of other family structures, or low-involved biological fathers. The adolescent children of highly involved biological fathers had significantly fewer behavioural problems on the outcomes measured, which were externalising behaviour (e.g. arguing, lying); delinquency; negative feelings (e.g. sadness, nervousness, tiredness); and internalising behaviour (e.g. being withdrawn;) (Carlson, 2006).

A methodologically robust longitudinal study of more than 7000 children in the UK assessed the difference between children of single mothers, mothers with stepfathers, children of biological parents who divorced, and children who were born into a household where their biological parents lived together and remained together for the first seven years of life of the child (Mariani et al., 2017). They found that compared to any of the other groups, children with a present biological father were significantly better at cognitive tasks (spatial problem solving using patterned squares), and less at risk of internalising issues, such as depression. These benefits might be due to better health and emotional support in families with biological fathers present. They also found that even when there was a divorce, children who had a biological father present were less likely to be obese, which the study authors suggested was because 'enforcement of rules is easier in households with biological fathers' (Mariani et al., 2017, p. 200).

Despite the social relevance of findings like these, a review of studies of father involvement on children suggest that 'Further studies [are] needed to clarify the role of biological fathers vs father figures' (Sarkadi et al., 2008,

p. 156). This was mainly because studies of fathers used a broad definition of 'father', which could include stepfathers and others. This definitional confusion is ongoing, e.g. the American Academy of Pediatrics' guidelines on fathers define fathers as 'the male or males identified as most involved in caregiving and committed to the well-being of the child, regardless of living situation, marital status, or biological relation' (Nierengarten, 2019, p. 1). Given evidence that the biological father can have a different impact on children than stepfathers, future research should make the distinction between biological father and father figure more clearly (*Theme: 'flawed definitions'*, in Section 13.2.4).

PARENTAL ALIENATION

Parental alienation occurs when one parent creates a negative narrative about the other, either deliberately in order to harm the other parent, or inadvertently. This often happens in the context of family breakdown, and the negative narrative is conducted in the absence of a reasonable basis to do so. Sometimes the parents' alienating behaviours are deliberate, with the intention of hurting the other ('target') parent, though sometimes the alienating parent is not aware of the impact on the child. Indeed, not all children exposed to alienating behaviours will become alienated. Signs of alienation are a child's strong alignment with one parent while rejecting a relationship with the other. The child's rejection is typically disproportionate, idealising the alienating parent and totally rejecting the target parent. In comparison, children who have experienced abuse from a parent might still want to see that parent, despite feeling uneasy around them. Children who are alienated aren't conscious of this process, but feel a strong need to reject the target parent (Whitcombe, 2013).

On the surface, the alienated child might seem to function well, though may show anger, withdrawal, aggression and other signs of disturbance such as depression and sleep disturbance. However, the longer term impact on the child in later life can be seen in mental health problems, substance abuse and impaired ability to sustain healthy work and personal relationships (Baker, 2005).

It is estimated that around 1.3% of parents in the US have children who were moderately to severely alienated, and these parents – at least half of whom are men – are at increased risk for depression, trauma symptoms and suicide (Harman et al., 2019).

Although parental alienation is a very significant child attachment issue, it has been a victim of gender politics, mainly because it impacts child access issues in family courts. The result is that it has been difficult to help children suffering from this condition, in part due to objections by activists to the inclusion of parental alienation as a diagnosis in the DSM and ICD (Whitcombe, 2013).

4.5.4 *Involuntary Childlessness*

Around 25% of men and 20% of women in Europe don't have children over their lifetime (Tanturri et al., 2015), and around 80% of this is involuntary. Involuntary childlessness can come about for various reasons, e.g. medical, social or sexual orientation-related (see also Section 10.2.1). A study of 396 men and women over the age of 50 found that having an anxious childhood attachment is significantly correlated with being childless (Hadley, Newby & Barry, 2019). Although younger men tend to be less interested in being fathers than older men, it is sometimes only in later life that the rewards of having children become apparent, and the costs of being childless are felt more consciously (Hadley, 2019). There is less research on childlessness in men than in women, possibly an example of gamma bias (see Section 2.5.5.1).

4.6 THE NEGATIVE DISCOURSE ON MASCULINITY

The word 'toxic' was voted *Word of the Year* in 2018 by Oxford University Press. This award is given to the word that most reflects the preoccupations of society that are likely to be of lasting cultural significance, so it is significant that in a year of news stories about environmental pollution, the phrase 'toxic masculinity' was rated second only to 'toxic chemicals'.

Most people want their children to grow up in a place where they will be happy and avoid stressful experiences such as prejudice and discrimination. Although masculinity in the past has been associated with positive traits, in recent years the academic and media discourse have become increasingly negative (see Section 12.5.2, and SPOTLIGHT box 12.4).

4.6.1 *What is it Like Growing up in a Culture that Distrusts Masculinity?*

Throughout history, men and women have faced difficulties of various kinds, some related to gender (e.g. men being drafted to war) and some related to biology (e.g. women and the dangers of childbirth). However, in recent decades boys have been growing up experiencing a new difficulty: being raised in a culture that sees maleness as a problem. For example, a study in New York of 237 children aged 5–11 reported that even when boys show a selfless concern for girls, it is considered 'benevolent sexism' (Hammond & Cimpian, 2020). Unstructured interviews with boys in high schools in the US and Australia found that boys want to support the #MeToo movement, but feel excluded (Reiner, 2020). For instance, in a discussion at a Baltimore high school of 'male power and privilege', boys found they were 'shut down' when they asked about the double standard of girls being allowed to hit boys but not vice versa. Similarly, in an Australian high school a boy who asked why girls can touch and kiss boys without asking, but not vice versa, was also shut down. Based on these examples, the impact of #MeToo on boys is to make them resent being shamed, confused, silenced and worried, to the point that they are becoming averse to romantic relationships.

This potential alienation of boys – from girls, from culture and even from their own masculinity (*gender alienation*) – has potentially serious psychosocial implications, but has received very little academic research. However, there has been some academic work indirectly related to this topic which is instructive. For example, boys are more quickly associated with negative attributes than are girls (Heyman, 2001), and sometimes when people are given a bad name they start to live up to it (Sharma & Sharma, 2015). Without being given a way to develop a healthy identity, many boys are likely to opt for an unhealthy identity (Nathanson & Young, 2009). A survey of 589 adolescent boys in the US found that those who experienced 'stress about being perceived as "sub-masculine" may be more likely to engage in sexual violence as a means of demonstrating their masculinity' (Reidy et al., 2015, p. 619). Social constructionists – who believe that masculinity is a social construct – believe that language doesn't simply describe the world, it constructs it. This being the case, social constructionists should be especially aware of the risks of using shaming language (*Theme: 'unintended consequences'*, in Section 13.2.1).

4.6.2 Are Boys Affected by the Narrative about 'Toxic Masculinity'?

No study to date has tried to assess the impact on boys of terms that are commonly used in Western culture, such as 'toxic masculinity'. However, an online survey, with 88% of respondents from Europe or North America, asked 203 men and 52 women their opinions on the popular narrative around masculinity, including what they thought the impact on boys might be (Barry et al., 2020). Around 90% of male and female participants agreed that the idea of 'toxic masculinity' changes the way we see all men. Both men and women moderately agreed that the term might be harmful to boys, and there was strong agreement that the term wouldn't improve men's behaviour. In contrast, terms like 'traditional masculinity' and 'positive masculinity' were seen much more favourably.

Without a doubt, research is needed to find out the impact on boys of the negative views of masculinity in Western culture. We can only speculate what the impact might be, but it is perhaps not difficult to understand why some boys retreat into a world of video games and other online distractions (*Theme: 'unintended consequences'*, in Section 13.2.1).

DO VIDEO GAMES CAUSE VIOLENCE?

In the US, 84% of adolescent boys and 59% of adolescent girls (aged 10–19) play video games (Bassiouni et al., 2019). Ever since Bandura's highly influential Bobo Doll study suggested that children imitate aggressive behaviour, it has been 'received wisdom' that depictions of violence in the media can influence young people to be violent (Bandura et al., 1961). Although the American Psychological Association has taken a firm stance against violent video games on the basis of the supposed link between violent video game exposure and aggressive behaviour, the evidence supporting this link is surprisingly limited (APA, 2015; Ferguson, 2020b). For example, a review of 25 years of research into violent video games concluded that 'evidence regarding the impact of violent digital games on player aggression is, at best, mixed' and that persistent claims of such a link damaged the credibility of research in this field (Elson & Ferguson, 2014, p. 33).

More recently, fears have arisen about the specific influence of gaming on gun crime, e.g. school shootings. A US study of two national samples of more than 50,000 adolescent boys and girls (around 13–16 years old) examined the relationship between the number of hours they played video games (on any device) and how often they brought a gun to school (Elson & Ferguson, 2014). After taking other factors into account (age, social background) the result was an unconvincing correlation between video game use and gun-related behaviours: low levels of gaming were correlated with a low chance of taking a gun to school, but higher levels of gaming were related to only a small increase in likelihood of taking a gun to school.

We know aggression and violence have many possible causes (see Chapter 8 and Section 4.4), but it seems that video games are at most a minor part of the problem. The 'moral panic' over video games is therefore ill-founded, except perhaps at the very highest extremes of use.

It should be noted that much of the narrative on video games overlooks the benefits of gaming, e.g. improving motor skills, selective visual attention and cognitive abilities (Bavelier et al., 2011). These benefits have even been useful clinically, e.g. in a video game that can help children with ADHD to control impulsivity (Crepaldi et al., 2020).

4.6.3 *Relationship Formation in the Twenty-First Century*

Young men are sometimes said to be more interested in video games and pornography than they are interested in girls. Indeed there is now a sizeable online community who call themselves MGTOWs ('Men Going Their Own Way'), who have turned their back on marriage and relationships in favour of casual sex, though some choose celibacy (Daubney, 2015). Similarly, an online community of self-described 'incels' (involuntary celibates) has emerged in recent years, these being young men who can't find a sexual or romantic partner (Yarrow, 2018). Sometimes the men who brave the world of dating resort to the techniques of 'pickup artists' (PUAs). Generally, men who fail to date women are looked down on, and those who use PUA techniques are distrusted. However, there is evidence that these behaviours are done more out of necessity than malice, and indeed there is some evidence that sometimes these groups serve to provide a supportive community in a competitive and unforgiving dating environment (Whitley & Zhou, 2020).

4.7 CONCLUDING REMARKS

Parents in the US are reporting that their boys are more likely than their girls to have serious emotional and behavioural difficulties (CDCMMWR, 2020). This chapter highlights many possible reasons why this might be happening, such as developmental disorders, deprivation or lack of a father at home. However, there is a strange lack of empathy for boys around these issues, and the potential impact of the negative discourse about masculinity is all but ignored. Instead there is a tendency to see boys and their life choices as the problem, and video games, school performance and even a child's choice of toy have become problematic. Furthermore, there seems to be an unwillingness to acknowledge possible causes of violence, such as childhood trauma and social deprivation, in favour of moral panics about video games. Ironically, true pathologies such as dad deprivation are given less importance than socially constructed pathologies such as toxic masculinity.

It makes sense that if we had a more realistic understanding of boys' behaviour, then we could support them in their vulnerabilities and promote their strengths in a way that could be to the benefit of all society. But at present we appear to be hindered by victim-blaming (*Theme: 'victim-blaming'*, in Section 13.2.3), and one might speculate that it is far easier for people to blame men and masculinity for antisocial behaviour than it is to fix the social conditions that create it.

4.8 SUMMARY

- This chapter has considered several topics in child development relevant to male psychology.
- Biological, evolutionary and social factors can all influence children's toy preferences.
- ASD and ADHD are more common in boys than in girls.
- Parenting and early adverse experiences can influence criminality and mental health.
- The positive impact of fathers – especially biological fathers – lacks research.
- The possible impact of the 'toxic masculinity' narrative on boys needs further research.

5 Education

CHAPTER OUTLINE

Perspectives in Male Psychology: An Introduction, First Edition.
Louise Liddon and John A. Barry.
© 2021 John Wiley & Sons, Ltd. Published 2021 by John Wiley & Sons, Ltd.

LEARNING OUTCOMES

By the end of this chapter, you should be able to:

1. Understand why boys are behind girls in education
2. Recognise sex differences in educational ability
3. Realise the implications of boys' underachievement
4. Recognise problems in teaching about gender
5. Know some of the solutions to the 'boy problem' in education

5.1 INTRODUCTION

This chapter will explore the reasons why boys have fallen behind girls in education since around the 1990s. The consequences of the gender education gap will be explored, and solutions suggested. Key issues highlighted include: an assessment of the benefits of male schoolteachers; the unrecognised impact of colour blindness on academic performance; sex differences in academic aptitude; problems with teaching about gender; university dropout; and the limits of our knowledge of the long-term consequences of boys' failure in education.

5.2 WHY ARE BOYS FALLING BEHIND GIRLS IN SCHOOL?

The academic performance of secondary school students in the UK has been higher for girls than boys since 1993 (Bramley & Rodeiro, 2014). A similar situation is seen in the US and other Western countries (Stoet, 2019). In developed countries across the world girls have surpassed boys in educational attainment for several decades, not only in tests of literacy – in which girls traditionally excel – but also in mathematics and science, which are subjects that boys traditionally have excelled in (Pekkarinen, 2012). Boys underperform academically compared to girls regardless of social background (Hillman & Robinson, 2016). This phenomenon can be seen in early education and continues through all educational levels (Stoet & Yang, 2016).

Despite some misreporting in the media (Stoet, 2017), the gender education gap is increasing. For example, according to a report by the Universities and Colleges Admissions Service, the gender gap in university enrolment doubled between 2007 and 2015 (Stoet, 2019). In the UK in 2015, for every 10 boys who entered university, 13 girls did so too (Stoet, 2019). Apart from the loss of potential economic benefits of a better educated workforce, educational underachievement can have personal costs to individuals and to society, especially when underachievement turns into delinquency (Shader, 2004).

There are several explanations for the gender education gap, any one of which may separately impact an individual boy, or they may act together, compounding the effect of each.

5.2.1 *Boys Spend Less Time on Homework*

Although boys might enjoy expending their energies in other ways (e.g. in team sports), a key issue in regard to school grades is that boys spend less time on homework than girls (Hillman & Robinson, 2016). This can't be dismissed simply as laziness, because several important factors that are beyond boys' control are involved, such as slower cognitive and emotional development. However, some factors are more controllable. During adolescence, overuse of video games by boys is a major distraction from homework (Lemmens et al., 2011). This not only uses up time that could be dedicated to homework, but also many boys will experience late nights and a lack of sleep that can impact cognitive ability (Stoet & Yang, 2016). Boys' overuse of energy drinks may also disrupt sleep patterns and concentration (Stoet & Yang, 2016).

5.2.2 *Boys are Less Inclined to Seek Help*

Although it is clear that boys often need help academically, from an early age up to university level, male students are less likely than female students to seek academic help (Kessels & Steinmayr, 2013). The first study to assess the degree to which help-seeking is associated with traditional gender scripts (Section 3.7.2.1) found that both male and female UK university students who scored higher on valuing 'mastery and control' of their feelings (a 'male script') were less likely to seek help (Brown et al., 2020). There were some interesting sex differences too: for male participants, being a 'fighter and a winner' predicted reluctance to seek help, whereas for female students, greater help-seeking was associated with more interest in creating 'family harmony' (a 'female script').

5.2.3 *Special Educational Needs are More Common in Boys*

Special educational needs (SEN) are more common in boys than girls (Department for Education, 2016). Dyslexia is twice as common and stuttering four times more common in boys than girls (Halpern, 2012). Colour blindness is around 16 times more common in boys than girls and is classified as an SEN. Although colour blindness can be detrimental to education, the DoE figures for SEN do not include it (see SPOTLIGHT box 5.1).

THE IMPACT OF COLOUR BLINDNESS ON SCHOOL CHILDREN

In the average school today, two or more children in each class will look into a box of coloured pencils and only be able to recognise around four of the colours (Todd, 2018). Their confusion is often perceived by teachers and schoolmates as a sign of a deficit in intelligence, or of being uncooperative.

Colour blindness affects 1 in 12 boys and one in 200 girls and often goes undiagnosed for years. Rather than seeing in black and white, colour blindness creates difficulty in distinguishing some colours from others. 'Red green' colour blindness is the most common form. Despite its name it affects not only seeing red and green, but other colours such as brown and orange.

This topic is generally overlooked in schools and by researchers, but a review identified the areas in which colour blind children of various ages typically struggle: differentiating team colours in sports; using colour in art; colour-coded graphs and charts used in mathematics, geography and other topics; reading stained slides under microscope, or identifying plant species in biology; difficulty with coloured coding and wiring in physics; reading litmus paper and identifying chemical solutions in chemistry (Chan et al., 2014). Furthermore, the needs of colour blind children are usually not taken into account in exams, where some aspects of the exam might need colour vision (e.g. a colour-coded chart in the exam paper).

The impact of problems with colour blindness typically endures throughout the lifespan. Many people are ashamed of their condition and find that it impacts quality of life in terms of their emotions, health and lifestyle, and especially their career choices (Barry et al., 2017). Given the huge number of people impacted by these problems throughout their lives, it is surprising that these issues generally pass without comment in science, academia and public discourse. It is true that men are unlikely to seek help for this problem, and this might be for various reasons, e.g. shame, fear of being ridiculed or realising that there is no cure so ultimately no help. In addition, it could be that our view of this condition is distorted by 'male gender blindness' – it is overlooked because it impacts mostly men (Seager & Barry, 2019).

5.2.4 *Maltreatment and Academic Achievement*

A literature review of studies (94% from US and Canada) found that academic achievement was adversely impacted by childhood maltreatment, especially maltreatment that occurred in multiple forms (particularly neglect) and started early in life (Romano et al., 2015). Maltreatment was associated with special educational interventions, poor grades across subjects and truancy. The review also found that the negative impact of maltreatment on education was greater for boys than girls, and worse at adolescence than for younger children.

5.3 MATHEMATICS VS READING

Males tend to do better at mathematics and worse at reading or verbal skills, than women (Stoet & Geary, 2018; *Theme: 'Yin and yang'*, in Section 13.2.4). The male-typical 'mathematics-tilt' predicts interest in STEM, whereas the female-typical 'verbal-tilt' predicts interest in the humanities (Stewart-Williams & Halsey, 2018). This pattern might be related to the fact that male researchers are more likely than women to use quantitative methods such as statistical analysis, and female researchers more likely than men to use qualitative methods such as interviewing (Thelwall et al., 2019).

The sex difference in reading ability is most likely a biological tendency in boys, related to the normal slower vocabulary development in boys and special educational issues such as dyslexia (see Section 5.2.3). Reading is a key skill for educational advancement, e.g. a boy who is very gifted in mathematics will struggle to progress in his educational development unless he can accurately read the exam paper. The male disadvantage in reading skills is in fact an important part of the reason for fewer men than women accessing higher education (Stoet & Geary, 2020a). However, this disadvantage is not explained by disorders such as dyslexia, but rather seems to be a general reading disadvantage that boys have compared to girls. It could be argued that schools should focus more on helping boys improve their reading skills.

An interesting exception to the 'boys are better at mathematics' rule is that girls aged 5–14 years old tend to do better than boys in tests of mathematical computation (multiplication, division etc) (Hyde et al., 1990). In contrast, from adolescence onwards, boys tend to do better in mathematical problem solving, which is the kind of reasoning ability that is extremely useful in STEM fields (Hyde et al., 1990).

5.3.1 *Does the Sex Difference in Academic Ability Vary by Culture?*

Many people presume that gender differences are simply a product of culture, so would guess that cultural differences – such as variations in gender equality in different countries – will impact female academic performance. A study of mathematics and reading performance of nearly 1.5 million 15-year-olds in 75 countries found that, regardless of a nations' gender equality indicators, boys scored higher than girls in mathematics, and lower than girls in reading (Stoet & Geary, 2013). The sex difference in mathematics was largest for the highest grades, but the size of the sex differences varied across nations, and countries with a smaller sex difference in mathematics had a larger sex difference in reading and vice versa.

A further study using an updated version of the same database found that using a combination of students' academic results and attitudes to academic work (e.g. enjoyment of reading), the sex of students across countries could be predicted with, on average, 69% accuracy (Stoet & Geary, 2020b). Furthermore, the degree of predictability of sex was largest in countries that showed the greatest gender equality (as measured by relative income equality, women's participation in the workplace and politics). The authors interpret these findings as possibly indicating that in more egalitarian countries, where education is not so much a way out of poverty as a way to improve quality of life, boys and girls are more free to express their underlying preferences for career / lifestyle path. These findings contradict the narrative about institutional sexism having a negative impact on the academic performance of girls (*Theme: 'don't make assumptions'*, in Section 13.2.5).

5.3.2 *Stereotype Threat and Mathematics*

Despite having good mathematical ability, girls may lack confidence in mathematics (Stoet et al., 2016). It is not implausible that if schoolgirls think girls are not as good as boys at mathematics, this mindset might cause anxiety and decrease performance in exams, and lead to a reluctance to take mathematics subjects compared to boys. However, a well-designed study of mathematics performance of 931 boys and girls (9–18 years old) in the US 'found no evidence that the mathematics performance of school-age girls was impacted by stereotype threat' (Ganley et al., 2013, p. 1886). Also, a meta-analysis of research on this topic suggests that 'stereotype threat' does not explain the gender gap in mathematics performance and achievement (Stoet & Geary, 2012). Why then is stereotype threat such a popular explanation for the maths performance of girls? There is some evidence that research on stereotype threat and gender is more likely to be published if the findings support the existence of the stereotype threat: this phenomenon is known as *publication bias* (Flore & Wicherts, 2015). If true, this means that claims tend to overestimate the importance of stereotype threat in explaining the performance of girls in tests of mathematics.

5.3.3 *Stereotypes and Bias Against Boys in Education*

A Norwegian longitudinal study of 563 high-school students aged 14–15 found that boys were less likely than girls to enter the pre-university college track (54% vs 64%), and more likely to drop out once they started (24% vs 14%) (Almås et al., 2016). This gender gap in dropping out of the college track was not explained in this paper, and could not be accounted for by demographics or personality characteristics. However, regarding the decision to choose either the academic or vocational track, the authors suggest that the school system stereotypes the choices of the boys as favouring vocational careers, and advises boys accordingly (Almås et al., 2016, p. 301).

An Israeli study of nearly 30,000 pupils in more than 300 schools examined data for three cohorts of Jewish secular high-school seniors in the years 2000–2002 (Lavy, 2004). Student matriculation exams were routinely graded in two ways: an external grade which is blind to name and sex of the pupil, and an internal grade which is non-blind. The pupil's final grade is a mean of the internal and external grades. This study found that boys were given lower grades in the non-blind assessments across all nine of the subjects studied. The researcher, having ruled out other possible explanations, concluded the discrepancy in scoring was a result of bias in the unblinded grading. A strength of this study is that it is a natural experiment. Another large natural experiment, this time of teaching accreditation exams for around 100,000 individuals in France, found a bias against male applicants on non-gender-blind oral tests compared to gender-blind written tests when applying for male dominated fields (Breda & Hillion, 2016). Not all research has replicated bias against males in exams, but the effect of methodological differences between studies might explain this.

5.3.4   Do Boys' Grades Improve by Having Male Teachers?

The notion that boys would do better in school if there were more male teachers is a popular one (see Section 10.5.2). Most research on this question comes from the US, where some studies find benefits of 'gender matching', but others do not (Diallo & Hermann, 2017). Findings from Europe are also inconsistent, but generally less supportive of the benefits of gender matching students and teachers.

Surprisingly, almost all studies of this question suggest that male teachers don't have a particular benefit for the grades of male students (Carrington & McPhee, 2008; de Salis et al., 2019; Francis et al., 2008; Hamilton & Jones, 2016; Moreau & Brownhill, 2017; Neugebauer et al., 2011; Watson et al., 2017). Some studies offer slightly more hopeful (or at least mixed) evidence (e.g. El-Emadi et al., 2019; Sullivan et al., 2010).

The largest study of this topic – 20 European countries – produced very mixed findings, partly because of differences between countries (Diallo & Hermann, 2017). This study used data from the Trends in International Mathematics and Science Study database, an international assessment programme that runs every four years. The main finding was that on average the students of female teachers achieved higher test scores than students of male teachers, and this benefit was mainly for female students. In Western Europe only, gender matching benefits students of both sexes; this effect was particularly high in England, and in fact eclipsed the generally positive effect of having a female teacher. The beneficial effect of having a female teacher was strongest in countries where teacher wages were especially high for women, suggesting that higher wages attract more able teachers. Also, the effect was strongest for low achievers, and – in Western Europe – for students with an immigrant background (they or a parent were born in another country).

It seems the idea of male teachers improving boys' academic performance has little or no evidence base. So an interesting question is: why do people keep suggesting that it is true? (*Theme: 'Don't make assumptions'*, in Section 13.2.5). Well, it is possible that male teachers are beneficial to boys, but just not in ways that translate into better grades. For example, male teachers might be more tolerant of boys' tendency to higher energy and rough-and-tumble play, and boys might be more willing to accept the authority of a male teacher (Stoet & Yang, 2016). Thus it could be that male teachers are beneficial by shaping the character of boys differently than female teachers do. This is a question that needs to be researched.

Another under-explored issue is that any benefits of male teachers might come from the masculinity that they bring to the classroom, and it could be that teaching, being a predominantly female profession, attracts men who are less masculine, or it could be that men feel pressure to rein in their masculinity in order to fit in (Msiza, 2019).

Although the overall evidence suggests little academic benefit to boys of having a male teacher, the persistence of the idea might stem from the recognition that father absence can have a major impact on educational achievement, especially for boys, so male teachers might make up for this absence in some way (Stoet, 2019). But perhaps that is asking too much of male teachers, and if boys need a male role model to help their grades, having one at home is more important than having one in the classroom.

5.4 WHAT HAPPENS TO BOYS WHO DROP OUT OF EDUCATION?

Fewer men than women are starting university, a trend that has increased in recent years (Stoet, 2019). For example, in US colleges, 42.6% of bachelor's degree students were male and 57.4% were female (US Dept of Education, 2020b). The response of many people is that if these are the life choices of the individual, so be it. However, there is not enough research to understand why men appear to be opting out of higher education, and what the consequences are for them and for society. An important issue is that we don't know what happens to male students who drop out of university.

5.4.1 *Dropping Out of University*

Boys are more likely than girls to drop out of school and university (Stoet, 2019). No surprise then that youth unemployment among 16–24-year-olds in England is higher among boys than girls (Clark, 2019b). The earlier children drop out from school, the more serious the problems (Stearns & Glennie,

2006), and for younger students, social deprivation plays a role (Bertrand & Pan 2013). A longitudinal study of 1,325 young people in the US found that high-school dropouts were significantly more depressed and reported lower life satisfaction than graduates at the time of their expected graduation (Liem et al., 2010). The fate of university dropouts is an area that needs more research. However, one reason to be optimistic is that for the first time in years, boys in the UK took up as many apprenticeships as girls did (Clark, 2019a), but this doesn't account for the numbers dropping out of university, or not applying in the first place.

5.4.2 'Failure to Launch'

In recent decades there has been a decline in independent living of young men. 'Failure to launch' is the unflattering term for young men who don't leave home and progress into adulthood (education/training, career, family etc) within the traditional timeframe. In the UK in the 1990s, most children left home before age 21, and in 2017 the typical age was 23 (ONS, 2019b). This phenomenon affects boys more than girls, and although Japan has a more extreme form of this in its culture called *hikikomori* (Furlong, 2008), in Western cultures this trend is probably mostly related to a lack of economic opportunities. The trend started in the 1980s mainly in Germany, Italy and Belgium, and less so in the UK and North America (Bell et al., 2007). The 2009 global recession increased the trend (Mykyta, 2012), and it has probably remained steady since then.

The phenomenon is primarily caused by practical issues, such as a lack of affordable housing (ONS, 2016). Other related factors are the fact that on average young women earn more than young men (see Section 7.5.4) so can better afford to leave home, and also single mothers in some countries (e.g. the UK) have special access to housing which makes it easier for them to leave home (ONS, 2016). However, other issues – perhaps psychological issues related to dropping out of higher education – may contribute to this being a predominantly male problem.

Although there is little research on this topic, some authors – often based on clinical experience rather than research – suggest that 'failure to launch' has one or more significant psychological components. For example, anxiety, depression, attention deficit hyperactivity disorder (ADHD), substance abuse and a lack of ambition (sometimes accompanied by a sense of entitlement) have been identified by a counsellor in the US (DeVine, 2013). Another view is that these young men have, on some level, rejected the role of adult male, perhaps seeing it as too difficult or not worth the effort (Farrell & Grey, 2019). In this regard, not launching might be seen as a decision rather than a failure. Other proposed causes include the lack of suitable male role models (see Section 5.3.4), education becoming less male-friendly, and biochemical imbalances caused by endocrine disruptors in the environment (see Section 10.2.3) and medications such as Ritalin (Sax, 2009).

To simplify this complex issue, it could be said that the problem is a combination of young men lacking the resources or ability to set up home elsewhere, or having a relatively comfortable lifestyle and insufficient motivation to leave. Overall the term 'failure to launch', though popularly used, is somewhat unfair, especially as it implies the fault is with the young man rather than complex economic and social forces.

The general question of why boys are 'failing to launch' needs a lot more research attention. Also to be considered are those who aren't ready to launch into life, but don't have the option of a home they can stay in. Similarly, some may start out in education, but then drop out but not have a home to fall back on. Without a fixed address their lives might drift unpredictably. This is a good example of where researchers need to make special efforts to reach the 'hard-to-reach' populations who might not be in a position to answer an online questionnaire, or might have no inclination to do so.

5.4.3   Autism and Homelessness Men

Young men with autism may find it hard to successfully launch into life. It can be hard for them to find work, and they are vulnerable to slipping into the poverty trap (Calsyn & Winter, 2002). Autism affects 1% of the population (Brugha et al., 2016). Severe cases are four times more common in males, and the less severe form (Asperger syndrome) is nine times more common in males (Barry & Owens, 2019).

Given the fact that most homeless people are male – especially rough sleepers – it is no surprise that autism is at least *12 times* more common in homeless people than the general population (Churchard et al., 2019). This high figure isn't explained by substance abuse, because substance abuse is less common in people with autism than other people (Butwicka et al., 2017). It is likely that the greater level of social isolation experienced by people with autism is the key: autistic people often have fewer people to turn to if things go wrong in their lives, such as their housing being threatened (Churchard et al., 2019). They are more likely to experience sensory difficulties (e.g. finding noise distressing), which makes living in shared accommodation or a hostel virtually impossible. Added to this, for those with cognitive impairments impacting their ability in tasks such as planning ahead, everyday independent living can become virtually impossible.

5.4.3.1   Interventions for rough sleepers

A group called Homeless Link (2015) has created practical guidelines on how to identify autism in homeless people, and how to communicate in a way that best facilitates support for the homeless person. However, much more needs to be done to identify the scale of the problem of autism in homelessness, and to develop evidence-based methods of helping these vulnerable people.

SPOTLIGHT BOX 5.2

MAKING CAREER CHOICES

The first steps into adulthood can involve tough decisions that may impact future happiness. Some research suggests that job satisfaction (an intrinsic motivation) is the best predictor of having a positive mindset in men (Barry, 2020), but when deciding on a job or career people usually also take income (an extrinsic motivation) into account. (Income is also a good predictor of job satisfaction (Barry, 2020)). So how can a young man find a balance between job satisfaction and income? Here is an example (Murray, 2008).

A high-school graduate enjoys tinkering with electrical and electronic gadgets and would like to be an electrician. However his parents advise him that the average income of a manager in an electronics company is about twice the average income of an electrician. This puts him in a dilemma. How does he decide what to do? Well, when it comes to anything electrical, he has excellent practical knowledge and skills compared to his peers, though is about average when it comes to interpersonal skills. This suggests he might be an excellent electrician, but an average manager. He looks online and finds that a top electrician makes only a little less than the average manager in a big electrical company. So his choice of career is based on whether it is worth earning a little less income to have a job he enjoys a lot more.

Real life is often more complicated than this example, and the range of options is likely to be wider than just two, so it's always worth discussing options with a professional careers advisor. They can help identify skill sets that will more accurately identify the most suitable career choice. For example, tests like the Armed Services Vocational Aptitude Battery, a test the US military use in recruiting, can identify relevant skills such as linguistic abilities, interpersonal skills, mental rotation ability and fine motor skills.

5.5 EDUCATION AND TRAINING ABOUT SEX AND GENDER DIFFERENCES

Readers of this book might find themselves thinking about the possibility of learning more about male psychology. At the time of writing, there is only one undergraduate module on male psychology in the world (at the University of Sunderland, UK), so a more widely available alternative – gender studies, which sometimes includes men's studies – might seem a suitable alternative. However, readers are advised that the two fields are very different from male psychology, as the next section demonstrates.

5.5.1 *Criticism of Gender Studies as Unscientific*

There have been claims that gender studies is an alternative and superior kind of science to traditional science, with its (allegedly) old-fashioned, bigoted and boring positivist methods (Söderlund & Madison, 2015, 2017; Madison & Söderlund, 2018). In response to this, two scholars in Sweden made an assessment of the quality of gender studies research (Söderlund & Madison, 2015, 2017; Madison & Söderlund, 2018). Based on 12,414 publications in the Swedish Gender Studies List, they found a range of shortcomings in gender studies compared to other fields in academia, including:

- **Less focus on science.** Gender studies articles had less of a focus on biology, genetics and individual/group differences than articles in other fields.
- **Less evidence.** In other fields, statements were more likely to be supported by arguments or references.
- **Less self-critical.** Papers in other fields tended to be more self-critical (e.g. mentioned limitations of their research) compared to gender studies.
- **Lower academic standard of publications.** 70% of publications in other fields were in peer-reviewed journals, compared to only 20% of gender studies publications. Most gender studies publications were book chapters, dissertations and conference contributions.
- **Fewer citations.** In gender studies, only 28% of articles were cited in other papers, compared to other fields in which 90% of papers were cited three times on average.

The authors concluded that gender studies articles were of lower scientific quality, and appeared to be more about relating the experiences and viewpoints of various groups of people rather than about comprehensive models of the real world. This does not mean that gender studies papers are of no value, just that their standard of scientific credibility is lower than in other fields.

Perhaps not unexpectedly, the critique was rejected by many scholars in gender studies, mainly on the grounds that the methods typically used in gender studies cannot meaningfully be compared to traditional scientific methods.

The credibility of gender studies and related fields that embrace postmodern and critical theory methods (see SPOTLIGHT box 6.1 and Section 11.4.3) was further called into question by the 'grievance studies' affair, where satirical versions of academic papers were accepted as genuine papers for publication in some journals, including gender studies journals. The accepted papers included one suggesting that dogs engage in 'rape culture' (Wilson, 2018), a rewrite of Adolf Hitler's *Mein Kampf* as a feminist struggle (Gonzalez

& Jones, n.d.), and one entitled 'The conceptual penis as a social construct' (Lindsay & Boyle, 2017). All of the papers were retracted by the authors upon acceptance, who also declared the hoax, explaining that their point was to expose how easy it was to get 'absurdities and morally fashionable political ideas published as legitimate academic research' (Cofnas et al., 2018).

Criticism and debate are accepted in science as important ways of developing theories and keeping knowledge updated, and without them science is in danger of becoming unscientific (Popper, 1959). In contrast, the response to the 'grievance studies' affair was defensive. Of course, there are examples of poor science across all of academia, but when these are found in most fields it is followed by much consternation and soul-searching, as in the case of the 'replication crisis' in psychology, and it is common for students of psychology in the UK to be taught about the perils of academic fraud in research (Fletcher, 2013).

For a field that has existed for decades, there is little interest in gender studies from most other academic fields (as shown by the low citation rate noted above). In spite of this, gender studies has a relatively large impact outside academia, on government, law, the media etc, impacting funding and policymaking (Geary & Stoet, 2020).

The growth in gender studies publications between 2000 and 2010 was more than double that seen in other academic fields (~12% compared to ~5%) (Söderlund & Madison, 2015, 2017; Madison & Söderlund, 2018). Ironically, publication of well-conducted scientific studies of sex differences is often made difficult because of an academic climate that is unfavourable to studies of this topic (Geary & Stoet, 2020).

It is important to note that criticisms of gender studies are not just academic tiffs of relevance only to dusty academics in ivory towers; much of our cultural attitudes towards men originate from gender studies, so we should insist these attitudes be based on good evidence. Unfortunately, many of the ideas that are problematic for men today (e.g. hegemonic masculinity, male privilege, patriarchy etc) have little scientific credibility, yet these ideas influence the media, politics, law and many areas of discourse. Debate and criticism is a cornerstone of science, but debate or even questioning of gender studies topics is often discouraged, and people who try to debate these issues are bullied (e.g. 'no platformed' or 'cancelled') or even fired (Pluckrose & Lindsay, 2020).

Gender is a topic of great interest to many people and could potentially make a wonderful contribution in the social sciences and almost every area of life. To be of real value, though, gender studies needs to learn from criticism and take some revolutionary steps towards being a discipline based on science.

MALE LECTURERS DISCUSS TEACHING ABOUT GENDER

Gunilla Risberg and colleagues interviewed 20 men (15 professors and 5 senior lecturers in health sciences) in a Swedish medical school. Although the men found gender an important topic, gender-related issues were seen as 'ideological and political… unscientifically presented', mostly concerning 'women's issues and to tend to involve "male bashing"' (Risberg et al., 2011, p. 618).

Some of the interviewees had 'concerns that gender-related issues would take too much time from "basic medical knowledge"' (Risberg et al., 2011, p. 617). There were also concerns that emotions were put before facts, leading to 'unscientific teaching approaches' (Risberg et al., 2011, p. 618).

The male lecturers said of female colleagues working with gender and gender researchers:

> Several feminists and gender researchers seem to belong to a special category of people who are dissatisfied with their situation and blame everything on their gender. They give many men an excuse to hold on to their prejudices and to continue their chauvinist attitudes.
>
> (Risberg et al., 2011, p. 618)

The authors suggest that the men didn't embrace gender-related issues because they had not been exposed enough to the subject. However, the male lecturers had lots of exposure, firstly because the teaching of a gender-related perspective has been mandatory in Swedish medical schools since the 1990s (indeed four of the men had taught gender-related material), and secondly because Sweden is perhaps the most feminist country that has ever existed.

The authors make several recommendations, including to 'establish gender as an area of scientific knowledge'. This is a valuable goal, but somewhat undermined in the context of some of the other recommendations, such as to 'Focus on the structural rather than individual aspects of power', which is influenced by unscientific ideas about patriarchy (see SPOTLIGHT box 12.1) based on critical theory (see Section 11.4.3).

The authors also observe that 'male teachers were taken more seriously than female teachers when teaching about gender', and therefore 'bringing more male teachers into gender education in medicine might improve the status of the gender-based perspective'. But bringing in more men 'may endorse the asymmetry of the respective status of men and women. The solution replicates the problem' (Risberg et al., 2011, p. 622; *Theme: 'the solution replicates the problem',* in Section 13.2.1).

The ambivalence shown by the male lecturers in the study by Risberg et al. (2011) is similar to that seen in the interviews with psychological therapists on sex differences in the needs of their clients (Holloway et al., 2018; Russ et al., 2015). In those two studies the therapists said they didn't like generalising about sex differences, but then went on to describe various sex differences.

It suggests that professionals are doing their best to see the world through the lens of gender studies in good faith, but find it a struggle to do so.

A paper from the US suggests two different tactics for increasing the impact of women's studies on universities: 'embracing the stereotypes of feminist professors as "scary" (or "man-hating," "lesbian," "hairy" and so on)' and 'training male students as viruses' because 'when men become feminist viruses, infecting and unsettling spaces where their privilege and dominance is assumed, the potential danger and impact is keenly felt' (Fahs & Karger, 2016, p. 947). The authors suggest training students to see gender and other aspects of life from the 'critical' perspective, which (as seen in Section 11.4.3) is political rather than scientific.

5.5.2   *Training for Interventions with Men and Boys*

The prevailing view of gender in education today (as seen in Sections 3.4.6 and 3.6.2.2) is: (a) it is primarily about women; (b) it is not about biological influences on gender; and (c) it tends to have a negative view of men and masculinity. Both within professional psychology and outside (SPOTLIGHT box 11.3), therapists and workshop leaders are being encouraged to view masculinity as problematic. This is of concern, especially where safety and efficacy have not been established.

5.6   WHAT CAN BE DONE TO PREVENT BOYS FROM FALLING BEHIND IN EDUCATION?

Because the reading skills of boys are generally behind those of girls, it has been recommended that boys should not be made to learn to read as early as girls, because early failure may be damaging to self-confidence (Curtis & editor, 2007). However, reading skills are so crucial to accessing higher education that it would be unwise to abandon efforts to improve them in boys (Stoet & Geary, 2020a). Suggestions to improve boys' educational performance include: don't start boys at school before age six, give more guidance to boys in secondary school and limit screen (TV and gaming) time for boys at all ages (Stoet & Yang, 2016). However, the 'boy problem' is complex, and resistant to apparently simple solutions (*Theme: 'don't make assumptions'*, in Section 13.2.5). For example, efforts to improve self-confidence in boys should recognise that there is a reciprocal link between self-confidence and achievement (Fraine et al., 2007). The following section will look at other factors that might help boys.

5.6.1 *Overcoming Biases will Help Boys*

Some authors believe that the issue of boys' underachievement is not important because there are more men than women in the very top positions in academia (Jóhannesson et al., 2009). This kind of argument is clearly unfair to the majority of boys, who should not be disadvantaged just because a minority of men are in top jobs. Part of achieving gender equality should – by definition – include recognising when boys are disadvantaged (UNESCO, 2018).

The help-seeking behaviour of both male and female students – but especially male – is related to specific gender-typical attitudes (Brown et al., 2020). Knowing this might offer useful insights for student support services, e.g. by reframing masculine values in a positive way when helping male students (see Section 9.6.2).

In another approach, rather than pathologising the behaviour of boys, we should look at how much of it is normal (e.g. high energy) and how much might be a sign that help is needed (e.g. developmental issues such as ADHD, or impact of trauma, neglect or abuse), and find ways of dealing with these in a constructive way. In many cases a strengths-based approach will be a good compliment to any other interventions required (see Figure 11.3). For example, recognising the potential benefits of ADHD can be a productive part of routine care (Chheda-Varma, 2019). Routine testing for colour blindness at the start of elementary schooling and more judicious use of colour in teaching and exams will help the 8% of boys and 0.5% of girls who are colour blind.

5.7 CONCLUDING REMARKS

In a world in which we are told that 'the future is female' (Valji & Castillo, 2019, p. 4), it is refreshing to be reminded 'don't forget the boys' (UNESCO, 2018, p. 1). That's because the problems boys have in education receive little attention, but when girls fall behind boys in any subject it is a cause for concern (Seager & Barry, 2019). This is not only an example of gamma bias but an example of delta bias, that girls are encouraged to engage in topics at which boys traditionally excel, and boys are encouraged to be less competitive and value domestic activities more (Seager & Barry, 2020). This raises the question of why we don't celebrate more the academic strengths of boys in STEM as much as we encourage girls to excel in this field. Academic underperformance is creating problems for women too, e.g. highly educated women tend to prefer an equally well-educated partner, so a dearth of well-educated men will have ramifications for relationship formation, family and community life (Birger, 2015). Indeed, there is a negative correlation between women's education and population growth, which might be an unintended consequence of the gender equality movement (Vollset et al., 2020). It is ironic that a study of 566,827 students aged 15 years old (49.8% girls) across 73 countries found that mental health was worse for girls in those countries with the highest levels of gender equality. The authors attributed this counterintuitive result to 'possible incongruence between expectations and reality in high gender equal countries' (Campbell et al., 2020, p. 1; Theme: unintended consequences in Section 13.2.1).

This chapter has emphasised the importance of education, but that is not to say that the only careers that are worthwhile are the ones that require a university education. Far from it – society would break down very quickly without the support of plumbers, mechanics, electricians, the emergency services, lorry drivers etc, most of whom are men. The point of highlighting the issue around education is that this field appears to have developed obstacles to the full participation of boys, such as not adequately helping boys with reading skills, and these issues need to be explored and rectified so that the brightest minds – both male and female – can fully develop their talents to the betterment of themselves and society. For many boys the alternatives to a fulfilling career might not be so good, and the consequences of underachievement have potentially damaging consequences for everyone.

5.8 SUMMARY

- This chapter has considered the relevance of male psychology to education in school and university.
- Developmental and other biological differences should be recognised. For example, higher energy and poorer reading skills need to be responded to by schools in a more productive way in order to get the most from boys.
- Popular ideas, such as improving boys grades by having more male teachers, should be revised in the face of research suggesting there is little benefit.
- Similarly, the strengths of boys in STEM subjects should be encouraged more.
- Bias against girls is so often the focus that bias against boys is overlooked.
- Gender studies would be more useful if it was more scientific.
- Research-based solutions are needed to address issues such as why so many young men today have lost a sense of ambition, and what happens to boys who drop out of college.

6   Sport and Exercise

CHAPTER OUTLINE

Perspectives in Male Psychology: An Introduction, First Edition.
Louise Liddon and John A. Barry.
© 2021 John Wiley & Sons, Ltd. Published 2021 by John Wiley & Sons, Ltd.

LEARNING OUTCOMES

By the end of this chapter, you should be able to:

1. Identify sex differences in interests in sport and exercise
2. Understand the reasons for these differences
3. Appreciate the arguments for and against sex segregation in sport
4. Recognise some of the variables that impact sporting performance
5. Know about the wellbeing and mental health benefits of sport and exercise

6.1 INTRODUCTION

Sports and exercise are an integral part of modern society, as well as billion dollar industries. Sport can be defined as an organised activity requiring physical skill where two or more individuals or teams compete to win, according to agreed-upon rules (Deaner et al., 2016). This differentiates sports from games that don't require physical skill (e.g. chess), and non-competitive physical activities, such as exercise. The world of sport and exercise is of importance not only to psychologists working with elite athletes, but also to the general population who want to improve their health, wellbeing and sporting performance.

This chapter looks first at sex differences in levels of interest and performance in sports, how much biological and evolutionary factors impact these and attempts to make sports more gender-equal. Factors that impact sports performance will be explored, including colour blindness and performance anxiety. The impact of homophobic chanting in football is also discussed. Finally, sex differences in the mental health benefits of different types of sports and exercise are examined.

6.2 SEX DIFFERENCES IN SPORTS INTEREST AND PARTICIPATION

It seems reasonable to suggest that men and women should be encouraged to engage in whatever sport that appeals to them and achieve as much as they are able to, whether that is fitness, gold medals or enjoyment. Sports have historically been dominated by men, though there have been efforts in recent years to increase female participation and spectatorship.

6.2.1 *Evidence of Sex Differences in Interest in Sports*

Although it is known that in ancient Sparta, girls competed in running and wrestling events, as a general rule historically and cross-culturally, women are less interested in sports, as participants and spectators, even when given opportunities for engagement (Deaner et al., 2016). It has been suggested that women would participate as much as men if they had the time, but women spend as much time on exercise as men, and in numerous surveys women express less desire than men to participate and excel in sports (Ellis et al., 2013). It could be suggested that women have less free time than men, so can't watch sports as much. However women watch as much TV as men, though fewer sporting programmes (Deaner et al., 2016). In a study of 37 countries, men were around three times more likely than women to report watching sports on TV, or participating in competitive sports, and six times more likely to participate in team sports (Apostolou, 2015). Women's sports consistently attract smaller audiences and are less profitable than men's sports (Deaner et al., 2016).

6.2.2 *Evidence of Sex Differences in Competitiveness and Risk-Taking*

Men are more likely than women to report taking risks in sports, not only in obviously dangerous sports such as rock climbing, but also in less risky sports. For example, male marathon runners more than female runners risk becoming exhausted early in the race by starting out at a fast pace (Deaner et al., 2015). Male athletes are more likely than female athletes to engage in sports for reasons of competition and desire to win, though a possible exception to this general rule is tennis, where one study found that female professionals scored higher in competitiveness than males (Houston et al., 1997).

A Spanish study of 435 boys and 417 girls aged between 12 and 17 found sex differences in the motivation to engage in physical exercise (Portela-Pino et al., 2020). Boys were significantly more motivated than girls by competition/social recognition/challenge, strength/muscle resistance, affiliation/fun/wellness and health emergencies. In contrast, girls were more significantly more motivated than boys by issues around body weight/body image and agility/flexibility. Three barriers presented significantly more difficulty for girls than boys: fatigue/laziness, body image/physical–social anxiety and obligations/lack of time. These gender difference show parallels with traditional gender roles, as described by Seager et al. (2014).

THE CRITICAL STUDIES PERSPECTIVE ON SPORT AND EXERCISE

In recent decades there has been a great deal of interest in women's participation in sports. Some important advances have been made. For example, before the 1980s, women were excluded from participating in long distance running at the Olympic Games on the premise that such events were too strenuous for women (Lovett, 1997). This has proved to be a false premise, and shows that taking an informed gendered perspective can be beneficial.

Generally speaking, men are more interested than women are in participating and watching sports (Deaner et al., 2016). Although taken for granted historically, in recent decades the reasons for this sex difference have come under scrutiny: 'critical studies of men, masculinity and sport culture have emerged … Drawing on various feminist, social constructionist, or poststructuralist theories of gender, these scholars argued that sport served to sustain symbolic idealisations of male power, normalise the marginality of women, and reinforce rigid status hierarchies among men themselves' (Matthews & Channon, 2019, p. 373). From this point of view women are seen as victims of sporting governing bodies which are part of 'the construction of women's bodies as athletically able but inferior to men, an arrangement formalized in codified rules and procedures and legitimized by external stakeholders' (Pape, 2020, p. 81).

The view of sports from the perspective of critical studies and the view from sports fans and athletes could not be more different. One group is concerned with sports as an arena where everyone being equal is the goal, and the other group sees sport as an arena where seeing who is best on the day is the goal. Other feminist ideas, such as the view that the gender pay gap is caused by sexism, are difficult to transfer to professional sports, where pay is based on performance and ticket sales. Things can become especially complex when academics claim that gender is only a social construct (Eagly, 2018), or the perplexing claim that gender created anatomical sex (see Section 6.3.1), which paves the way for the argument that people who are genetically male but identify as female should be able to compete against women in sports (*Theme: 'unintended consequences',* in Section 13.2.1).

Without a doubt, interest in women in sports has changed the face of sports in recent years. This is to the benefit of many, and women in the US today earn about 60% of sport and exercise degrees (Nuzzo, 2020b). Nowadays women's participation in sports is widely incentivised. In comparison, men in the UK these days are no longer doing enough physical activity to even maintain health (Public Health England, 2019). (See also Section 12.2)

6.3 EXPLANATIONS FOR SEX DIFFERENCES IN SPORT

The cross-cultural pervasiveness of sex differences in sports suggests biological / evolutionary roots. Thus although cultural transmission of sporting interest clearly plays a role (e.g. fathers encouraging their sons to support the local team), other aspects of sporting interest might be more related to evolutionary purposes (e.g. contact sports that might be related to hunting or fighting skills).

6.3.1 *Biological Explanation for Sex Differences in Sport*

A biological variable related to sporting ability is prenatal exposure to testosterone, which increases aptitudes that are useful in many sports, such as interest in rough-and-tumble play (Frisén et al., 2009). Prenatal exposure to testosterone is associated with three-dimensional mental rotation ability (Barry & Owens, 2019), which is probably useful in tracking objects as they move through the air, as might happen in many sporting activities. Also, testosterone contributes to muscle strength, an obvious advantage in many sports.

There may be an interesting reciprocal relationship between prenatal testosterone contributing to interest in sport, and success in sport increasing testosterone levels postnatally. The *challenge hypothesis* is the phenomenon whereby testosterone increases in reaction to achieving dominance, and decreases in reaction to a loss of status. Lots of research confirms this: e.g. a meta-analysis of 49 studies with more than 2500 participants found that on average, for both men and women, winners of competitions show a larger increase in testosterone than the losers, and real-world studies find larger effects than laboratory studies (Geniole et al., 2017). It should be noted though that these changes in testosterone are relatively small compared to the very large naturally occurring sex difference in testosterone levels seen in healthy men and women.

6.3.2 *Evolutionary Explanation for Sex Differences in Sport*

There is plenty of research evidence supporting the hypothesis that sporting ability has an evolutionary basis (see Deaner et al., 2016). Firstly, successful male athletes – and even men described as being athletic – have greater access to mates because sporting ability is related to 'good genes' and likelihood of healthy offspring. However, if sport is mainly a type of courtship display, this doesn't explain why women are less interested in sport than men are. On the other hand, women's participation in *display sports*, such as gymnastics or figure skating, that emphasise feminine movements, is easy to see as court-ship display. Supporting this idea, women in 24 of 37 countries surveyed were significantly more likely than men to say they participate in sports 'to look good' (Apostolou, 2014).

Other evolutionary hypotheses are that sports are physical competitions for status, in a format that is less deadly than war, or that sports, especially team sports, are related to readiness to engage in tribal warfare (Lombardo, 2012). This could explain why sometimes sports fans can be very aggressive towards each other. The *development of skills hypothesis* (described in Dean-er et al., 2016) suggests the evolutionary function of sport is that it helps people to develop skills that might be useful to the community, such as hunting and protection from invasion. Sports can build character, self-disci-pline, coping with defeat, co-operation and following rules and instructions. The *development of skills hypothesis* has the advantage of being applicable to women to a greater degree than other hypotheses.

6.3.3   *Influence of Socialisation on Sporting Interest*

In contrast to the evolutionary / biological view is the suggestion that sporting interest is caused by socialisation, and because girls are encouraged to play different sports to boys, this causes the sex differences that are observed worldwide. This social-determinist view has the appeal of being easy to understand and is popularised in the media, but even a little knowledge of biology demonstrates that it cannot be the sole explanation (see Section 6.3.1). A more informed view is that socialisation shapes biological forces, resulting in the sex differences in sports we see around the world. Thus even with social forces encouraging girls to engage more in male-typical compet-itive sports, there is evidence that men continue to show more interest than women in participating in competitive sports (Deaner et al., 2014).

6.3.4   *Biases in Presenting Gender Differences in Sports*

If all athletic activities are taken into account, then the sex difference in par-ticipation in sports is small. However, this analysis obscures the large sex differences in competitive rather than non-competitive sports, and the sex difference in team sports compared to individual sports (Apostolou, 2014).

The tendency to obscure sex differences is called beta-bias (Hare-Mustin & Marecek, 1988). This is common in gender studies, and examples are easy to find. For example, Title IX is a US federal law that legislates equal oppor-tunity for women in educational settings, including athletics. Arguments for Title IX that suggest it is a 'false premise' that women are less interested in sports (e.g. Samuels, 2003) are showing beta-bias, and ignore a large evidence base of research to the contrary (e.g. the review by Deaner et al., 2016).

Beta-bias is also seen where women's performance in sport compared to men is blamed on stereotypes about performance ('stereotype threat', e.g. Gentile et al., 2018) rather than actual sex differences in performance. For example, although phrases like 'you throw like a girl' can be used as an insult (especially during competition between men, to anger and disconcert an opponent), it is nonetheless true that sex differences in physiology means that men and women throw objects differently in a variety of ways (Lombardo & Deaner, 2018). Although it is true that performance anxiety will reduce performance, the problems caused by 'stereotype threat' are likely to be overestimated (see Section 5.3.2) and eagerness to read about it has probably led to publication bias (Flore & Wicherts, 2015).

6.4 MAKING SENSE OF SEX-SEGREGATION IN SPORTS

Many people will recognise that, generally speaking, a biological man will tend to have an advantage over a biological woman in most sporting competitions, for reasons related to biology. This next section will look at some of the reasons why sport is segregated by sex, and will examine some of the attempts to close the performance gap.

6.4.1 *Sex-Segregation: The Basics*

Sports performance relies on a range of variables, including training, diet and motivation. Before puberty, mixed-sex sports interactions are common because in childhood, sex differences relevant to sports are less likely to impact sports performance. After the onset of puberty, single-sex settings begin to be applied to sports where sex differences are expected to play a significant role in sporting proficiency. Where differences are not deemed to have an effect on performance outcome (e.g. horse racing), men and women can compete against each other. Some sports have mixed events where each competing team has the same number of men and women (e.g. tennis mixed doubles).

6.4.2 *Should we have Sex Segregation in Sports?*

As a general rule, elite male athletes show around 10–12% performance advantage over elite female athletes (Coleman et al., 2020). Men tend to outperform women in athletics because of natural advantages such as larger and more powerful muscles, better oxygen consumption and greater bio-mechanical efficiency (Keenan et al., 2018). If men and women competed together, the top women athletes might find themselves no longer in the top ranks. For example, using data for athletics events worldwide, the fastest time for the 400-metre run for women was beaten by more than 4000 different men and nearly 300 different boys (males under age 18) (Coleman et al., 2020). Although in some events women athletes do very well (e.g. the pole vault), it seems fair that in events where one gender has a significant advantage over another, men and women should compete separately. (*Theme: 'one-size-fits-all'*, in Section 13.2.4).

The reason for the male advantage in sport is not just the benefits in terms of muscle mass, but the benefits of prenatal exposure to testosterone, which programmes the foetus to develop a more athletic body postnatally (Coleman et al., 2020). Therefore people who are born male (generally speaking, have a Y chromosome) have a large advantage over people who are born female (generally speaking, have no Y chromosome), even if the latter is taking a testosterone supplement. Does this mean that men and women should not compete together in sport? That is something for the sports governing bodies to decide, but a variety of evidence suggests this would put women at a disadvantage (Coleman et al., 2020). However, in adolescence it is more possible, though rare, for girls to beat boys in contact sports. For example, Michaela Hutchison in Alaska became the first girl to ever win – in competition with boys – a state-wide high school wrestling title in 2006, followed by Heaven Fitch, who achieved the same in North Carolina in 2020 (Gerken, 2020).

6.4.3   *Closing the Sex Difference Performance Gap*

Apart from sex differences, a host of other variables (e.g. training, diet, motivation) can have an important influence on performance. We can see from the previous section that even among elite athletes who are maximising the benefits of training, diet etc, there is still a sports gender gap in elite athletes. This suggests that environmental factors don't compensate for innate differences. Nonetheless, there is evidence that the greater resources being put into women's sports can change performance. For example, in the US the Title IX gender equality programme has increased participation and incentives (e.g. scholarships) for women's heavyweight rowing, and this has seen an improvement in women's performance relative to men's heavyweight rowing (Keenan et al., 2018). However, this improvement needs to be seen in the context of declining performance in both men and women for this event over the period studied (1997–2016). The cause of this decline is unclear, though raises the question of whether incentives for women act as disincentives for men in some way, perhaps indirectly – though the relationship might be correlational rather than causal, and an adequate research design would be needed to address these complex issues.

6.5 PERFORMANCE ISSUES

Performance can be influenced for better or worse by a huge range of variables, including practice, drugs and even spectators (see Section 6.5.2). Almost all athletes experience anxiety – at some level – before a competition, or even before training, but there is evidence that various cognitive and behavioural techniques, including hypnosis, can help significantly enhance performance (Cripps, 2012). This section will explore some issues that impact sports performance relevant to male psychology. This topic is potentially very wide, and what is presented in this section introduces just a few topics, two of which are underexplored (colour blindness (see SPOTLIGHT box 5.1) and homophobic chanting) and another – the psychology of 'choking' under pressure – which is of perennial interest to fans and players alike.

SPOTLIGHT BOX 6.2

IMPACT OF COLOUR BLINDNESS ON SPORT

Colour blindness impacts 8% of men and 0.5% of women. This is typically 'red-green' colour blindness, though in reality the experience is one of being unable to distinguish between reds, greens, oranges, browns and some combinations of colours, e.g. red on black.

From an early age, colour blindness can impact a variety of experiences related to sport. Common examples are struggling to distinguish between teams due to lack of distinction of colours, being unable to see infographics on TV or problems seeing the colours of balls, especially in dim or artificially lit conditions. Other problems crop up in various ways, e.g. the London 2012 Olympic Games used a red track, making it difficult for colour blind spectators to see athletes properly. A blue track would have avoided this issue.

Although the problems associated with colour blindness are still overlooked in almost all areas of life, since 2015 a charity called *Colour Blind Awareness* has been advising the football industry, including UEFA and FIFA, on how to help colour blind supporters and players. Interest in making these improvements has expanded in the UK to lawn tennis, rugby and even croquet.

Colour blindness is an example of a seldom recognised problem that faces mostly men. It is probably a good example of male gender blindness, though its low profile is not helped because men don't tend to complain.

6.5.1 *Yips and Choking*

To succeed in professional sport is to succeed under pressure, but striving too hard can backfire and lead to *paradoxical performance*, and losing when expected to win. *Choking* in sports is predominantly experienced as a psychological symptom (anxiety). Repeated experiences of choking can lead to *the yips*, in which performance anxiety is combined with physical reactions such as small muscle spasms (e.g. in the wrists of golfers).

A survey found that 39% of 86 golfers and 68% of 69 archers self-reported experiencing yips or choking (Clarke et al., 2020). Participants who experienced choking had significantly higher scores for physical concerns, cognitive concerns, social concerns, fear of negative evaluation, private self-consciousness, non-display of imperfection, concern over mistakes, parental expectations and doubts about actions, and significantly lower levels of conscientiousness. Participants who experienced the yips had significantly higher social anxiety, non-display of imperfection and perfectionistic self-promotion, and significantly lower scores for conscientiousness (Clarke et al., 2020).

Performance anxiety can be related to perfectionism, but the research findings tend to be mixed on this point (Klämpfl et al., 2013). The study by Clarke et al. (2020) suggests that perfectionism is related to choking but not to the yips, in that three perfectionism measures (concern over mistakes, parental expectation and doubts over actions) were related to choking but not the yips.

6.5.1.1   Sex difference in sporting anxiety

Although women tend to score higher than men on tests of anxiety, including sporting anxiety, there is very little research on sex differences in choking under pressure in sports. A study of 300 university athletes found that women experienced external and internal sources of choking more than men, but only slightly so (Adegbesan, 2007). One small study found a slight tendency for self-consciousness being more likely to affect performance for females and trait somatic anxiety more likely to affect performance for males (Wang, 2002).

6.5.2   Homophobic Chanting in Football

> I remember we played an away game once … the other team had a young goalkeeper, about 18. We sung that he 'takes it up the arse' for quite a long time. It obviously affected him, he conceded two soft goals afterwards, and we won the game.
>
> –An example of homophobic chanting given by a football fan
> (Magrath, 2018, 716)

In the UK, football (also known as soccer) is the sport most participated in (Magrath & Stott, 2019). There are currently no openly gay professional players in the top divisions of UK professional football (Magrath, 2018), possibly because the homophobic treatment of Justin Fashanu in the 1990s – whose life ended in suicide – may have deterred other footballers from being openly gay (Magrath, 2019). This tragic end to a brilliant career has been bad for the image of football, and many people would feel more proud to be a football fan if the sport were more inclusive. Although homosexuality was illegal for men in the UK until the 1960s, most adults these days don't care very much whether a man is gay or not, not only in the general UK population (Watt & Elliot, 2019) but even among schoolboys in the UK (McCormack & Anderson, 2010). For these reasons, the phenomenon of homophobic chanting at football matches seems out of step with the times, and its continued existence has been the subject of criticism.

The quote at the start of this section is from an interview study of 30 male football fans. On first reading, the main theme of the quote appears to be homophobia. However, further thought reveals another layer of meaning, and offers an insight into a hidden function of homophobic chanting: it is a device used to disconcert the opposing team in order to gain a competitive advantage (Magrath, 2018). The actual sexual orientation of the player targeted is not usually a consideration, and all 30 of the football fans interviewed said they weren't homophobic and that they accepted homosexuality in football.

Of the 30 fans who said they engaged in homophobic chanting, five said the purpose was to pick on a player they didn't like or to disconcert the other team, especially if there was a history of rivalry between the teams. In fact, the themes of taunting were not just about homosexuality, but could be on a variety of topics: being bald, having ginger hair, having an unusual haircut, distinctive facial features, unusual boots etc. Thus homophobia is part of a range of themes used as leverage to upset the other team or their fans, and is best understood in terms of context and underlying intent rather than just the overt words (McCormack et al., 2016). It is an expression of competitiveness in a context where winning the game is much more highly valued than egalitarian views of equality and inclusiveness (Magrath, 2018). Nonetheless, the fact that homosexuality can be used as an insult is increasingly anachronistic, and the fact that homophobic taunting is often about putting opponents off their game does not justify its use.

6.5.2.1 Would increased visibility of gay fans reduce homophobic chanting?

Despite the existence of homophobic chanting, it is interesting that around a third of the football fans interviewed said homophobic chanting was rarely heard (Magrath, 2018). Less than a fifth of them participated in it, and all of the fans claimed not to be homophobic (Magrath, 2018). Furthermore, all 30 of the interviewees said they would stop homophobic chanting if they knew there were gay fans around, raising the possibility that if there were more openly gay fans at football matches, there would be less homophobic chanting. In support of this idea, a UK university-based study found that a lecturer being openly gay helped to reduce homophobia in 106 undergraduate sports science students (Batten et al., 2020). Although potentially useful, further research is needed to find out how much these findings generalise to the football stadium. Features of the role model (confidence, charisma, humour, leadership etc) would also need to be controlled in order to measure their impact on the reduction of homophobia. Features of the target audience should be considered too, because although attitudes to homosexuality have become less negative in the UK since the 1990s, the change has been smaller in some demographics, most likely due to religious beliefs (Watt & Elliot, 2019).

6.5.2.2 Campaigns to reduce homophobia

The perhaps surprisingly low levels of homophobia reported by the 30 football fans could potentially be due to recent campaigns to reduce homophobia (Magrath, 2018). The FA has tried several policies over the years, though without empirical assessment of outcomes. The latest intervention, *Opening Doors and Joining In*, was designed to eliminate homophobia, biphobia and transphobia in English football, through education, visibility, partnerships, recognition, reporting discrimination and monitoring. This was the first anti-discrimination policy to be empirically tested, and it was found that 41 of the 53 fans interviewed weren't aware of the new policy, a situation that would not help improve reporting of instances of abuse (Magrath & Stott, 2019). One solution suggested by fans and the campaign group *Kick It Out* was more proactive stewarding at matches. The assessment of *Opening Doors* concluded that homophobia in football is best tackled by: (a) authorities taking a more nuanced understanding of homophobic chanting (as discussed above); (b) stopping relying on education programmes to reduce homophobia when there is little evidence of their efficacy; (c) tailoring policy to specific points where homophobia arises, rather than a blanket policy for all people and situations; (d) regulating homophobia at the match, and researching the outcomes; (e) retrospectively identifying offenders by CCTV (Magrath & Stott, 2019).

6.5.3 Paradoxical Performance

A general interpretation of the Yerkes-Dodson law would predict that apart from very simple tasks, if you try too hard at a complex task then it is likely to backfire (*Theme: 'unintended consequences'*, in Section 13.2.1). Trying too hard to be a winner (e.g. 'fighter and winner', Seager et al., 2014) can backfire, and working too hard, trying to be too much of a tough guy, trying too hard to control emotions etc will be successful up to a point, but will eventually backfire. This is similar to the idea of 'rigid demands' in REBT (see Section 12.6.3) and applies as much to sport as to anything else. In fact, at one time the Yerkes-Dodson law was the dominant explanation of the arousal–performance relationship in sport psychology (Raglin, 1992). It makes intuitive sense, and indeed empirical evidence has been found to support the inverted U-shaped trend in relation to cognition, though less so for motor performance (Raglin, 1992).

The classic explanation for the underlying mechanism is that at low levels of anxiety (or 'arousal' in the literature) the focus is too wide, and at high levels of anxiety the focus becomes too restricted; thus there is a 'Goldilocks' level which is somewhere in between (Easterbrook, 1959). The optimal level of anxiety in a given sport varies by individual and by sport (Furst & Tenenbaum, 1986), though age and degree of experience in a sport do not seem to influence the inverted U shape (Raglin, 1992).

Although there is surprisingly little research on whether there is a sex difference in the impact of the Yerkes-Dodson law in sports or other realms, this effect might be used to explain the phenomenon of 'stereotype threat', where performance is worse when stereotypes about a demographic are invoked (Hirnstein et al., 2014). Thus it could be that if women think they are expected to perform less well in sports, this causes them anxiety, which impairs their performance.

6.6 SPORT AND EXERCISE FOR MENTAL AND SOCIAL WELLBEING

Sport can provide a career for a lucky few, and healthy recreation for the masses to watch or participate in, right throughout the lifespan. This section will focus on mental and social wellbeing benefits of sport and exercise.

6.6.1 *Wellbeing Benefits of Being a Sports Fan*

There can be little doubt that being a fan of team sports offers a good opportunity to experience ingroup favouritism and outgroup bias, of the kind predicted by social identity theory (Tajfel & Turner, 1979). Research suggests that the social wellbeing benefits of being a fan are mainly seen in identification with the local team rather than as a fan of a distant team (Wann & Weaver, 2009). Especially for men who have few other outlets for emotional expression, singing, chanting and shouting together at a sport event can be good way to release tension in a socially acceptable way, and this catharsis might explain why one study found that sports fans experience less depression and alienation than people who aren't interested in sports (Wolensky, 2018).

6.6.2 *Wellbeing Benefits of Exercise*

There is a great deal of evidence that physical activity can improve mental health and wellbeing, meaning it is especially useful for people who can't take medication for their mental health, or prefer not to discuss their feelings.

Various reviews of controlled trials have found benefits of physical activity for anxiety, depression and post-traumatic stress disorder compared to non-active control groups (Thomas, 2020). Even more impressively, reviews have found that clinical trials for people suffering from common mental health disorders have found similar levels of benefits for physical activity compared to standard treatments such as cognitive behavioural therapy (CBT) (Thomas, 2020). A systematic review of interventions combining physical activity and psychotherapy (usually CBT) found that the benefits of the intervention did not seem to be related to the type or duration of the psychotherapy or physical activity elements. The changes most likely to promote wellbeing were increased feelings of self-efficacy, autonomy and being supported, regardless of the frequency, intensity, time or type of intervention (Thomas, 2020). The finding regarding 'being supported' suggests that therapeutic alliance was a factor here too (see Section 11.4.5).

6.6.2.1 Sex differences in wellbeing benefits of exercise

A population survey of 3368 Belgian men and 3435 women aged 25–64 found that all levels of physical activity, from low to high, had a positive impact on mental health (Asztalos et al., 2010). However they also found interesting sex differences: for men, participation in vigorous-intensity physical activity was significantly associated with lower feelings of depression, anxiety and somatisation (i.e. physical symptoms of stress). In contrast, for women, walking was significantly positively associated with emotional wellbeing. The researchers suggest that walking while alone provides women with an opportunity for reflection, and walking with others provides social interaction and bonding. This study may well provide useful insights into general advice for men and women, but it has some limitations that should be noted. Although it controlled for age and socioeconomic class, it did not control for other possible factors that might have had an impact on mental health, such as recent life events or health status. Also, it is a cross-sectional survey analysed using logistic regression, so does not prove causality, e.g. we can't tell whether walking more often makes women happy, or whether happy women walk more often.

Running is another popular activity for men and women. *Parkrun* is a free 5-km run which takes place every week in more than 1000 locations around the world. It is not a competition and anyone can take part, including those with disabilities. On registration, participants receive a barcode which is used to record their running time. A UK study of 7308 adult parkrunners found that 76% of regular runners and 87% of occasional runners reported increased wellbeing attributable to the parkrun (Stevinson & Hickson, 2014). Additionally, 87% of regular runners and 85% of occasional runners reported an increased sense of community. An Australian study of 337 male and 538 female parkrunners found that women reported a significant mental health benefit of parkrun, whereas for men the community connection of parkrun was significantly associated with wellbeing (Grunseit et al., 2018). This association was not explored further in the survey, though it could be speculated that parkrun is for men a 'running Shed' that reduces social isolation.

6.6.3 *Engaging Men's Mental Health Through Sport and Exercise*

A survey of men in the US found that sports was a significant predictor of men's mental positivity (Barry, 2020). Because men tend to seek 'talking cures' less than women do (e.g. Holloway et al., 2018), interventions that don't require the sharing of distressing feelings are potentially more attractive to men. Sports are a good alternative to video games for boys, and can be a healthy way to use excess energy, especially in those with attention deficit hyperactivity disorder (Chheda-Varma, 2019). Socialising might be an important aspect of interventions for men (e.g. Grunseit et al., 2018), so team sports could be an ideal way to combine the benefits of exercise and informal socialising. On the other hand, for some men more challenging sports, such as boxing or martial arts, might be preferred.

6.6.3.1 *All to play for football (ATPF)*

All to play for (ATPF) is part of the Men's Wellbeing Project based in Norfolk, UK (Kingerlee et al., 2019). It aims to help participants improve their emotional, physical and social wellbeing through a free weekly game of football (Abotsie et al., 2020). Over a period of around two years, 142 men who identified as possibly 'finding life a bit difficult' attended free weekly afternoon football sessions with a professional coach with experience of working with men's mental health. There was no formal commitment to the group and mental health disclosure was optional. After 60 minutes of football, players could go to a drop-in session and talk to any of a range of people: a psychologist, a mental health nurse, men who have experienced mental illnesses, financial advisors, employment advisors and addiction support.

Comparing baseline measures to 12 weeks post involvement, of the 42% who returned their questionnaires, 67% reported improved fitness, 67% made new friends, 58% reported reduced anxiety and stress and 42% reported improved mood. Also, many participants reported contacting services for stress management, mostly mood/anxiety management support and drug and alcohol support services. Qualitative outcomes found that participants had benefited in terms of self-belief, enjoyment of the friendly and non-judgemental atmosphere of the programme, a reduction in feeling isolated, a feeling of being able to access other services and an improvement in physical and mental health.

ATPF demonstrates that football can be a successful way to engage men who are 'hard to reach' in terms of dealing with their mental health issues. This programme utilised various aspects known to help men's mental health (Liddon et al., 2019): a low 'barrier to entry' to the programme in terms of no requirement for mental health disclosure; an indirect approach (via football rather than a clinic); focus on 'fixing the problem', not just focusing on emotions; and engaging as a team (see Figure 11.3). In collaboration with a range of other organisations (such as *Active Norfolk*, the *Premier Sports Foundation*, *Norwich MIND*, the *Football Development Centre* and *Change, Grow, Live*), the success of this pilot study has led to the establishment of three more groups across the Norfolk area.

6.6.3.2 *Walking football for older men*

For people over the age of 50 in the UK, an alternative to football is 'walking football'. This a slowed-down version of ordinary football where, as the name suggests, players walk rather than run. Research has found benefits in terms of wellbeing (Reddy et al., 2017). Most of the participants in walking football are male, and it offers wellbeing benefits to those who would be considered hard to reach in terms of accessing mainstream health services. More research would be welcome to explore the potential benefits of this increasingly popular activity.

IS BOXING GOOD FOR MENTAL HEALTH?

Male depression can sometimes be expressed through aggressive or even violent behaviour (Zierau et al., 2002), and it is often said anecdotally that boxing is a good way to help wayward working-class boys to channel aggression and learn to be more disciplined. However these days there are concerns about chronic traumatic encephalopathy (CTE), and despite the fact that a systematic review of amateur boxing concluded that 'there is no strong evidence for brain injury' (Loosemore et al., 2007, p. 812), the British Medical Association has been campaigning since 1982 to ban boxing on medical grounds (White, 2007). Arguably, the decision to box should be an issue of informed consent.

Boxing and martial arts have a special place in the male psychology of sport because boxing – like martial arts – epitomises an archetype of the masculine fighter and winner (Seager et al., 2014). However, the belief that a man should be a fighter and winner can – if held too rigidly – become more a burden than an asset (see Sections 12.6.3 and 6.5.3). This psychological truism is understood by the average person too, as shown by a vignette study where participants suggested that beliefs such as '*I absolutely have to win*' were associated with the suicide of a fictional boxer (Sporrle & Forsterling, 2007).

There is likely to be a difference between the impact of competitive boxing on mental health and the benefits of boxing as a method of exercise. For example, the pressure on professional fighters to continue even when hurt, and the disappointment of losing a key fight, weigh heavily. So although a champion fighter might feel on top of the world after winning a fight, the lows of eventually losing or retiring at a relatively early age represent a potentially severe downside.

There is evidence for mental health benefits of martial arts (Wang et al., 2015), and for 'Rock Steady Boxing' training for people with Parkinson's disease (Meinert & Hatkevich, 2019). Despite anecdotal evidence for the potential benefits of boxing on mental health, it is an under-researched area and no peer-reviewed publications exist. However, a UK pilot study of 24 participants found their wellbeing had improved significantly after a 16-week boxing programme (John & Mansfield, 2018). Further research on this topic could highlight a valuable way to support the mental health of men who might otherwise be uninterested and 'hard to reach'.

6.7 CONCLUDING REMARKS

One of the interesting aspects of this chapter is that it highlights how large some sex differences can be, and how much a male psychology perspective brings to understanding them. The contrast between the subjective experience of sports from the perspective of the player or fan, and the critical perspective from gender studies, is so vast as to almost constitute different worlds. Whereas for many people sports is a source of joy and adds meaning to life, to others it is a problematic arena of sexism and hegemonic masculinity. It would be interesting to see a critique of gender studies from the point of view of sports fans.

Other material in this chapter will have been especially of interest to sports coaches and players, e.g. the section on choking and the yips. The section on homophobic chanting shows that some things are more complex than they appear on the surface. It would be interesting to see research on how much the masculine protector role (Seager et al., 2014a) might be employed as a way to protect gay fans. This might work especially well for fans who support the same team, because of the added potential ingroup favouritism.

A final observation is that although men are said not to empathise as much as women do, sports fans – predominantly male – appear to very powerfully experience the highs and lows of the players, and of fellow fans. Perhaps this is another example of sex differences in the expression of a characteristic, which can be seen so often (see e.g. Section 11.4.1; therapy is feminised, Figure 11.3).

6.8 SUMMARY

- Different theories (biological, evolutionary and social) each have something to say about the reason for sex differences in interest in sport and exercise.
- The gender studies view of sports was assessed.
- Reasons for sex segregation in sports were discussed.
- Sports performance issues were described.
- The benefits of sport and exercise focusing on mental and social well-being were discussed, including examples of sex differences.
- Examples of sport and exercise interventions for mental health were discussed.

7 The Workplace

CHAPTER OUTLINE

Perspectives in Male Psychology: An Introduction, First Edition.
Louise Liddon and John A. Barry.
© 2021 John Wiley & Sons, Ltd. Published 2021 by John Wiley & Sons, Ltd.

LEARNING OUTCOMES

By the end of this chapter, you should be able to:

1. Understand why men and women tend to gravitate to different occupations
2. Be familiar with the evidence that men gravitate to working with 'things' rather than with people
3. Understand what unconscious bias is, and how it can work against men in the workplace
4. Know about gender equality schemes and reasons behind the 'sexist' pay gap
5. Learn about banter, bullying and wellbeing in the workplace

7.1 INTRODUCTION

Employment and job satisfaction are important for men's wellbeing (Barry, 2020). This should be good news for men in fulfilling jobs, but if their wellbeing depends too much on their job, they are at the mercy of employment conditions that are probably beyond their control. This chapter will address topics impacting men's experience of work, such as the factors that affect wellbeing at work, changes in the nature of the modern workplace, sex differences in occupational choices (including working in psychology), gender-related bias in the workplace, gender equality schemes, banter and bullying.

7.2 SEX DIFFERENCES IN OCCUPATIONS

7.2.1 *Male/Female-Dominated Fields*

Women tend to do more healthcare, early education and domestic jobs ('HEED' jobs) than men do (Block et al., 2019). Since the 1970s, the labour market for many male-dominated occupations – especially working-class/manual jobs in manufacturing – has grown smaller (Bureau of Labor Statistics, 2017). In contrast, not only have female-dominated jobs expanded, but women today dominate the majority of industries – mainly in health and social care – that are predicted to have the highest job and wage growth in the US up to 2028. Men have made little progress entering female-dominated occupations, though in contrast women have made significant progress entering male-dominated occupations that require a high degree of education (Croft et al., 2010).

7.2.2   Why do Men not Enter Female-Dominated Fields?

Possible reasons that men tend not to enter female-dominated fields are that jobs there pay less, have fewer benefits and might be seen as too feminine for men. A meta-analysis of studies over several decades found the impact of unemployment on mental health was significantly worse for men than for women (Paul & Moser, 2009), but for those who are ready to make career changes, unemployment significantly increases the likelihood of men entering female-dominated jobs (Yavorsky & Dill, 2020). Evidence for systematic advantages for men in traditionally female jobs is limited, and the sociologist who originally theorised the 'glass escalator' for men in 1992 accepts the concept now is of limited validity, because it was originally based on assumptions about the stability of employment, nature of bureaucratic hierarchies and widespread support for public institutions which can no longer be taken for granted (Williams, 2013).

It is interesting that the lower number of men than women in helping professions is attributed – by men and women – to internal factors such as choice, whereas the lower number of women in science, technology, engineering and mathematics (STEM) fields is attributed to external factors such as discrimination against women or stereotyping (Block et al., 2019; *Theme: 'victim blaming'*, in Section 13.2.3). People tend also to see it as less important to get men into HEED jobs. Note that the term 'choice' is appropriate in the context of gender and occupations, because although choices are limited to some degree by various factors (e.g. social background), research shows that the more gender egalitarian a society, the more gender-typical the choice of career (Stoet & Geary, 2018). This suggests that the more choice women have over their lifestyle and career, the more fully they can express their career preferences.

7.2.3   Why are There More Men Than Women in Non-organic STEM Fields?

Although there are many voices in the media, academia and the gender equality industry (e.g. Equality Challenge Unit, 2013) saying that there are more men in STEM because women are kept out in various ways (e.g. 'unconscious bias' against women), there is evidence that on the whole there are roughly equal numbers of men and women in STEM, when people sciences are taken into account (Funk & Parker, 2018; HESA, 2018). When STEM is categorised as organic vs people sciences, familiar gender differences emerge: there are more men in non-organic STEM areas (geoscience, engineering, economics, mathematics/computer science and the physical sciences) but around equal numbers – or more women – in people-orientated sciences (life science, psychology and social science) (Ceci et al., 2014).

It appears that men and women often make different career choices based on interests (see Section 7.3.1) and other aspects of a job. For example, an interview study of male and female doctoral chemistry students found that the female students were less keen than the males on pursuing a career in chemistry because the job was seen as solitary; entailed long hours, stress and a competitive culture; and was not conducive 'with other aspects of their life, particularly relationships and family' (Newsome, 2008, p. 7). Despite the lower uptake of women to chemistry being a matter of lifestyle choice, nonetheless this study has been taken as evidence of systematic sexism, and is even recommended reading in gender equality circles (Oxford Research & Policy | Resources for Athena SWAN and Juno, 2017).

7.3 SEX DIFFERENCES IMPACTING OCCUPATIONAL CHOICES

7.3.1 *Sex Differences in Jobs Related to Things or People*

Jobs can be categorised into six types: Realistic (things, gadgets, outdoors); Investigative (STEM, social sciences, medicine); Artistic; Social (helping people); Enterprising; and Conventional jobs (well-structured environments, especially business). These interests can also be seen as existing on a *Things–People* dimension and a *Data–Ideas* dimension (Prediger, 1982). Placing jobs on the Things–People spectrum finds the most strongly thing-orientated jobs are machinist, engineer and physical scientist, whereas the most strongly people-orientated jobs are school teacher, social worker and clergy ('psychologist' is in the top third of people-orientated jobs; Lippa et al., 2014). It is well-established that when asked to place themselves on the People–Things dimension, men are more thing-orientated and women more people-orientated, and this difference can be quite large (Cohen's $d = 1.29$; Lippa, 2006). A meta-analysis of 81 studies from 1972 to 2007, with a total of more than half a million participants, found that men showed stronger Realistic (i.e. things) interests ($d = 0.84$) and Investigative ($d = 0.26$) interests, and women showed stronger Artistic ($d = -0.35$),

Social ($d = -0.68$) and Conventional ($d = 0.33$) interests. Scores on measures of interest in engineering ($d = 1.11$), science ($d = 0.36$) and mathematics ($d = 0.34$) are also higher in men (Su et al., 2009). Analysis of US Bureau of Labor Statistics data for 60 occupations from 1972 to 2010 found that the People–Things orientation of occupations has become a stronger predictor of sex difference in job choice over that time (Lippa et al., 2014). Also in that period, women's participation in thing-orientated occupations has remained consistently low.

The sex difference in Things–People interest can be seen among researchers. A review of 508,283 articles in the database *Scopus*, covering the full spectrum of science subjects for the 12 months of 2017, found that male researchers are more likely to use quantitative methods such as statistical analysis, and female researchers to use qualitative methods such as interviewing people (Thelwall et al., 2019; see Section 5.3).

A survey in Sweden of 2400 new graduates of engineering, law, law enforcement, social work and psychology found that those in gender-atypical occupations tended to display gender-atypical personality traits (Grönlund & Magnusson, 2018). For example, men overall were more risk-taking than women, and psychology – a female-dominated profession – tended to attract risk-averse men and women. In contrast, the police force attracted risk-taking men and women (see Section 3.3.3).

It is notable that the male-typical interests lead to jobs that generally have higher salaries. Some might argue this is evidence that women's interests are financially undervalued, though we should note that the male-typical interests tend to lead to occupations that are more technical and, by and large, cost more to train in (Hemelt, 2018).

WHY ARE THERE NOT MORE MALE PSYCHOLOGISTS?

Based on what we know about the Things–People effect, we might predict that there would be fewer men than women in a relatively people-orientated field like psychology. However some aspects of psychology are less people-orientated than others, e.g. IT, data analysis and non-clinical roles such as lecturing. Nonetheless, the number of men graduating in the US with psychology bachelor's degrees decreased from 55% in 1971 to 21% in 2018 (Digest of Education Statistics, 2018).

In the UK, the BPS has recommended that gender quotas be used in two ways: to increase the number of male undergraduates, and to increase the number of women in the very highest positions in academia (Gale, 2017). However, gender quotas don't address the question of why men are increasingly unrepresented in psychology. This is an important issue, and might be connected to why not only are there fewer psychologists who are men, but there are fewer psychology clients who are men. It might also be connected to the claim that 'feminists have made it possible for women to not only invade the (traditionally male and pathologizing) field [of psychology], but to radically take it over' (Fahs & Karger, 2016, p.945). This claim is of concern both because psychology is described as 'traditionally male and pathologizing', and also because this 'invasion' brings with it the sociopolitical lens of 'critical theory', which has resulted in encouraging a negative view of masculinity in psychology (see Section 11.4.3). Whether this 'invasion' is part of the cause of men's exodus from psychology or not, gender quotas – based on the presumption that unequal numbers mean unfair treatment – don't seem a sensible solution because, for example, although men might be persuaded to train in psychology, this risks replicating the 'leaky pipeline' seen for women in STEM when other career or lifestyle choices are made (see Section 7.7).

There are fewer male psychologists than female, but beyond their being a numerical imbalance, is there an actual need for more male psychologists (Barry et al., 2016)? One way to look at this is as a question of meeting the specific needs of the job, in other words, if men are needed because they bring qualities to psychology that aren't found in women, or because there is demand from clients for psychologists who are male, then this justifies increasing the representation of men in psychology.

What happens to the men who apply for clinical psychology posts? In the UK, Clearing House data shows the proportion of male and female (and 'prefer not to say') applicants to clinical psychology doctorates in the UK. Each year around 84% of applications are unsuccessful. Between the years 2005 and 2018, although men were in a minority of those applying to be clinical psychologists (16.8% of all applicants were male) they had less chance of being accepted on the training course (15.2% of the successful applicants were male) than were female applicants (Villanueva, 2019). (For contrast, see Ceci et al., 2014, and see Table 7.2). Given the scarcity of psychologists who are men, this trend against male applicants should be treated as a potentially important issue for psychology as a profession.

7.3.2   Differences in Leadership

A study of 577 European executives (434 male, 143 female) and 52,139 non-executive employees (34,496 male, 17,643 female) found that female executives scored higher on male-typical traits than women who weren't executives (Wille et al., 2018). Although the male and female participants were similar on most personality traits, the sex differences in traits relevant to leadership were smaller among executives compared to non-executives. Male and female executives tended to show a 'leader personality' archetype, focused on assertiveness, high-level strategic thinking and decisiveness. Despite the relevance of these differences to evolutionary theories of sex differences, the authors said the results 'generally supported a gender-similarities perspective' (Wille et al., 2018, p. 220) (*Theme: 'cognitive biases'*, in Section 13.2.5).

7.4   UNCONSCIOUS BIAS IN THE WORKPLACE

It is sometimes claimed that women's careers are held back by patriarchy or institutional sexism (Eagly, 2018). For example, it is said that 'unconscious bias' based on stereotypes about women means they are less likely to be hired in male-typical fields, and that people hiring for such posts should prepare themselves by 'for example, reading about famous female scientists/leaders and set[ting] an implantation intention (e.g. "think female think leader")' (Equality Challenge Unit, 2013, p. 8).

7.4.1   *Criticisms of the Implicit Association Test (IAT)*

A: *Well, we're academics, so we know we're pretty objective when it comes to research.*

JB: *We think we are, but what if collectively we can't see our biases about gender?*

A: *Oh yeah, but we have unconscious bias training for that.*

JB: *But what if that is part of the bias?*

A: *[Silence]*

JB: *What if not recognizing gender differences is a cognitive bias. What if this bias is causing us to do more harm than good?*

A: *[Silence]*

– Conversation between John Barry and another attendee at the *Nuffield Foundation Family Justice Observatory* meeting at UCL in 2017, https://www.bps.org.uk/blogs/dr-john-barry/gender-blindness-not-blindfold-impartiality

Unconscious bias (or implicit bias) is the notion that, regardless of our conscious thoughts and feelings, we hold biased judgements against people who are different to us. Implicit bias is often measured using the Implicit Association Test (IAT), popularised by Greenwald et al. (1998), in a paper which is the third most cited in the high-ranking *Journal of Personality and Social Psychology*. In brief, the IAT requires participants to rapidly pair positive and negative words to different categories of demographics (e.g. men and women), and their score is based on differences in how many negative words have been assigned to that demographic. (For a detailed description of the IAT procedure, see Johnson, 2017).

Even though many people find taking the test distressing – especially if they see themselves as unbiased but the test suggests otherwise – the IAT is widely used in the workplace and elsewhere (Blanton et al., 2009). Also, the tests have been controversial for various reasons. For example, IAT scores are a poor predictor of actual behaviour, and contradictory findings from the same participants are possible depending on how data are analysed (Blanton et al., 2009). It has been found that higher bias scores can be caused by a person's motivation to control their bias (Vanman et al., 2004). Another criticism is that the test often finds 'false positive' results, partly because it forces participants to choose between words like 'good' and 'bad' in situations where they don't think either word applies.

Perhaps the main problem with the IAT is that it can identify statistical realities as bias, e.g. people taking the IAT generally associate women more quickly with literature than with science, which is interpreted by the IAT as an implicit bias against women in science, even though this pattern of scoring reflects actual sex differences in occupations (Nosek et al., 2002). It could be argued that the fundamental problem with the IAT is of 'construct validity', i.e. the IAT doesn't appear to be a valid measure of bias (Schimmack, 2019). Despite these problems, the IAT is still in popular use.

7.4.2   *Understanding Unconscious Bias in the Real World*

A study often cited as proof that unconscious bias is a barrier to the careers of women found that when academic staff are given job application forms containing identical information, they favour male candidates over female (Moss-Racusin et al., 2012). However, a larger replication found that the 'unconscious bias' was 2:1 against men (Williams & Ceci, 2015). Unconscious biases no doubt exist, probably because we can navigate the world more easily if we work from cognitive 'rules of thumb' rather than by taking each situation as a unique case to be figured out. Thus if we see someone running past us dressed as a firefighter, we presume there is a fire somewhere, and we don't first stop to think whether the person is an actor late for a disaster movie, or an office clerk with strange fashion sense. Similarly, if we hear the term 'plumber' we think of a man, which seems reasonable because almost all plumbers are men. According to the IAT, we are biased to presume a plumber is male. However, if such opinions are based in reality, it is unreasonable to treat them as if they are wrong, either factually or morally.

There is also a question mark over how manifest these biases are in daily life. For example, if they are only manifest by being teased out by an IAT, and even then not very convincingly, then how much do they translate into real-world discrimination? A survey in the US asked 490 female and 919 male students (engineering graduates and undergraduates) about discrimination against women on the engineering programme: 57% of male students and 26% of female students estimated there was virtually no such discrimination from other engineering students, and 51% of male students and 77% of female students estimated there was virtually no such discrimination from engineering instructors. Less than 2% of male and female students thought that virtually all students and instructors discriminated against women at least occasionally. If true, this implies that discrimination, like crime, is not widespread, but is concentrated in a minority of people (perhaps similar to the '80/20' rule (Sanders, 1987)).

Furthermore, there is evidence of serious *unintended consequences* of trying to tackle such biases: a series of experiments found that videos highlighting the widespread nature of sexism in STEM fields had the effect of making women feel they didn't belong in STEM, and made them less interested in challenging sexism in STEM (Moss-Racusin et al., 2018; Pietri et al., 2019) (*Theme: 'unintended consequences',* in Section 13.2.1).

7.5 UNCONSCIOUS BIAS AGAINST MEN IN THE WORKPLACE

Many modern workplaces now have 'gender equality' programmes which support women's careers in STEM, the boardroom and other high-status areas where women have historically been less represented.

7.5.1 *The Expansion of Gender Equality Schemes*

The original idea of Athena SWAN in 2005 was to get more women into occupations where there were far fewer women than men. Originally, the fields focused on were science, technology and engineering (STE), but over time this was extended to include mathematics (STEM), then medicine (STEMM), and since 2015 the scheme has been extended to all areas of academia, including arts, humanities, social science, business and law departments. Note that women were already over-represented in the humanities at that time.

Athena SWAN has also spread to Ireland and Australia and plans to spread to India. Similar schemes have taken off worldwide. Title IX began in the US 1972 as a 37-word clause asserting gender equality in educational programmes or activities funded by the Federal government. In 2011 this was extended to dealing with allegations of sexual harassment on campus, but due to increasing criticisms, such as the overly inclusive interpretation of sexual harassment (see Section 8.4.3.2), it has been reined in somewhat (US Dept of Education, 2020a).

It is difficult to assess the impact of equality schemes on academia, e.g. whether academic output is improved in any way, or whether the costs of the schemes (e.g. a time-consuming box-ticking exercise which detracts time that could be devoted to scientific research) are justified in other ways

(Tzanakou, 2019). However, equality schemes exist in many realms these days, including the business world, where profit is higher on the list of priorities. In business, the *KLD STATS* assess social performance on seven dimensions, including diversity. A 14-year longitudinal assessment of 1889 US public firms found 'firms that increase board diversity suffer a decrease in market value and that this effect is amplified for firms that have received higher ratings [on KLD STATS] for their diversity practices across the organization ... every increase in the number of female directors may lead to a 2.3% loss of market value, which could amount to hundreds of millions of dollars' (Solal & Snellman, 2019, p. 1270 and 1278). The authors explained that 'a gender-diverse board is interpreted [by investors] as revealing a preference for diversity and a weaker commitment to shareholder value' (Solal & Snellman, 2019, p. 1270). (*Theme: 'unintended consequences'*, in Section 13.2.1).

7.5.2   *Unconscious Bias Against Women, or Conscious Bias Against Men?*

In France, 85% of newly appointed judges are women, and it has been suggested that this is because gender quotas discourage men from applying for those jobs (Evening Standard, 2015). In Sweden – which is probably the country that has most experience of gender equality policies – some men have expressed ambivalence about working in environments where gender equality is a tangible part of daily life (Risberg et al., 2011).

To date, research asking men their opinions of gender equality programmes are noticeably lacking. Clearly, some research is needed on this topic, because if men experience gender equality schemes as not simply beneficial to women but as detrimental to men, this needs to be addressed in some way. This issue might have relevance to university dropout and 'failure to launch', so research on this topic is important (see Section 5.4).

In the US, a nationally representative longitudinal survey of 239 male and 78 female lawyers found that even after controlling for other variables, very early career experiences of discrimination in the workplace can impact aspirations and long-term career (Azmat et al., 2020). The study also found that higher early career aspirations were the key to greater likelihood of men's promotion later in their careers, and there was no evidence of any systemic or institutional advantage to helping men rather than women in their careers. It appeared that small differences in preferences early in their career impacted aspirations, which in turn increased effort and commitment to being promoted. This echoes the way that multiple relatively small sex differences in traits (*Theme: 'the difference that makes the difference'*, in Section 13.2.4) and attributes can add up to create a large difference when considered as a profiles (Kaufman, 2019), and can impact sex differences in career trajectory (Ceci et al., 2014; Williams & Ceci, 2012).

7.5.3 Are Men Exploited in the Workplace?

The current social trend towards looking up at the 'glass ceiling' means our attention tends not to go to the 'glass cellar', the place in which men do the dirty and dangerous jobs (Farrell, 2001). The majority of workplace deaths are male, a figure that has remained stable over the years (HSE, 2019).

7.5.4 The Gender Pay Gap

The famous lament 'There are three kinds of lies: lies, damned lies, and statistics' is attributed to British Prime Minister Benjamin Disraeli, and this sentiment is no less true anywhere than the confusion over the gender pay gap. (For an accessible explanation of the gender pay gap, see the video by economist Professor Thomas Sowell on this book's companion website).

Before looking at actual statistics, for the sake of clarity, here is what the UK's Office for National Statistics (ONS) says: 'The gender pay gap is calculated as the difference between average hourly earnings (excluding overtime) of men and women as a proportion of average hourly earnings (excluding overtime) of men's earnings. It is a measure across all jobs in the UK, not of the difference in pay between men and women for doing the same job ... For age groups under 40 years, the gender pay gap for full-time employees is now close to zero ... women over 40 years are more likely to work in lower-paid occupations and, compared with younger women, are less likely to work as managers, directors or senior officials' (ONS, 2019a).

Table 7.1 shows that the median pay gap for full time work is 8.6% in favour of men, and that for part time work is 4.4% in favour of women. The

TABLE 7.1 *Gender pay gap, illustrating* Simpson's paradox.

Hourly pay excluding overtime, median, April 2018 (share of employees)	Men	Women	Pay gap
Full time	14.81	13.54	8.6%
	(85% of men)	(58% of women)	{ = (14.81–13.54)/14.81}
Part time	9.07	9.47	-4.4%{ = (9.07–9.47)/9.07}
	(15% of men)	(42% of women)	
All	14.00	11.50	0.179
	100% of men	(100% of women)	{ = (14.00–11.50) { = (9.07–9.47)/9.07}

Source: ONS 2018 (Athow, 2019). https://blog.ons.gov.uk/2019/04/16/decoding-the-gender-pay-gap-how-a-bletchley-park-codebreaker-helped-explain-a-strange-paradox/.

overall pay gap is 17.9%, which is higher than would be intuitively expected (called *Simpson's paradox*) because there are more men in full time work (Athow, 2019).

Key points in understanding the pay gap are, firstly, that it does not take into account the different pay for different types of jobs that men and women choose to do (Section 7.3.1). Secondly, it doesn't take into account the levels of seniority in those jobs. Thirdly, women tend to choose careers that allow them to more easily take time off and career breaks for child rearing. For example, there are proportionally more female school teachers than IT developers and taking time out from a fast-developing field like IT can set a person's career back more than a less fast-developing field like school teaching. The fact that librarianship pays less well than IT, and attracts more women than men, is typical of the factors that cause the gender pay gap.

SPOTLIGHT BOX 7.2

SEXISM AGAINST MEN IN HIRING

It is not uncommon to find popular psychology articles with titles like 'Why You Should Hire Women Over Men, According to Science' (Tsipursky, 2020). Typically, the evidence presented in these articles is unconvincing. Let's look closer at the Tsipursky article.

Firstly, implicit bias is given as an explanation for discrimination against women, but – predictably – there is no consideration of whether 'stereotyped' concepts of women (e.g. being more family-orientated) might actually be based in reality. Secondly, three studies are cited, each of which are based on women's opinions, rather than objective evidence, of why their careers are not going as well as they would like, e.g. 'doing all the right things needed for advancement' (published in 1992) or 'having to work harder to overcome a variety of barriers, such as being excluded from informal networks and getting less mentoring than men' (published in 2000) or 'experiencing discrimination much more frequently than men' (published in 1990). These complaints are not only from an era, two or three decades ago, that is incomparable in terms of today's widespread uptake of gender equality schemes (e.g. in the UK since 2005), but also the complaints are highly subjective. Moreover, in today's workplace men could reasonably argue that, in a world of programmes to enhance women's careers, they are the ones experiencing institutional discrimination.

The article concludes by saying that when hiring 'you should always give preference to women ... I would prefer to hire women over men, and recommend other males do the same.' If this comment was made about women, it would be considered sexist and career-ending for the author. However, it is accepted as just another part of the narrative, promoted in academia, the media, government and the legal system, that women – not men – are the victims of gender-based prejudice (Fradera, 2017).

In contrast with this popular narrative there is good evidence that there is 'no real-world hiring data show[ing] a bias against hiring women' (Ceci et al., 2014, p. 101). In an impressive 67-page review exploring a range of explanations for the position of women in academia, from innate abilities based on prenatal testosterone levels to whether better male networks explain males' higher rate of publication, they conclude that 'invitations to interview for tenure-track positions in math-intensive fields – as well as actual employment offers – reveal that female PhD applicants fare at least as well as their male counterparts in math-intensive fields' (Ceci et al., 2014, p. 75). Table 7.2 shows that in each of the six STEM fields assessed, women were disproportionately given interviews, and disproportionately offered jobs. For example, in electrical engineering, 11% of applicants were women, but 19% of them were invited to interviews, and 32% were subsequently offered jobs. This can be contrasted with the experience of men applying to be clinical psychologists (SPOTLIGHT box 7.1).

TABLE 7.2 *Bias against hiring men in STEM (from Ceci et al., 2014).*

Woman in academic science: a changing landscape

Field	Mean percentage of female applicants	Mean percentage of women invited in interview	Offered position
Physics	12%	19%	20%
Biology	26%	28%	34%
Chemistry	18%	25%	29%
Civil engineering	16%	30%	32%
Electrical engineering	11%	19%	32%
Mathematics	20%	28%	32%

Note: Data shown here were drawn from sections 3–10 and 3–13 of 'Gender Differences at Critical Transitions in the Careers of Science, Engineering and Mathematics Faculty' (National Research Council, 2010).

In Sweden, women's careers have been given preference over men's for the past three decades, yet less than a third of professors are women. Some claim that this reflects institutional bias against women, with women being held to higher standards before being made professor. However, analysis of academic publications at the time of being made professor, in both medicine and the social sciences, showed that male faculty had 64–80% more publications and 42–260% more citations than did female faculty (Madison & Fahlman, 2020).

7.6 WELLBEING IN THE WORKPLACE

Work is an important part of wellbeing for many men. However, the workplace has changed a lot for men in recent decades, in many ways for the worse. The next section explores factors associated with wellbeing and stress, in the workplace.

7.6.1 *The Changing Face of the Workplace*

The US between 1979 and 2010 saw a trend, across age groups and educational levels, for men's wages to decrease and women's increase (Autor & Wasserman, 2013). Men still account for 95% of workplace fatalities (HSE, 2019) despite the shift in many countries from traditionally male jobs in manufacturing and mining to more gender-neutral work, such as office work or the service industry. Although correlation does not prove causation, these changes have coincided with a rise in suicide in traditionally male industries since the 1980s (Roberts et al., 2013).

A survey of 4000 men aged 18–75 in the UK, US, Australia and Canada found that about a third of men said they always or frequently felt stressed because of their work (Movember, 2019). Around half of men surveyed felt they couldn't take time off work if stressed, and worried about what colleagues would say about them if they did. About a third worried that discussing their mental health could have a negative impact on their career.

7.6.2 *The Relationship Between Men, Work and Mental Wellbeing*

A survey of 2000 men (mean age 42) in the British Isles followed up by a survey of 5000 men (mean age 33) in the US (Barry, 2020) found that by far the strongest predictor of mental wellbeing (measured using the Positive Mindset Index), in the UK and every region of the US, was job satisfaction. This correlation was independent of a range of other demographic variables.

In the US, the values most predictive of job satisfaction were 'making an impact on the company's success', followed by 'good pay', 'chatting with co-workers', 'using my own unique talents' and 'work–life balance'. There was some regional variation, with 'making an impact on the company's success' being the strongest predictor of job satisfaction in the Northeast, then Midwest, South, then West.

These findings could suggest that mental positivity is strongly linked to the provider role (Seager et al., 2014). Although it might be attributed to socialisation, the fact that it was the strongest predictor across 7000 men in two geographical regions albeit both in the West – might indicate a deeper, perhaps evolutionary, influence, especially when put in context of broadly similar findings worldwide (Ellis, 2011). The relevance of job satisfaction to mental positivity also has clinical relevance, and therapists should be aware of any employment issues in their male clients, even if not part of their presenting problem.

7.6.3   Banter in the Workplace

According to the Merriam-Webster dictionary, banter is defined as 'to speak to or address in a witty and teasing manner'. Although we have 'all met the office joker [who keeps] the mood light … Most of us have also met the one who takes it "a step too far"' (Wise 2016, p. 481).

In the following section it is important to make the distinction between something intended to be lighthearted, on the one hand, and bullying on the other (see Section 7.6.4). Bullying is not acceptable, but to some degree subjective perception makes this issue complicated because what seems like bullying to one person might be intended as friendly banter to another.

Although some people take the view that 'the meaning of the communication is the response you get' (Freeth, 2008, p. 166), others take the more everyday understanding that if a comment is genuinely intended as humour, then reasonable allowances should be made to accept it as such. Banter has, in recent times, got a bad reputation as 'a way of expressing disgust and hatred with an exit strategy: "just joking"' (Wise, 2016, p. 498). There is a lot of research on workplace humour, and plenty of opinion expressed in the media, particularly about banter and sexism.

7.6.3.1   The social complexity of banter

Banter is more complex than is often portrayed, and 'seems to cause both job satisfaction and dissatisfaction for both men and women' (Bjerke & Rones, 2017, p. 2). For example, in the military, humour can be part of the socialisation process which regulates the effective functioning of the unit while allowing a controlled way of coping with and criticising their circumstances (Godfrey, 2016). Indeed, it has been found in the US Military Academy that new cadets were less likely to drop out if they used humour as a coping strategy (Priest & Swain, 2002). On the other hand, banter can seem threatening, and there is a drive to remove banter from the workplace. For example, Ann Francke of the Chartered Management Institute suggested that chatting about sports in the workplace makes women feel left out and is a 'gateway to more laddish behaviour' and therefore to be discouraged (BBC News, 2020). This is unfortunate because 'chatting with workmates' has been found to be related to men's job satisfaction and wellbeing, so putting restrictions on talk about sport – especially as sport is also a major interest of many men – might reduce men's wellbeing (Barry, 2020).

7.6.3.2   *Positive aspects of banter*

Although the focus of research and media discussion is on the damaging aspects of banter in the workplace, there is evidence that it can have a positive impact. Banter has been found to be positive in various workplaces, e.g. construction and construction management (Ponton et al., 2020).

An interview study of 39 employees (18 male and 21 female) at all levels of three IT companies in New Zealand found that banter – or 'taking the piss' – was almost continuous in the workplace (Plester & Sayers, 2007, p. 163). The study found that the six main functions of banter were: making a point; boredom relief; socialisation; celebrating differences; displaying a work hard–play hard culture; and highlighting and defining status. Apart from when it was used to deliver a 'barbed' message, or for those not yet socialised into the ingroup, the laughter generated by banter was considered an important part of dealing with the stresses of work.

There is evidence that humour in the workplace increases creativity, especially 'liberating humour', which facilitates seeing things in a new way and may include broaching socially sensitive concerns and taboo topics (Lang & Lee, 2010). This might be especially useful in jobs where innovation and creativity are valued.

7.6.3.3   *Banter across cultures*

Most research on banter is based in the West, but research with blue-collar workers in Singapore suggests that in some respects the phenomenon is universal (Wise & Velayutham, 2020). An example of Singaporean banter is the Pilipino hospitality worker who calls the Indian chef 'lolo', which she tells him means 'handsome'. When the chef finds out that it actually means 'granddad', he makes enquiries with others about Pilipino vernacular and begins calling her 'lola', which means 'grandma'.

The authors suggest that the Singaporean banter lacks the harsh disparaging element described in some Western studies of banter (Wise & Velayutham, 2020). This might be true, but it is difficult to generalise about cultures, e.g. although English and Australian humour is Western and have a shared history, the styles are not identical (Sinkeviciute, 2017). The type of work is probably a major influence on the type of communication, including banter, with more dangerous or highly stressful jobs – much of which involves work done by men – lending themselves more to 'gallows humour'. For example, in the emergency services gallows humour 'is a bona fide coping mechanism which can contribute to the resilience, health and wellbeing of emergency services personnel but one which, to the uninitiated, may appear callous and uncaring' (Christopher, 2015, p. 610). Thus it is possible that the association between men and challenging humour came about because some of the most dangerous and stressful jobs are done mostly by men.

It could be that learning to work in different types of job is like working in different cultures, with different norms and customs (see Section 9.6.2). For example, a female gym instructor at a mixed-sex gym in the UK said of the humour from men there: 'at first I didn't really like it, and then like I just joked back and I found that joking back actually made me more not on edge and I didn't feel threatened by them' (Clark, 2018, p. 11). Banter in situations like this might feel uncomfortable, at least at first, but it suggests that a function of banter might be to signal willingness to be part of an ingroup (Plester & Sayers, 2007).

As can be seen, banter is a complex phenomenon. Trying to understand banter is not the same as condoning bullying, and in an ideal world misunderstandings of the intent of communication would not occur. From a practical standpoint, it would be useful for people to both make an effort to respect the sensitivities of others, and make an effort to not be too easily offended. This is easier said than done, and constraint, resilience and forgiveness are powerful attitudes that workplaces might benefit from encouraging.

7.6.4 *Bullying in the Workplace: are Women More Likely to be Victims and Men Bullies?*

The evidence regarding sex differences in bullying at work is mixed. Some studies find men are more likely than women to be bullies, but this might be an effect of rank rather than gender: men are more likely to be in supervisory or managerial roles, and these roles give more opportunity to bully (Zapf et al., 2003). In samples that are predominantly female, women are more likely than men to report being victims (Zapf et al., 2003). There is a possible impact of gender differences in reporting; based on what we know about sex differences in help-seeking, women are more willing than men to report experiencing problems related to stress, in contrast to men who don't want to be seen as weak. Also, sex differences in type of aggression might influence the likelihood of reporting of bullying: male aggression is typically more overt and easily identifiable, whereas female aggression is more indirect (see Section 8.2.4); thus male bullying is more obvious and might be more likely to be reported for that reason (Zapf et al., 2003).

WORKPLACE SUPPORT FOR MEN'S MENTAL WELLBEING

It is important that people who experience stress at work receive treatment that will help them. A longitudinal study of 2300 participants on a UK Employee Assistance Programme (EAP) found that immediately after therapy (brief counselling), men and women appeared to benefit equally (Wright & McLeod, 2016). However, at the six-month follow-up assessment the male participants had relapsed to their previous levels of poor mental health, unlike the female clients, who had maintained their gains.

These results should be very interesting to therapists, and this study is especially valuable because the outcomes of psychological therapies are not routinely disaggregated by gender, because generally the assumption is made that men and women benefit equally (Parker et al., 2011; *Theme: 'don't make assumptions',* in Section 13.2.5). It also highlights the danger of beta bias, and the importance of sex differences research, which has been promoted in medicine since 2001 (see Section 3.6.2.2).

The results of Wright and McLeod's study might also explain, at least in part, why men are less likely than women to seek psychological help; not only does therapy typically take a 'talk about your feelings' approach, whereas men often prefer a 'quickly fix the problem' approach (Liddon et al., 2019), but this study suggests that talking therapies might not work as well for men as for women. Men are also less likely to seek help if they think they won't be listened to (Hashi, 2019), especially if they are concerned that they will be blamed for their problem (McNeely et al., 2001). This means that even programmes that are very good in other ways might not help men if they don't take a male-friendly approach to therapy.

Apart from the option of therapy, if stress is work-related then practical solutions might be considered first, e.g. a reduction in hours or other change in work practice. Other everyday solutions can help reduce stress too, e.g. exercise. If therapy is needed, there are male-friendly approaches that can be considered (Liddon et al., 2019).

7.7 CONCLUDING REMARKS

This chapter has explored some interesting topics, such as banter, bullying and workplace stress. Much of the chapter has focused on the way in which sex differences in interests and abilities influence the types of jobs and lifestyles that men and women gravitate to. This could be celebrated as an example of complementary differences (*Theme: 'yin and yang',* in Section 13.2.4), but on the contrary the trend these days is to think of these sex differences in outcome as being the result of unconscious bias or institutional sexism, and the solution is to socially engineer a different outcome though equality schemes and unconscious bias training. But because people are so focused on the presumed disadvantages of women, we don't seem to notice the ways in which men are disadvantaged (see Section 2.5.5.1).

Most people support the basic idea of equal opportunities (Barry et al., 2020), and consequently many people say 'yes' when asked if they support gender equality schemes (Block et al., 2019). However, there may be unintended consequences (*Theme: 'unintended consequences'*, in Section 13.2.1) for men, but these are often unresearched and go unnoticed, except in occasional glimpses, such as the suggestion that gender quotas are putting men off applying for jobs (Evening Standard, 2015) and that incentives for women might have an indirect negative impact on men (Keenan et al., 2018). In the spirit of the solution replicating the problem (*Theme: 'the solution that replicates the problem'*, in Section 13.2.1), the 'old boys network' (school friends or alumni helping each other in adulthood) has been outlawed, and replaced by gender equality schemes that are in effect an 'old girls network' (Nielsen, 2015).

It is noticeable that gender equality in practice seems to apply only to the very top jobs held by a tiny minority of men; gender equality is not about the equal representation of women in the ranks of plumbers, bin men or building site workers, or others in much more numerous dirty or dangerous jobs. Equality schemes receive millions of dollars in funding from bodies such as the National Science Foundation to promote women in STEM (National Science Foundation, 2017). At the same time, the equality industry takes up a huge amount of a university's admin capacity in various ways, e.g. applying for Athena SWAN awards, creating workshops, compiling statistics etc. Although these changes bring diversity awards, the investment is not necessarily recouped financially, as found by the experience of award-winning boardroom diversity initiatives in the US (Solal & Snellman, 2019).

The 'leaky pipeline' is an unsurprising outcome of cajoling women into careers they are not committed to (Gino et al., 2015; Metcalf, 2010; Royal Society for Chemistry, 2008). Somehow the familar drop-out of women from STEM careers appears to perpetually baffle supporters of the gender equality industry (Nurse, 2014), who don't seem to realise that only a minority of women prefer a career to a family (Hakim, 2000). As Richard Lippa put it: sex differences in preferences for types of job 'undoubtedly have substantial societal consequences, affecting women's and men's behavior in the workplace and in close relationships' (Lippa, 2006, p. 639). For the same reason, efforts to pipeline men into female-typical jobs are likely to spring leaks too, and in psychology the underlying reason for men's flight from the field of psychology careers needs to be investigated as a first step before any action is taken.

It seems ironic that we are constantly directed to focus on presumed 'unconscious bias' against women when there is institutional bias against men, called 'equality' schemes, as well as other evidence of bias against men (Williams & Ceci, 2015). Because gender bias is so misunderstood, the proposed solutions tend to fail. For example, a meta-analysis of 492 studies (with over 87,000 participants) found that unconscious bias training did not change behaviour (Forscher et al., 2019), and in fact might even exacerbate biases (Dobbin & Kalev, 2018). For these reasons the UK government has decided to stop giving it's employees unconscious bias training (Lopez, 2020). But meanwhile boys are still lagging behind girls in education, and girls are encouraged into STEM careers even though boys tend to excel in STEM subjects (delta bias, see Section 2.5.5.2) and could definitely do with some encouragement. Overall, the workplace appears to be a place where bias is all too common, and it seems that the majority of men and women don't benefit from the present set of 'equality' initiatives.

7.8 SUMMARY

- This chapter has assessed sex differences in occupations, e.g. the predominance of men in science-related fields, with fewer in psychology.
- The relationship between sex differences in interests and sex differences in job choice was explored.
- Unconscious bias, as an explanation for sex differences in occupations, was evaluated.
- Men's mental health at work, banter and bullying were also discussed.
- Gamma bias in relation to gender equality schemes, the supposed sexism of the gender 'wage gap' and bias in hiring were explored.

8   Forensics and Crime

CHAPTER OUTLINE

Perspectives in Male Psychology: An Introduction, First Edition.
Louise Liddon and John A. Barry.
© 2021 John Wiley & Sons, Ltd. Published 2021 by John Wiley & Sons, Ltd.

LEARNING OUTCOMES

By the end of this chapter, you should be able to:

1. Know about sex differences in criminal behaviour
2. Understand the possible causes of sex differences in criminality
3. Recognise how bias in research has shaped our view of male criminality
4. Appreciate the reasons that male victims may be reluctant to seek help
5. Know some of the ways in which male criminality might be reduced

8.1 INTRODUCTION

Understanding male offending (and why it is much more likely than female offending) is the most important explanatory task for all theories of crime.
                                                                –Durrant, 2019, p. 603

Criminal psychology is arguably the most challenging area for psychologists. Not only are the causes of criminality complex, multifactorial and difficult to research, but advocating therapy as a way to reduce criminality can be greeted with suspicion both by offenders – who may deeply distrust psychologists as authority figures – and by the general public – who might prefer to just 'throw away the key' on men they find frightening.

Chapter 4 described some of the factors in childhood that influence the development of criminality. The present chapter looks at some of the other possible causes of criminality, including the role of biological and social factors, and examines gender differences in criminality. Therapeutic approaches to working with male offenders are considered. The *male psychology* perspective adds to the existing literature by highlighting important issues related to criminality in men that are sometimes minimised or overlooked, e.g. the general tendency of people to see men as perpetrators and women as victims.

Although most of this chapter describes contextual risk factors, this is not to imply that exposure to a risk factor inevitably leads to criminality, or that people don't have any free choice in whether they offend or not. Also, knowing the reasons for criminality does not imply that people should not be punished for crimes (Whyte, 2010). We know however that in general men are seen as being more agentic than women, both by themselves and by others, so are more likely to be seen as morally responsible for wrongdoing (Reynolds et al., 2020).

8.2 SEX/GENDER DIFFERENCES IN CRIMES

8.2.1 *A Minority of Men Commit the Majority of Crime*

It has been known for a long time that most criminals are men. Most crime is committed in adolescence and early adulthood, but those who start on the path to crime at a young aged tend to continue through their life, committing 77% of crime at an estimated cost in England – in each offender's lifetime – of £1.3–2.3 million (Williams et al., 2018).

The fact that most criminals are men is such a powerful idea that it often seems to morph into the sense that most men are criminals. However, this is a major fallacy, because only a relatively small number of male offenders commit the majority of offences, especially the most serious ones (Martinez et al., 2017). This pattern is reminiscent of the Pareto principle, or '80/20 rule', where for most phenomena 80% of effects come from 20% of causes (Sanders, 1987). In the case of crime, however, the number of causes (i.e. offenders) tends to be fewer than 20%. For example, a Swedish study found that less than 1% of men were responsible for more than half of all violent crime (Falk et al., 2014).

SPOTLIGHT BOX 8.1

A CLASSIC STUDY OF WORKING CLASS CRIME

A classic study in criminology was the Cambridge Study of Delinquent Development (West & Farrington, 1973). This was one of the first longitudinal studies of the causes of crime, and followed 411 typical working-class schoolboys from the age of eight in the UK (South London). Most were born in 1953, 87% were White British and more than 90% were from two-parent families. On average, officially recorded criminal careers began at age 17, ended at age 23 and included 4.5 criminal convictions. The most persistent offenders were usually those who started youngest. By age 32, 37% had a conviction, mostly for theft, motivated by economic gain. By the age of 40 just 6% of the sample committed half of all officially recorded offences. In contrast to the chronic offenders, the careers of the adolescent offenders were short lived.

In many ways this study was an early example of good methodology: it had a large sample size, followed participants longitudinally (so that cause and effect relationships between variables could be identified) and 'triangulated' the view of criminality by measuring it from different perspectives (court records, validated questionnaires, interviews etc). Every study has limitations, and the most obvious ones in this study were that it was based on a white working-class population of men born in London in the 1950s, so might not generalise very well to other populations, such as people in multicultural London today. Also, the study did not include girls – probably because men are more associated with crime than women – which means the study doesn't identify whether there are important differences in the development of criminality in boys compared to girls.

8.2.2   *Violence and Gender*

Globally, 95% of individuals convicted for homicide and 75% of victims of homicide are males (Butchart et al., 2014). The ratio of male to female victims of homicide ranges from 7.9 in the Americas to 2.22 in Asia (United Nations Office of Drugs and Crime, 2014). In Europe, a decline in male offending over the past 600 years means that the gender homicide gap had narrowed significantly. This decline is probably due to punishment increasingly being handled by the state rather than individuals, improved standards of living, and reduced social inequality (Durrant, 2019).

The crimes of girls are more often nonviolent compared to boys (Zavlek & Maniglia, 2007). Some research suggests that female criminals use violence if necessary, but where possible will minimise risk by employing other strategies, e.g. 'acting bad', selecting female targets or relying on men's reluctance to use violence against women (Kruttschnitt, 2013). However, the gender crime gap is closing: in the US between 1985 and 2009, delinquent crimes among girls increased by 86% (from 222,900 to 415,600), but for boys the rates of delinquency increased much less, by 17% (from 932,300 to 1,088,600; Puzzanchera et al., 2012).

8.2.3   *Gender and Types of Crimes*

In general, the gender gap in crime tends to be largest for sexual and serious violent offences and smallest for the least risky and dangerous crimes, such as shoplifting and embezzlement (Durrant, 2019). Numbers of female criminals have increased, however, in activities such as methamphetamine sales and human trafficking (Kruttschnitt, 2013).

8.2.4   *Indirect Aggression*

In everyday life, indirect aggression is sometimes demonstrated in passive-aggression (e.g. expressing aggression through refusing to talk) or relational aggression, when false rumours are spread about someone to cause them harm (see SPOTLIGHT box 8.2). Some meta-analyses have found that females are more likely than males to use relational or other indirect aggression during early to mid-adolescence (Archer, 2004) though less so in adulthood. This might be because girls mature socially and physically sooner than males, giving them an advantage in terms of the sophistication of bullying strategies used. An example of this is cyberbullying (see Section 8.3.6.2.2). The suggestion that women are better able to conceal their criminality than men is not a new one (Pollak, 1950), and female criminals have been said to find ways other than direct violence in order to intimidate (Kruttschnitt, 2013).

8.2.5   *Slow Violence: Recognising Subtle forms of Violence*

Criminologists generally focus on overt forms of violence, and less often consider more subtle forms of violence. For example, 'slow violence' is a term coined to explain phenomena such as carcinogenic pollution and over-prescription of opioids, 'whose calamitous repercussions are postponed for years or decades or centuries' (Nixon 2011, p.1). However the term could be applied to some types of social phenomena, such as the spreading of malicious rumours or the impact of destructive parenting on childhood development (Section 8.2.4).

A study that might show evidence of the impact of slow violence is a five-year longitudinal study which assessed the impact of criticism between 867 couples in the US, aged 57 to 85 at the start of the study (Bookwala & Gaugler, 2020). It was found that, after controlling for other relevant variables (education, health status, medication use), being criticised by one's partner was significantly correlated with death five years later, regardless of the sex of either partner. The findings were interpreted as probably the result of stress on the cardiovascular system and health behaviours (such as smoking cigarettes, exercise and eating habits), though a limitation of the study was that the cause of death was not known because of restrictions on the data available to the researchers.

8.3 CAUSES OF MALE CRIMINALITY

8.3.1 *Gendered Crime Across the Lifespan*

This section will assess the various causes of male criminality, sometimes looking at the causes of female criminality in comparison. Apart from being male, the other two consistent predictors of crime are being an adolescent or young adult, and being from a disadvantaged background (DeLisi & Vaughn, 2016).

Although sometimes this turns into a 'nature vs nurture' debate, it should be borne in mind that both innate and social factors are likely to influence criminality. Causes of criminality is a highly complex issue, and it could be, for example, that epigenetic effects of social disadvantage might be passed from parents to offspring and have a different impact on sons compared to daughters (Scorza et al., 2019).

8.3.2 *Impact of Nature vs Nurture*

In the past, testosterone was said to explain men's violence (Theme: don't make assumptions in Section 13.2.5). This relationship in humans has not received strong support empirically (e.g. Book et al., 2001) and in the past few decades it has become fashionable to view men's violence as the result of socialisation. Such ideas have their roots in sociology and gender studies, though are also influenced by social learning theory, e.g. Bandura's classic Bobo Doll study of how children imitate aggressive behaviour (Bandura et al., 1961).

In the 1970s, feminist criminologists began calls to 'feminise' male socialisation in order to reduce male criminality (Heidensohn, 1995), and suggested masculinity should be examined in order to understand the roots of male criminality (Messerschmidt, 1993). Masculinity, and 'toxic masculinity', have today become popular ways to explain criminality in men (Kupers, 2005).

Ultimately, explanations that rely exclusively on ideas of social construction are reductionist explanations, but from this point of view the universality of the gender 'crime gap' is explained – perhaps counterintuitively – as evidence of the influence of culture (Harrower, 2001) rather than biology. Theories based on socialisation don't fully explain the size and prevalence of the gender crime gap, nor how it is possible that men could be socialised in the same way across history and across the world, given the variation in types of societies. It is more likely that nature and nurture have a reciprocal impact: 'Many gender differences tend to be "amplified" via socialisation practices: initially small or medium differences in temperament lead to large differences in behavioural outcomes' (Durrant, 2019, p. 601; Theme: difference that makes the difference in Section 13.2.4). It makes sense for biology and the environment to be considered in any explanation of complex behaviours, such as criminality. For example, a hand gesture in one culture might be friendly, but the same gesture in another might cause great offence, triggering a fight or flight response and violent behaviour (Richerson & Boyd, 2008).

8.3.3 Sex Differences in Onset and Life Course of Criminality

Some authors suggest that responses to negative life events vary significantly by gender, and lead to different types of criminality (Kaufman, 2009; Piquero & Sealock, 2004). However, relatively little research has investigated this question, and there has been a heterogeneity of methodologies which makes it difficult to form clear conclusions. Some longitudinal research (the Dunedin Birth Cohort Study, the Boricua Youth Study and the Criminal Career and Life Course Study) suggests that, overall, criminality has similar causes in both genders, though the effect on men might be more dramatic, e.g. they may more often become high-rate offenders (Block et al., 2010; Jennings et al., 2010; Piquero et al., 2005; and see Section 8.3.5). Several researchers suggest that offenders who start at an early age (<age 14) tend to be lifelong criminals (Moffitt, 1993). Some research suggests that males are more likely than females to begin a criminal career early (Piquero & Chung, 2001; D'Unger et al., 2002), whereas others find this early-start pattern for both sexes (Mazerolle et al., 2000; Odgers et al., 2008). However, evidence that women tend to have a later offending onset than men is increasing (Block et al., 2019; Eggleston & Laub, 2002). Why this gendered pattern might exist is an ongoing matter of investigation and will be explored in more detail later in the chapter (see Sections 8.3.5 and 8.3.6.1.4), after we first look at some of the theoretical explanations for criminality.

8.3.4 Evolutionary and Genetic Explanations

Compared to women, men have in general a lower capacity for self-regulation, a greater motivation to engage in high-intensity activities and lower levels of fear; these factors combined can contribute to the sex differences in antisocial and criminal behaviour, according to some theorists (Eme, 2018). These differences are related to neurobiological functioning, hormone levels, the stress response system and autonomic arousal (e.g. heart rate). One view is that the sex difference in criminality is largely innate, related to male risk-taking, status-seeking, sexual motivation and physical aggression towards other men (Durrant, 2019). However, genetic studies appear to support a 'nature plus nurture' view of criminality. A meta-analysis of 51 twin and adoption studies found that upbringing was a slightly better predictor of antisocial behaviour than genetics (Rhee & Waldman, 2002). The strongest influence on antisocial behaviour was environmental variables of the kind that were experienced by some family members but not others (moderate effect size, 0.43); the second strongest influence was 'additive genetic' influences, i.e. effects of alleles from different loci which 'add up' in their influence (moderate effect size, 0.32). (*Theme: 'difference that makes the difference'*, in Section 13.2.4). Overall, the influences of nature and nurture were found to be similar.

Two large birth cohorts found a small but statistically significant correlations between genes associated with educational achievement and risk of a criminal record (Wertz et al., 2018). These findings were similar in males and females, and remained after controlling for the influence of socioeconomic deprivation and parental anti-social behaviour. Effect sizes were similar across the two cohorts, and because the cohorts were from different decades and geographical locations (the Dunedin cohort of 918 children born in the early 1970s in New Zealand, and the Environmental Risk cohort of 1999 twins born in the UK in the mid-1990s), the findings supporting the case for the influence of genes.

8.3.5 *Sex Difference in how Trauma Causes Delinquency*

Although the factors that cause delinquency might be the same for boys and girls, some evidence suggests that the effect is different on boys compared to girls, with a wider range of negative outcomes for boys (Durrant, 2019). Some sex differences are probably more to do with the extent and timing of the trauma rather than its presence or absence, e.g. the extent of child sexual abuse (CSA) is sometimes more severe in girls, which might explain why CSA is more common in female offenders (Conrad et al., 2014). Adverse childhood conditions are more likely to lead to greater risk-taking, antisocial behaviour and intra-sexual aggression in males, and greater depression and anxiety and antisocial behaviour in girls (Ellis & Del Giudice, 2019).

Around a third of boys and half of girls in detention in the US show clinical levels of trauma symptomology (Kerig & Becker, 2010). A study of adverse childhood experience (ACE) scores of 22,575 juvenile delinquents found that, controlling for other factors, the more childhood traumas experienced as a child, the more likely the child would go on to be a serious, violent and chronic offender (Fox et al., 2015) (see Section 4.4.3).

8.3.6 *Lifespan Approach: Causes and Consequences*

The following sections are broken down into childhood, adolescence and adulthood, and will look at some causes and consequences of criminality, as well as well as differences in victims/perpetrators.

8.3.6.1 Childhood

This section will outline some of the main factors that are implicated in the development of criminality in childhood (see Section 4.4). These include prenatal factors, the environment, attachment, parenting, witnessing domestic violence (DV), traumatic experience such as physical or sexual abuse, peers, school and bullying.

8.3.6.1.1 Prenatal environment and development of criminality

It is well established that prenatal conditions can influence the health and behaviour of the offspring in adult life (Barker, 1990). Antisocial personality disorder (APD) might be associated with severe prenatal nutritional deficiency in the first or second trimesters of pregnancy (Neugebauer, 1999). Substance abuse can have damaging effects; for example, fetal alcohol syndrome can cause the child cognitive and behavioural limitations that endure through life (Brown et al., 2014). Many studies have found that offenders who start their criminality at a young age tend to have, among other problems, neurocognitive difficulties (e.g. Jennings & Reingle, 2012), which is suggestive of prenatal developmental problems. These studies raise the possibility that those who start criminality early in life may have suffered from poor prenatal environment, whereas the adolescent-onset offending may be caused by life events postnatally. Some evidence suggests that paedophiles show signs of developmental disorder, such as atypical white brain matter, which suggest poor prenatal conditions (Fazio, 2018). These various studies suggest that the prenatal environment might be significant in causing problem behaviour across the lifespan.

A study of 216 Danish births found that the trauma of a difficult delivery, in combination with having one or more parent with schizophrenia or a personality disorder, may cause neurological dysfunction, leading to impulsivity or low intelligence and recurrent violent behaviour (Kandel & Mednick, 1991). These findings are interesting, but need to be replicated.

8.3.6.1.2 Lead and crime

Lead is a potent neurotoxin capable of reducing grey matter volume and disrupting mood, executive functioning and decision making. A survey of 4704 children in the US found that lead concentrations in blood were significantly correlated with attention deficit hyperactivity disorder (ADHD) (Braun et al., 2006). There is evidence that lead poisoning influenced the rise in crime in the twentieth century, and restrictions on lead influenced the fall of crime in the 1990s (Gesch, 2013); until the 1980s, lead was routinely added to petrol, and data over several decades and several countries show a strong correlation between crime – especially murder – and childhood exposure to lead (Nevin, 2007). Interestingly, men are more influenced by lead poisoning than women, which may contribute to differences in crime trends. It is possible that epigenetic changes mean that the impact is transgenerational (i.e. acquired in one or both parents and passed onto their children).

8.3.6.1.3   *Social variables that reduce antisocial behaviour*

Antisocial behaviour can be reduced by good family and school bonds in childhood, and work and marriage in adulthood (Hoeve et al., 2012). Structural disadvantages such as poverty, income inequality, joblessness and single-parent households impact male and female criminality, though possibly to different degrees (Kruttschnitt, 2013). Poverty is an important variable, e.g. after-school activities can keep children out of trouble, but can be expensive.

8.3.6.1.4   *Child sexual abuse: sex differences in outcomes*

Some research suggests that sexually abused youths show more criminality, especially aggression, than nonabused youths (Chen et al., 2010). Although the majority of people who experience CSA do not go on to become criminals (Leach et al., 2016), retrospective studies show that up to 70% of sex offenders have experienced CSA and people who experience CSA are more likely to commit crime (Jespersen et al., 2009). One study found that 52% of personality-disordered sex offenders had been sexually abused in childhood by a female abuser acting independently of men (Murphy, 2018).

Various studies have found that for girls, CSA is associated with low self-esteem, poor interpersonal functioning, distress, and externalising behaviours such as promiscuity (Conrad et al., 2014). For boys, CSA or other types of abuse are associated with substance use, aggressive criminal behaviour and sexual risk-taking (Conrad et al., 2015). The experience of CSA for girls tends to start earlier, go on for longer and be more severe than the abuse of boys, which probably is more traumatising for girls, and leads them to behaviour (e.g. elopement, truancy and aggressive or assaultive behaviours) that bring them to the attention of the courts moreso than boys.

Several studies have found that rates of post-traumatic stress disorder (PTSD) and sexual assault are significantly greater among female delinquents compared to male (e.g. Adams et al., 2013; Conrad et al., 2014). Girls may be differentially affected by their trauma history (perhaps depending on type of trauma), which may lead to gender differences in pathways to PTSD or other life consequences, such as repeat offending and chronic substance use (Abram et al., 2007).

Conrad et al. (2014) conducted a retrospective study of 454 juvenile offenders – 240 males, 162 females – aged 11–17 in the US between 2006 and 2008, followed up for 12 months. Of these, 60% were white, 18% Latino and 6% Black. Significantly more of the girls than boys had experienced CSA (23% vs 8%) (though see Section 8.5.2). Males had higher rates of recidivism (32%) than females (22%) but the only two significant predictors of recidivism were having an externalising disorder and being a female victim of CSA. Male recidivism was related to substance use and a history of more past offences.

One review of gender and crime concluded that 'there is growing evidence that many (but not all) of the central theoretical correlates of crime (poor parenting, low self-control, delinquent peers, and economic disadvantage) are gender invariant [the same for boys and girls] but that the mediators of these experiences, which may include opportunities for reacting to these stressors, may not be' (Kruttschnitt 2013, p.296).

8.3.6.1.5   Age at onset

Many researchers agree that early signs of delinquency may predict long-term criminality, but many criminal careers start in the teenage years and end in the early 20s (Moffitt & Caspi, 2001). Boys are ten times more likely than girls to have childhood-onset delinquency, but only slightly more likely to have adolescence-onset delinquency. Early-onset offenders are more likely to show signs of neuropsychological deficits (Gesch, 2013b; see Section 4.4).

8.3.6.2   Adolescence

8.3.6.2.1   Peers and school

Falling into 'bad company' can lead to delinquency, perhaps through social learning. Some offenders grow up in an environment of 'antisocial models', with criminal parents, siblings, friends, and schoolmates in criminal neighbourhoods (Farrington, 1995). Although schools themselves might have little effect on delinquency, problems at home, or an academically unstimulating environment at home, can impact school behaviour and grades.

One of the most worrying aspects of school life today is violence at school. In the US, school shootings have been attributed to various factors, including 'dad deprivation' of children, i.e. children growing up without the guidance of a father (Farrell & Grey, 2019).

8.3.6.2.2   Bullying and cyberbullying

Bullying is an intentionally hostile behaviour over a period of time against someone in a lesser position of power (Burger et al., 2015). It can be difficult to differentiate bullies and victims. For example, boys are more likely than girls to be bully-victims, i.e. sometimes bullies and sometimes victims (Yang et al., 2016). Also there is a personality type characterised by seeing oneself as a victim (Gabay et al., 2020).

A meta-analysis of 122 studies found males were more likely to cyberbully than females during later adolescence and into college age, whereas prior to age 11 'girls are clearly more likely to cyber-bully others than males' (Barlett & Coyne, 2014). It can be difficult to know the true identity of those involved in online bullying, and although it is sometimes presumed that abuse of women is more likely to be done by men or right wing activists, this can be inaccurate (Ferguson, 2020a); one study of Twitter found that half of misogynistic tweets (verbal attacks on women using terms like 'slut') were done by young adult women (Dale, 2016). Although the term 'cyberbullying' is not used in law, people in the UK are protected by law against online harassment, malicious communication etc (Metropolitan Police, 2014).

8.3.6.2.3   ADHD, risk-taking and impulsive behaviour

Men in general are more inclined than women to take risks, and both ADHD and risk-taking are more common in men and are related to offending behaviour (Durrant, 2019; Eme, 2015), possibly because impulsive people don't think enough about the consequences of their actions (Farrington, 1995). A longitudinal study found that boys who went on to become delinquents were rated as 'daring' by parents and peers, and 'hyperactive with poor concentration' by their teachers (Farrington, 1995). They tended to be impulsive on psychomotor tests and personality questionnaires. Hyperactivity at age 8–10 predicted juvenile convictions independently of conduct problems at age 8–10. These boys also tended to be unpopular with their peers (Farrington, 1995). However, risk-taking may also be of evolutionary advantage in some contexts (Durrant, 2019), e.g. the emergency services consist of people who are willing to take risks for others in dangerous situations.

8.3.6.2.4   Autism spectrum disorder (ASD)

ASD is around 4–9 times more common in men than women (Barry & Owens, 2019). Some people with ASD show challenging behaviours, e.g. the tendency to rigidly adhere to rules or routines or misunderstanding social situations might lead some people with ASD to frustration and aggression (King & Murphy, 2014). Also, lack of empathy in ASD (or more correctly, impaired 'theory of mind') might contribute to offending, and social naiveté might lead to vulnerability to being manipulated into offending (van Wijngaarden-Cremers, 2019).

8.3.6.2.5   Domestic violence and intimate partner violence in adolescence

An epidemiological study of five European countries (Bulgaria, Cyprus, England, Italy and Norway) found that witnessing intimate partner violence as a child increased the risk of perpetration of intimate partner violence as an adult (Gil-Gonzalez et al., 2008). The study surveyed 4500 adolescent boys and girls aged 14–17 for experiences of interpersonal violence and abuse (IPVA), and found that 53–66% of young women and 32–69% of young men reported experiencing at least one form of IPVA (online, emotional, physical or sexual). In each country, between 9% and 22% of young women and 8% to 15% of young men reported physical violence. The rates were highest in England and Norway (see Section 8.3.6.3.1).

8.3.6.2.6   Substance abuse

A longitudinal study of 1806 boys and 1808 girls aged 12–17 found a strong correlation between substance use and delinquent behaviour (Begle et al., 2011). They also found that girls who engaged in risky behaviour (substance use and delinquency) were not at increased risk for later sexual abuse.

8.3.6.3 Adulthood

This section looks at predictors of criminality that are usually seen in adulthood. Many of these are linked to the experience of trauma, brain damage and other risk factors from earlier life. This section also looks at the consequences of criminality, e.g. sentencing and prison, and related issues.

8.3.6.3.1 Domestic violence and intimate partner violence

In England and Wales 7.5% of women and 3.8% of men experience domestic abuse, and around a third of DV victims are male victims of female violence (Office for National Statistics, 2019). Many male victims don't report being a victim for fear of not being believed (Powney & Graham-Kevan, 2019). Indeed, men who report being a victim often find themselves accused of violence, and might even be arrested (Tsui, 2014; see Section 12.6.1).

The discourse around DV typically portrays men as the perpetrators and women the victims, and indeed 74% of DV homicides in England and Wales are female victims of male perpetrators (Office for National Statistics, 2019). DV can result in mental health injury too, including suicide, and although it is extremely difficult to assess this empirically, it has been estimated that when suicides related to DV are taken into account, the number of deaths related to DV is higher for men than women (Davis, 2010). There is some evidence – as demonstrated in the large collection of research with of a total of 371,600 men and women – that in relationships, women are as physically aggressive, or more aggressive, than men (Fiebert, 2010). However, the male perspective is generally not taken into account in feminist research (Dutton & Corvo, 2006; Powney & Graham-Kevan, 2019). It is likely that the cognitive distortion *gamma bias* has a role in making it difficult to see women as perpetrators (Seager & Barry, 2019). This is problematic for various reasons, including that treatment of female offenders is unlikely to happen if their violence is not recognised and addressed, and human nature being what it is: 'People hit and abuse family members because they can' [get away with it] (Corry et al., 2002).

8.3.6.4 Prison

In total 95% of the UK prison population is male (GOV.UK, 2018), and at least 50% of prisoners have common mental health disorders, such as anxiety, depression and PTSD (National Audit Office, 2017). Male prisoners are six times more likely to die by suicide than men in the community, and notably female prisoners are around a third more likely than male prisoners to die by suicide (National Audit Office, 2017). In England, around half of adults and three quarters of minors released from custody reoffend within a year, costing around £10–13 billion annually (Williams et al., 2018). Prison is an opportunity to improve mental health and to reduce criminality, but this opportunity isn't being successfully implemented for men or women in prison in the UK.

8.3.6.4.1 ASD in the criminal justice system

A systemic review of people with ASD in the criminal justice system (CJS) found that people with ASD are somewhat over-represented in the CJS, with the overall prevalence rate above 1% (King & Murphy, 2014). Those with ASD committed a range of crimes and there seemed to be similar predisposing features (e.g. childhood physical abuse and neglect) to non-ASD criminals. Research findings in this area are limited by the fact that most of the studies have small sample sizes and use a variety of methodologies. Some authors suggest that psychiatric comorbidity with ASD might lead to crime (Newman & Ghaziuddin 2008). One study found high rates of co-morbid psychosis and personality disorder, but explained this as sample bias due to the samples being derived from prison populations (King & Murphy, 2014).

There are more male than female arsonists in the general population. Although a Swedish study of 155 male and 59 female arsonists found a higher rate of Asperger's in arsonists (Enayati et al., 2008), other studies do not support this finding (King & Murphy, 2014).

8.3.6.4.2 Brain damage and violence

Boys are more inclined to rough-and-tumble play, but it is only in adolescence that the odds of having a traumatic brain injury (TBI) doubles in males compared to females (Williams et al., 2018). Men and women with TBI appear to suffer similar effects on offending behaviour (Williams et al., 2018). A review concluded that damage to the focal orbitofrontal area (just above the eye sockets) is specifically associated with increased aggression – though not necessarily actual violence – probably due to impaired decision making ability (Brower, 2001). Brower estimates that the risk of violence from someone with focal frontal lobe damage is about 10% higher than the general population. Research in prison populations shows that TBI is unusually common in male and female offenders. A study of 287 male prisoners found that violent prisoners were nearly twice as likely compared to other prisoners, and five times more likely than controls, to have abnormalities in regions associated with empathy (Schiltz et al., 2013). A weakness of research in this area is that the direction of causality is sometimes hard to identify, i.e. whether the brain abnormality caused the violence, or was the result of violence.

8.3.6.4.3 Brain damage and antisocial personality disorder (APD)

A meta-analysis estimated that APD is 56% genetic in origin, 11% due to family socialisation and 31% due to life events (e.g. head injury; Ferguson, 2010). Men are more likely to be diagnosed with APD than women are, and evidence from MRI research suggests this is mostly due to gender differences in the volume of the orbitofrontal (just above the eye sockets) and middle frontal regions of the prefrontal cortex (left and right sides of forehead; Raine et al., 2011). However some research suggests this difference may be caused, in part, by substance misuse (Schiffer et al., 2011). Overall there is evidence for certain types of brain damage being associated with violence, but other factors (e.g. substance abuse) should be taken into account.

8.3.6.5 *Later life*

After the age of 18, men become less aggressive and impulsive, and social outcomes are best for those who marry and have job stability, and worst for those with a criminal conviction (Farrington, 1995). (See also Barry, 2020).

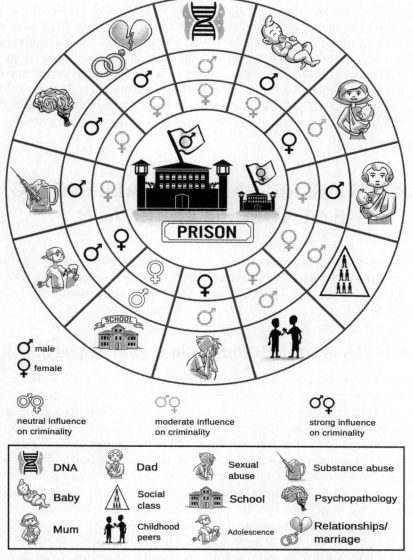

FIGURE 8.1 *Description of sex differences in the factors that influence criminality over the lifespan.*

In Figure 8.1, the size of the effect is a qualitative estimate, based on the literature cited in this chapter and the Developmental chapter (see Section 4.4). When the symbol for male or female is white, this indicates the variable has little or no potential effect (positive or negative) on engaging in criminality (see school in Fig. 8.1); grey indicates a moderate potential influence (positive or negative) (e.g. dads for girls); black indicates a strong potential influence (positive or negative) on engaging in criminality (e.g. dads for boys).

Although we know something about the variables that predict criminality, we are less sure about how these interact with each other. In general we know that there is an additive effect of ACEs on criminality, and that issues like the severity of adversity is an important variable. Thus although Figure 8.1 depicts what could, for some people, be a developmental sequence of traumas, it is likely that any one or two of these factors might be sufficient in causing criminality. It is important to bear in mind that other variables might have an influence too, which may decrease the development of criminality (see Section 8.6).

8.4 CRIME RESEARCH: CHALLENGING THE GENDERED APPROACH

Some experts suggest that evidence shows there is a need to move on from the traditional gendered approach to crime, for example, not seeing DV as a 'battered women' issue but as an issue that impacts both men and women (Bates & Taylor, 2019; Powney & Graham-Kevan, 2019).

8.4.1 *Generational Changes in Sexual Aggression*

Different recent generations have been classified, often with slight variations in the boundary years, as Baby Boomers (born 1946–1964), Generation X (born 1965–1981) and Millennials (1982–1999). An intergenerational study comparing 697 people born between 1945 and 1984 (Baby Boomers and Generation X) to 774 people born between 1985 and 2004 (Millennials) explored the use of several types of sexual aggression: unwanted verbal pressure, arousal techniques, coercion, alcohol or drugs, force or other pressure to have sexual contact (Anderson et al., 2020). The sample was American, heterosexual, mostly Caucasian and recruited from Amazon's *MTurk* participant pool, a crowdsourced online sample of the type commonly used in consumer research.

It was found that sexual aggression tended to be much less commonly used by Millennial men and much more often by Millennial women than had been the case in previous generations. For example, the percentage of older participants who had ever used pressure or force to have sexual intercourse with someone was 5.9% men and 3.1% women, but in Millennials the percentage was 7.8% women and 4.1% men. In other words, the rates of pressurised/forced intercourse by women had more than doubled across generations. This trend was similar for all types of sexual aggression measured. The authors suggest these findings reflect a loosening of the 'traditional sexual script' which in previous generations dictated that men be the initiators of sexual activity. The findings are controversial, and questions over their generalisability from the MTurk sample will no doubt be raised, though such samples have been found to yield results similar to those from other samples in psychology studies (Paolacci et al., 2010; see Section 8.5.2).

8.4.2 *Physical Abuse is More Likely to Create Violent Boys than Violent Girls*

Begle et al. (2011) conducted a longitudinal study of 1806 boys and 1808 girls between ages 12 and 17, examining the link between high-risk behaviour (i.e., alcohol use, substance use, delinquent behaviour) and victimisation (either sexual abuse, or abuse such as physical abuse/assault and/or witnessed violence). Measurements were taken at two timepoints, around 15 months apart. Sexual abuse was limited to analysis of girls' data, due to the low incidence ($N = 6$) of boys reporting new sexual victimisation at 15-month follow-up. Data were analysed using structural equation modelling. The study found not only that the effect of victimisation happened relatively quickly, i.e. within the 15-month trial period, but that there were important sex differences. Some previous research had found that girls, but not boys, who were exposed to abuse (where sexual and physical abuse were not differentiated) were more likely to engage in high-risk behaviour later in adolescence (Krischer & Sevecke, 2008; Widom et al., 2006). The study by Begle et al. (2011) found this pattern was true of boys, except that boys who were victims of physical abuse were subsequently more likely to engage in risky behaviours that would – unlike the girls – lead them into further violent situations, e.g. gang activity. The study did not find the same pattern for girls who were victims of physical abuse, but found that girls who were exposed to sexual abuse were more likely to engage in later alcohol and substance use, but less likely to engage in delinquent behaviour. The gender difference due to physical violence was – according to the authors – found because of methodological strengths of their study compared to others, mainly due to assessing the impact of different types of abuse separately, unlike some other studies (e.g. Simpson & Miller, 2002), using a longitudinal rather than cross-sectional design, and including male and female participants. So although the sample size turned out to be too small to test all hypotheses due to drop-out at 15 months, the study is a good model for other research in this field.

8.4.3 *Understanding Gamma Bias in the Context of Crime*

Gamma bias is a type of cognitive distortion in which aspects of our perceptions of men and women are magnified or minimised (Seager & Barry, 2019). For example, we tend to notice problems more – such as being the victim of crime – when they impact women than if they impact men. Also, we tend to view bad behaviour – such as violence – as being less acceptable when done by men than by women (Reynolds et al., 2020).

Crimes by girls are more often nonviolent (Zavlek & Maniglia, 2007), but crime by girls increased in the US between 1985 and 2009 by 86%, compared to an increase in crime by boys by 17% during that period (Puzzanchera et al., 2012). However, based on US data sources, some authors emphasise that even though violence by girls has increased, there are a list of mitigating reasons for this (Zahn et al., 2008). Firstly, violence by girls is usually simple assault (i.e. without a weapon or causing serious damage) rather than the more serious violence seen in men. Secondly, the increase is the result of increased public focus on violence by girls, increased reporting of girls and changes in enforcement policies regarding girls. Moreover, 'Findings that girls are particularly likely to act violently in certain settings or under certain conditions affirm the importance of examining the context of violence for insights into why girls are sometimes violent' (Zahn et al., 2008, p. 11). Examples given are girls being violent due to being victimised in low-income neighbourhoods, self-defence against peers or to gain status. Girls' violence in the home can be 'a defence against or an expression of anger stemming from being sexually or physically abused by members of the household', or 'striking back against what they see as an overly controlling structure'. 'When girls fight at school, they may do so as a result of teacher labelling, in self-defence, or out of a general sense of hopelessness' (Zahn et al., 2008, p. 15).

This paper should be praised for highlighting the influence of the social context on violence. Focusing on the influence of the context on violent behaviour rather than focusing on the person leads to a less blaming attitude, and this seems only fair when a person's behaviour can be explained, at least in part, by social forces that are out of their control (Maruna & Mann, 2006). It is especially empathic to take into account the social context in cases where girls commit violence to gain status, or out of feelings of anger or hopelessness, rather than self-defence.

If criminologists were to extend this level of empathy to violence by boys, it would represent a huge paradigm shift. At present however, the idea of 'striking back against what they see as an overly controlling structure' in the home is, in contrast, exactly the opposite of how men's violence is seen. In, fact it is a cornerstone of the highly influential Duluth model of DV that men use violence as a means to control women, even in cases where the man claims he is the victim (Powney & Graham-Kevan, 2019). This apparent double-standard in understanding violence by women compared to men makes sense when viewed as an example of gamma bias, and raises the question of how much people consider the context rather than the person for the explanations typically given by men for their violence e.g. 'due to provocation' if the fight is one-on-one, or 'to help a friend' in the case of group fights (Farrington, 1995).

8.4.3.1   Feminist research

A strength of feminist research is that it highlights the contextual reasons for women's criminality, leading to campaigns promoting options other than prison for women (Ministry of Justice, 2019b). Mainstream criminology was criticised by feminists for neglecting to focus on the causes of criminality in women and the gender gap in crime (Daly & Chesney-Lind, 1988). However, much of feminist research uses female-only samples (e.g. Siegel & Williams, 2003) and 'males are routinely left out of the studies' (Kruttschnitt, 2013; Theme: the solution replicates the problem in Section 13.2.1).

Between 1996 and 2011 around 35% of articles on gender and crime came from a feminist perspective (Kruttschnitt, 2013), but feminist criminology has done little to uncover the extent of female crimes such as DV (see Section 8.3.6.3.1) and infanticide (see Section 4.4.5). Interesting research on 'offending pathways' tends to be qualitative, and while these studies are important in describing women's lived experiences and are valuable in early-stage research, they don't tell us whether claims about gendered pathways are confirmed by statistical testing (Salisbury & Van Voorhis, 2009). Thus much of this research is adding to a gender studies literature base that is already of questionable scientific quality (see Section 5.5.1). For example, some authors base their research on the notion of how women 'do gender' in the process of committing crimes (e.g. Messerschmidt, 1993), which is very popular in gender studies but tends to reinforce a social reductionist viewpoint.

Despite some strengths, a major limitation of the feminist approach is the tendency to not recognise that the factors that influence criminality in women may also do so in men. For example, in a sample of female offenders, variables such as child abuse, DV and educational/employment problems were said to 'create unconventional pathways to recidivism not typically observed with men' (Salisbury & Van Voorhis, 2009, p. 559). In contrast, other researchers have found: 'When males' experiences are systematically compared with those of females, either the effects of abuse, and many of the other predictors of serious juvenile offending, do not vary significantly by sex of the offender … or the variations are related to the extent and timing of the life trauma rather than to its presence or absence' (Kruttschnitt, 2013, p. 398). Although the experiences of men and women are not identical (e.g. the impact of father absence on boys), it seems only reasonable that because the causes of criminality are so similar for men and women, the conclusions of feminist researchers – that female offenders should receive 'humane correctional environments and interventions' (Salisbury & Van Voorhis, 2009, p. 563) – should equally apply to male offenders.

8.4.3.2   *Operational definitions and 'linguistic inflation'*

How something is defined is crucial to how we understand it (Theme: flawed definitions in Section 13.2.4). If harsh words are defined as violence then almost everyone has committed violence at some time, and the rate of 'violence' is inflated. To avoid misunderstandings over different interpretations of words, psychologists usually clearly define ('operationalise') definitions (see also Section 12.3.7; Begle et al., 2011; Conrad et al., 2015).

Precision is especially important when it comes to legal definitions because there are life-changing consequences for the victim and the accused. For example, rape is a serious crime whether the victim or perpetrator is male or female. Although it is known that men can be forced to penetrate women (Weare, 2018), some psychologists argue that "It is inappropriate to consider as a rape victim a man who engages in unwanted sexual intercourse with a woman" (Koss 1993, p. 206). This definition makes male victims disappear, and impacts how they are treated in law and even therapy.

8.5 VICTIMS' PERSPECTIVE: BARRIERS TO SEEKING HELP

Help-seeking behaviour is a theme that runs through most of the topics in male psychology. In relation to crime, help-seeking refers both to victims of crime and to perpetrators. (see Sections 11.5.1.3, 11.5.2 and 12.6.1).

8.5.1 *Help-Seeking in Domestic Violence*

Western culture has become much less tolerant of violence against women by men, but tolerance for violence by women against men has only recently started to become questioned in mainstream discourse (ManKind Initiative, 2015). Women are often seen as non-violent, and female aggression to men is often seen as self-defence (Johnstone & Boyle, 2018; Mildorf, 2007; Shum-Pearce, 2016), or even humorous (Hine & Arrindell, 2015). Male victims are seen more negatively than female victims (Arnocky & Vaillancourt, 2014), and are more prone to being disbelieved (Tsui, 2014) or blamed for the violence against them and thought of as the perpetrator (Hine & Arrindell, 2015; Lewis & Sarantakos, 2001; Tsui, 2014).

Negative experiences of help-seeking compound the trauma of being a victim of DV, and can cause an increase in alcohol abuse (Douglas & Hines, 2011). Male victims often find little support from social services and the CJS, which are focused on helping female victims (Hines & Douglas, 2009), causing men to feel shame, embarrassment and anxiety (Tsui et al., 2010) and to fear they won't be supported by healthcare services (Brogden & Nijhar, 2004). A large, nationwide study of help-seeking by male victims of domestic abuse in the US found that 40% of the participants did not disclose the abuse even when their injuries were queried by clinicians (Douglas & Hines, 2011).

8.5.2 *Help-Seeking for Male Rape Victims*

Viewing sexual violence as a problem only affecting women can isolate and silence male victims (Davis, 2010). Shame is a key factor in the underreporting of this crime. The impact on a man's sense of masculine identity (Seager et al., 2014a) and the associated shame will make it difficult for a man to discuss this experience with anyone else (e.g. the shame that the protector was unable to protect themselves) (See Section 11.3.4.). Male victims of sexual violence may be traumatised by the event, but feel isolated due to being blamed and disbelieved by others (Lowe & Balfour, 2015). Fear of ridicule, blame or accusation can inhibit help-seeking (Lisak, 2005). Men may have anxieties about appearing not only unmasculine, but appearing feminine and weak (Addis & Mahalik, 2003). In a UK study of 154 male victims of rape by women (Weare, 2018) where a man is forced to penetrate a woman with his penis without his consent, being disbelieved is a barrier, especially as UK law does not, to date, permit women to be charged with rape (Anderson et al., 2020).

MALES AS PERPETRATORS/FEMALES AS VICTIMS

As a general rule, men are more likely to be seen as perpetrators of crime, and women as victims. In a six-part study with 3137 men and women in the US, China, Norway and Canada it was found that judgements about morality, fairness, responsibility, sympathy, punishment and compensatory aid revealed cognitive bias favouring women, to a degree that was disproportionate to the occurrence of these issues in everyday life (Reynolds et al., 2020). Thus in identical situations, men are judged more harshly than women, which has implications for criminal justice issues.

Child sexual exploitation

Although research sometimes highlights how women are disadvantaged by interpretations of their behaviour, an issue that is not usually highlighted is that way in which boys can be disadvantaged compared to girls when it comes to identifying CSA, with boys more often seen as being criminal or 'boys being boys', whereas girls are seen as victims and offered help. These differential interpretations might have a significant impact on the path someone is streamed into, with the girls being offered support and the boys punishment.

False allegations of sexual offending

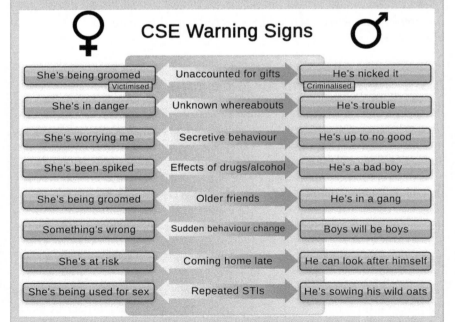

FIGURE 8.2 *Gamma bias in the interpretation of behavioural warning signs of child sexual exploitation (CSE) (adapted by kind permission of psychotherapist Phil Mitchell based on his clinical observations).*

Being accused of wrongdoing or crime whether false or not, accounts for around 9% of suicides (Callanan & Davis, 2009). False allegations of rape are a recognised phenomenon (Berne, 1968; Collins, 2019). According to the UK's False Allegations Support Organisation (FASO), there isn't currently reliable data on false allegations because the police and other relevant authorities don't keep such information and have been accused of not always following up on complaints of false allegations. Weare (2018) says 1.5% of her 'forced-to-penetrate' sample were threatened with false allegations of rape, which is ironic, seeing as the men were assaulted by the women. A contentious legal issue is whether the accused in such cases should be allowed the same anonymity as the accuser (Rumney & Fenton, 2013).

8.6 CRIME REDUCTION STRATEGIES

This next section offers some insights which might be valuable in helping to prevent crime and recidivism. Any of the suggestions below could potentially help with female offenders too.

8.6.1 *Intervene at an Early Age*

Knowing the best point to intervene at in the lifespan (shown in Figure 8.1) to make the most impact is an issue that needs more research. There is evidence that some pathways to crime start early in life, and others in adolescence. Those who begin criminality early in life tend to go on to be the most persistent offenders, so it would make sense to see how effective it is to prioritise these boys for prevention and treatment (Farrington, 1995).

ADHD is sometimes cited as one of the risk factors for criminality. However, many people with ADHD can learn, with support, to harness their symptoms and excel in fields such as sports, the military, music etc (Chheda-Varma, 2019).

8.6.2 *Involve Mothers*

The most persistent offenders are males who start their criminal careers early in life. Some research has found that these offenders more often show signs of neurocognitive problems, and are of smaller stature, both of which indicate the possibility of suboptimal prenatal environment (Farrington, 1995). Further research is needed on this topic, and if the link is confirmed, then health promotion campaigns could encourage healthier pregnancies in vulnerable populations, e.g. women of childbearing age with substance abuse problems. Relevant services could work together on supportive health promotion campaigns to improve nutritional intake etc.

8.6.3 *Involve Fathers*

Delinquency is more prevalent in boys, and we know that suboptimal attachment to fathers is a risk factor, therefore interventions for delinquency in boys should involve the fathers (Hoeve et al., 2012). Evidence exists that when fathers attended a parent training, children benefited more than when the mothers alone attended (Lundahl et al., 2008). This contrasts with other advice based on the 'gender similarities hypothesis', e.g. 'Contrary to the expectations of many developmental psychologists, the differences between mothers and fathers appear to be much less important than the similarities' (Lamb, 2004, p. 10; see Section 13.2.5 and SPOTLIGHT box 3.3). More research is needed on the impact of father-involvement on criminality in order to be able to give more evidence-based advice, which might help in the creation of important interventions.

8.6.4 *Mentoring*

Some community projects and charities are leading the way in helping boys off the pathway to becoming offenders. For example, *Lads Need Dads* is an award-winning project that offers a mentoring scheme in Essex, UK. Other projects help to make sure that young offenders stop reoffending. For example, the UK-based charity *Journeyman UK* uses rites of passage and other male-friendly interventions to help young men understand how good men contribute to society. Using the PMI questionnaire, an audit of the Journeyman programme found a significant benefit of their intervention (Doyle & Doyle, 2018). Another UK charity, *A Band of Brothers*, uses an intensive rite-of-passage programme to help young offenders in the CJS make a transition to an adulthood that has a sense of connection and purpose. These three projects use mentoring to guide boys to being stable adults, and use male-friendly methods, though are small community operations with little or no funding.

8.6.5 *Creating a Stable Family Background*

Stable relationships and jobs are important factors in reducing criminality (Farrington, 1995). If the parents are involved in DV, this impacts the children, so effective interventions for DV are needed. At present, interventions are almost exclusively aimed at men, and are based on the Duluth model (Powney & Graham-Kevan, 2019). However, interventions based on the Duluth model are relatively ineffective, so it is recommended that better inter-ventions are used, e.g. relationship enhancement, which a meta-analysis found to be twice as effective as interventions based on Duluth (Babcock et al., 2004). Safe and effective programmes should be made available to female offenders too.

8.6.6 *Sentencing*

Athough there are interesting exceptions (Barry, Seager et al, 2020), men are seen as more responsible for their actions than women and more likely to be seen as blameworthy than are women (Reynolds et al., 2020). Gamma bias is likely to influence sentencing (see Section 8.6.8) and perceptions of sentencing. Longer sentences for men are typically attributed to men's crim-inality being worse (magnification), and perceptions regarding leniency to women (e.g. due to childcare responsibilities) are played down, i.e. minimisa-tion (Kruttschnitt, 2013). However, if women are said to be just as capable of doing good things (e.g. being a CEO or a professor), then why are they not seen as just as capable of bad, e.g. perpetrating DV.

Some of the characteristics of people with ASD are likely to impair their fitness to plead, culpability, criminal responsibility and ability to survive prison, but these special issues are not always taken into consideration in legal proceedings (Allen et al., 2008).

8.6.7 *Male-Friendly Therapy for Prisoners*

A potentially very effective crime reduction strategy is to improve the mental health of prisoners. Improving physical health is likely to help improve mental health and reduce recidivism too (Williams et al., 2018). However, although men 'are the main participants in offender rehabilitation programmes, and re-offend at higher rates than females' (Durrant, 2019, p.603).

Standard therapies seen in forensic psychology in the UK are Diagnoses (NICE Clinical Guideline for APD), Behaviour (e.g. Life Minus Violence for aggression) and Environment (Positive & Proactive Care; See, Think, Act). However, only around 30% of male prisoners access recommended ther-apies. Those who do may experience barriers regarding problems with talking about their issues, due to humiliation, embarrassment, professional language used and concern that incriminating information will be used legally against them. These can lead to aggression, withdrawal or superficial engagement (Clark & Fallon, 2019).

Many psychologists in a UK prison setting, or other clinical setting outside private practice, are probably in a diagnostically driven service with an almost overwhelming number of patients, and have been trained to focus on their client as someone with a specific mental health condition that requires a specific pathway to a specific outcome. In reality, then, thinking about them also as a man, or in terms of their masculinity, with specific preferences for therapy, might seem to add to the workload rather than open up opportunities for a quicker route to better outcomes (Clark & Fallon, 2019).

Formulation of therapy usually doesn't take male-typical communication into account (e.g. Johnstone & Dallos, 2014). Prison doesn't very effectively prevent reoffending, but it is possible that effective psychological formulations of therapy, taking a positive masculinity into account, could help reduce mental health and reduce reoffending (see Section 11.6.1.2). Some of the men most in need of therapy might be some of the most challenging as clients in therapy. Many law-abiding people have little sympathy for them, so the challenge for therapists is especially great.

For men who feel that being violent and aggressive is part of their masculinity, or an act they need to perform to get them through the dangers of prison life or street life, one suggestion is to use approaches such as acceptance and commitment therapy, which focus on meaning, values and identity to support the development of a healthier masculine identity (MacQueen & Fisher, 2019, p. 613).

8.6.8 *Politics*

In the UK, there are around 20 times more men in prison than women (GOV. UK, 2018). The UK government recognises that women who commit crime have suffered various types of abuse in their past, and they see the solution to women's reoffending as holistic community services rather than prison. They have invested £5 million in these services over a two-year period (Ministry of Justice, 2019b). This plan is based on the government's Female Offender Strategy (Great Britain & Department for Work and Pensions, 2018), which is the product of campaigns for women's prisons to be shut down for all but the most notorious murderers, and reopened as men's prisons (Corston, 2007). Instead of prison, the plan is for women to have community centres, either residential or day centres. However, despite the fact that there are around 20 times more male prisoners than female, there is no corresponding government strategy for men. Indeed, the UK government is investing £2.5 billion to build prisons for 10,000 more men (Ministry of Justice, 2019a).

Men are more visible as criminals, partly due to their crimes being more obvious and more often involving risk-taking and overtly aggressive and violent behaviour. However, research on DV shows that although women are also capable of violence, it tends to be less easily recognised (see Sections 8.4.3 and 8.5.1). It is plausible that politicians may feel pressure to take a 'lock 'em up' attitude to men, and a more sympathetic attitude to women.

Even though the evidence shows that criminality in men and women has comparable causes, women's criminality is typically seen as the result of forces outside their control, whereas men are made to take full responsibility. This might be a gendered 'fundamental attribution error' where men are seen as more to blame for problems they experience. In fact, men face bias at every level when it comes to crime, from cautions, to arrests, to imprisonment, to sentencing, to discharge (Collins, 2019).

Although there are more men than women in politics, male politicians don't fight for men specifically, though many female politicians fight for women specifically. Presumably this is in line with the wishes of the electorate, but a step forward, as suggested by the UK charity The Men & Boys Coalition, would be to change the title of the Minister for Women and Equalities to the Minister for Equalities, with a clear remit to include male inequalities in their activities (Men & Boys Coalition, 2020).

SPOTLIGHT BOX 8.3

CAN GOOD NUTRITION REDUCE VIOLENCE?

There is some evidence that poor nutrition is associated with antisocial behaviour (Gesch, 2013b). This hypothesis was tested in a double-blind, placebo-controlled RCT with 231 young (18–21 years) adult male prisoners in the UK (Gesch et al., 2002). Participants spent an average of 142 days in the clinical trial, half taking a nutritional supplement and half on placebo. Those on vitamins and minerals committed 26.3% fewer offences. The improvement in those taking supplements for at least two weeks was a 35.1% reduction in offences, whereas there was no significant difference for the placebo group. Psychological measures (e.g. anger, anxiety and depression) were also taken, but unlike the significant changes in behaviour, there was no significant impact of treatment on self-reported mood.

These findings have been replicated by the Dutch Ministry of Justice; its double-blind RCT of 231 young (18–25 years) male prisoners reported a significant reduction of incidents of aggressive behaviour, disruption and drug possession in the nutrients group (Zaalberg et al., 2010).

The effect of the intervention on behaviour might be via benefits of essential fatty acids, selenium, magnesium and iron to the central nervous system, cerebral blood flow and neurotransmitters (Gesch, 2013b).

One interesting aspect of both of these studies is that the changes were seen in actual behaviour, not self-report of behaviour or changes in mood. The lack of change in their psychometric scores in both studies could indicate that the prisoners were not trying to please the experimenters (social desirability bias), or perhaps that the prisoners were not in touch with their feelings, which might be the result of having to strategically reduce displays of emotion and become more masculine for self-protection in a prison environment (Phillips, 2001) though the need for such strategies is likely to vary based on how dangerous a given prison environment happens to be.

8.7 CONCLUDING REMARKS

Criminology is a vastly complex field, and this chapter merely scratches the surface of some key issues. One of the greatest challenges to psychologists is to develop a capacity for empathy with people – often men – who have committed terrible crimes (Rubinstein, 2010). Understanding and empathy doesn't mean condoning criminality, of course.

We know that the majority of crime is committed by a minority of criminals, most of whom are men. We also know that those who start their criminal career early in life are the ones who are most persistent, and these people are also usually men. Many of these early starters show neurocognitive issues, suggestive of prenatal developmental problems. It seems therefore that interventions at two levels are most needed: preventative measures aimed at the social level, and male-friendly interventions in the prevention and treatment of criminality.

The view that 'most criminals are, and always have been, men' is easy to see (Cain, 1989, p. 4). However, like the rabbit/duck illusion, there is more to this picture if we only take enough time to look. Generalisations about the criminality of men (or women, or any demographic) don't really help much in understanding the roots of crime, or help us see more than the most overt forms of crime. Individuals need to take responsibility for their actions, but this is a complex feat when variables that are beyond their control contribute to their behaviour. If we are serious about reducing crime, and the misery it causes for criminals and victims, then part of the solution is to move beyond an attitude of blame and towards an attitude of developing a clear-minded approach to the difficult task of developing practical solutions.

8.8 SUMMARY

- In some respects, men and women tend to commit different types of crimes
- There are some differences between men and women in the causes of criminality
- Gamma bias influences our view of criminality
- There are various challenging obstacles to men seeking help, even if they are the victim rather than perpetrator of crime
- Criminality might be reduced by a number of strategies e.g. reducing 'dad deprivation', and increasing the availability of male-friendly interventions for offenders

9   The Military

CHAPTER OUTLINE

Perspectives in Male Psychology: An Introduction, First Edition.
Louise Liddon and John A. Barry.
© 2021 John Wiley & Sons, Ltd. Published 2021 by John Wiley & Sons, Ltd.

LEARNING OUTCOMES

By the end of this chapter, you should be able to:

1. Recognise the different types of warfare, and the relevance of psychology
2. Know about PTSD and other mental health issues related to modern military service
3. Understand the specific obstacles to seeking help for military personnel
4. Be familiar with different interventions for different issues in the military
5. Recognise the potentially positive impact of military life

9.1 INTRODUCTION

In the UK there are around 200,000 personnel in the armed forces – of whom around 90% are male – and around 2.6 million veterans (Eldridge & Fraser, 2019). Sometimes military psychology is presented as a harrowing caseload of disturbed men with broken lives, haunted by traumatic memories of warfare. This view – often found in dramatic stories in the news, TV and cinema – is only one side of the story, however (Ministry of Defence, 2018). There are many facets to warfare, and likewise there are many facets to military psychology. For example, it's obvious that war can be waged with tanks and guns (the physical domain), but wars can also be heavily influenced by propaganda (the informational domain), and the mindset of the soldier is always a crucial element (the cognitive domain) (Le Roux, 2007).

This chapter will cover some issues that might be considered perennial in military psychology (e.g. combat-related post-traumatic stress disorder (PTSD)) but also covers some newer developments in the military, such as psychological aspects of being a drone pilot, psychological warfare (*cyber warfare* and psychological operations (*PsyOps*)) and other issues that are less discussed, e.g. the mental health benefits of military service.

9.2 WARFARE

War can take place on many levels. This section will focus on two of clear relevance to psychology: information warfare and PsyOps.

In this chapter, unless the context suggests differently, the terms 'military' and 'soldiers' are used loosely to refer to people in the army, navy and air force.

9.2.1 *Information Warfare*

War is most obvious in its physical form, but in recent times cyber warfare has moved from science fiction to stark reality. Today, an attacker can – almost literally at the flick of a switch – disable a country's power supply, financial system and communications, leaving the enemy nation in a damaged and disorientated state (Matthews, 2013). Similarly, military aims can be achieved by the spread of ideas online. For example, political elections can be subject to foreign influence through social media, achieving military objectives such as weakening military alliances or weakening the morale of a nation (Matthews, 2020). This important new front in warfare has interesting implications for how much traditional masculine values are still needed in the military today: warfare is increasingly about cyber activities that can be conducted without the use of physical force from behind a desk.

9.2.2 *Psychological Operations (PsyOps)*

Psychological operations, known as PsyOps or PSYOPS, is one aspect of information warfare, and can be defined as 'planned and co-ordinated psychological activities, including political, economic and military actions' that aim to influence 'emotions, motives, objective reasoning and ultimately attitudes and behaviour to secure the achievement of national and military objectives' (Le Roux, 2007, p. 223). The scope is so wide that in some ways PsyOps can best be defined by their effect rather than the method used to achieve the effect.

Although we usually think of warfare as physical combat, as far back as ~ 500 BC the military strategist Sun Tzu recognised that battles can be won or lost in the psychological realm (Tzu, 2003). An example of Sun Tzu's maxims is 'One hundred victories in one hundred battles is not the most skillful. Subduing the other's military without battle is the most skillful' (Tzu, 2003, p. 168). War can be played out in the 'cognitive domain' through intangible elements such as leadership, morale, camaraderie, training and experience and public opinion. An example of PsyOps that precedes even Sun Tzu is from

1245 BC, when Gideon confused the opposing army at night by using lamps and trumpets, creating the illusion that his army was much larger than the enemy's.

An important part of PsyOps is understanding the psychology of one's own forces, and making sure morale and wellbeing are supported. 'No matter how good your leaders, training, equipment and firepower are, if the hearts of your soldiers are not in the fight you will have little success' (Le Roux, 2007, p. 226). Examples include making sure they are motivated, mentally healthy and not feeling isolated (especially if overseas), and making sure complaints about leadership are taken seriously. It is also important to understand the impact of the contradictory pressures of being a soldier during peacetime, sometimes called 'peacekeepers' syndrome'.

9.2.3 *Propaganda and Fake News*

Propaganda can be a powerful weapon of war. Feature films were famously used successfully as propaganda on all sides of the Second World War (Koppes & Black, 1990). A recent example of PsyOps in action was Operation Burning Hawk during the Gulf War, which attempted to persuade Iraqi soldiers to surrender, using TV and radio and dropping 30 million leaflets from military aircraft (Pop, 2017). The result of this operation was that more than 60,000 Iraqi soldiers surrendered. This shows a great advantage of PsyOps: conflict can be resolved or avoided without a single shot being fired. Another advantage is that PsyOps can be very cost effective compared to conventional weapons – Operation Burning Hawk was more effective than conventional warfare, and accounted for only around 1% of the total cost of that war (Pop, 2017).

PsyOps can be used to create a positive or negative impression, and can be used defensively or offensively. At the strategic and operational level of war, media such as newspapers, the internet, radio and television can be exploited. At the tactical level, personal communications can be used, e.g. phone calls and emails.

PsyOps are a regular feature of modern communications. For example, 'fake news' can be used to spread 'weaponised information' by paid trolls, or by chatbots controlled by artificial intelligence, or by those who genuinely believe the stories (known cynically as 'useful idiots') (Sample et al., 2019). Computational linguistics algorithms can help identify fake news, but by the time fake news has been circulated in the mainstream and social media, and shared and reshared, it is difficult to undo the damage done by widespread misinformation (Sample et al., 2019).

Sometimes propaganda is not so much about influencing public opinion on a topic as it is a reminder of the power of the state. For example, the population of a country might totally disbelieve the propaganda broadcast on state television, but the aim of the propaganda might be simply to demonstrate the power of the state, through showing total control over mass media (Huang, 2015).

PsyOps is not just about attack, it is also about defence, and it is considered vital to maintain continuous vigilance to PsyOps attacks. States that are not well versed in PsyOps are 'vulnerable to external forces seeking to undermine the morale and culture of their people and the authority of their governments' (Le Roux, 2007, p. 223). Such attacks may go undetected unless leaders at all levels are trained to recognise them as such, which means relevant information needs to be relayed up the chain of command by trained intelligence officers. PsyOps personnel need to have specialised training and experience in relevant topics, such as journalism, scriptwriting, communications, language, broadcasting and designing and printing of leaflets, posters and use of loudhailers.

A limitation of PsyOps is that unlike conventional warfare, usually 'the results of a psychological campaign are not instantly obvious, they cannot be scientifically evaluated and measured' (Pop, 2017, p. 109). Sometimes the results are more immediately obvious, though, e.g. the surrender of troops after Operation Burning Hawk.

9.3 MENTAL HEALTH PROBLEMS AND TRAUMA RESPONSES TO MILITARY SERVICE

Mental health is recognised as a crucial element in the modern military. As well as PTSD (see Section 9.3.2), there is evidence that common mental disorders (CMDs, i.e. depression and anxiety disorders) are more common in the military. For example, a large academic study in the UK of more than 6000 serving military personnel found about twice the rate of CMDs than seen in more than 7000 civilians, even after controlling for demographic factors (Goodwin et al., 2015). This study did not control for the impact of experiencing military combat, but Goodwin et al. suggest the most likely reason for higher CMDs was stressors seen more in the military, such as moving house frequently and the constant possibility of deployment to combat duty.

This chapter will focus on some aspects that are less explored, such as gender differences in PTSD and PTSD related to modern non-combat warfare.

9.3.1 *Research into Mental Health in the Military*

Before looking at the research on this topic, a note of caution: sometimes findings are inconsistent across studies in this field. This is due to research being conducted from different institutions, e.g. the Ministry of Defence

(MoD) in the UK tends to find lower rates of mental health in the military than research by charities or universities (Ministry of Defence, 2018). These difference appear for various reasons. In the UK, veterans are more likely to seek help outside the MoD – perhaps because clinics outside the MoD allow anonymity – and civilian clinicians are less likely to diagnose PTSD (Ministry of Defence, 2018). Data recording in primary care is sometimes incomplete, partly because some veterans are reluctant to disclose their military status (because of stigma, security fears etc), and partly because clinicians don't enter relevant codes in the IT systems. A similar situation is true of suicides, where such deaths do not record that the deceased was military personnel.

The country where the research was conducted can make a difference too. For example, rates of PTSD in serving personnel are 0.2% in the UK, 6% in Canada, 8.7% in Australia and 12.6% in the US. The rates are higher for veterans, and this is often attributable to different levels of deployment, e.g. the US has lengthier tours of duty than the UK. Also, the US collects data on mental health anonymously, unlike the UK, which may encourage more reporting of mental health problems in the US.

9.3.2 *Post Traumatic Stress Disorder (PTSD)*

Military combat is a significant cause of PTSD in the military. Symptoms of PTSD, which can include 'flashbacks', nightmares, sweating, trembling, withdrawal, hyperarousal (feeling 'on edge'), anxiety, depression and substance abuse, have been described throughout the history of war. PTSD was called 'shell shock' in the First World War and was the cause of a third of all medical discharges. The name came from the incorrect hypothesis that the symptoms were caused by physical bruising of the central nervous system by proximity to an explosion. Nonetheless shell shock was often seen as a sign of weakness by military authorities, sometimes leading to the firing squad rather than psychological intervention. In the Second World War the diagnosis changed to 'combat fatigue', and the source was attributed to child development issues. The condition became better understood in the Vietnam War, when it became known as PTSD.

Research with UK armed forces personnel suggests the rate of 4% PTSD following deployment (a rate similar to the general population) increases to around 7% in combat troops (Fear et al., 2010). Interestingly, exposure to combat is not generally associated with an increase in anxiety and depression (Fear et al., 2010).

9.3.2.1 *Sex Difference in PTSD*

In the general population of US, the lifetime prevalence for PTSD is twice as high for women as men: 2–13% for men and 5–27% for women, depending on variables such as diagnostic criteria (Jones, 2015). A longitudinal study of 9960 children and adolescents in the UK found that this sex difference did not exist in childhood, but emerged in adolescence (Haag et al., 2019).

Some interesting information about sex differences in veteran PTSD came from a small interview study of four men and four women veterans of the US forces with PTSD (Jones, 2015). Interpretative phenomenological analysis (IPA) of the interviews identified some interesting sex differences. The male veterans talked about a sense of individual self as separate from the collective unit, a sense of pride that protected their sense of self during and after their combat experiences and a sense of hope about their recovery. The themes that came up for the female veterans were their identity as a woman within the military, acknowledgement that trauma due to sexual violence was more likely for women than men and resilience despite multiple traumatic experiences. Three themes were common to both men and women: anger, avoidance and support/vulnerability. In general terms, the men's themes were individualistic and action-oriented, whereas the women's themes were around diversity and the experience of multiple traumas.

The topic of sex differences in combat-related PTSD is little researched, and although the study by Jones (2015) was small and conducted for a doctoral thesis it has provided some relatively good information, compared to some other studies that have been conducted (see SPOTLIGHT box 9.1).

SPOTLIGHT BOX 9.1

THE PARADOX OF LOWER PTSD LEVELS IN FEMALE VETERANS: THE 'HEALTHY WARRIOR EFFECT'?

Although it is known that in the general population, women suffer twice the rate of PTSD that men do (Haag et al., 2019), there is surprisingly little quantitative (statistical) research on sex differences in PTSD related to combat. What published studies are available, when taken together, seem to suggest that female veterans are less likely than male veterans to experience combat stress.

Back in the 1990s, a team from Central Michigan University complained that there was not enough research on women veterans of the Vietnam War because 'the unique war zone stressors that were encountered by women in Vietnam' such as 'fear for one's safety' and 'personal discomforts and deprivations' were underexplored (King et al., 1995, p. 185). Consequently, the NIMH funded a study of 300 male and 108 female Vietnam veterans. One of their findings was that, surprisingly, there were higher levels of PTSD in male than female veterans. This finding is less surprising when you realise that the study did not take into account combat exposure, even though most of the men in the study had been in combat, whereas most of the women were nurses in non-combat roles who generally saw no violence (King et al., 1995).

A study conducted psychiatric assessments of male and female veterans, and found that 77% (7 of 31) of the men and 3% (1 of 31) of the women were diagnosed with PTSD (Grossman, 1997). Again, this difference is less remarkable when taking into account that all seven of the men with PTSD had seen high levels of combat, whereas none of the 31 women had been in combat.

A decade or so later a study of 1032 male and 197 female veterans returning from Iraq and Afghanistan found that the women were significantly less likely to screen positive for PTSD (21% vs. 33%). Although the authors suggest this is possible evidence of "the 'healthy warrior effect' (the disproportionate loss of psychologically unfit personnel early in training) [which] might even the playing field for men and women deployed", it is more plausible that the finding is an artefact of the researchers not controlling for the effect of combat exposure (Haskell et al., 2010, p. 270).

A study of 498 male and 352 female veterans of Iraq and Afghanistan found mean PTSD scores higher in men who smoked tobacco compared to women who smoked tobacco (men = 47.3; women = 43.8), but the opposite in non-smokers (men = 50.5; women = 53.0; Gross et al., 2020). This seems interesting, though taking smokers and non-smokers together (data not presented by Gross et al.) there is little sex difference (men = 48.9; women = 48.4). However, a key issue is this study did not take into account the impact of combat exposure on PTSD scores; mean combat exposure scores were much higher in men whether smokers (men = 25.3; women = 12.8) or non-smokers (men = 23.6; women = 9.9), making it likely that men's higher PTSD scores were due to their greater combat exposure. It is possible that men with PTSD were more likely than other soldiers to be smokers.

In summary, these studies present data showing that female veterans experience lower rates of PTSD than male veterans. However, none of these studies made it adequately clear that the female veterans were much less likely than the men to have experienced combat duty.

To be fair, the main focus of most of these studies was not sex differences in PTSD, but it seems quite an oversight that all four papers mention the noteworthy finding that female veterans have lower PTSD scores but, instead of explaining clearly that the most likely cause was the sex difference in combat experience, three of the papers left the reader to draw their own conclusions, and one of the papers (Haskell et al., 2010) attributed the finding to the 'healthy warrior effect'.

Two of the papers (Haskell et al., 2010; Gross et al., 2020) were published in *the Journal of Women's Health*, which might explain the lack of focus on men, but for all four papers it is ironic – given that the subject was soldiers – that the key variable they overlooked was experience of combat. No doubt these oversights were unintended, but they demonstrate the pitfalls of not being alert to beta bias in research (*Theme: 'cognitive biases'*, in Section 13.2.5).

9.3.3   *Drone Pilots and Moral Injury*

Drones, or, more properly, unmanned aerial vehicles, allow operators to safely kill with incredible precision (Matthews, 2020). However, these weapons are not without controversy because, for example, of the psychological dangers of being a drone operator: such soldiers may suffer rates of PTSD-like symptoms similar to PTSD rates among those involved in direct combat. This PTSD-like condition has been called 'moral injury', and can occur when soldiers observe or participate in actions that impact their sense of ethics (Matthews, 2020). This is a newly identified condition and at the time of writing it isn't clear whether PTSD and moral injury are qualitatively different, and our knowledge on this point has important implications for whether different methods of prevention and treatment are needed (Matthews, 2014). It is likely that moral injury is more of an existential crisis than the more visceral trauma typically associated with direct combat, though moral injury can also result from direct combat, related to, for example, strong feelings of disillusionment if military leaders are seen as incompetent or dishonest (Matthews, 2018). Indeed, moral injury can occur in the absence of combat of any kind, as long as the sufferer has a strong sense of violation of their moral standards, combined with a strong sense of powerlessness and hopelessness (Matthews, 2018). The concept of moral injury can be generalised to civilian organisations where people feel, for example, that profit is put before safety.

9.3.4 *Who is Vulnerable to Mental Health Problems in the Military?*

Although a soldier not being deployed when fellow soldiers are can leave a sense of disconnection and unfulfilment (Ministry of Defence, 2018), clearly the stress of combat – even when virtual – can lead to mental health issues. For example, UK forces deployed in Afghanistan and Iraq had double the rate of PTSD (6.9% vs 3.6%) and alcohol misuse (22% vs 11%) as those not deployed (Ministry of Defence, 2018). Apart from this, there are a range of other issues that might cause mental health issues, and the factors in the general population that are associated with mental health also impact military personnel. There are also variables which predict mental health that are specific to the military: being in combat; being army or RAF personnel; reservists; and those who leave the services in less than four years (Hacker-Hughes, 2017; Ministry of Defence, 2018). The fact that longer-serving personal are less likely to have mental health problems could suggest that military service doesn't completely explain mental health issues.

Some conflicts are particularly traumatic. For example, although those UK forces deployed to operations in Afghanistan and Iraq in 2004–2009 showed a 4% rate of PTSD – similar to the general population – those deployed between 2014 and 2016 had a rate of PTSD of up to 9% (Ministry of Defence, 2018). In the US military, the suicide rate climbed steadily after the start of the Iraq and Afghanistan conflicts (Schoenbaum et al., 2014). For those with a pre-existing vulnerability, combat may aggravate the condition, but on the other hand the camaraderie of belonging to a cohesive group may reduce the condition (Ministry of Defence, 2018; see also Section 9.6).

FORGOTTEN WARRIORS: PRISONERS, HOMELESSNESS AND SUICIDE

Experience of military combat increases the risk of PTSD. Those with combat experience are twice as likely to report violence on return from deployment than non-combatants (KCMHR, 2018). Although the causes of imprisonment, homelessness and suicide are complex, for many servicemen with combat experience, untreated or unresolved PTSD can play havoc with their lives and the lives of those around them, leading to lives spiralling out of control.

Aggression, violence and substance abuse can be difficult for family, friends and strangers to deal with, and they distract attention and sympathy from seeing that these behaviours might be symptoms of PTSD or depression. If these problems aren't successfully treated by the helping professions, or are not resolved with the support of friends or family, then these men might well find themselves on a fast track to dire circumstances.

Prison

The largest occupational group in UK prisons, at around 3.5%, is of men who have served in the armed forces. These men are less likely than other prisoners to be in prison for theft. In fact, servicemen have a lower lifetime rate of criminal convictions than civilians. However, servicemen are more likely than other prisoners to be there for a sex offence, or violence against the person (KCMHR, 2018). The violence appears to be a result of pre-enlistment problems (social deprivation, previous convictions), alcohol and PTSD.

Homelessness

A meta-analysis of 31 studies of veterans in the US found that they were more likely to become homeless than other men (Tsai & Rosenheck, 2015). A study of homeless men (125 military veterans and 228 non-veterans) in Florida in the US found that having substance use or mental health problems was the main cause of homelessness in 28% of military veterans compared to 8% of non-veterans (Dunne et al., 2015).

Suicide

In the US and UK military, rates of suicide are typically lower than in the general population (Ministry of Defence, 2018; Schoenbaum et al., 2014). Exceptions to this rule are men below the age of 20, young veterans (aged 16–24) and early service leavers (Ministry of Defence, 2018). It is likely that this increased risk is associated with pre-existing issues (see Figure 8.1). After the Iraq and Afghanistan conflicts began, suicides in the US military increased steadily, and exceeded the demographically matched civilian rate in 2008 (Schoenbaum et al., 2014). Apart from being male, the main predictors of suicide in the US army were being Caucasian, junior enlisted rank, recent demotion and current or previous deployment.

> **The challenge of having empathy for challenging men**
>
> The male-typical expression of depression (see Section 11.2), and the symptoms of PTSD, may involve aggression and substance abuse and other challenging behaviour. Some men may have these issues as a result of the stress of military combat. Although it is easier to have sympathy for someone who expresses their mental health problems by weeping and seeking help, it seems only fair to men who have risked their lives for others to find it in ourselves to step back from their challenging behaviour and ensure their problems are treated by mental health professionals.

9.4 HELP-SEEKING

It is estimated that around 60% of UK military personnel with mental health issues do not seek psychological help, which means the true rate of mental health conditions could be up to 8% in serving personnel, and up to 10% for combat veterans (Ministry of Defence, 2018). On the other hand, the prevalence of help-seeking from specialised psychiatric services is similar in UK armed forces personnel (3.2%) and the general population of the UK (3.5%; Ministry of Defence, 2018).

9.4.1 *Obstacles to Help-Seeking in the Military*

Evidence suggests that similar obstacles exist in the military and general population (Fikretoglu et al., 2008), though there are some specific issues for military personnel, outlined below.

9.4.1.1 *Not recognising there is a problem*
Some personnel don't recognise symptoms of mental health problems in themselves, or don't realise they need treatment (Fikretoglu et al., 2008). This has also been seen in the general population (Liddon et al., 2017).

9.4.1.2 *Military masculinity*
It is not a pun to say that soldiers tend to be more psychologically defended than other men (Kingerlee, 2019). Where does this psychological armour come from? 'Historically, hyper-masculine gender norms have been explicitly used by the military to socialize soldiers into an idealized culture of "warrior masculinity," presenting the soldier as the ideal of the strong and stoic male', and this reduces their capacity for help-seeking (Shields & Westwood, 2019, p. 417). However, the prevalence of help-seeking is only slightly lower in the UK armed forces than in the general public, so we should perhaps not over-emphasise

the size of the barrier created by military masculinity (Ministry of Defence, 2018). However, the constant pressure to make sure you 'square your shit away' (keep your feelings and behaviour under control), though vital to the safety of comrades and the success of a combat mission, can make it shameful to admit being 'weak' and in need of help. In short, it is a lot to ask someone who has been immersed in a culture of loyalty, and trained to kill without mercy, to sit in a comfy chair and talk about his feelings (doubts, fears, regrets) about what he has had to do for his country. In fact, it is said that some veterans would rather go into battle than talk about their psychological issues (Kingerlee, 2019). Rather than risk reputation by opening up to colleagues or within the military healthcare system, or risk being misunderstood by discussing with a civilian therapist, how much easier it must be to keep these feelings at bay with alcohol, which is 'the traditional refuge of military men through the ages, to quell his symptoms' (Eldridge & Fraser, 2019, p. 271).

9.4.1.3 Stigma

The popular expectation is almost that veterans will end their careers in the military as 'mad, bad or sad', which stigmatises veterans and may even discourage them from seeking help (Ministry of Defence, 2018). Stigma is not the main barrier to help-seeking, though it can be an issue, especially to those seeking help for the first time (Ministry of Defence, 2018). However, if therapy is fully endorsed by the chain of command, this reduces stigma (Jones et al., 2018). Stigma in the forces is more intense during deployment, but when not deployed is probably similar to the general population. The Royal Foundation's *Heads Together* and other campaigns such as the MoD's *Promote and Prevent* have helped to destigmatise mental health issues in the armed forces (Ministry of Defence, 2018).

9.4.1.4 Help doesn't seem to be available

A problem reported across the UK is that veterans can also feel let down by the health services when they don't receive the priority care they are due according to the Armed Forces Covenant, because of NHS commitments to equality and clinical need (Ministry of Defence, 2018). In the UK, provision of PTSD help for veterans can take too long and varies across the UK (Ministry of Defence, 2018). However, increases in use of Defence Medical Services might reflect recent improvements in the time taken to find help, and reduction in perceived stigma (Ministry of Defence, 2018).

9.4.1.5 Negative attitude to treatment

Veterans are put off from seeking help if they have been unable to access care when they need it or found it to be ineffective (Ministry of Defence, 2018). The lack of understanding from civilian clinicians of the veterans' experiences can be off-putting, especially at first contact (Ministry of Defence, 2018). Risk of damaging reputation with colleagues and the military can also be a barrier to help-seeking (Eldridge & Fraser, 2019).

9.4.2 'Hard-to-Reach' Men and Survivorship Bias

It often seems that men fly under the radar when it comes to mental health care. Firstly, men tend to deal with stress in ways outside healthcare (e.g. at the gym), and symptoms of their stress (e.g. aggression) are not always recognised as such by health professionals and not detected by standard tests of depression.

Some men put off therapy until they have exhausted all other options, and some men don't seek therapy at all, even if it is offered to them (Bilsker et al., 2018). We should not take a rejection of help to mean they cannot be helped or don't want to be helped – there are various reasons why help is refused (see Figure 12.1). It could be that the timing of the offer, or the type of help offered, impacts their decision. Some men in prison might be especially concerned that what they say will be used as evidence against them, or fear the consequences of being misunderstood by other prisoners as colluding with officials.

Although we can identify the obstacles to treatment by asking people in surveys, how do we know the obstacles for men who don't respond to surveys, who don't seek help from professionals or from anyone? This is an important issue, because at present our therapies and the pathway to therapies are based on what we know of clients, but the 'hard-to-reach' men are perhaps the group most at risk of tragic consequences – and yet we know very little about them. The situation is reminiscent of US Secretary of Defence Donald Rumsfeld's comments in the build-up to the Iraq war: 'there are known unknowns; that is to say we know there are some things we do not know. But there are also unknown unknowns – the ones we don't know we don't know' (Shermer, 2005). At present our therapies are based on people who have symptoms typical of a mental health problem, recognise their symptoms, seek help, show up for therapy and stay the course until it's complete. It could be that we need an entirely different approach for those people who have atypical symptoms (e.g. physical aggression), don't recognise themselves as having a mental health issue, refuse counselling and end up in trouble.

The phenomenon of *survivorship bias* is relevant to this issue. An example from the Second World War illustrates the point. In the effort to make aircraft more resilient to anti-aircraft fire, the initial idea was to look for the damaged places in the planes that returned from a mission, and reinforce those places on other aircraft. However it was pointed out that identifying the location of damage in aircraft that had survived attack (*survivorship bias*) was less informative than identifying the location of damage in aircraft that had *not* survived the attack. This was impossible because those aircraft were lost, so the solution was to add armour to the parts that were unscathed on the aircraft that returned from combat (Wald, 1980). Extending this example to men's mental health: we should not base our knowledge of men's mental health so much on the men who seek help and attend therapy, but should also try to discover the problems of men who don't seek therapy, and may instead 'crash and burn'.

Based on this way of seeing things, we should identify the type of damage seen in men in prison, homeless men and completed suicides (suicide notes, or other information) and unexplained deaths, e.g. road traffic death with no obvious cause. For example, we might see some of the factors related to crime (see Figure 8.1) as the type of damage we don't see so much of in male clients who seek therapy. Similarly, a review of research into suicides found that the majority of suicides were precipitated by relationship problems (40%) or work/money problems (22%; Callanan & Davies, 2009; see Section 11.3.2 for further details of causes). However, the percentages don't add up to 100% for the various causes, and it could be that this missing information is also key to understanding the gaps in our knowledge of service provision for hard-to-reach men.

9.5 INTERVENTIONS FOR VETERANS

In the UK in 2017 the MoD and the National Health Service published a four-front strategy to help the mental health of the armed forces. The strategy aims to take a research-based approach to *Promote, Prevent, Detect and Treat* mental health problems (Ministry of Defence, 2017). This strategy includes not only clinical interventions delivered through a system of Departments of Community Mental Health, but also support from non-clinical sources, including health promotion, training and education, welfare support and online resources (see also Section 9.5.4). There is also a 24/7 helpline for serving personnel and their families, in partnership with the charity Combat Stress.

9.5.1 *Male-Friendly Approaches to Therapy with Veterans*

Military training encourages men to control their feelings and not discuss their fears; this helps them to be good soldiers but is less useful in making them good clients for psychological therapy. Emotional self-disclosure and self-reflection are not priorities for a soldier, and even if they get to the point of seeking therapy, they are less likely to engage fully and are more likely to drop out (Shields & Westwood, 2019). Although some approaches to therapy encourage a rejection of traditional masculinity (APA, 2018), others suggest that there is much more to be gained by embracing the strengths inherent in masculinity and helping men to deal with their feelings without feeling that they are abandoning their masculinity (Englar-Carlson, 2006). For example, helping veterans to realise that regaining mental health can be a battle that requires courage and is a sign of strength is a way of working with the grain of masculinity (Shields & Westwood, 2019; see Section 9.6.2).

9.5.2   *Drama-Based Interventions*

The Veterans' Transition Programme (VTP) involves the therapeutic re-enactment of battle trauma, with a supportive group of facilitators (Westwood et al., 2010). Key to the programme is creating a supportive environment, aided by six to eight fellow veterans, over several weekend sessions. The 'course' (a term that for male clients was preferable to 'therapy programme') follows a number of steps, and involves activities such as writing about one's experiences and reading them aloud to the group, which helps to normalise such experiences and the psychological consequences of the experiences.

The main part of the course is the therapeutic enactment of the traumatic event, leading to letting go of negative feelings, such as shame and guilt ('dropping the baggage'). The success of the VTP, including its low drop-out rate, has inspired similar programmes, such as Action-Based Group Therapy (Kingerlee et al., 2019).

9.5.3   *The Veterans' Stabilization Programme*

One of the problems experienced by people with PTSD is a tendency to react too quickly, and overreact, to situations that they previously would not have taken much notice of. For example, they might be enjoying a party, a camera flash goes off nearby, and this triggers a fight or flight response (a rush of adrenaline, the mind racing, feelings of aggression or anxiety, etc).

The Veterans' Stabilization Programme conceptualises PTSD symptoms, such as hyper-vigilance, as 'disorders of speed' (Kingerlee et al., 2019). The VSP is a 16-week outpatient treatment programme that trains veterans to be able to make the transition between military and family life by slowing their thinking, as well as learning to control the use of substances and to recognise and deal with psychological 'Trojan horses' such as 'paranoid' thinking.

The VSP is part of a wider set of interconnected programmes which offers a relatively comprehensive care network for veterans and their families in the Norfolk area of the UK. The other two programmes are The Walnut Tree Project, a clinic offering a range of treatments to veterans (e.g. CBT, coaching, mindfulness) in a relaxing setting, and the Community Response Team, an out-of-hours team that delivers professional and peer support in a response car to veterans registered with The Walnut Tree Project.

Another treatment that has been used with veterans is eye movement desensitisation and reprocessing (EMDR). EMDR reprogrammes traumatic memories of battle – which might be complicated by difficulties from childhood – so that they are manageable (Kingerlee, 2019). This therapy is recommended for use with general PTSD in many countries, though there have been no randomised clinical trials (RCTs) with US veterans to date.

9.5.4 *Alternatives to Psychological Therapy*

Asking someone to talk about feelings that they don't want to talk about is demanding, and therapies that require veterans with PTSD to face the source of, or even re-experience, their trauma are even more demanding and may lead to drop-out (Steenkamp et al., 2020). For veterans with PTSD in the US, the Department of Veterans Affairs and Department of Defence recommend prolonged exposure (PE) therapy and cognitive processing therapy, which have shown good results in RCTs with civilians. A review of studies of treatments for PTSD in US veterans found that these interventions were not significantly more beneficial than some other standard treatments that are not trauma-focused (Steenkamp et al., 2020). It seems likely, then, that, given the complexity of PTSD, veterans should be offered alternatives to trauma-focused therapies, especially if they are considering dropping out of a trauma-focused programme. A study of 230 Iraq War veterans with possible PTSD found that 68% experienced partial or full reduction of symptoms after three years (Rona et al., 2012). However a major weakness of this study is that it did not assess whether the veterans received therapy or not.

The MoD offers non-clinical support for mental health too, e.g. health promotion, training and education and online resources. Examples of online resources are Joint Forces Command's *Wellbeing Online* and the *Big White Wall*, which provide anonymous online guidance. Recent examples are *START Taking Control* by the Stress and Resilience Training Centre, *Operation REGAIN* (Royal Navy), *Operation SMART* (Army) and *SPEAR* (RAF; Ministry of Defence, 2018).

A study in the UK of 250 veterans found that Armed Forces and Veterans' Breakfast Clubs contribute to wellbeing by providing mutual support and a safe space to talk and share experiences with similar others (McDermott, 2020).

9.5.5 *Helping Veterans with Hearing Loss and Tinnitus can Improve Mental Health*

Hearing loss is the most common medical issue facing military veterans, impacting around 300,000 veterans in the UK (Royal British Legion, 2018). Hearing loss is more than three times more common in veterans than in the general public. Many veterans don't seek help for their hearing as it is seen as a relatively minor problem. A specific problem common in veterans is auditory processing disorder (APD), which reduces the ability to distinguish between competing noises. For example, a veteran with APD might struggle to hear someone speak if there is background noise. Hearing loss in veterans is associated with lower quality of life both physically and mentally (Hawkins et al., 2012), though more research is needed to fully understand this issue (Alamgir et al., 2016).

9.6 POSITIVES OF MILITARY PSYCHOLOGY

The military has some obvious benefits in terms of the defence and security of the nation. However, there are other benefits of the military that are often overlooked, such as useful community support in peacetime activities. The idea of mental health benefits of the military is surprising to many people, who might associate the military with violence and PTSD.

9.6.1 *Applications of Military Psychology to Everyday Life*

The military is often required to push technology to extremes, and consequently is often at the forefront of new developments in technology. In a similar way, military psychology is often about pushing soldiers and leaders to their limits and thus is sometimes found at the forefront of innovations in personal development and leadership training, and findings in this field can be applied in other fields, such as sports and business. For example, requirements for rigorous selection procedures for entering the military mean that some of the tools developed for the military, such as the Armed Services Vocational Aptitude Battery, are valued and used in job selection in non-military industries (see SPOTLIGHT box 5.2).

It is interesting to consider that technologies developed for warfare can often be translated for use in civilian life. For example, the US army seeks ways to enhance soldiers' cognitive, physical and social development, particularly character development, which can be used outside the military to improve behaviour in civilian life, especially in business, sports, and education (Matthews, 2020). Another example is that movies have been used as propaganda to influence people in wartime, and 'information-entertainment' has been used extensively around the world to promote prosocial behaviour via television soap operas (Bandura, 2003; see Section 10.6). Even Sun Tzu's classic book *The Art of War* has been re-packaged as a guide to dealing with the battles of everyday life (Tzu, 2003).

9.6.2 *Therapy Working with the Grain of Military Masculinity*

The link between the army and masculinity is pervasive, and can be seen in boys' play behaviour and the cultural celebration of war heroes. Military life is almost a different culture to civilian life, and indeed it could be said that therapists can expand their cultural competencies by learning effective ways of working with men in the military.

During combat it is arguably an evolutionary necessity for a soldier to suppress emotions, such as fear and disgust, that would reduce their ability to cope effectively. Thus military training encourages what might be seen as hypermasculine qualities, such as stoicism under pressure. Although this training works in creating soldiers who function well in combat situations, these soldiers might experience psychological injury in combat, and their training might then become counterproductive. For example, a soldier who is traumatised in battle might feel reluctant to seek help if he feels it is a sign of weakness, or if he feels it is letting his comrades down.

The usual 'social script' in regards to psychological therapy is that the client lets the therapist control the situation, introspects and talks about their feelings, admits to feelings they feel ashamed of, and generally puts themselves in a vulnerable position emotionally. This is somewhat in contrast to how many men deal with their feelings, especially in the military.

To help overcome this mismatch between masculine norms and therapeutic norms, one widely reported tactic is to ensure that specific words are avoided and replaced with more neutral or more earthy language. For example, the term 'therapy' can put some men off seeking psychological help, whereas taking 'a course' where you can 'drop your baggage' (Shields & Westwood, 2019, p. 430) and 'unfuck your shit' (Lea et al., 2020, p. 536) can be more appropriate for some men. These changes might help reduce the contrast between masculine norms and therapeutic norms demonstrating sensitivity to the military culture of men and facilitating a good therapeutic alliance.

Note that changing terminology is superficial unless it is part of a sincere effort to 'meet men where they are at': a review of the elements that create male-friendly therapy concludes that empathy for men is crucial (Liddon et al., 2019).

There are many possible ways of helping men with help-seeking (Brown et al., 2019; Liddon et al., 2019). For example, reframing help-seeking in masculine terms might appeal to veterans. An example of reframing the traditional male gender scripts is: (a) seeking help means you are taking control of your feelings (*mastery and control* script); (b) which means that you are better able to take care of others who rely on you (*provider and protector* script); (c) and means you will be able to get back to being a fighter and a winner again (*fighter and winner* script) (Seager et al., 2014). Various techniques have been reported by clinicians to have been useful in therapeutic contexts, but clinical trials on their efficacy are needed.

9.6.3 A Fresh Start

Many who join the military are from disadvantaged backgrounds, have lower levels of educational attainment, have histories of childhood adversity and enlist as a last resort or as a fresh start (Gee, 2007). The army will give many recruits not only a sense of the value of teamwork, but a camaraderie that might feel like their first real family, and bonds that might last a lifetime. In terms of social identity theory, personnel will have the benefits of a strong ingroup identity (Tajfel & Turner, 1979).

9.6.4 Military Life can be Good for Mental Health

Given some of the negative images of veterans in the media and popular culture, it is surprising that although the rates of mental illness have nearly doubled in the past decade among serving UK personnel (Ministry of Defence, 2018), military life can be good for mental health. An online survey of 5000 men in the US measured the variables that predicted mental positivity (Barry 2020). The 94 men (1.9% of the sample) currently serving in the military had a higher mean ($\pm$ standard deviation) Positive Mindset Index (PMI) score (4.3 $\pm$ 0.8) than the mean for the whole sample (3.7 $\pm$ 0.8), and being currently in military service was a significant predictor of PMI after demographic variables were taken into account.

So what might explain these positive findings? The MoD suggest that the support and sense of community in the military is protective of mental health, even against suicide (Eldridge & Fraser, 2019; Ministry of Defence, 2018). The military services provide many conditions that are conducive to mental health, such as stable employment with career opportunities, housing, strong leadership and a sense of unit cohesion (Ministry of Defence, 2018). Although deployment and combat are generally found to increase the likelihood of PTSD, in some circumstances more experience of operational tours is associated with increased psychological wellbeing (Hacker-Hughes et al., 2005), which might be because personnel who are more psychologically resilient remain longer in the military (Ministry of Defence, 2018). For example, elite units in the US (e.g. Special Forces) experience less than half the rates of PTSD of regular combat units, despite their greater exposure to danger. This is said to be due to a combination of the more careful screening before entry to elite units, and the fact that once accepted into the unit they experience strong leadership and *esprit de corps* (Matthews, 2018). This echoes the most usual explanation for good mental health in the armed forces: the military environment gives men a strong sense of ingroup acceptance (a 'band of brothers') and of being part of something larger and more important than oneself. A similar effect of groups has been noted outside the military (Englar-Carlson, 2006), suggesting that men like groups in general (e.g. group sport). In a sense, the military might be considered the ultimate 'men's shed', where men co-operate in interesting activities and extreme experiences often with high-tech equipment, creating bonds that often endure through the rest of their lives.

9.7 CONCLUDING REMARKS

Although there is room for improvement in harmonising research on mental health in the military across universities, charities and the military themselves (Section 9.3.1), there is room for optimism that the military can offer an environment where men have an opportunity to 'be all they can be' (as the US recruitment advert famously put it), while minimising any detrimental impact to their mental health. Clearly, there can be incredible challenges in being in the armed forces, but also it seems that modern armies are taking seriously the challenges of supporting their personnel. This includes some examples of therapeutic approaches that recognise masculinity can be used productively in therapy.

In this and other ways, the military is at the leading edge of developments in psychology, as it is in technology.

If we accept that the military is an inevitable part of dealing with threat in an imperfect world, then we are in a better position to recognise the benefits it might have for the rest of society, both in war and in peace.

9.8 SUMMARY

- War in the psychological domain has become more relevant today than ever, and has implications for military masculinity
- Psychological injury is a perennial issue, even when warfare is conducted remotely
- It is important that obstacles to help-seeking by military personnel are recognised by health professionals
- Promising new approaches to therapy for military personnel exist and should be tested in clinical trials
- There are positives of the military that tend to be overlooked and undervalued in civilian life

10 Health and Wellbeing

CHAPTER OUTLINE

Perspectives in Male Psychology: An Introduction, First Edition.
Louise Liddon and John A. Barry.
© 2021 John Wiley & Sons, Ltd. Published 2021 by John Wiley & Sons, Ltd.

LEARNING OUTCOMES

By the end of this chapter, you should be able to:

1. Understand the relationship between testosterone and health in men
2. Recognise why masculinity can support health and help-seeking behaviour
3. Assess the argument that men get preferential treatment in health research
4. Be familiar with how men are viewed by healthcare authorities
5. Appreciate some of the better ways to promote health to men

10.1 INTRODUCTION

Men suffer from health inequalities across a spectrum of issues: life expectancy, cancer, heart disease, accidents and suicide (Banyard, 2007; Nuzzo, 2020a). These and other health issues continue to disproportionately impact men (Affleck et al., 2018). This might partly be due to risky men's behaviour and lack of using health services, but also 'it might be that the problem with men's health is that this area is far less defined compared to women's health which has a focus around reproductive issues' (Banyard, 2002, pp. 147–8). Only in recent years has men's health come on the gender inequality radar, but at present a 'victim-blaming' approach is taken, with masculinity often seen as the cause of the inequalities. There are calls to disaggregate data by gender, but in a culture of victim-blaming, a greater focus on men is not necessarily helpful (see e.g. the reaction to COVID-19; SPOTLIGHT box 10.2).

    This chapter will look at some reproductive health issues, the relationship between masculinity and health behaviour, the question of bias in research, bias in healthcare and strategies to improve men's health.

10.2 REPRODUCTIVE HEALTH AND WELLBEING

In medicine, women's reproductive health tends to get more attention than men's. In many ways this is perfectly understandable, given that women's reproductive health involves the hugely complex phenomena of menstruation, gestation and childbirth. Nonetheless, it could be said that men's reproductive health could do with more attention, because some serious issues tend to be overlooked, most notably prostate cancer.

10.2.1 *Male Infertility*

In couples who are seeking assistance in becoming pregnant, around a third of infertility is cause by male issues, a third by female issues, around 15% by some combination of male and female issues, and about 15% by unknown causes (American Society for Reproductive Medicine, 2019). The most common cause of male infertility is varicocele, which is like a varicose vein in the scrotum, and can reduce sperm quality and production. Varicocele explains about 35% of cases of male infertility. Around 25% of male fertility can't be explained, and the remaining 40% is due to various other conditions, including the effects of treatment for prostate cancer, and low testosterone (Machen & Sandlow, 2020).

Given the sex differences in human reproduction, it should be no surprise that 'it is essential that infertility counselors be aware of how men and women experience infertility differently' (Peterson et al., 2012, p. 245). In general, women tend to experience more distress, anxiety and depression than men, and use avoidant coping (e.g. avoiding being around people with children), whereas men use stoicism and problem-solving strategies, e.g. focusing on reproductive technologies (Peterson et al., 2012). Sometimes these different ways of coping can lead to an 'emotional trap', with the man trying in vain to fix the woman's emotional response, and the woman feeling that her emotions are being invalidated (*Theme: 'yin and yang'*, in Section 13.2.4).

10.2.2 *Low Testosterone, Fertility Problems and Loss*

Despite men's reproductive biology being relatively simple in comparison to women's, sperm production is a complex process, involving testosterone and other pituitary hormones, mainly follicle stimulating hormone. For this reason, although testosterone 'is an absolute prerequisite for sperm production' (Ismael et al., 2017, p. 628), it is an oversimplification to say that low testosterone causes infertility, or that taking testosterone supplements will improve sperm production.

Testosterone decreases with age, partly due to normal biological ageing processes, but also due to other factors. A study in the US followed 1667 men aged 40 to 70 between 1987 and 2004 (Travison et al., 2007). They found a decrease in testosterone of around 20% total testosterone and – more importantly – 32% decrease for free testosterone (which is more biologically active), partly related to an increase in chronic illness, obesity, stopping smoking and increased medication use. They also found that 'loss of spouse was associated with declines in total serum T [testosterone] comparable to that associated with approximately 10 yr of aging' (Travison et al., 2007, p. 549). This finding shows that testosterone can rise or fall in response to psychological factors, perhaps via a similar mechanism to the challenge hypothesis (see Section 6.3.1).

Other factors can reduce testosterone, and there has been some concern about a trend towards lower testosterone levels in recent decades worldwide. However, the trend is not as clear as some media headlines suggest. For example, although studies of Danish and Finnish men have found declines in testosterone (Andersson et al., 2007; Perheentupa et al., 2013), a large US study of men between 1991 and 2004 (Nyante et al., 2012) did not replicate the trend found by Travison et al. (2007). The reason for this is unclear, however, and could not be adequately explained by differences between the two studies in ethnic composition or geographic spread.

Changes in testosterone levels and fertility are most likely related to lifestyle factors, as described by Travison et al. (2007), but they might also be influenced by the presence of the presence of endocrine disruptors in the environment (Sharpe, 2017).

10.2.3   BPA and Endocrine Disruptors

Formerly popularly known as 'environmental oestrogens', endocrine disruptors are chemicals that have the potential to alter the endocrine system, including sex hormones (testosterone and oestrogen).

There are several types of endocrine disruptor (e.g. synthetic progestins such as medroxyprogesterone acetate), but the most widely known is *bisphenol A* (BPA), a chemical widely used in manufacturing and commonly used to line tin cans and plastic containers. It can 'leach' from these under intense heat or due to degrading with continued use, and can be found in the urine of 93% of Americans. BPA becomes inactive in the human body within a few hours, though some people may be more vulnerable due to, for example, having a slow metabolism. The evidence for the impact on fish is much stronger than that for humans, because if the water is polluted with an endocrine disruptor, then fish are constantly exposed to it. Nonetheless, the problem of endocrine disruptors is potentially significant enough that the European Parliament approved a resolution in 2019 to take preventative action (Barry, 2019).

PCBs (polychlorinated biphenyls 153) are common in plastics, rubbers and pigments used in household products. A study of 557 men in the US (average age 46 years old) found there was a significant correlation between lower testosterone levels and higher serum (blood) levels of PCBs (Leong et al., 2020). However, in this study the relationship between PCBs and testosterone became non-significant when age and body mass index (BMI) – which were both negatively correlated with testosterone – were taken into account.

It could be that the effect of endocrine disruptors on humans comes from combinations of endocrine disruptors rather than any individual chemical, and the most likely effect is an increase in type 2 diabetes (Lee et al., 2014). It is well-recognised that men with type 2 diabetes have moderately lower levels of testosterone than healthy men, probably mostly due to the complex effect that increased visceral (stomach) fat seen in diabetes has on the pituitary gland, reducing the production of luteinising hormone, which leads to reduced testosterone production (Grossmann, 2011). Men with type 2 diabetes may experience fertility problems due, in part, to the negative impact of reduced testosterone on sperm quality (Ding et al., 2015).

10.2.4 *Erectile Dysfunction*

Erectile dysfunction (ED) is the inability to have and maintain an erection. A review of research on ED found the main causes were age, physical health (diabetes, cardiovascular disease, obesity, prostate cancer), mental health (anxiety, depression) and lifestyle (heavy drinking and smoking) (Kessler et al., 2019; see Section 10.2.5). Demographic factors were related to ED, too: men who were single, separated or divorced, unemployed or of low socio-economic status were at increased risk. Prevalence varies worldwide, partly due to demographic and health differences in each country, and probably also in part due to differences in self-report of this sensitive topic, and perhaps also due to genetic differences. The prevalence of ED in the six global regions is: Africa 24–59%, Europe 10–77%, North America 21–58%, South America 14–55%, Asia 8–71%, Oceania 40–61%.

ED is successfully treated by sildenafil (Viagra) in 85% of cases, even though the cause in about 40% of cases is psychological issues, which can be categorised as performance anxiety, or recent stressful life events, or vulnerabilities from childhood and adolescence (Leiblum, 2006). If ED happens with a partner but not while alone, the cause of ED is most likely psychological.

It has been suggested that an increasing number of young men have ED due to internet pornography use, e.g. through developing expectations that are unrealistic in real life. However, the evidence for this is inconsistent, and it could be that in some cases pornography is blamed when other issues, such as relationship problems, are the true cause (Fisher & Kohut, 2017). Further research is needed on this complex topic. There are lots of successful treatments for ED (NHS Inform, 2020). A meta-analysis found good evidence for the success of medication, psychological therapies or exercise (Allen & Walter, 2019).

10.2.5 *Prostate Cancer and Mental Health*

Prostate cancer is the most common type of cancer in men, affecting one man in eight. It is the third most common cause of cancer death in the UK, with around 11,700 deaths annually (Cancer Research UK, prostate, 2020). To put this in perspective, there are 11,400 breast cancer deaths per year (Cancer Research UK, breast, 2020). Compared to white men, the rates are higher in Black men and lower in Asian men (Gannon, 2019).

The prostate is a small gland under the bladder, in front of the rectum, surrounding the urethra. It can become enlarged in later life and interfere with urination, but without causing health problems. However, enlargement can also be cancerous. Men seek help relatively late for prostate cancer, in part due to embarrassment (especially if a digital rectal examination is needed) and fears of other invasive tests. Help-seeking for prostate cancer can also be lower in men with lower education, because of difficulty understanding the complexities of information about prostate cancer (Baratedi et al., 2020). Other barriers to help-seeking are that the symptoms are not very obvious or may even be absent, and that the most common screening test, the PSA, is not very accurate (Gannon, 2019). Some new tests promise much greater accuracy, but are not yet widely available (Klotz et al., 2020).

Prostate cancer has been called 'a couple's disease' because the support of a partner is so important at all stages, from decisions over help-seeking to diagnosis and beyond, where a supportive partner can improve physical health, mental health and quality of life (Gannon, 2019). The treatment side effects can be a difficult experience, especially where surgery or medication cause ED (see Section 10.2.4), which can impact the man's sense of masculinity. Because testosterone is associated with the development and course of prostate cancer, a treatment approach in about 50% of cases is to cut off the body's production of testosterone using androgen deprivation therapy (ADT), which improves symptoms and increases survival time (Connolly et al., 2012). However, ADT highlights the importance of testosterone to men's health and wellbeing, and the effects of losing testosterone include ED, genital shrinkage, loss of libido, hot flashes, osteoporosis, loss of muscle mass, breast enlargement, anaemia, fatigue, risk of diabetes, risk of cardiovascular disease, mood swings, tearfulness, depression and possibly cognitive issues (Gannon, 2019). Compared to other treatments (e.g. prostatectomy or radiotherapy), patients on ADT have relatively low health-related quality of life (HRQoL) scores (Bacon et al., 2001).

10.3 MEN'S HEALTH BEHAVIOURS AND MASCULINITY

It has become fashionable in recent years to blame a number of men's behaviours (e.g. smoking, diet etc) on problems related to masculinity.

10.3.1 *Hegemonic Masculinity and Health Behaviour*

The study of men's health has been influenced by the concept of hegemonic masculinity, which sees men as enculturated in behaviours characterised by domination, subordination and oppression (Connell, 1995). Based on these ideas, some influential papers (e.g. Courtenay, 2000) have promoted the idea that men's health problems are a result of masculinity. For example, risk-taking can incline men to substance abuse and dangerous occupations, and self-reliance and control of feelings causes reluctance to seek help. Even when men are engaging in healthy behaviours such as sport and vigorous exercise (see Section 6.6.2.1), Courtenay (2000) suggests these activities involve too much risk and injury compared to, say, aerobics or healthy eating.

10.3.2 *Men's Masculinity Bad, Women's Masculinity Good?*

One view of mental and physical health is that it is a matter of balance, or homeostasis. It has been said by many authors, including ancient philosophers, that a healthy balance for men involves more masculinity than femininity, and a healthy balance for women is more femininity than masculinity (Jung, 1969) (*Theme: 'yin and yang'*, in Section 13.2.4). It is interesting that women today are increasingly engaging in traditionally masculine practices, such as drinking, smoking and fighting (Sloan et al., 2010). Some authors regard these as positive signs of liberation from the traditional female role: 'In fact, girls are sometimes rewarded for performing masculinity, that is, by enacting stereotypical masculine behaviors, such as not crying when hurt or by taking risks' (Levant et al., 2019, p. 163).

10.3.3 *Is Masculinity Bad for Health Behaviour?*

It is popularly held these days that masculinity is bad for health behaviour. For example, a survey of 148 men aged 18–78 concluded: 'The findings support previous research which has found that traditional masculine gender socialization and social norms models encourage men to put their health at risk' (Mahalik et al., 2007, p. 2201). However, a review of studies with the widely used Male Role Norms Inventory (MRNI) questionnaire found that 'Traditional masculinity ideology as measured by the MRNI was not associated with engaging or not engaging in preventive health behavior' (Levant & Richmond, 2007, p. 141). Furthermore, a survey of 1233 male, female and trans patients found that for the male-identifying participants (trans and biological men) traditional masculinity, measured on the MNRI, had a protective effect on general health and mental health (Levant et al., 2019).

It is interesting that the view of masculinity as potentially good for health behaviour is relatively absent from the literature. This is probably because there is so much research that seems to prove that masculinity is bad for health behaviour, though there is reason to be cautious about this research. In brief, the main weaknesses are a distorted definition of masculinity, sample bias (young men from the US) and 'research paradigm fixation' leading all studies to use similar methods and come to similar conclusions (see SPOTLIGHT box 12.1).

10.3.4 *Masculinity can be Good for Health*

Some psychologists have taken a positive approach to examining potential strengths of masculinity in promoting health. Interviews and focus groups with 140 men in the UK aged 15–35 found they viewed their bodies as projects by which to express their identity, but without being too obsessive or vain about health and appearance (Gill et al., 2005). Two UK interview studies, of 30 men in total aged around 30, found that although men took care of their health, they played down the significance of their health behaviours and believed that discussing their health was unmasculine. They justified their healthy behaviours in terms of 'action-orientation, sporting targets, appearance concerns and being autonomous' (Sloan et al., 2010, p. 783). These attitudes might appear flippant, but 'the masculinity-health behaviour relationship is complex, and more research is required to investigate further the ways in which masculinities are deployed in discussions of both healthy and unhealthy lifestyles … the masculinity=poor health behaviour relationship can be considered facile' (Sloan et al., 2010, pp. 798–9).

10.3.5 *Traumatic Brain Injury, Coping and Masculinity*

Men are more likely than women to have dangerous occupations and engage in rough sports, which contributes to the greater risk of traumatic brain injury (TBI) in men. Masculinity can influence the course of recovery from TBI in several ways. For example, TBI might cause failure to live up to traditional male roles such as being a provider and protector, and may reduce help-seeking. Conversely, research suggests that masculine ideals such as striving for success, power and competition, winning and seeking status can all help achieve positive outcomes post-TBI (MacQueen & Fisher, 2019). For example, an interview study of ten men aged 21–67 years with TBI concluded that masculine identity can be a valuable resource in the reconstruction of self-identity in recovering from TBI, and can help promote engagement and adjustment and achieve meaningful rehabilitation outcomes (MacQueen et al., 2020).

MASCULINITY AND HELP-SEEKING FOR HEALTH PROBLEMS

The 1990s saw the beginning of interest in the psychological aspects of masculinity. However, this body of work created a deficit model of masculinity, with masculine traits seen as problematic socialisations. This view remains prevalent today. The influential work of Addis and Mahalik (2003) suggested that for men to seek help they need to overcome the masculine values which pressure them to not seek help. According to this view, seeking help means showing emotional vulnerability to others, which is in conflict with masculine ideals such as being in control of one's emotions. This view of masculinity is generally unchallenged in psychology, academia and the media. It sounds plausible, but does it tell the whole story?

Addis and Mahalik (2003) noted that advertisers were both supporting and challenging traditional constructions of masculinity by asking men to 'step up to the plate' in seeking help for their health, which suggests that masculine values might be used to encourage men's health. So what does research in health psychology tell us about men's help-seeking?

Some research is interpreted as implying that masculinity is bad for help-seeking for health issues. For example, an interview study of ten men in the UK with eating disorders found that help-seeking is delayed by beliefs that eating disorders are a 'female' condition (Räisänen & Hunt, 2014). In one sense these men are correct – 75% to 90% of people with eating disorders are female, and it could be that greater awareness that men can have eating disorders might help men to recognise that they have relevant symptoms and thus can seek help. The barrier to help-seeking in this situation, then, is as much about a lack of information than concerns about 'reduced masculinity' (Griffiths et al., 2015, p. 2).

Other research suggests that men don't seek help because of stoical reluctance (Mansfield et al., 2005). Although this may be true in some cases, other reasons need to be fully considered, or else we run the risk of victim-blaming. For example, although Mansfield et al. (2005) recognised that there were concrete barriers (such as financial restrictions) that prevented men from seeking help, these have tended to be underplayed in the literature on men and help-seeking. For example, it is seldom recognised in any literature that men are 16 times more likely to be colour blind than women are, and colour blindness can make it difficult to recognise symptoms that would otherwise prompt a consultation, e.g. blood in faeces, jaundice or skin discolourations (Barry et al., 2017). It could be that the willingness to blame problems on masculinity leads to a restricted awareness of other issues.

Studies of the impact of masculinity on help-seeking for health issues tend to find a mix of benefits and barriers (e.g. Gough, 2013). For example, de Visser and McDonnell (2013) did a mixed-methods survey of English university students (503 women, 228 men, aged 18–25) and found that 'Young men's concerns about masculinity could be harnessed to encourage healthy "masculine" behavior. However, such approaches may not be effective for men who eschew traditional definitions of masculinity' (de Visser & McDonnell, 2013, p. 5).

There is more research on the impact of masculinity on help-seeking in mental health than physical health, and further examples will be given in the next chapter (see Section 11.5). Given the evidence that masculinity can be used in a positive way, it makes sense for psychologists today to research the most effective ways in which masculinity can be harnessed to help men's health (Kiselica & Englar-Carlson, 2006).

10.4 HEALTH RESEARCH

There is a surprising amount of misunderstanding about the role of men in health research, as is evidenced in this section.

10.4.1 *Should We Measure Sex and Gender in Health Research?*

Sex and gender can sometimes interact in unexpected ways. For example, there are biological sex differences in pain pathways, but also gender differences in how pain symptoms are reported (Tannenbaum et al., 2019). An idea that is increasingly used in health research is treating sex and gender as two separate predictors of health outcomes. A Canadian study of acute coronary syndrome (ACS) and major adverse cardiac events (MACEs) assessed 273 women and 636 men aged 18–55 prospectively over four years (Pelletier et al., 2016). Gender was measured using a composite of instruments, including the masculinity and femininity subscales on the Bem Sex Role Inventory. They found no sex differences in relapse or death rate. However they found that regardless of biological sex, masculine characteristics were less associated with recurrent ACS and MACE compared with feminine roles and personality traits. Thus a man with a high femininity score was more at risk of relapse, and a woman with a high masculinity score was less at risk. This paper suggests that like sex hormones, masculinity and femininity have a healthy balance in men and women (*Theme: 'yin and yang'*, in Section 13.2.4).

A potential drawback of this approach is the measures that might be used. For example, some measures define masculinity negatively (e.g. as homophobic playboys), and it is likely that these negative attributes are more associated with poor outcomes than masculinity itself.

10.4.2   *'Male Bias' in Clinical Trials*

In 2006 a London hospital ran a clinical trial of TGN1412, an experimental drug for leukaemia and rheumatoid arthritis. There were eight men in this Phase I clinical trial, two of whom were received a placebo. Each were paid £2000. Almost immediately upon administration of the drug, the TGN1412 participants felt ill. Before long, blood pressure dropped and organ failure began, accompanied by swollen tissue. In some cases there was grotesque swelling of the head, leading to the research being known popularly as the 'elephant man' trial. The six participants needed treatment in intensive care and only recovered after several weeks in hospital. Some participants were still experiencing long-term problems years later, caused by the 'cytokine storm' triggered by being administered TGN1412 (Sandilands et al., 2010). Even these days, when patient safety is a priority in research, this story demonstrates the potential dangers of participation in clinical trials, especially at the early stages of research.

The stages of research go in 'phases'. After trials have passed safety standards with animals, when a drug is being tried with humans for the first time, it is called a Phase I clinical trial, with the aim of testing safety and side effects in humans (Cancer Research UK, 2014). Phase II and Phase III trials still have potential risks, though these are reduced by what is learned in Phase I. Historically and today, the participants in Phase I clinical trials are usually men. This probably – at least in part – can be attributed to men's greater willingness to take risks, as well as the medical profession's greater willingness to take risks with men rather than women. According to a review of research in the US Food and Drug Administration (FDA), with a total of 185,479 participants between 1992 and 2015, about half of participants in the later phases were women (48% in Phase II and 49% Phase III trials) and 78% of participants in Phase I trials were men (Labots et al., 2018). Because Phase I trials are usually smaller than other phases, women made up 47% of participants in the FDA trials overall. The conclusion of this review – that there is 'no evidence of any systematic under-representation of women' in clinical trials (Labots et al., 2018, p. 700) – is similar to that of a Cochrane review of 311 randomised controlled medical trials (Wallach et al., 2016).

10.4.3   *Have Men Been Unfairly Favoured in Clinical Trials?*

In recent years an important issue has been raised: 'the consideration and inclusion of men overshadowed women in clinical research design and conduct' (Liu & DiPietro Mager, 2016, p. 2), and this is said to have resulted in important gaps in knowledge about women's health. The factors claimed to have contributed to this are outlined in bold italics below, followed by an evaluation of each claim.

Claim 1: *White males were considered to be the 'norm' study population.* This claim doesn't take into account that it is normal practice to take as your reference group, or norm, whichever happens to be the largest group in your study, which – for various reasons unconnected with prejudice against women – could be male (Strand & Cadwallader, 2011).

Claim 2: *'A type of observer bias, male bias, in assuming a male's attitude in conducting trials.'* What this claim means exactly is unclear, but Liu & DiPietro Mager (2016) cite another paper which describes 'male bias' as 'observer error caused by adopting a male perspective and habit of thought' (Mastroianni et al., 1994, p. 8). Again, this isn't explained fully apart from questioning whether scientific objectivity can be achieved because of unconscious biases, and the paper doesn't mention 'male bias' at all. However, a section describes 'cross-cultural differences between men and women', claiming that the values, beliefs, and imperatives for women are organised around '"giving" to and serving others' whereas 'men's lives – with their focus on "doing" – are psychologically organized against the principle of giving to others. Men's images revolve around selfseeking achievement and competition' (Mastroianni et al., 1999, pp. 46–7). Thus although 'male bias' is not defined adequately, the claim appears to be that research by men is biased due to a selfish and competitive attitude. This claim seems an unfair and cynical attitude to take to health researchers, especially when an alternative interpretation is that male researchers traditionally protected women from being put at risk in risky clinical trials.

Claim 3: *'Researchers often thought that women would have the same response as men from drugs in clinical trials.'* In fact, it turns out that there are very few differences in how men and women respond to drugs in clinical trials, according to two studies with a combined total of around 336,000 male and female participants (Labots et al., 2018; Wallach et al., 2016). Of course the differences in responding are of importance too, as we now know (*Theme: 'difference that makes the difference'*, in Section 13.2.4).

Claim 4: *'They also viewed women as confounding and more expensive test subjects because of their fluctuating hormone levels.'* Concerns about fluctuating hormones as a confounding variable are perfectly valid: hormones can have a powerful biological impact, and because women's hormones fluctuate markedly across the menstrual cycle (see Figure 24.17 in Molnar & Gair, 2019) and show individual differences in these fluctuations too, it would be huge challenge to researchers to take this into account in a way that did not introduce a potentially unmanageable financial cost and a huge amount of variance into the data, with an impact on statistical analysis. So this issue is a mostly a practical issue rather than a moral one, although routinely spending a large amount of funding to try to identify sex differences, when in fact sex differences happened very rarely, is an ethical issue that could weigh against including women, unless there were good reason to believe that a specific drug might produce a sex difference in responding. Interestingly, women's health in the US has received more funding than men's health, and has done for years (Nuzzo, 2020a; see Section 10.4.4); which may be partly attributable to the relative complexity of women's health compared to men's.

Claim 5: '*Concerns of potential reproductive adverse effects led to policies and guidelines that considered pregnant women as a "vulnerable population" and, subsequently, excluded these women from research and restricted the ability of women of child-bearing potential to enroll in trials, especially in early stages of research.*' The foetus is vulnerable to biochemical influence, and drugs can have unpredictable consequences, e.g. thalidomide caused many children to be born with truncated limbs. Including pregnant women in trials would be a risk to them, their unborn child and their reproductive future. Unless the study is specifically about some aspect of pregnancy, including pregnant women would be too risky. For similar reasons, women of reproductive age are risking their fertility by taking part in clinical trials. Men of reproductive age are taking this risk too, but this risk is generally deemed more acceptable. [*Themes: 'gamma bias'* in Section 2.5.5.1]

Claim 6: '*The quality of knowledge related to women's health was lacking due to the exclusion of women in research.*' In fact, two large studies of this topic found that significant sex differences rarely occurred, and one stated that there were no differences large enough to impact treatment recommendations (Labots et al., 2018; Wallach et al., 2016).

In conclusion, blaming men or patriarchy for gaps in our knowledge about women's health is a false accusation based on faulty assumptions, especially as almost half of clinical trial participants are women, although 78% of participants in the most risky trials are men. It seems to be an example of gamma bias that lobbyists complain that women are excluded from clinical trials to the disadvantage of women, without seeing that men are bearing the brunt of risk – especially in Phase 1 clinical trials, where they predominate. Without a doubt, in any areas where there are sex differences related to healthcare, every reasonable effort should be made to fill in these gaps. However, this should be done without the outdated narrative of misleadingly and unnecessarily blaming men or 'male bias'. If there is any male bias connected to this issue, it is probably a bias in favour of protecting women and foetuses from the risks of clinical trials.

10.4.4   Gender and the 'Health Paradox'

Men in the US have worse health outcomes than women, but national offices focus their resources on studying and promoting women's health (Nuzzo, 2020a). This 'health paradox' has been shown in the past 50 years by the greater focus on women's health in research. This is demonstrated in various ways: the finding of around five times more mentions of 'women's health' than 'men's health' in the PubMed and MEDLINE databases, the greater number of journals dedicated to women's health than men's health (ten times more) and more specialist care for women's health in the US (three times more women's health than men's health centres). 'Such evidence contradicts the notion women have been discriminated against in health research' (Nuzzo, 2020a, p. 47).

An assessment of 134 countries found that countries with medium or high levels of human development tend to show disadvantages for boys and men, usually due to underinvestment in preventative health care (Stoet & Geary, 2019). However, men's poor health is often explained as being men's fault, a narrative which ignores other causes of men's problems, so is an explanation based on victim-blaming (SPOTLIGHT box 10.2 and Section 11.5.3.3).

10.5 HEALTH SERVICES AND PUBLIC HEALTH

It is fair to presume that everyone's health needs are recognised by the major healthcare bodies. However closer inspection reveals that gender bias can be found both within healthcare bodies and the narrative around health.

10.5.1 *Healthcare Practitioners*

Although men's relative lack of use of healthcare services is often attributed to stoicism or some other aspect of male-typical behaviour, in some cases evidence suggests that they might seek help more if they were more certain to receive help (Section 12.6.1). For example, some research suggests that general practitioners did not take male victims of domestic violence by women as seriously as female victims (Mildorf, 2007).

10.5.2 *Sex of the Doctor*

In psychology there doesn't appear to be a clear pattern of preference for the sex of the therapist (Liddon et al., 2019). For example, in an online survey of 232 women and 115 men, 62% of men and 61% of women did not mind whether the therapist was male or female. Of the rest of the respondents, 22% of men and 34% of women preferred a female therapist, and 17% of men and 5% of women preferred a male therapist (Liddon et al., 2017).

By contrast, in medicine there has been the radical suggestion that women are better suited to being doctors than men are, because men are socialised to be tough and unemotional, whereas women are socialised to be caring (Gray, 1982). Roter et al. (1991) suggest, echoing the words of Gray (1982), that 'all patients, but especially women, should seek out female doctors' (Roter et al., 1991, p. 1092). They justified this claim by reference to their US study of consultations by 101 male and 26 female doctors with their patients, 228 men and 309 women. It was found that compared to male doctors, female doctors conducted longer visits (22.9 vs 20.3 minutes) (Roter et al., 1991). Whether this 12% difference made any improvement to the consultation is an interesting (though unasked) question, but perhaps more important was the finding that male doctors spent two minutes more on average with male patients compared to female (21.5 vs 19.4 minutes), while female doctors spent on average one minute more with female patients compared to male (23.3 vs 22.3 minutes; Roter et al., 1991, p. 1087). Although apparently not quite statistically significant ($F(1,515) = 2.9$, $P < .09$), it is surprising that this finding was not given more prominence by Roter et al., because it casts a very different light on the idea that women spend more time with patients, and could have inspired further research into, for example, why female doctors spend less time with male patients. However, Roter et al. overlooked this finding, as did subsequent authors who cited the paper – including widely read papers such as Cooper-Patrick (1999), which has been cited over 2000 times.

Thus the idea that female doctors give longer consultations has been perpetuated, with the implication that women are better doctors, furthering the notion that, as Gray (1982) suggested, medical schools should socialise male students into 'losing some "maleness" and gaining some "femaleness"' thereby gaining more 'care, warmth, patience and love' (Gray, 1982, p. 169).

In the decades since then, the idea that women are better communicators has become an article of faith, even though most studies find only a weak same-sex preference for physician unless the presenting problem is sex-specific (Roter & Hall, 2006). This is an example of the influence of gamma bias on research, where the positive female finding is highlighted and the positive male finding is minimised.

10.5.3 *Men's Health and Self-Management*

Around 15 million people in the UK have a long-term condition (LTC), such as hypertension, diabetes or heart disease. Most of these are men, but less than a third of those using self-management of their condition are men. Given the costs of providing services, the future of LTC support is likely to be self-management (Coulter et al., 2013).

A meta-analysis assessed randomised controlled trials (RCTs) of self-management support interventions for LTCs (Galdas et al., 2015). Of the 40 studies, 28 were based in the US or Canada, and the rest in Europe. The most common disease type for men in these studies was prostate cancer (15 of 40 studies).

The meta-analysis found some sex differences in the benefits of different interventions.

Physical activity (in an exercise class or by one's self) had moderate benefits regarding HRQoL ($d = 0.54$) and fatigue in men ($d = 0.41$), and large benefits for depression for women ($d = -1.07$).

Education (taught course or materials provided) had moderate benefits for HRQoL ($d = 0.36$) and fatigue in men ($d = -0.36$), and no significant benefits for women.

Peer support (support group or buddy scheme) showed small benefits for HRQoL ($d = 0.23$) and depression ($d = -0.23$) and a moderate benefit for self-efficacy ($d = 0.57$) in men, and a small benefit for women for depression ($d = -0.32$) and fatigue ($d = -0.29$).

Healthcare professional monitoring and feedback showed small and non-significant benefits for men and women.

These findings reinforce the idea that men and women may respond differently to different types of interventions. Some of the findings echo other research, e.g. that informational support is liked by men more than women (Liddon et al., 2017). However, the meta-analysis was hampered – as many studies are – because in some studies data from men and women were combined and could not be disaggregated (*Theme: 'one-size-fits-all'*, in Section 13.2.4).

SPOTLIGHT BOX 10.2

'MORE MEN ARE DYING, BUT WOMEN ARE THE REAL VICTIMS': A PANDEMIC OF GAMMA BIAS

As of May 2020, around 65% of deaths internationally from the COVID-19 coronavirus were male. In normal circumstances men tend to die younger than women, and when this is taken into account in the COVID-19 data the mortality rate for men approaches double that for women: 0.47% deaths of men and 0.26% deaths of women (ONS, 2020).

From the start of the pandemic, the reaction from the media, politics and even healthcare showed evidence of gamma bias (Barry, 2020b). The greater number of male deaths was minimised by a number of methods, e.g. by a focus on other contributory factors such as age and obesity, or by focusing on mortality by ethnicity, although these also reflected greater male mortality (ONS, 2020a). Another example was focusing on the infection rate – which is similar in men and women – rather than the death rate (Stokes, 2020).

Another aspect of gamma bias has been to magnify examples of women's inconvenience caused by the pandemic, for example, having a greater burden of domestic work than men (Lewis, 2020), or feeling more worried than men about infection risk and unemployment (Guardian, 2020).

This narrative came from the media, politics and even health authorities. For example, a leading health journal suggested that men's COVID-19 deaths were related to 'behaviours associated with masculine norms' (Lancet, 2020, p. 1168). For example, men wash their hands less, thus increasing the chance of infection, and smoke cigarettes more than women do, thus weakening the lungs' capacity to deal with infection. However international sex differences in smoking in various countries do not map well to sex differences in rates of COVID-19 mortality in those countries, so smoking doesn't explain the mortality gap. Also men and women are infected in equal numbers, but men die more, so hand hygiene doesn't explain the sex difference either (Barry, 2020b). Nonetheless, at the time of writing, medical journals are still publishing papers that, although they contain some good science, also contain unjustified speculation that smoking, handwashing and slower help-seeking might be factors that contribute to COVID-19 mortality in men (Gebhard et al., 2020).

A more credible explanation is the long-established fact that women's immune response is, due to having two X chromosomes, stronger than men's – an advantage common in all mammals (Xirocostas et al., 2020). This explanation should be the most obvious, especially given the record of a similar gender mortality gap for similar infections, such as SARS, MERS and swine flu (Chen, 2017). However, victim-blaming of men (see Section 11.5.3.3) for male-typical risk-taking behaviour appears to have been the default explanation. This seems especially distorted given that risk-taking behaviour is extremely beneficial to society, especially in times of danger, such as in the emergency services, which are populated mainly by men (Careersmart, 2020).

Although not new, this victim-blaming narrative has at least highlighted real-world example of gamma bias in action. Previous examples are easy to find, e.g. the *New York Times* report that 'alcohol deaths have risen sharply, particularly among women', ignoring the fact that the male death rate for alcohol deaths is twice that of women (New York Times, 2020).

No doubt time will show the true extent of contribution of various risk factors to COVID-19 mortality, but at the time of writing (June 2020) it doesn't seem likely that men's lack of hand washing or inclination to smoking are likely candidates for their higher mortality. If there is a gender-related lesson to be learned from the COVID-19 pandemic, it is that gamma bias exists on a global scale, and the scale of the suffering of men does not reduce it.

10.6 HEALTH PROMOTION AND HELP-SEEKING

Most people want to be healthy, so one would expect that promoting good health to people would be an easy thing to sell. Indeed, based on *social learning theory*, soap operas have for years been successfully used to promote family planning, health, gender equality and pro-social values in non-Western countries (Bandura, 2003; Fox, 1996). For example, viewers of *Hum Log* – India's first soap opera – reported stronger beliefs in family planning and gender equality (Brown & Cody, 1991). However, the reality of health promotion – especially to men – is not a success story. As seen in the following sections, men don't always respond to health messages in the way that advertisers would like.

10.6.1   *Sex Differences in Food Preference*

It has been found that females – young and old and across various nations – show more interest than males in eating fruit and vegetables (Cooke & Wardle, 2005; Prättälä et al., 2007). The idea that people should eat '5 a day' portions of fruit and veg has been promoted in many countries since around 2001 (WHO, 2004). However, most people don't meet the 5-a-day guideline (Cassady et al., 2007); one study based in the North of England intended to recruit ten men who followed this advice, but could not find any such men and had to revise down the recruitment criteria to '3 per day' (Sloan et al., 2010). What might explain this apparent failure of health promotion?

A study of women across 23 countries found they prefer food that is healthy (Wardle et al., 2004). In contrast, men across several countries like food based on taste and portion size rather than health (Sloan et al., 2010). These cross-cultural differences suggest that the sex difference in food preferences might be influenced by something deeper than socialisation. Could this reflect evolutionary differences in food preference?

There is some evidence that women eat more fruit and vegetables than men do because of the different nutritional benefits to women of the weak oestrogenic effect of flavonoids found in these foods (Marino et al., 2011). Also, primate research suggests that meat is an important protein source for the male-dominated activity of hunting (Fahy et al., 2013), and sharing meat with females increased mating success (Gomes & Boesch, 2009). Given the associations with promoting strength and creating pair-bonds, it is not so surprising that eating red meat is considered masculine (Roos et al., 2001). It might even be associated with wellbeing: a review of 18 studies including a total of 85,843 women and 73,232 men concluded that abstinence from meat is associated with increased anxiety, depression and self-harm (Dobersek et al., 2020).

Perhaps public health promotion campaigns should be careful not to fall into the trap of 'healthism', where it is presumed that the public will make the moral and rational choice to engage in healthy habits (Crawford, 1980). This is especially true given that health advice from different sources can be contradictory or even turn out to be wrong (Pietilä, 2008).

Also, there is no doubt a certain amount of gamma bias in health promotion campaigns, in which there is an implicit assumption that women's preferences are wise and men's are foolish (*Theme: 'One-size-fits-all'*, Section 13.2.4).

10.6.2 *Family Meals & Nutrition*

Much of traditional family routine is based around meals, and in some cultures especially, a mother's love can be expressed through food (Gesch, 2013b). One aspect of family breakdown that is not taken into account is the impact on the diet of the family. Nutritional intake can impact antisocial behaviour (Gesch et al., 2002), so it would be interesting to know whether family breakdown has a negative impact on the quality of food intake, and if this has an impact on delinquency.

SPOTLIGHT BOX 10.3

EIGHT LESSONS FOR PROMOTING MEN'S HEALTH

Based on 20 years of work in community-based men's health promotion in Canada, Prof John Oliffe, founder of the University of British Columbia's *Men's Health Research* programme, suggests eight guidelines (Oliffe et al., 2019):

1. **Tailor your programme to specifics of the group** in terms of sex, race, culture, socioeconomic status, education and income levels, and the specific masculine roles, relations and identities. For example, the *DUDES* club offered homeless men the opportunity to discuss health issues at a venue where they could also get a free haircut and hot meal.
2. **Men connect by 'doing'**, so emphasise activities rather than talking candidly about health. Men also connect by talking – sometimes using humour – and through silence, a time where they can process their thoughts by themselves.
3. **Respect the right to silence or to talk**, while creating space where anyone can express their feelings if they want to e.g. the *DUDES* club has a motto – 'leave your armour at the door'.
4. **Speak the language.** Technical jargon and medicalised language will put some men off, especially working class men.
5. **Use men-friendly community-based spaces**. Hosting your intervention in a comfortable environment can aid recruitment, bypasses doctor-patient hierarchical dynamics, and reduces concerns about institutionalised healthcare.
6. **Collaborative leadership.** Teach men to take control – become the leader – of their own wellbeing. Community-based programmes can run for longer if they 'train the trainer', so that participants can become leaders on subsequent programmes.
7. **Formal evaluation of the programme is critically important.** This should be in place from the start (e.g. a qualitative pilot study) and progress to more rigorous methods e.g. pre-post, and eventually RCT. It is important that key information is measured without being burdensome to participants (see Section 11.6.3.4).
8. **Play to the programme's strengths and recognise the programme's limitations**. Community programmes are often best thought of as 'pop-ups', seeding ideas for further projects, rather than being in themselves long-term

and expanding nationally or internationally. Few community programmes are lucky enough to have a committed source of funding to support a realistic business plan. Even successful programmes might not easily expand e.g. the *Man up Against Suicide* photo exhibition was expanded from in-person to online/social media platforms, which didn't work very well and depleted time and funding which could have been used for further in-person photo exhibitions.

These guidelines echo findings of other projects. For example, *connecting by 'doing'* is fundamental aspect of e.g. Men's Sheds. *'Speaking the language'* is recognised in the Veterans Transition Program (Shields & Westwood, 2019), where the emphasis is not on completing a course of 'counseling psychology and intensive group therapy', but on '"dropping your baggage" and "unfucking your shit"' (Oliffe et al., 2019). Thus those who are 'carrying a lot' can use the tactic of 'release' without feeling emasculated. 'Male friendly spaces' have been successful in other realms, e.g. health promotion to African-American men in a barbershop context has proven successful.

These eight lessons represent a valuable basis for future research. It is possible that an even more male-centric approach would yield greater improvements (see Figure 11.3). Further research is needed.

10.7 CONCLUDING REMARKS

There are a number of myths and misconceptions around men, masculinity and health. Some of these relate to the structure of healthcare itself. For example, an unintended consequence of having fewer women in clinical trials is a lack of knowledge of the impact of some interventions on women (e.g. Liu & DiPietro Mager, 2016). It's true that our knowledge would be greater had more women been participants in trials, but it would be harsh to interpret this as the result of 'male bias' against women. Indeed, we have seen some evidence of gamma bias in healthcare, e.g. the notion that people should seek female physicians because they are much more caring and better communicators than men.

There seems to be a lot of evidence highlighting the ways in which masculinity can prevent help-seeking for health problems, but other research has been overlooked. For example, masculinity can promote help-seeking, though other barriers may prevent men from finding help. Overall, we can conclude that 'the *masculinity=poor health behaviour* relationship can be considered facile' (Sloan et al., 2010, pp. 798–9; italics added) and we should look for more effective ways to encourage men to engage with traditional health services. Credible solutions might be found in some of the suggestions in the next chapter (e.g. Section 11.6.3) or in the development of community-based men's health promotion programmes. It is encouraging that the Irish, Quebec and Australian governments have national men's health strategies, and WHO Europe has published an overarching men's health strategy.

10.8 SUMMARY

- This chapter has considered various psychological aspects of men's health, including the role of testosterone, health behaviours, bias in research, the relevance of the sex of the practitioner and the influence of health promotion on help-seeking.
- Testosterone is important for men's physical and mental health.
- Masculinity is related to health in interesting ways, e.g. food choices.
- Men have taken a lot of risks as participants in clinical trials.
- A subtle bias against men exists in various ways in healthcare.
- Health promotion campaigns might be more successful if they understood masculinity better.

11 Mental Health, Therapy and Support Services

CHAPTER OUTLINE

Perspectives in Male Psychology: An Introduction, First Edition.
Louise Liddon and John A. Barry.
© 2021 John Wiley & Sons, Ltd. Published 2021 by John Wiley & Sons, Ltd.

LEARNING OUTCOMES

By the end of this chapter, you should be able to:

1. Understand issues related to men's mental health, such as being able to:
2. Identify male depression
3. Understand the causes of suicide, some of the signs of suicidality and approaches to prevention
4. Recognise the problem with some current approaches to men's psychology based on masculinity
5. Understand issues with research on men's help-seeking
6. Know how to create a male-friendly therapy

11.1 INTRODUCTION

Tom is drinking too much. His partner finally persuades him to stop going to the pub with his friends and see a psychotherapist. Tom is slow to open up in therapy, and often talks off-topic or makes jokes. The therapist feels treatment is not going well. They mutually decide to terminate therapy. Tom's drinking gets worse.

– Vignette from a male psychology workshop by
Martin Seager and John Barry

The prevalence of common mental health disorders has increased in the past three decades. In the UK around one in five men and women aged 16–64 has at least one mental health condition, such as depression, anxiety, phobia, obsessive compulsive disorder or panic disorder (Public Health England, 2019). These rates have increased due to Covid–19–related issues (Public Health England, 2020).

Some mental health issues show sex differences. For example, women are twice as likely as men to experience major depression, and 75% of substance abuse is by men (Affleck et al., 2018). However, only around 30% of people who use mental health services are men (Smith et al., 2013). Despite the fact that around 75% of suicides are male (Affleck et al., 2018), men are less likely to seek help than women are. For example, one study found that 50% of women who committed suicide had previously seen a psychiatrist, psychologist or any other mental health professional, whereas only 29% of men had (Kung et al., 2003). The lack of treatment of men's mental health issues is one of the key issues in male psychology.

There is evidence that one of the most consistent predictors of successful outcomes in therapy is not the type of treatment (counselling, psychotherapy etc), but the quality of the therapeutic alliance (Del Re et al., 2012). This chapter discusses ways in which both treatment and alliance can be improved to make therapy more male-friendly.

11.2 MALE TYPICAL PRESENTATION OF MENTAL HEALTH ISSUES

People in general tend to think they know what mental illness looks like. If someone is depressed they look sad and cry, if someone is psychotic they wander around shouting at the sky, etc. These stereotypes might seem hackneyed, but in a way you can't blame non-professionals for having simplified views of things that they are not experts in. But what if even mental health professionals are influenced by stereotypes too? This section looks at whether we have stereotypes about mental illness that prevent us from identifying mental health problems in men.

11.2.1 *Is Male Depression Different to Female Depression?*

There is a worrying paradox at the heart of clinical psychology: we know that around half of completed suicides are linked to depression (Möller-Leimkühler, 2003), and that women experience double the rate of depression that men do, but why then do men commit three quarters of suicides? This paradox raises the question of whether men experience a high degree of depression, but not in a way that is detected by researchers and mental health services. There might be several other explanations, but the following section explores the possibility that men experience depression in a way that is not detected by traditional depression questionnaires.

11.2.1.1 *Characteristics of male depression*

A narrative review of clinical issues in men's mental health concluded improving men's anger coping skills was one of the key tasks (Bilsker et al., 2018). But the clinical phenomenon of 'male depression' is more than just anger management, and is said to be characterised by 'externalising symptoms', such as irritability, substance abuse, fighting and other risk-taking behaviours (Brownhill et al., 2005). It may also include distraction coping strategies, such as using video games or sex/pornography (Liddon et al., 2017).

Although 'male depression' is not yet widely accepted as a diagnosis, there is increasing evidence that it is a valid clinical phenomenon (Talarowska et al., 2018). It could be that male depression is commonly overlooked because depression questionnaires typically don't ask about 'acting out' symptoms of depression, and that male depression is recorded instead as substance abuse disorder or criminality.

A large European study found that men often attribute depressive symptoms to work stress or physical illnesses, particularly heart and blood pressure problems, whereas women attribute depression to relationship problems or illness/death in the family (Angst et al., 2002). Although this tendency to experience psychological issues as physical symptoms (somatisation) could be viewed as indicating poor emotional awareness (Brown, Sagar-Ouriaghli, & Sullivan, 2019), it might also be viewed, more pragmatically, as just a sex difference in the expression of depression.

When levels of depression are measured that include symptoms of acting out, the sex difference becomes negligible. One study, of 2382 men and 3310 women, found that when a depression measure – the Male Symptoms Scale – included acting out among the symptoms of depression, men showed slightly higher rates of depression than women (26.3% of men and 21.9% of women; Martin et al., 2013). Within this scale, men scored significantly higher on the questions on anger attacks, substance abuse and risk-taking behaviour, whereas women scored significantly higher than men on stress, irritability, insomnia and lack of interest.

The clinical applications of male depression scales are potentially important. For example, an Italian sample of 326 male and female psychiatric patients found that the Gotland scale of male depression was reasonably accurate in correctly identifying men who had made recent suicide attempts (Innamorati et al., 2011). A more recent male depression scale –

the Male Depression Risk Scale – has shown even better accuracy in a sample of 1000 Canadian men (median age 49.6 years old), which suggests that measures of male depression might be useful in preventing suicides (Rice et al., 2019).

11.2.1.2 *Can women suffer from male depression?*

The concept of male depression can be useful for women too. Not all women will experience depression in the way women typically do, and depression in these women therefore risks being overlooked. A German study of 518 male and 500 female students found that many women experience male-type depression, which the authors speculated might be the result of increased male-typical patterns of social behaviour by women (e.g. social acceptance of aggression), combined with increased exposure – compared to men – of chronic stressors such as entrance to the workplace, single motherhood and caregiving for elderly or other family members (Möller-Leimkühler & Yücel, 2010). Demographics of the sample (age and social class) might also have influenced the findings.

11.2.1.3 *Postnatal depression in men*

Postnatal depression (PND) is mostly thought of as being an issue experienced by women, but a meta-analysis has found that 10.4% of men experience this too – or at least a male version of it – especially in first-time fathers (Paulson & Bazemore, 2010). Possible causes are the major changes to sleep, financial pressure and social support. It can start as early as the first trimester of pregnancy, and peaks when the child is 3–6 months old. A review paper concluded that PND often goes undetected in men, and can make women's PND worse, as well as impact the mental health of the children (Goodman, 2004).

11.2.1.4 *How do we identify depression in men with postnatal depression?*

The definition of a construct can make a huge difference to how we perceive a phenomenon, how we research it, and in some cases whether we perceive it all (*Themes: 'flawed definition'*, in Section 13.2.4 and beta bias in Section 13.2.5). The Edinburgh Postnatal Depression Scale (EPDS) asks ten questions (see Table 11.1) about symptoms typical of depression. The EPDS doesn't ask about issues specific to babies etc, so is a good comparison to a questionnaire on male depression, the Gotland scale, which includes some of the key experiences said to occur in male depression, such as irritability, aggression, overworking and alcohol consumption. These two measures were used with the same participants in a GP-recruited sample of 3258 men in Denmark. It was found that 8% men were diagnosed with

TABLE 11.1 *Comparison of two measures of depression, one for general use in detecting perinatal depression (EPDS) and another sensitive to 'male depression' (from Madsen, 2019) Stress.*

EPDS ('traditional' depression)	The Gotland scale ('male' depression)
• Unable to laugh or see funny side of things • Cannot look forward with enjoyment to things • Blamed myself unnecessarily when things went wrong • Have been anxious or worried for no good reason • Have felt scared or panicky for no good reason • Felt things have been getting on top of me • Have been so unhappy that I have had difficulty sleeping • Have felt sad or miserable • Cried because I was unhappy • Had thoughts of hurting myself	• Lower stress threshold/more stressed • Aggressive, acting out, difficulty with self-control • Burnout and emptiness • Unexplainable fatigue • Irritable, restless and frustrated • Difficulty in making everyday decisions • Sleeping problems too much/too little/restless/ difficulty in falling asleep/walking early • Feelings of unrest/anxiety/discomfort, especially in the morning • Excessive consumption of alcohol and pills and/or hyperactive/works hard and is restless, jogs, etc • Behaviour changed so you are difficult to deal with • Feel yourself or others regard you as gloomy, negative • Feel yourself or others see you as self-pitying, complaining • Family tendencies to abuse, depression, suicide

perinatal depression using the EPDS, but using the male-specific Gotland scale 23.5% of men were diagnosed with depression (Madsen, 2019).

In other research the Gotland scale questions concerning use of alcohol were said to have 'hit the nail on the head' for some depressed men (Strömberg et al., 2010, p. 262). It also compares very well to the widely used Beck Depression Inventory (BDI) in the detection of moderate and severe depression in men, and has the appeal of being more brief than the BDI.

11.2.2 *Substance Abuse*

Substance abuse is twice as common worldwide in men than in women (Ellis, 2011). For example, cannabis use and dependence is generally around twice that of women (Affleck et al., 2018). Cannabis tends to be seen as a mild drug, but in fact it can have serious psychological effects, mainly because the psychoactive effects have become stronger over the years. The abuse of drugs of various kinds is implicated in a large proportion of mental illness, violence, robbery and death of men, e.g. around 80% of deaths in British Columbia from the opiate fentanyl – which is now more popularly used than heroin in some countries – are male (Bilsker et al., 2018).

Although moderate social use of alcohol can bring psychological and emotional benefits (Dunbar et al., 2017; Emslie et al., 2013), alcohol abuse is said to have the worst impact on mental health of all substances (Bilsker et al., 2018). Internationally, deaths by alcohol are six times higher in men than women (Rehm et al., 2009) and alcohol has been implicated in some suicides (Moreira et al., 2015). Some research suggests that treatment of alcoholism is less successful in men than women, though other research suggests no sex difference in outcome (Bilsker et al., 2018).

One explanation for the higher rates of substance abuse in men is that socialisation to Western gender role norms teaches men dysfunctional coping strategies, such as alcohol consumption to cope with distress (Bilsker et al., 2018). There is some truth to this, but the existence of male substance abuse across cultures, despite many cultures being different to one another in various ways, suggests that the male tendency to substance abuse could also be inherent to some degree (Ellis, 2011).

SPOTLIGHT BOX 11.1

HOMELESSNESS AND MENTAL HEALTH

At any one time in the UK there are around 5000 rough sleepers and additionally at least 250,000 with no stable accommodation (Duffy & Hutchison, 2019). This latter group is sometimes referred to as the 'hidden homeless'.

Around 85% of rough sleepers are men and almost half of rough sleepers have mental health needs (Duffy & Hutchison, 2019). The most frequently cited reasons for male homelessness are relationship breakdown, substance misuse or leaving an institution (e.g. prison, care or hospital) (Brown et al., 2019). Other reasons include a history of childhood abuse and neglect, which is seen in 80% of homeless people (Torchalla et al., 2012). These traumatic experiences can create in victims an association between home and distress (Duffy & Hutchison, 2019). Other types of trauma prior to homelessness are also common (e.g. military-related PTSD), and indeed the tough and unpredictable life experienced by rough sleepers can also lead to trauma (Buhrich et al., 2000).

The other 'hidden homeless': people with ASD

Autism is four times more common in men than women, and Asperger Syndrome – the milder form of autism – is nine times more common in men (Barry & Owens, 2019). People with autism tend to have difficulty living with others due to sensitivity to noise and difficulty socialising, and are more likely to be unemployed. This means autistic people often lack social and financial support in times of difficulty, and are more vulnerable to becoming homeless (Churchard et al., 2019).

Once homeless they may lose touch with other support systems and are less able to seek help when they need it. This is why people with ASD, most of whom are men, who are homeless are 'the other hidden homeless'.

Homeless people with autism have, despite their greater needs, few resources specifically for them. The UK charity Homeless Link has created guidelines on how to identify autism in homeless people, and the specific communication skills to approach and support homeless people with autism (Churchard et al., 2019).

11.2.3 *Interventions for Rough Sleepers*

Many people become homeless because of psychological problems. However, getting a roof over someone's head is often seen as more important than understanding what is going on inside someone's head, for example, problems related to childhood attachment (Seager, 2011). It's 'as if the physical shelter provided by the roof was more important than any psychological shelter that might be provided under that roof from the relationships formed between that person and the others who live there' (Seager, 2011, p. 183). According to Seager, homeless people need a home – a place where they can feel a consistent and stable attachment. Hostels can adopt a range of measures to become psychologically informed environments for homeless people (Phipps et al., 2017), such as reflective practice for staff as a way to step back and think about how to cope with the challenges of their work. Hostel staff can get to know residents sufficiently only if there are not too many, so the maximum number of residents should be no more than the size of a very large family (8–12) (Seager, 2011).

11.3 SUICIDE AND MEN

11.3.1 *The Gender Paradox in Suicide*

More women than men are diagnosed with major depression, yet more men end their life by suicide. This is a pattern that replicates in most countries worldwide. Although 75% of suicides are male in the UK and US, and more in many other countries (discussed below), there is 'surprisingly little research and few preventive efforts specifically targeting male suicide' (Bilsker et al., 2018, p. 591).

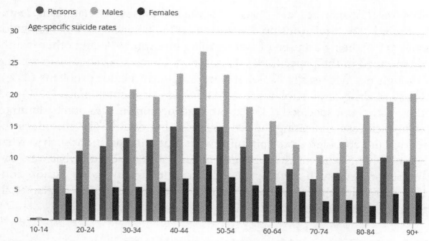

FIGURE 11.1 *Suicide rates across the lifespan, with sex differences (ONS, 2019c).*

11.3.1.1 *Suicide rates across the lifespan, with sex differences*

Figure 11.1 shows the sex difference in suicide rates for the UK across age groups. It can be seen that suicide rises from adolescence to its highest point in middle-aged men (45–49 years old), then falls off, until beginning to increase again in those in their late 70s, to a second peak in elderly people in their 90s (ONS, 2019c). At all age points, the suicide rate is higher in men.

11.3.1.2 *Cross-cultural differences*

According to World Health Organization (WHO) statistics for 2016, Eastern European countries have the highest gender suicide gaps; the very highest is Ukraine, with a suicide rate 7.34 times higher for male than for female suicide (GHO, 2017). The ratio of male to female suicide is lower in Western countries: 3.4 in the UK, 3.3 in the US, 3.0 in Sweden, 3.0 in Spain, 2.9 in Australia, 2.8 in Germany and 2.6 in Canada. Of 182 countries, only seven countries – mostly Asian – have higher rates in women, and then only very slightly higher. China is one of these countries, and there used to be a relatively high rate of suicide by young women in rural areas by swallowing pesticide, which is a readily available source of poison (Page et al., 2017). However, since the modernisation of China in recent years, this practice has lessened and suicide rates are now very similar in men and women.

11.3.2 *Causes of Suicide*

Various causes of male suicide have been suggested. A review of research into suicides, including suicide notes, of 621 cases of suicide in Ohio, US, found that the most frequent reasons for suicide are relationship or work/money problems (Callanan & Davis, 2009). The main causes were relationship/family discord (22%), relationship dissolution (18%), financial crisis (11%), work issues (11%), being accused of wrongdoing or crime (9%) and other factors not specified in the paper (29%). Chronic problems associated with suicide – though not necessarily causal – were long-term health problems (28%), history of drug or alcohol abuse (21%), history of mental illness (17%) and other factors not specified (34%). Note that the percentages don't add up to 100 in each case, indicating the presence of other causes. The chronic problems are not considered precipitating events, but raise questions such as what the underlying cause of the substance abuse issues were, and what were the precipitating events (if any) for mental illness. Interestingly, the authors conclude that 'suicide cases with and without notes are essentially similar' (Callanan & Davis, 2009, p. 55823).

11.3.2.1 *Relationship problems and suicide*

The most common reason for suicide is relationship problems, accounting for 40% of suicides (Callanan & Davis, 2009). Family breakdown is usually stressful for all involved, but men in this context are twice as likely to experience depression compared to women, possibly in part due to men's greater reliance on their spouse's network for social support than vice versa (Rotermann, 2007). It been estimated that male suicides can be related to domestic violence, but the numbers are difficult to identify with certainty (Davis, 2010). Men can suffer extreme stress due to losing child custody and having a negative experience in the family courts (Barry & Liddon, 2020), and these experiences can lead to substance abuse and even suicide (Felix et al., 2013). An estimate based on data from the US National Longitudinal Mortality Study suggests that, after taking age, education and income into account, divorced men are at nine times higher risk of suicide than divorced women (Kposowa, 2003).

11.3.2.2 *Family court and access to children*

The distress of family breakdown for men can be considerable (Collins, 2019). For example, a longitudinal study of 26 fathers dealing with the aftermath of family breakdown in the UK family court system found that repeated experiences of child access problems and family court problems were associated with chronic - almost clinical - levels of distress, as measured using the Positive Mindset Index (Barry & Liddon, 2020). It is known that family breakdown can lead to distress and even suicide (Sullivan, 2019). Some evidence suggests that men are more vulnerable in family/relationship breakdown than women. For example, divorced men are significantly more likely than married men to die from cardiovascular disease, hypertension and stroke and substance abuse, and are also more prone to depression and suicide than married men (Felix et al., 2013). The contribution of the various elements of a breakup to depression and suicide are only partially understood. There is some evidence that loss of children is a contributor (Shiner et al., 2009), but many aspects of the contributing factors are uncertain. For example, the timing when suicide is most likely to occur (e.g. during separation, during the family court process or years afterwards), and the degree to which preexisting personality factors such as low agreeableness (Stack, 2016) or rigidity of gender-typical thought patterns (Seager et al., 2014) impact depression and suicide, are unclear.

It is also important to consider disruption of the child's attachment to the father, because evidence suggests that the quality of childhood attachment is related to suicide risk (Zortea et al., 2019), though research typically does not differentiate between the impact of attachment to the father compared to the mother in these studies (see Section 4.4.1).

11.3.2.3 *Work/financial problems and suicide*

The second most common reason for suicide is work/money problems, accounting for 22% of suicides (Callanan & Davis, 2009). Although job satisfaction is strongly linked to having a positive mindset (Barry, 2020), work stress and unemployment can lead to serious mental health problems and suicide especially in men, which is why in times of economic recession, the gender suicide gap increases (Möller-Leimkühler, 2003). The type of occupation can be a relevant factor: some jobs involve pain-habituating and fear-habituating experiences (e.g. military training or combat experience) which leave men less averse to death and with an acquired capability for suicide (Bryan et al., 2010).

There is possibly an effect of generation on differences in suicide, related to financial issues. Generation X consists of the people born between around 1965–1980. In some countries (e.g. UK, Canada) it appears that this generation of men is more likely to die by suicide than older or younger generations (respectively, 'Baby boomers' or 'millennials'). The reasons for this are not fully known, but might be related to the relatively high uptake of opiate use by this generation in their early adulthood (Public Health England, 2018), or unemployment/financial problems that have recurred in the lives of people of this generation (BBC News, 2019).

11.3.2.4 *Pollution*

There is some evidence that lead poisoning can cause neurological damage and violent tendencies (Gesch, 2013) and anxiety and suicide (Fonseka et al., 2017). In some cases lead poisoning can be passive (e.g. from petrol fumes) or it can be active (e.g. inhaling petrol fumes to achieve intoxication) (Fonseka et al., 2017). General air pollution has also been associated with depression and suicide; a meta-analysis found that the risk of suicide is higher on days when coarse particulate air pollution (PM_{10}) levels were high over a three-day period, compared to the risk after less polluted periods (Braithwaite et al., 2020).

11.3.2.5 *Physical health problems and suicide*

Long-term health problems were associated with 28% of suicides, though were not necessarily the cause (Callanan & Davis, 2009). Analysis of 14,103 suicides in Denmark between 1995 and 2015 and a large sample of the general population found that physical health problems were a greater risk to men for suicide than to women (Gradus et al., 2020). Psychiatric disorders were also a predictor of suicide in men and women in the Danish study.

11.3.3 *Relationship Between Masculinity, Mental Health and Suicide*

Since the introduction of the deficit mode of masculinity in the 1990s, it has become the received wisdom that masculinity is a cause of mental health problems in men, including suicide (Kalish & Kimmel, 2010). However, the evidence for this unconvincing (see SPOTLIGHT box 12.2 Masculinity research: a review and critique and SPOTLIGHT box 11.3 The Man Box) and better research needs to be done, including research on the potential benefits of masculinity to mental health. For example, feeling good about masculinity is good for men's self-esteem (Burkley et al., 2016), and masculinity can be protective against suicidality (Mansdotter et al., 2009). Controlling for other variables, self-esteem and Positive Mindset Index (PMI) were significantly predicted by having a favourable view of traditional masculinity, in 203 men predominantly from the UK and North America (Barry, Walker et al., 2020). The mean age in this sample was 45 years old, which is around the age most at risk for suicide in men. PMI is inversely correlated with suicidality (Seager et al., 2014) which suggests that traditional masculinity might be protective against suicidality.

11.3.4 *Relationship Between Shame and Suicide*

Shame is like guilt, except that shame involves denigration of the self (Barr, 2004). It has been said that shame is the core emotion for understanding men (Englar-Carlson, 2019).

Although masculinity can be beneficial for men who feel they are living up to the standards of masculinity (e.g. Seager's gender scripts of being a fighter and winner, being a provider and protector and being able to control one's feelings), the major downside is the potential for shame for those who aren't able to meet these standards (Seager et al., 2014). For example, failing to be able to control one's feelings in a stressful situation can lead to shame.

There are many examples of how violating the gender scripts can lead to shame. Men with Traumatic Brain Injury (TBI) can feel shame at having to be reliant on others (MacQueen & Fisher 2019), thus failing in the provider role. Men in the military may be especially prone to shame due to pressure to not let themselves or others down (Eldridge & Fraser, 2019), or surviving when others in their unit have died (Shields & Westwood, 2019), thus violating the fight/win role and protector role. Shame is not just created internally, though. For example, realistic fear of an unsympathetic or even hostile reception from helplines or other services can exacerbate shame felt by male victims of domestic violence (Powney & Graham-K, 2019).

An important difference between Seager's interpretation of shame and sociocultural interpretations, such as that put forward by Kimmel (1994), is that the potential for shame is archetypal rather than socially learned. This is an important difference because it explains why efforts to get men to seek help and 'just open up' tend to fail, because this is inviting men to violate their instincts in a way that will make them feel ashamed (Seager, 2019). The sociocultural view implies that shame is the unnecessary product of not living up to unnecessary rules about manhood, which trivialises men's feelings of shame, and even implies that men should be ashamed of being ashamed.

SPOTLIGHT BOX 11.2

TRAUMA, SHAME, ANGER AND THERAPY

Trauma and shame in angry young men

People who are prone to shame are not inclined to talk about their shame, instead hiding away or becoming angry or aggressive with others. This may be particularly true in young men who have been exposed to violent trauma, often very early in life, who might also engage in criminal activity and experience anxiety, depression, eating difficulties, school truancy, self-harm, or substance use. However help-seeking tends to be much lower, and suicide higher, in these individuals. Studies have found that feeling guilt prevents further wrongdoing, but feeling shame does not, and in fact is associated with denial of responsibility and recidivism (Smith et al., 2019).

Reducing shame in therapy

'Positive masculinity is a counterbalance to shame ... offering growth, hope, expectancy, and encouragement to men by focusing attention on what is possible and healthy in their lives' (Englar-Carlson, 2019, p. xi). Therapy with men should be done bearing issues around masculinity and shame in mind. There are various ways of dealing with this, mostly based around harnessing useful aspects of masculinity. For example, men with TBI should be encouraged to take an active, if not leading, role in therapy (MacQueen & Fisher, 2019).

Much of the evidence suggests that men who feel shame act out in unhealthy ways, e.g. through aggression, violence or withdrawal. This suggests we should be careful not to shame men, for example, by promoting narratives such as toxic masculinity (Barry, Walker et al., 2020) or depicting men as foolish or other negative ways in the media (Nathanson & Young, 2001, 2006). Shame is a driver of destructive behaviours that can have negative consequences for everyone (*Theme: 'Unintended consequences',* 13.2.1).

11.3.5   *Women and Shame*

The idea of shame regarding not living up to gender norms is likely to impact women too, and it could be that trauma or difficulties related to the female gender scripts (i.e. beauty, fertility and family harmony) have a corresponding effect (Seager et al., 2014). It is also possible that both men and women react to feeling shame related to gender archetypes by withdrawing and not wanting to talk about their feelings. For example, an Australian longitudinal study of 86 men and 72 women reported feeling significantly more shame than men did one month and 13 months following the loss of their child, at between 20 weeks of pregnancy and 4 weeks after birth (Barr, 2004). Women's shame in this case might be related to the female gender scripts regarding fertility and family harmony.

11.3.6   *Suicide Prevention*

Although most suicides are by middle-aged men, much of the suicide prevention research has focused on young adults and teenagers (Bilsker et al., 2018). Some of the ways to prevent suicide are indicated by the causes of suicide. For example, if relationship problems are implicated, then ways to maintain healthy relationships are valuable.

11.3.6.1   *Marriage*

The importance of relationship stability to mental health is well established in the general population of men in the US and UK (Barry, 2020) and most research has found that in general an enduring marriage reduces the likelihood of men committing crime (Farrington, 1995; Durrant, 2019).

11.3.6.2   *Signs of suicidality*

Identifying signs of suicidality can be notoriously difficult. Good advice is to be watchful of suicidality in men going through a crisis, even though they may appear calm and rational (Bilsker et al., 2018). Men who experience suicidal thoughts are less likely than women to use mental health services (Hom et al., 2015). It can be difficult to distinguish between normal fluctuations in mood and those indicating suicide risk, and often the signs are subtle and only recognised in retrospect. A review of male suicide identified three main signs associated with completed suicide: anger, direct statement of suicidal intent and not seeing solutions to problems (Hunt et al., 2017). Other signs might include a change to a more positive mood, agitation, or talking about death or suicide in relation to themselves or someone else.

11.3.6.3 *Understanding transition from suicidal ideation to suicidal behaviour*

The integrated motivational–volitional (IMV) model of suicidal behaviour suggests that suicidal ideation is caused by a sense of being defeated and having no way out. Various moderating variables are said to influence whether suicidal ideation goes on to become completed suicide (O'Connor & Kirtley, 2018). The main moderators are access to the means of suicide, whether family member or friend has died by suicide, lack of a fear of death, having a plan, impulsivity, imagining being dead and a history of suicidal behaviour. This theoretical model has some empirical support, though prospective studies are needed to test how much the predictions of the model are proved in the real world.

11.3.6.4 *Ways to reduce suicide risk*

Interviews with 35 men in Australia who had attempted suicide, as well as interviews with 47 family and friends, identified several ways to interrupt progression to suicide. Practical help and emotional support was important, including 'helping men to focus on obligations and their role within families' (Player et al., 2015, p.1). Helping men to identify small achievable goals created a 'positive momentum'. Similarly, a survey of 251 Australian men who had attempted suicide found that 67% said that 'thinking about the consequences for their family' reduced the likelihood of future attempts (Shand et al., 2015, p. 4). The importance of family in being protective against suicide has long been recognised (Durkheim, 1897).

11.3.6.5 *Religion and suicide*

Although in declining popularity in some Western countries, there is some evidence that the beliefs and sense of community of religion promote resilience and a barrier to suicidality. A study of 1098 adolescents in the US found that commitment to religious beliefs was associated with less depression and suicidality (Greening & Stoppelbein, 2002). A cross-cultural study found that people who attempted suicide (n=2819) were less likely to be religious than others (n=5484). This was a statistically significant effect in Estonia, Brazil, Iran, Sri Lanka, and South Africa, though not in India or Vietnam (Sisak et al., 2010).

11.4 THERAPIES: CAN WE DO BETTER?

Despite evidence that men have a range of mental health issues (see above), men seek help for these less than women do. What can be done to improve this situation?

11.4.1 *Therapy is Feminised*

Mental health services providers have been criticised for taking a one-size-fits-all approach to therapy that is based on the needs of the average female client (Morison et al., 2014). This model – which might not fit all women – is of therapy as a talking cure where the client discusses their feelings (Ogrodniczuk et al., 2016). The historical reasons for therapy being formulated in this way are a matter for debate, but it could be based on Sigmund Freud's clinical experience, which used predominantly middle-class female clients in Vienna.

The different needs, in general, of men and women can be summarised by the idea that *men want a quick fix to their problem and women want to explore their feelings* (Holloway et al., 2018). Whether this sex difference is caused by nature or nurture is a moot point, though from a practical and empathic standpoint it makes sense to 'meet the client where they are at', i.e. conduct therapy in a way that the client is ready to. However we should be careful not to presume that men don't benefit from talking about their feelings, and approaching this aspect of therapy indirectly can help this important process begin (see Figure 11.3). So although a nuanced approach will help men to open up, with most psychologists being women and with services relying on a 'feminised' style of therapy (emphasising talking about feelings etc), some men get the sense that mental health services are not really for them, and one study found that suicidal men were at increased risk of sex and drug use when faced with intolerant attitudes from health care providers.

Male stoicism is sometimes blamed for men's mental health problems and lack of help-seeking, but rational emotive behaviour therapy (REBT) is a very effective therapy, yet is based on the philosophy of the stoics. It teaches people not to ignore their feelings, but to cope with them by putting them in perspective (see Rethinking stoicism 12.6.3). Stoicism – like anything – can be used in a negative way, but if men tend to cope using stoicism then it makes sense to harness this as part of therapy rather than dismiss it as a faulty aspect of masculinity. Other treatment approaches that are solution-focused rather than emotion-focused might be useful for men too, such as life coaching (Russ et al., 2015), hardiness training, self-efficacy or more recent approaches such as resilience training (Hoelterhoff & Chung, 2020; Reivich et al., 2011; Robertson et al., 2015).

The elements that help to make therapy male-friendly are discussed below (see Figure 11.3) after an exploration of recent trends in psychology for men (*Theme: 'One-size-fits-all'*, 13.2.4).

11.4.2 *Therapy for Men: Survey of APA Psychologists*

A survey of 475 psychologists from the APA aimed to identify practices that would be helpful or harmful in therapy for men and boys (Mahalik et al., 2012). Most respondents were male (64%), mean age 53 years old, white (87%), heterosexual (82%), with an average of 19.5 years in practice, seeing 17 clients per week, mostly in private practice (59.14%), using an integrative/eclectic orientation (55%) or cognitive behavioural therapy (CBT) (30%). In total 49% considered therapy with men one of their areas of specialisation, having seen around 100–250 male clients during their career. Apart from being a mostly male sample, they were probably a fairly representative sample of US psychologists (see SPOTLIGHT box 7.1: Why are there not more male psychologists?).

Ten themes emerged from qualitative analyses. The issue most frequently endorsed by participants was 'Emotions in Therapy'. This issue included ideas such as 'practitioners shouldn't think that clients who have difficulty exploring their feelings are unsuitable for therapy'. This is a key issue (e.g. Holloway et al., 2018), and despite being the theme most endorsed by participants, it was ranked by the researchers as fifth out of ten, for reasons that were not made clear.

Besides the ranking of the themes, the choice of which material to exclude was interesting. As part of the content analysis/review process, the researchers excluded some material in order to maintain the research focus on gender-relevant issues in working with males, rather than focus on general therapeutic practices. This was unfortunate because it meant excluding some key themes in male psychology, such as 'positively relating to the client, therapist relationship and process problems [i.e. the therapists' ability to engage with different kinds of clients], not shaming clients, being knowledgeable to the trauma histories of abusive males...' (Mahalik et al., 2012, p. 594; see SPOTLIGHT box 11.2; Section 11.4.5; Figure 11.3). The exclusion of these themes means the findings and conclusions of the study are not entirely based on the information given by the study's participants. Had this information been included, the conclusions of the study might have been more helpful for male clients.

The decision-making regarding exclusion might be connected to something recognised by the researchers as a weakness of their study:

'the themes identified may be idiosyncratic to the researchers involved in data synthesis. For example, all researchers were pro-feminist White males who bring a critical perspective on traditional gender roles. To address this, we relied on a rigorous process of cross-checking and auditing' (Mahalik et al., 2012, p. 601). 'Critical' here is not used in the everyday meaning of the word. Taking a *critical perspective on traditional gender roles* means making the radical assumptions that (a) gender roles are harmful, and (b) gender roles are social constructs, without biological influence. These assumptions recur in other recent approaches to men's mental health, and are discussed further below (see Section 11.4.3).

Regardless of whether the therapists who participated in this study took a *critical perspective* on traditional gender roles or not, the information they gave was interpreted through the critical lens. This in itself would make the focus on social constructionist material unsurprising, and the decision to exclude some very interesting and relevant material. The claim that the cross-checking and audit of the themes was 'rigorous' means less because it was done by members of the research team all of whom shared the same viewpoint, thus the findings inevitably reflect their pro-feminist critical perspective on traditional gender roles.

This was a potentially very valuable study, and a reanalysis of the raw survey data by a less radical research team might produce quite different findings.

11.4.3   *What is the Critical Perspective on Traditional Gender Roles?*

Criticism, in the sense of analysis and evaluation, is essential to science, but the term 'critical' has a totally different meaning when it comes to gender studies and an increasing number of other fields in academia (Pluckrose & Lindsay, 2020). Critical theory has its roots in the Marxist idea of using criticism with the aim of eroding the power of one class over another (see also Section 12.2). From the critical perspective, any gender inequality is seen as the result of power imbalance and oppression, rather than biological factors or personal preferences. Citing several authors on the topic, Blyler (1998) says: 'the critical perspective is concerned not with describing and explaining a given aspect of reality, but rather … [the] relationship between knowledge and politics', hence its rejection of "the innocence and neutrality of knowledge" … Critical research, therefore, aims at empowerment … and emancipation: By "introduc[ing] radical doubt into sedimented modes of thought," critical research "foster[s] the kind of self-reflection that enables us to recognize how it is that common sense understandings of the world arise"' (Blyler, 1998, p. 36). In other words, the critical perspective does not aim to be objective and scientific, let alone aim for common sense, but aims to 'emancipate' people from scientific and common sense views of the world by introducing 'radical doubt' into studies of gender, or whatever field of study it is applied to. In relation to the study by Mahalik et al. (2012), the influence of the critical perspective means that the research is not intended to discover something new and objectively real, but has a quasi-political aim of causing people to doubt their ideas about masculinity, and 'emancipate' men from traditional gender roles. Similar concepts inform other material relevant to male psychology, such as the 'critical realism' which informs the Power Threat Meaning Framework (PTMF) (Johnstone & Boyle, 2018, p. 57).

This critical perspective has increased in influence in the social sciences and other academic subjects (Pluckrose & Lindsay, 2020). For example, one paper promoting the critical perspective claims that 'women's studies pedagogies have equipped students with the necessary tools to see any field, any course, and any future career through a critical lens', making it 'an infectious discipline – one that serves not only as a virus that attaches to the "host" bodies of other disciplines and disrupts and infects them, but one that fundamentally alters the cell's blueprint and directs it to a new purpose' (Fahs & Karger, 2016, p. 945). This purpose is in contrast to what is being attempted by biological and evolutionary approaches to psychology, which aim to be as objective and scientific as possible. It would be very helpful if all papers were as open as that of Fahs and Karger in declaring their aims. Critical theorists have become more vocal in declaring their position in the last few years, meaning that at least we are in a better position to be able to distinguish which research aims to meet the standards of science and which does not.

11.4.4   *The APA Guidelines on Therapy for Boys and Men*

Division 51 (Men and Masculinities) of the *APA guidelines for psychological practice with boys and men* includes some material of value (American Psychological Association, Boys and Men Guidelines Group, 2018). For example, Guideline 5 encourages the involvement of the father in raising children, and Guideline 9 offers some good advice on creating a male-friendly therapy. However, the APA guidelines cite Mahalik et al. (2012) several times, and the guidelines replicate the flaws of the critical perspective.

The introduction to the guidelines states that 'socialization for conforming to traditional masculinity ideology has been shown to limit males' psychological development, constrain their behavior ... and negatively influence mental health ... and physical health ... Indeed, boys and men are overrepresented in a variety of psychological and social problems' (American Psychological Association, Boys and Men Guidelines Group, p. 3). However, evidence that masculinity causes mental health problems does not have a very convincing evidence base (see SPOTLIGHT box 11.3), and in fact there is evidence suggesting that traditional masculinity might be good for self-esteem (Burkley et al., 2016) and mental positivity (Barry, Walker et al., 2020), and even protective against suicidality (Mansdotter et al., 2009). Previous chapters have shown there are a variety of explanations other than masculinity for physical health problems and social problems. For example, the causes of some learning difficulties (e.g. dyslexia) are unlikely to be related to gender socialisation (see Section 5.2.3). In fact it seems odd to focus on masculinity – which is potentially helpful to men – when other issues that are potentially damaging, e.g. the role of trauma in male violence, are more likely to be related to mental illness.

Let's look now at the key weak points in the guidelines.

APA Guideline 1

The critical perspective is most apparent in Guidelines 1 and 3. The first guideline states that 'masculinities are constructed based on social, cultural and contextual norms' (American Psychological Association, Boys and Men Guidelines Group, p. 6). Although socialisation influences the expression of masculinity, the assumption that this is the only influence on masculinity is false, as is demonstrated by the abundant evidence for the biological influences on masculinity (see Section 3.7.2.1). This is an important issue for therapy, because the presumption that masculinity is merely learned implies that it can merely be unlearned, without recognising that male biology and evolved traits cannot be simply unlearned. Using a talking therapy to change innate factors is swimming against the tide of evolutionary forces. For example, if men have an innate tendency towards being competitive, then treating competitiveness as a flawed aspect of traditional masculinity is not only incorrect, but also alienating for a client who has experienced – from childhood onwards – competitiveness as a fundamental and positive part of their life.

APA Guideline 3

The third guideline claims that on average, 'males experience a greater degree of social and economic power than girls and women in a patriarchal society' (American Psychological Association, Boys and Men Guidelines Group, p. 9). Although this statement might be true in some parts of the world or at a different point in history, it is difficult to justify this statement with regard to modern countries such as the US. In fact men are disadvantaged in many countries worldwide today, especially those with medium to high levels of development (Stoet & Geary, 2019). Guideline 3 is influenced by gamma bias, magnifying advantages that men have and minimising disadvantages, and simultaneously minimising advantages that women have and magnifying disadvantages (Seager & Barry, 2019). Many examples can be cited, e.g. magnifying the greater number of men in top jobs and minimising equality schemes promoting women into top jobs, or minimising the existence of male victims of domestic violence (at least 30% of victims are male) and magnifying the plight of female victims (see Sections 8.3.6.3.1 and 2.5.5.1). A survey of 107 therapists found those who practice male-friendly therapy (Guideline 9) were significantly less likely to believe in the social construction of masculinity (Guideline 1) and a harmful patriarchy (Guideline 3), casting doubt on the coherence of the APA guidelines (Barry et al, in press).

Although practitioners are free to follow these guidelines or not, the APA is a major accrediting body which means its guidelines will be on the curriculum of many trainings and adopted by many trainees accordingly. In the UK, a widely promoted document contains sentiments similar to the APA's Guidelines 1 and 3 (see pp. 124–8 of the long version (412 pages in total) of the PTMF; Johnstone & Boyle (2018)). There is also a version in Australia (APS, 2017), suggesting masculinity is a social construct, is restrictive and may cause problems such as homophobia, violence against women etc.

11.4.5   *Impact on the Therapeutic Alliance*

The therapeutic alliance – the bond of goodwill and empathy between client and therapist – has been consistently found to contribute moderately (Pearson's $r = {\sim}.3$) to the success of therapy, regardless of what type of psychological intervention is used (Del Re et al., 2012). An online survey of 1000 Canadian men found that they were more likely to opt for individual psychotherapy or medication if they had positive perceptions of the patient–doctor relationship (Kealy et al., 2019). One of the findings of a systematic review of 71 studies was that men have less confidence in mental health professionals than women do (Prins et al., 2008). It makes sense therefore that therapists should be careful not to engage in practices that might undermine therapeutic alliance. For example, the 'patriarchy' narrative seems to cast the average man in an unfavourable light, and unless the client explicitly rejects patriarchy and traditional masculinity, it is difficult to see how it might enhance the therapeutic alliance with the average man. To take two examples, it has been claimed that masculinity/patriarchy are an impediment to women's careers (Rao, 2016), and can cause problems in relationships (Johnstone & Boyle, 2018). However, how might a male client feel who has work or relationship problems, and is told by his therapist that his masculinity is part of the problem? A survey asked 203 men how happy they would feel if problems with their job were blamed on their masculinity: 86.7% said they would feel unhappy or very unhappy. A similar question about blaming their masculinity for relationship problems found 87.5% of men would feel unhappy or very unhappy. The 52 women in the survey were just as unhappy when asked the same questions: 94.1% said they would be unhappy or very unhappy if their femininity was blamed for job problems, and 84.6% if blamed for relationship problems (Barry, Walker et al, 2020). These findings clearly indicate that people are unhappy about their gender being blamed for their problems. Although these questions were not asked specifically in relation to therapy, it is easy to see how blaming gender could alienate clients and even potentially be harmful: 'in disparaging masculinity as a whole, whether explicitly or implicitly, advocates can do real harm to boys and men themselves, particularly those who cannot live up to these new gender roles' (Ferguson, 2018). This makes guidelines 1 and 3 questionable in terms of Principle A of the APA Code of Ethics, which states that 'Psychologists strive to benefit those with whom they work and take care to do no harm' (APA, 2002, p. 1062). Similarly, the BPS says: 'Conversion therapy is the term for therapy that assumes certain sexual orientations or gender identities are inferior to others and seeks to change or suppress them. It is unethical, potentially harmful and is not based on any reputable evidence' (BPS, 2019, p. 3). Given that men are already less likely to seek help for mental health issues than are women, it is difficult to justify such guidelines, especially in the context of therapy when people are psychologically vulnerable.

It is likely that male clients might be perplexed to find themselves cast as privileged and powerful, especially if their presenting problems are relatively common issues for men, such as being unemployed or being the victim of domestic violence by a woman (around 30% of domestic violence victims are male). In therapy in general, it is considered problematic if therapists impose their beliefs on the client, don't respect the client's gender identity or encourage the client to blame others for their problems (Shenfeld, 2019). Therapists therefore need to be aware of any assumptions about masculinity that may cause them to see clients in a biased way (Liu, 2005). This applies to therapists of all therapeutic perspectives.

11.5 MALE HELP-SEEKING AND MENTAL HEALTH ISSUES

In various parts of the world, men use mental health services less than women do. For example, North American men are about half as likely to use mental health services as women are (Affleck et al., 2018). In the literature on help-seeking for major depression, the barriers are: being young or elderly, being male (sometimes attributed to hegemonic masculinity) belonging to certain ethnic groups and having a lower educational status (Magaard et al., 2017; Wong et al., 2017). Other issues can impact help-seeking, such as men's tendency to see depression as less severe or more brief than women do (Edwards et al., 2007) and men's mental health issues being asked about less and diagnosed less than women's in primary care (Affleck et al., 2018). This section looks at the causes of men's help-seeking for psychological support.

11.5.1 *Masculinity and Help-Seeking For Mental Health*

It has become so commonplace to say that masculinity is bad for help-seeking (e.g. Möller-Leimkühler, 2002) that it is more or less taken as a given. However, various factors influence help-seeking, such as occupation, ethnicity and especially age.

11.5.1.1 *Occupation*

The review by Clement et al. (2015) found that mental health stigma is generally ranked much higher among military personnel than in other occupations or demographics, especially in relation to concerns about anonymity and employment-related discrimination (Ministry of Defence, 2018). Interestingly, health professionals reported that shame, embarrassment and negative social judgement were barriers to them for mental health help-seeking (Clement et al., 2015).

11.5.1.2 *Ethnicity*

Taking men and women together, the review by Clement et al. (2015) found a large negative association between stigma and help-seeking in Arabic students (Israel/US) and Asian American people (US). There was a small negative association for African American people (US), but there was no association for Latino, Cuban and Puerto Rican people (US). This latter finding is interesting, given the reputation for machismo of Latin American men (Opazo, 2008).

11.5.1.3 *Age and masculinity as barriers to help-seeking*

A meta-analysis of 41 studies of help-seeking for psychological and medical issues found the main barriers were: '(1) embarrassment/anxiety/distress/fear related to using health-care services; (2) need for emotional control/guarded vulnerability; (3) viewing symptoms as minor and insignificant, and (4) poor communication/rapport with health professionals' (Yousaf et al., 2015, p. 271). The authors commented in the conclusions that the findings 'support the theoretical view that adherence to traditional masculinity norms reduces men's willingness to seek help' (Yousaf et al., 2015, p. 272).

Of the 41 studies, 16 were on psychological health, and in these studies the barriers were discussed in terms of masculine norms preventing help-seeking, and emotional control. These studies were also, in most cases, samples of young men in their early 20s in the US. In one case the sample was of high-school football players in the American Midwest with a mean (SD) age of 15.7 (1.3) (Steinfeldt & Steinfeldt, 2010). The studies with older samples revealed fewer issues with masculine norms, but other issues emerged. For example, an Australian study (Cusack et al., 2006) and a Canadian study (Johnson et al., 2012) of men, aged around their mid-30s on average, found that the key contextual barrier was the lack of a collaborative bond with the therapist (see also Section 11.4.5).

11.5.1.4   *Age, stigma and help-seeking*

A review of the impact of stigma on help-seeking found an effect of age, such that men and women under 18 years old tended to feel more acutely than older people discomfort about not being 'normal' if they had a mental health problem (Clement et al., 2015). At this young age, when identity formation and wanting to 'fit in' are important, it's a normal part of development for masculinity attitudes to intensify across early adolescence (Galambos et al., 1990), and these attitudes tend to decrease from early adulthood and older adulthood (Rice et al., 2011; Smiler, 2006). For men in the military it is more normal for strong identification with masculinity norms to continue into adulthood, though for some men this level of identification with masculinity can be associated with depression (Rice et al., 2011).

These findings suggest that it is normal for young men, typically going through a turbulent period of identity formation and social pressure, to display problems with mental health and help-seeking. It is surprising that the link between age, masculinity and help-seeking is so often overlooked in research, and that the common assumption is that masculinity *per se* reduces help-seeking (see SPOTLIGHT box 12.2).

Although studies of help-seeking and masculinity in young men are definitely of value, the findings don't seem to generalise very well to older men. To be of value, future research on this topic needs to clearly delineate the impact of age on the relationship between masculinity and help-seeking.

SPOTLIGHT BOX 11.3

THE MAN BOX

The Man Box is a concept used for 'gender transformative interventions and programs', i.e. the idea is that it is used to change masculinity in various non-clinical settings, such as mentoring programmes and workshops (Heilman et al., 2017, p. 5). The idea is influenced by sociologists R. W. Connell (who invented hegemonic masculinity) and Michael Kimmell (see Section 12.2.1) and funded by the multinational consumer goods company Unilever.

According to the Man Box idea, masculinity is rigid and keeps men stuck in a box emotionally. 'The seven pillars of masculinity' are said to be rigid, and cause depression and suicidality. The pillars include acting tough, being homophobic and being aggressive and controlling towards men and women. A survey of around 3675 men in the US, UK and Mexico found higher Man Box scores were correlated with depression and suicidality, as measured by the Patient Health Questionnaire-2 (PHQ-2; Heilman et al., 2017).

However, there are several problems with the Man Box:

- The Man Box is a social construct, and defines masculinity in an unrealistically negative way.
- Most participants in the Man Box study didn't identify with the 'pillars of masculinity' questions. For example, 20% or fewer agreed that 'men should use violence to get respect, if necessary' or that 'a husband shouldn't have to do household chores' (Heilman et al., 2017, p. 9).
- Psychologists familiar with REBT know that any ideas that are held rigidly can cause mental health problems stressful (Seager et al., 2014), which applies as much to masculinity as to any other values.
- Correlation between Man Box scores and poor mental health does not prove that poor mental health is caused by higher Man Box scores. More likely explanations are that one or more other variables influence Man Box scores and mental health scores. For example, men suffering from PTSD, or male-typical depression, might score higher on the Man Box questions about aggression, thus have worse mental health scores (see Section 11.2.1.1).
- The sample was of young men (aged 18–30), ~75% never married, and ~50% with any education beyond high school. As seen elsewhere, masculinity scores in young men of college age tend to be much higher than in other men. In other words, the Man Box findings probably don't generalise to men over around age 30.
- There were unusually high levels of depression and suicidality in the Man Box sample. Normally, only 6.5% of men of this age would score over three on the PHQ-2 depression scale (Löwe et al., 2010), but in the Man Box study 71% of men in the US and UK had a depression score of three or more. The authors acknowledged that this was 'extremely high'. Such unusually high mental health scores mean that the findings of this study can't be generalised to the average man, whether young or more mature.

By contrast, much more emotional maturity was found in two large surveys of older men (average ~37 years old), in the US and UK, around half of whom were married and had a college education or higher (Barry 2020). These two surveys didn't ask questions related to hegemonic masculinity, and those participants probably wouldn't have identified with the hegemonic questions any more than the majority of men in the Man Box study did. Nonetheless, the minority 20% of Man Box views are presented as representative of all men.

The Man Box reports states that the authors want to 'create a world free from violence', but it is questionable whether this report, being based on a sample of young men with a high rate of mental health problems, applies very much to the rest of the world (Heilman et al., 2017, p. 5). In the real world women commit violence too (see Sections 8.4.3 and 8.3.6.3.1), but the Man Box report shows gamma bias in acknowledging only violence by men.

In theory, virtually any intervention can be made male-friendly (see Figure 11.3), and the basic idea of getting young men to question their values around antisocial behaviours could be of benefit. However, the idea of blaming antisocial behaviours on masculinity risks making men feel ashamed of a core part of themselves. As noted previously, shamed men are more likely to be violent (SPOTLIGHT box 11.2).

11.5.2 *The Impact of Stigma*

In their meta-synthesis of 144 studies of the impact of stigma related to help-seeking for mental health, men were more likely than women to report stigma-related barriers, and more likely to report difficulty talking to health professionals (Clement et al., 2015). Of the 44 studies specifically on barriers to help-seeking ($n = 60,036$ male and female participants), the review found stigma had a moderately negative impact on help-seeking, compared to other barriers, and was ranked only fourth as a barrier (cited by 21% of participants). The main barrier, reported by 32% of participants, was general 'disclosure concerns' regarding confidentiality. The second barrier, reported by 23% of participants, was 'anticipated/experienced employment-related discrimination'. Third (22% of participants) was 'anticipated/experienced prejudice/negative social judgment' (Clement et al. 2015, p. 22). This meta-synthesis provides valuable information, but would have been improved had they been able to disaggregate all the findings by gender, but could do so only 35% of the studies.

11.5.3 *Improving Help-Seeking in Men*

There are signs that men today take their mental health more seriously (Barry, 2020) and there are success stories in the world of men's help-seeking. For example, perhaps because of public health campaigns like *Beyondblue*, the proportion of men in Australia who are getting help for their mental health problems increased from 32% to 40% between 2006 and 2012 (Harris et al., 2015). There is some evidence that men will join a therapy group when it is to support other men rather than for themselves (Sierra Hernandez et al., 2014; Shields & Westwood, 2019). This spontaneous supportive behaviour might be seen as an example of the traditional male protector role (Seager et al., 2014).

11.5.3.1 *Role models and credible sources as facilitators of help-seeking*

Some research suggest that role models and people considered credible sources can act as facilitators of help-seeking (Sagar-Ouriaghli et al., 2019). For example, endorsement of mental health treatment by leaders in the military (Section 9.4.1.3) and business organisations (Russ et al., 2015) can be very helpful. This might in part be due to reducing employee fears about the impact of disclosure on their career prospects (Clement et al., 2015).

A systematic review and synthesis of nine studies found that several strategies improve men's mental health help-seeking (Sagar-Ouriaghli et al., 2019). These included 'using role models to convey information, psychoeducational material to improve mental health knowledge, assistance with recognizing and managing symptoms, active problem-solving tasks, motivating behavior change, signposting services, and, finally, content that built on positive male traits (e.g., responsibility and strength)' (Sagar-Ouriaghli et al., 2019, pp. 11–12). Assessment using a novel Behaviour Change Technique taxonomy indicated that these various processes – in various combinations – helped improve aspects of help-seeking. The review by Sagar-Ouriaghli et al. is interesting in highlighting how little research has been done on this important topic. More good quality research projects, followed by a meta-analysis, are needed in this field.

11.5.3.2   *Promoting male help-seeking*

A multi-phase assessment of proven strategies of mental health promotion aimed at men suggested various ways to make strategies more male-friendly (Robertson et al., 2018). The suggestions are similar to those for physical health promotion (Oliffe et al., 2019; see SPOTLIGHT box 10.3).

Theoretical models have sometimes been applied to promoting help-seeking for mental health issues. The Theory of Planned Behaviour (TPB) is a popular model of cognition used widely in health promotion and advertising. Using material based on the TPB, videos presented to 97 male and 131 female US psychology students showed mixed success (Demyan & Anderson, 2012). The intervention was successful in making attitudes to help-seeking for psychological support more positive, and men reported being more likely than women to seek treatment, but only if they were experiencing clinical levels of distress and had a prior history of seeking help. For men and women, barriers to help-seeking, such as treatment fears, help-seeking stigma and disclosure distress, did not significantly change.

11.5.3.3   *Suicide, health promotion and victim blaming*

The billboard in Figure 11.2 is from the *US Agency for Healthcare Research and Quality*, was designed to reduce male suicide by encouraging men to seek help. Their slogan was *This year thousands of men will die from stubbornness*, and the spray painted response was *No we won't*. This neatly demonstrates two things: firstly, men's supposed stubbornness is blamed for their suicides. Secondly, if you blame people for their problems they are unlikely to respond positively. Thirdly, the fact that women's health is handled with greater sensitivity to social factors that cause problems (Whitley, 2018) hints at an unconscious bias against men. This can be seen as an example of the gender empathy gap (Collins, 2019), and is an aspect of the wider *gamma bias* that is not difficult to find in our culture (Seager & Barry, 2019) (Section 2.5.5.1).

FIGURE 11.2 *Graffitied billboard. The advertising campaign was by the US Agency for Healthcare Research and Quality, designed to reduce male suicide by encouraging men to seek help.*

11.5.4 *Impact of Men's Mental Health in the Media*

There is undoubtedly intuitive appeal in the idea that stories about the mental health problems of celebrities would be a good way of raising awareness, reducing stigma and increasing acceptance of the normality of mental health problems. One would expect a greater openness to seeking therapy, or talking with friends or family about these issues, thus reducing the intensity of the problems. For example, it has been speculated that more men have sought therapy as a result of the TV show *The Sopranos* (Barry & Seager, 2014), which depicted a fictional hypermasculine mob boss, Tony Soprano, in therapy. It makes intuitive sense that this might be a good example for hypermasculine men, but given that Soprano's therapy is depicted as ultimately unhelpful, and some of the issues he raised in therapy, such as being the victim of domestic violence, were either not treated seriously or ignored, it would be surprising if this depiction encouraged men to therapy.

There is little actual research on the influence of media coverage of mental health issues, but what exists suggests that the influence tends not to be positive, perhaps because the stories are so tragic. For example, in the six months following the death of comedian and actor Robin Williams there was an increase of nearly 10% in suicides in the general population of the US (Fink et al., 2018). A large study lasting five years recorded more than 80,000 crisis episodes in two London NHS Foundation Trusts. The researchers found that higher volumes of depression and schizophrenia tweets on Twitter, in response to stories about mental health in the media, were associated with higher numbers of same-day crisis episodes at the hospitals (Kolliakou et al., 2020). The authors interpreted the findings as evidence of media reports influencing mental health problems rather than increasing help-seeking for existing mental health problems.

11.5.5   *Negative Experiences of 'Opening Up'*

Men with masculine norms can be more inclined to seek professional help after talking with a female relative e.g. mother or partner (Lane & Addis, 2005). A survey of 4000 men in the UK, US, Canada and Australia (1000 men aged 18–75 in each country) found that 57% were relatively comfortable speaking with a doctor at a doctor's surgery (Movember, 2019). Of the men surveyed, 50% said they had a positive experience of opening up to someone about a problem, but 41% said they regretted opening up. Of these, 45% said their regret was because the person they were talking to did not seem to respect them or care about their problem, and 30% said it was because the person did not take them seriously. In all, 53% of these men said this experience would definitely or probably prevent them from opening up again. However, of the men who had a negative experience of talking openly, 52% also had a positive experience of doing so too; 65% of these men felt better after talking, 50% felt they could handle their problems better, 40% had ideas for how to improve their situation and 34% felt closer to the person they talked to. This study indicates that following advice to just talk about your problems doesn't always lead to help.

11.5.6   *Help-Seeking and Victim-Blaming*

In general, men tend to be seen as responsible for maintaining their physical and mental health, which means that when their health fails for whatever reason, the responsibility falls to men. Taking responsibility is good where appropriate, but if there are other reasons for a man's ill health, for example, lack of suitable healthcare, then holding him responsible for his ill health is 'victim-blaming' (Whitley, 2018). The victim-blaming approach probably contributes to men's lack of help-seeking, to poor therapeutic alliance and to drop-out from therapy (Whitley, 2018). This approach takes a narrow view of the causes of men's mental health problems, which results in a narrow range of solutions. For example, in men's mental health the strategy often seems to rely on repeating unsuccessful strategies, e.g. urging men to 'talk more', probably creating a 'leaky pipeline' of men not getting much from therapy, and dropping out.

The focus on reforming masculinity to reduce mental illness can be seen as an example of victim-blaming, even if couched in the notion that it's not men's fault that they are socialised into a dysfunctional traditional masculinity. The

APA, APS, PTMF (Section 12.3.1), European Parliament (Basterrechea, 2016) and World Health Organization (Manandhar et al., 2018) take a predominantly negative view of masculinity. However, not all organisations take this view. For example, in the UK, the Male Psychology Section of the British Psychological Society takes a more humanistic view of masculinity (similar to the positive psychology/positive masculinity (PPPM) approach: Section 11.6.1.2), and the Men's Health Initiative of British Columbia (Bilsker et al., 2010) recognises the problem of alienating men by undervaluing male traits.

If men are concerned they will seem weak by seeking therapy, and this is a legitimate concern if others – including employers – see it as a weakness then it makes sense to focus on the structural aspect of this issue, not just focus on the level of masculinity. But if we do focus on masculinity, rather than try to persuade men to restructure core parts to their being, it is much more in keeping with the principle of empathy in therapy to understand their point of view and try to work 'with the grain' where possible, by finding ways in which their masculinity can help them deal with their problems effectively.

11.5.7 'Hard-to-Reach' Men

The wind speed of the strongest tornados is a challenge to measure because the measuring equipment gets destroyed in the maelstrom. Similarly, we don't really know the problems of men who don't seek therapy, even though it is possible that they experience the most severe difficulties of anyone. An important issue in help-seeking research is to find out more about those who are least likely to seek help. This is a difficult issue. For example, autism is at least *12 times* more common in homeless people than in the general population (Churchard et al., 2019) and being homeless and autistic probably both make help-seeking more difficult (see Section 9.4.2).

11.6 MALE-FRIENDLY THERAPIES FOR PSYCHOLOGICAL AND EMOTIONAL WELLBEING

The previous sections raise the question of whether men would be more likely to seek psychological help if it were more male-friendly. Although 'many countries have mental health strategies that acknowledge gender differences, very few articulate strategies aimed at men' (Bilsker et al., 2018, p. 594). What kinds of changes would they need to make to accommodate men's mental health in clinical settings? The following section shows how a therapy doesn't need to change radically to become more male-friendly.

11.6.1 *What is a Male-Friendly Therapy?*

Men will often only seek counselling as a last resort (Russ et al., 2015; Bilsker et al., 2018). Apart from other barriers to help-seeking (see Section 12.6.1) it could be that men would be more willing to seek help if male-friendly options were more available and visible (Liddon et al., 2017).

11.6.1.1 *What does a male-friendly therapy look like?*
Evidence suggests that there are few sex differences in the type of therapy preferred, though it appears men like support groups more than women do, probably due to the emphasis on sharing information rather than feelings, and there is a statistically non-significant trend towards women liking psychotherapy more than men do, probably because it is more feelings-focused relative to some other therapies (Liddon et al., 2017).

Probably more important than the type of therapy is how male-friendly the therapist makes the therapy. The elements that help to make a therapy more male-friendly are identified in Figure 11.3 and outlined in the remainder of this chapter.

11.6.1.2 *Positive psychology/positive masculinity (PPPM) approach*
The PPPM approach (Kiselica & Englar-Carlson, 2010) suggests that better rapport and outcomes can be achieved by focusing on the potential strengths rather than the weaknesses of traditional masculinity. There is some evidence suggesting that PPPM values can be successful in building rapport with male clients, and further research would be helpful to explore the range of applications of this approach (Kiselica, 2008).

11.6.1.3 *Male-friendly approaches applied to existing therapies*
More generally, male-friendly approaches, such as those described in Figure 11.3, have already been applied in various ways to existing therapies, e.g. Cognitive Behavioural Therapy (CBT; Cairns & Howells, 2019; Chheda-Varma, 2019), adaptations of CBT (using the Threat Reaction/Threat Response model; Kingerlee, Abotsie, et al., 2019a); Cognitive Analytic Therapy (Kingerlee, Cawdron, et al., 2019b); Compassion Focused Therapy (Smith et al., 2019); Acceptance and Commitment Therapy (Bolster & Berzengi, 2019); Existential Therapy (Groth, 2019); and Eye Movement Desensitisation and Reprocessing (Kingerlee, 2019), and more. In other words, there isn't a specific male-friendly therapy as such, just ways to make any therapy more male-friendly.

Approach	Element	Application
Therapist	Empathy.	The key element for therapeutic alliance. Must be authentic.
	Client-centred.	Resist making assumptions e.g. if client says he is a victim of domestic violence, don't presume he is a perpetrator.
	Value masculine norms.	Respect masculine norms e.g. controlling feelings: 'seeking help means you are taking control of your feelings, and then better able to fix the problem'.
	Utilisation.	Use client's characteristics to their benefit e.g. if interested in sports, use sports as a metaphor for recovery.
	Demographics.	Understand specific issues based on age, background, education, ethnic group, sexuality, disability etc.
	Sex of therapist.	Check whether the client would prefer a male therapist.
Therapy	Indirect approach.	Start with solution focused approach and direct therapy to feelings only when client is ready to. Client may prefer to fix the problem rather than discuss feelings.
	Group.	Offer all-male groups as well as one-to-one therapy.
Techniques	Language.	Some language can be off-putting for men e.g. 'therapy'. Use other terms e.g. 'strategies for living'.
	Banter.	Men might use humour to deal with stress, build rapport & communicate meaningful information.
	Non-verbal communication.	Eye contact might be uncomfortable for men, especially if rapport is not established.

FIGURE 11.3 *Elements that help to make a therapy more male-friendly (based on Liddon et al., 2019).*

11.6.2 *Recognising and Valuing Different Coping Strategies*

Boys and girls aged seven, in a story completion task, indicated using different coping styles for stressful situations, with boys using more self-care and displacement strategies (e.g. watching TV) and girls finding it less easy to resolve distress (Del Giudice, 2008). In light of this perhaps we should not be surprised if men and women tend to have different coping strategies too.

11.6.2.1 Masculinity, coping and stress

It should go without saying but not all men are the same, so when it comes to dealing with stress they might use various strategies, from seeking a therapist to seeking alcohol (Bilsker et al., 2018). Strategies such as substance abuse, stoicism, shunning outside help, and risky behaviours – especially when done rigidly, in a context of social isolation and withdrawal from relationships – are said to increase the risk of suicide (Bilsker et al., 2018). However, there is evidence that traditional male coping can be positive e.g. social drinking in pubs (Dunbar et al., 2017), or reframing help-seeking as taking responsibility for being healthy in order to take care of others (the provider role) (Roy et al., 2014), or being brave or strong (Erdem et al., 2020). Another example is of taking control, where giving men control over choosing their own treatment plan can potentially help with uptake to therapy (Pollard, 2016).

An important point is the context of the behaviour. Similar to how the fight-or-flight response is adaptive in emergency situations where strength and adrenaline are needed but not situations where quiet reflection is needed, male-typical coping strategies can be adaptive in some situations, e.g. staying calm and stoical in an emergency situation, or taking a brief period of isolation to relieve stress (Bilsker et al., 2018). However, the value of these strategies is lost when used rigidly or excessively, which can lead to a wide range of negative consequences (Bilsker et al., 2018). The context is important too, e.g. there are times when stoicism and problem solving are not what is needed (see 'emotional trap' in 10.2.1 Male infertility).

11.6.2.2 Banter: male communication and coping

The adage goes that men bond by insulting each other but they really don't mean it, whereas women bond by complimenting each other but they really don't mean it. There is probably a similar sex difference in enjoyment of banter as there is in humour, where men may enjoy sexual jokes more than women do (Hofmann et al., 2020).

Both men and women highly value talking with friends as a coping strategy (Liddon et al., 2017) but it is likely that men and women tend to communicate in slightly different ways. Men appear to value banter as an indirect way of dealing with feelings without having to be vulnerable or emotionally intimate, and this communication style can be seen in male-centric places like the barbershop (Roper & Barry, 2016). Although banter has been criticised in the media, it can be a creative and constructive form of communication too (see Section 7.6.3). Banter can be seen as a male-typical communication, which in therapy can act as an indirect and informal way to lead onto more difficult topics, in or outside therapy (Liddon et al., 2019). Banter is not the same as bullying (see Section 7.6.4), and is not the same as telling a joke, but it is sometimes seen by therapists as a barrier to meaningful communication. However, sometimes if the client starts treatment with banter, or by talking about apparently irrelevant topics (e.g. sports, hobbies), this can be an opportunity to build rapport and create a male-friendly space in which more central issues can emerge. If the therapist understands how to work with banter, this can help build or strengthen the therapeutic alliance.

There is some evidence that men like therapy groups more than women do (Kiselica & Englar-Carlson, 2010; Liddon et al., 2019). This might be because groups allow for an exchange of information rather than focus on feelings, and all-male groups allow for a more free type of communication than the traditional therapeutic dyad, where the group can move from an apparently superficial information exchange and banter into a deeper exploration of difficult feelings and back to surface level again, all in the context of support and empathy (Seager & Thümmel, 2009).

SPOTLIGHT BOX 11.4

OLDER MEN USE MASCULINITY IDEALS TO COPE WITH DEPRESSION

A systematic review and meta-synthesis of 34 qualitative studies by Silvia Krumm and colleagues at Ulm University in Germany concluded that 'Traditional masculinity values might serve as barriers but also as facilitators to adaptive coping strategies in depressed men' (Krumm et al., 2017, p. 107).

Six of the 34 studies, mostly interview studies and one focus group, indicated benefits of traditional masculinity ideals. The men in these studies were usually from a mix of backgrounds, with the average age being around 45. A Swedish study of 12 men (mean age = 48) found that taking control through finding information and relying on one's own strengths and resources were helpful strategies (Skärsäter et al., 2003). A study of 24 middle-aged Finnish men found that they overcame their problems by activities such as chopping firewood, playing in a rock band and motor biking (Valkonen & Hänninen, 2013). A study of 16 depressed men from around the UK (aged 30–75 years old) found they valued 'being one of the boys', benefited from seeing depression as a heroic struggle that made them stronger as a person and enjoyed a sense of control of their condition when coming off medication (Emslie et al., 2006). Three other studies (two of Canadian men, and one of Scottish men) found some participants saw treatment-seeking as active, rational, responsible and independent action (Sierra Hernandez et al., 2014; O'Brien et al., 2005; Johnson et al., 2012).

It is notable that although some other studies of mature men didn't find benefits from traditional masculinity in terms of coping, none of the studies of younger men were described as using masculinity in a positive way.

Although Krumm et al. (2017) were cautious about encouraging the use of traditional masculinity as an intervention because it might put 'pressure on men to meet hegemonic ideals [and] reproduce traditional gender relations and power imbalances', the interpretation of the research presented in the present book suggests that these fears are unfounded (Krumm et al., 2017, p. 122). It is probably safe to take the findings of Krumm et al. at face value and recognise that traditional male values – self-reliance, action orientation, working as a group, enjoying being a fighter and winner and taking control – can be used in a positive, beneficial way. Like any set of values, masculine ideals can be used in a helpful or unhelpful way.

11.6.3 *Interventions for Men's Mental Health Outside the Therapy Room*

Mental health isn't just derived from therapy. In a broad sense, anything that gives life meaning is good for mental health, so an important task for each person in life is to find out how they can bring meaning to their life (Frankl, 1985). For men, important sources of mental health are job satisfaction and relationship stability (Barry 2020). Playing sports or being a supporter can also be good for mental health (see Section 6.6.1; Barry 2020).

In many ways the profession of mental health is behind the times when it comes to men's mental health, and many community-based organisations and charities are showing the way forward.

11.6.3.1 *Barbershops*

It is a popular idea in African American culture that men make a visit to the barber an enjoyable male-only social event where banter is accepted and enjoyed. Research in the UK found support for this, in that Black male participants reported significantly greater wellbeing benefits from visiting the barber compared to white men (Roper & Barry, 2016).

The 'Lions Barber Collective' in the UK has utilised the barbershop as a place in the community where men can talk in an informal environment, and where topics related to mental health might arise. The Lions Barber Collective has developed *BarberTalk*, an adaptation of the Safe Talk suicide prevention training, to help barbers to recognise when a customer needs help, ask direct questions, listen with empathy and know how to signpost to relevant resources (City of London Corporation, 2019).

11.6.3.2 *Men's Sheds*

Concern for men's health in Australia in the 1990s sparked the Men's Sheds movement, which has since grown internationally, especially in the UK, Ireland, Canada and New Zealand. These are not literally sheds, but are communal spaces, typically workshops dedicated to practical activities. Crucially, these spaces allow men to interact with each other, developing friendships and social support without these spaces being given the potentially stigmatising label of 'therapy'. Also, there is evidence that Sheds are especially useful for veterans, retired or unemployed men, as they give a sense of purpose and a substitute for the routine of work, which is central to masculine identity (Waling & Fildes, 2017).

While anecdotally Sheds are beneficial in reducing the mental health impact of social isolation, and might therefore be justifiably socially prescribed, research evidence is needed. A scoping review of the literature on Sheds and wellbeing, based on 16 peer-reviewed papers, concluded that the studies left room for improvement in terms of reliance on self-report measures, small sample sizes and/or low response rates, lack of clarity regarding demographics of participants and Sheds and a lack of assessment of physical health benefits (Kelly et al., 2019). Although some of these points are useful to future researchers, the criticism of reliance on self-report is probably too strict, given that the area is relatively new and that self-report is the most usual way of measuring wellbeing. Also, although only three of the 16 studies had sample sizes over 50, the remaining 13 studies were qualitative in part or wholly, so a relatively small sample size is appropriate. Perhaps of greater concern is that 14 of the 16 studies used either bespoke or qualitative measures, which means their findings are more difficult to compare to research that uses validated questionnaires. Future research on Sheds would benefit by using validated questionnaires, and another improvement would be to measure benefits of Shedding longitudinally, something done in only one study to date.

11.6.3.3 *Social drinking in the pub*

Although heavy drinking can have disastrous consequences on many levels (physical, mental, social, legal etc), there is evidence that moderate social drinking can have benefits for wellbeing. (This double-edged quality is reminiscent of the toast by cartoon character Homer Simpson: 'To alcohol! the cause of, and solution to, all of life's problems!' (Groening, 1997).) Social drinking can help build a support network and foster a feeling of being connected with the community (Dunbar et al., 2017). The pub can be a place where men find it acceptable to talk about their feelings (Emslie et al., 2013).

However high-risk alcohol use, which is more common than alcoholism, is a serious issue that therapists should be aware of in their clients (Bilsker et al., 2018).

11.6.3.4 *Other possible community-based activities for men*

It stands to reason that any community-based business that offers a safe place to talk might be useful in the same way the barbershops can be. For example, job centre workers, bartenders and others might adapt their own versions of Safe Talk. Such interventions should be assessed using validated measures in order to find out how well they work. Randomised controlled trials are not essential, because even simple assessments – if conducted properly – can be of great value. For example, using a brief and user-friendly validated measure, like the Wellbeing Benefits of Everyday Activities Scale (Barry & Roper, 2016), before and after the intervention could be a useful litmus test to indicate where further research is needed. Until being assessed in some way, community-based programmes remain 'promising but unproven' (Bilsker et al., 2018).

It is possible to view any activity that brings people together as a 'Shed'. In some ways Sheds are just a way of bringing men together for an apparently everyday activity, but the activity gains meaning by taking on a social aspect. This implies that an activity that a man finds meaningful will be enhanced by adding a social dimension. After all, it is a truism that if someone is able to find a meaning in their life, it can be very beneficial in terms of mental health (Frankl, 1985). One activity that has traditionally given meaning to men's lives is military, which can be meaningful in many ways (e.g. camaraderie, serving one's country, interesting activities etc). The possibilities are endless, including getting involved in organising community-based activities that help others find meaning.

Without having a meaningful and productive activity to turn to, men often drift into other groups that offer meaning and support, even if these don't appear particularly meaningful to outsiders. Men who don't see value in traditional relationships might become pick-up artists (i.e. use seduction techniques for sex rather than building lasting relationships) (Whitley & Zhou, 2020) or turn their back on relationships altogether, as in the Men Going Their Own Way movement. Others might find a sense of meaning in gangs. These are all areas that psychologists working in the community might help with.

11.7 CONCLUDING REMARKS

Many readers will now see the case study of Tom, presented at the start of this chapter, in a different light. For example, Tom's drinking might now be seen more as a symptom of distress, and talking to his friends in the pub might be seen as a way of coping. Tom's lack of progress in psychotherapy no longer seems entirely his fault, and the end of his therapy sessions should not have signalled the end of the road for his mental health.

It has been described as an 'emotional trap' in couples counselling when the woman wants to talk about her feelings but her male partner wants to fix her feelings using male-typical coping strategies (Peterson et al., 2012; see Section 10.2.1). It is interesting that the same issue applies to therapy for men, but in reverse: psychologists are predominantly women who try to help men by using the 'female-typical' approach of talking about feelings. This may indeed help lots of men, but many more men might benefit by having the option of a more male-friendly approach. A review of 23 studies in the US, UK and Australia found that for minority ethnic groups, taking the client group's views on board improves therapy in various ways (Aggarwal et al, 2016).

This and other issues (e.g. the measurement of male depression, or seeing masculinity more realistically) is not dissimilar to that described in 1977 by Carol Gilligan, who said of her developmental work that girls and women communicate *In a Different Voice*, and noted that this difference was easily overlooked if the male 'voice' was taken as the standard (Gilligan, 1977). This is a good point, but it seems that four decades later the roles have been reversed and 'the solution has replicated the problem' (*Theme: 'solution replicates the problem'*, in Section 13.2.1).

For men, not only is there a stigma attached to seeing a therapist, but arguably many of men's everyday recreational activities (watching football, going to the pub, hunting) have become stigmatised in recent years, and male-only spaces banned (Nathanson & Young, 2006). An example of a well-received intervention is from the Campaign Against Living Miserably (CALM), who created a link between the pub and the CALM helpline by putting their contact details on beer mats in pubs (Liddon et al., 2019). But more often, media campaigns tend to be more sympathetic to women with mental health problems than men, and need to be careful not to give the impression of simply berating men for not behaving more like women (Affleck et al., 2018). The move to making therapy more male-friendly is comparable to the change suggested by the Institute of Medicine in 2001, who highlighted the importance of recognising sex differences in health conditions (Pardue & Wizemann, 2001). Although men have been said to be 'confused about how psychotherapy actually works' (Englar-Carlson, 2006, p. 27), they might be more interested in finding out if they knew that help was being made more male-friendly.

11.8 SUMMARY

- Men's mental health is a key topic in male psychology both in the potential impact on men's lives and the degree to which improvements can be made
- Mental health problems might present differently in men than women e.g. male depression might present as aggression more than low mood
- It is important to recognise the possible social causes of male suicide e.g. distress due to family breakdown and loss of contact with children
- Theories of masculinity based on critical theory / patriarchy theory have become popularised, but cast men in a unsympathetic light and their impact on the therapeutic alliance are doubtful
- A more male-friendly approach to therapy is suggested
- Masculinity is said to reduce men's help-seeking behaviour, but there is evidence that the opposite may be true

12 Regarding Masculinity

CHAPTER OUTLINE

Perspectives in Male Psychology: An Introduction, First Edition.
Louise Liddon and John A. Barry.
© 2021 John Wiley & Sons, Ltd. Published 2021 by John Wiley & Sons, Ltd.

LEARNING OUTCOMES

By the end of this chapter, you should be able to:

1. Understand the criticisms of how 'masculinity' is defined
2. Know how masculinity is seen differently in different institutions
3. Recognise the influence of evolution/biology on masculinity
4. Understand the obstacles to men seeking help for psychological issues
5. Understand how masculinity changes over the lifespan
6. Recognise the strengths and limitations of masculinity as a concept in psychology

12.1   INTRODUCTION

What are little boys made of? Slugs and snails and puppy dog tails.
                                              – Popular nursery rhyme

The topic of masculinity crops up in several of the chapters in the present book in different ways, but because it has become a hot topic – not in psychology so much as in social sciences, the media etc – it gets a special chapter of its own.

12.1.1   *Do Men Want to Talk About Masculinity?*

When men seek therapy it is often for issues that are related to traditional masculinity, e.g. work-related stress or unemployment, which are both related to the provider role. However, how much do male clients want to talk about their masculinity?

A study of 713 English university students found that men scored significantly higher on traditional male attitudes and interests (e.g. drinking alcohol, competitive sports) but attached significantly less importance to their gender identity than did women (de Visser & McDonnell, 2013). This finding could be a clue that just as some men think discussing their health is unmasculine (Sloan et al., 2010), the same is true of discussing masculinity. This idea is supported by research for an Australian multimedia intervention about male suicide which found that the term 'masculinity' was off-putting for some men, and that compared even with reluctance to talk about suicide, 'engaging men in talking about masculinity presents a bigger challenge' (Schlichthorst, 2019, p. 399).

One of the founders of the deficit view of masculinity, Michael Addis, suggests that in the absence of empirical research to confirm any benefits of using the term 'masculinity' in therapy with male clients, 'we will continue to question whether talking about "masculinity" per se is necessary for working effectively with men in a clinical setting, or whether it might in fact be a distraction' (Addis, 2010, p. 112). In other words, even prominent researchers of masculinity recognise that men don't like talking about it. So why the reluctance?

There is probably a sense that being male comes with a built-in navigation system that is designed flexibly in order to adapt to different environments, such as variations in different cultures. No matter what the environment, the navigation system helps the man get through perennial challenges and opportunities that will come up in his life e.g. relationships, survival, and community. This system has been streamlined over millennia to optimise performance, and though nothing is perfect, it works fairly well.

If you are not born male it must be difficult to understand what it is like to be male, and some people might see differences in how men behave and presume that masculinity is simply a learned behaviour. They might not like some aspects of masculinity, and seek to change these, not realising that beneath the apparent cultural flexibility are much deeper roots (see Section 3.7.2.1).

This chapter will discuss the questions: What do we mean by 'masculinity'? Where does it come from (nature/nurture)? Does it change with age? How is it applied in psychology? Is it a useful concept in general and in psychology? What is the narrative about masculinity in academia, the government, the media and other aspects of our culture and environment?

12.2 WHAT DOES SOCIOLOGY SAY?

One would expect sociology to focus on the sociocultural influence on masculinity, but it tends to go further than this, in a general denial of biological influences, coupled with a unfavourable view of masculinity.

12.2.1 *Hegemonic Masculinity*

The concept of 'hegemonic masculinity' derived from Marxist ideology (Gramsci, 1971) is a hostile view of masculinity, seeing it as being about power relations and the domination of women (Connell, 1995). However, this theory overlooks the possibility that masculinity is flexible (Ridge, 2019) and ultimately of benefit to women, the family unit and society (Brown, 2019). The definition of masculinity by Connell is like a straw man argument, i.e. it constructs a pantomime villain version of masculinity from negative aspects of human behaviour, apparently in an attempt to prove that masculinity is essentially negative.

12.2.2 *Masculinities*

Although masculinity can be defined in a way that is recognisable across most cultures throughout history (e.g. Seager et al., 2014a), masculinity is flexible in that it can be expressed in different ways. Some theorists use the term 'masculinities' to emphasize the view that masculinity should not be treated as a unitary phenomenon, and examples of cross-cultural and historical variation are given as examples. This should be fine, except the concept of multiple masculinities is often used to undermine objective evidence of a uniting biological aspect to masculinity. Like the postmodernist philosophy of Foucault, who is paraphrased as saying 'There is no Knowledge; there are knowledges ... Instead of Truth, there are truths' (May, 1993, p. 2), 'masculinities' prioritises the subjective over the objective, so that 'masculinity has essentially become what different theorists and their followers say it is' (Ridge, 2019, p. 218).

The term 'masculinities' was popularised by sociologist R. W. Connell, the same person who coined the term 'hegemonic masculinity'. Like intersectionality, 'masculinities' has the effect of dividing men into demographic silos and treating them as if they have little in common except a struggle for power.

12.2.3 *Critical Perspective on Masculinity*

The critical perspective on masculinity began as critical theory, an offshoot of Marxism (Gramsci, 1971). In contrast to the aim of science, the aim of the critical perspective is empowerment and emancipation. This idea was adapted from a political struggle based on class to a personal struggle based on gender. Gender is presented as a restrictive social construct that people need to question, criticise and liberate themselves from (Pluckrose & Lindsay, 2020). It was adopted in sociology by feminist academics (Millett, 1970) and became influential in gender studies, and then the social sciences in general. It has even spread to science, technology, engineering and mathematics (STEM) subjects, which is remarkable because the aims of critical theory are incompatible with the aims of science (Ramos, 2020).

The idea of being empowered and liberated by breaking free of restrictive social norms has an obvious appeal, not unlike the appeal of 'hooray' words such as 'love' and 'freedom', which can be tagged onto any policy, no matter how draconian (Whyte, 2010). So it is not surprising that the critical perspective has become popular in the media and culture, where 'woke' critical ideas have become popular in recent years.

A good example of the subtle but widespread influence of the critical perspective on our view of masculinity is the study by Mahalik et al. (2012; see Section 11.4.3). It is also concerning that these ideas, including patriarchy theory, have been applied to our understanding of domestic violence, through what is known as the Duluth model (Section 8.4.3), which has led to inadequate psychological interventions for male offenders and a lack of therapy for female offenders.

WHAT DO WE MEAN BY 'PATRIARCHY'?

Like 'toxic masculinity', 'patriarchy' is a popular buzzword in sociology and the media, and increasingly in some parts of psychology. Patriarchy means literally *the rule of the father*, and historically has referred to 'a community of related families under the authority of a male head called a *patriarch*' (OED, 2020).

A modified concept of patriarchy was introduced to feminism by sociologist Kate Millett in her book *Sexual Politics*, which made the claim, based on Marxist ideas about the oppression of workers, that women were oppressed by men through the traditional family unit (Millett, 1970). Millett was active in the anti-psychiatry movement and rejected the diagnosis and medication of her 'manic depression' because she perceived these interventions as 'destroying personality' (Millett, 2008). Her theory of patriarchy was eagerly adopted and developed by other feminists, along with influential ideas such as R. W. Connell's 'hegemonic masculinity' (Connell, 1987). So popular has Millet's theory become that many people today think of patriarchy as a 'system of social structures and practices in which men dominate, oppress, and exploit women' (Walby, 1989, p. 214).

This conception of patriarchy has also influenced the field of psychology, to such an extent that according to the APA's Division 51 guidelines, in reference to the US today: 'Although privilege has not applied to all boys and men in equal measure, in the aggregate, males experience a greater degree of social and economic power than girls and women in a patriarchal society' (APA, 2018, p. 9).

The concept is familiar to many, having been popularised in the media, so it is almost taken for granted as being true to some degree. However, what is the evidence for the existence of this system of oppression of women? In most countries women can vote, own property, earn equal pay (Section 7.5.4), drive a car, and have freedoms undreamed of by women – and men – throughout history. In fact, women have rights and privileges that men don't have, e.g. preferential access to children and property after family breakdown, schemes to help them into lucrative careers, and are not pressured to take dangerous jobs (Creveld, 2013; Dench, 1998).

Although there are oppressed and exploited women at the bottom of society, there are arguably more men there, as shown by men's shorter lifespan, more homelessness, harsher prison sentences, more social isolation etc. It is possible to pick evidence for or against men or women being more oppressed, and this probably shows that each are oppressed in different ways. It is likely that selective attention and gamma bias (see Section 2.5.5.1) are behind many of the diatribes against patriarchy.

Modern examples of patriarchal societies are known, e.g. Afghanistan under the Taliban (Murray, 2009), but the rallying cry of 'smash the patriarchy' (Bulbeck, 2010) is seldom heard in those places. Instead it is heard in universities in the West, where the closest thing resembling a patriarchy is the traditional family unit, with the father as main wage earner. Thus in modern Western terms, smashing the patriarchy means smashing ordinary families, resulting in divorce, 'dad-deprived' children, and the spectrum of associated social problems (see Section 4.4.7) that also impact the wellbeing of women (Venker & Schlafly, 2011).

George Orwell once wrote regarding a conspiracy theory: 'One has to belong to the intelligentsia to believe things like that: no ordinary man could be such a fool' (Orwell, 1945). In modern Western cultures, complaints about patriarchal oppression of women are probably a result of *confirmatory bias* (seeing only those things than confirm your hypothesis), and closer to conspiracy theory than science, and arguably not the most solid basis for clinical practice by professional psychologists (see Section 11.4.4).

But what if patriarchy theory completely misunderstands men? What if the vast majority of men don't want to have power over others, and are very happy to have just enough stability in aspects of their lives that are important to them – some job satisfaction, being a good husband and father etc – to get by? In which case, perhaps the psychology of the average man is not represented at all by theories of masculinity and patriarchy, which project a demonic stereotype of men, instead of the more modest reality.

12.3 WHAT DOES PSYCHOLOGY SAY?

To the degree that mainstream psychology takes notice of men's psychology at all (which is relatively little), it tends to take the social constructionist view i.e. the 'nurture' side of the 'nature/nurture' debate.

12.3.1 *The Social Constructionist View*

This point of view, and its consequences, are outlined in this influential paper on men's studies (see Section 2.5.1): 'Men's studies are an extension of women's studies – an attempt to examine how masculinity is a social construction and often has a negative effect on men's lives and their mental health ... When we approach men's mental health from an essentialist [biological/evolutionary] perspective, we are more likely to view the dark side of masculinity as an unfortunate, but relatively inevitable, outcome of male heritage. However, when we approach the matter from a social constructionist perspective, we are more likely to offer ambitious programs to change our culture and enhance men's psychological well-being' (Brooks, 2001, pp. 287 and 292).

This approach has not so much inspired 'ambitious programmes' so much as it has fed into the narrow 'paradigm fixation' that researchers were warned about in the 1990s (Good et al., 1994; see SPOTLIGHT box 12.2). Certainly this narrow and negative view has inspired little that is likely to enhance men's psychological wellbeing. Clinical trials of brave new therapies are conspicuously absent after decades of the New Psychology of Men and men's studies. It seems likely that a negative view of masculinity based on the false premise that masculinity is a social construct with no biological input has produced research of questionable value, and built upon this are guidelines of questionable value (e.g. the APA in the US (Guidelines 1 and 3)) and PTMF in the UK (pp. 124–8 of the long version) and the APS in Australia.

12.3.2 *Masculinity, Health and Age*

A point that is not generally recognised in the literature on masculinity – for example, the APA guidelines on men and boys – is that extremes of masculinity are usually seen in young men of college age rather than more mature men. However, one of the leaders in masculinity research, Prof Ronald Levant, has pointed out that 'older men tend to endorse traditional masculinity ideology less than their younger counterparts' (Levant & Richmond, 2007, p. 140). He has described this in other papers too, e.g. 'Berger et al. (2005) found that age was a significant contextual predictor of positive attitudes toward help-seeking. Future research should also use more diverse samples. College students, predominantly white and middle class, tend to be younger and to experience themselves as invulnerable; hence, health issues simply may not be salient to them. In addition, for college students the participation in risky behavior may be related to factors other than the variables of interest in the present study (for example, different norms for drinking behavior)' (Levant & Richmond, 2007, p. 142). This typically overlooked age-related finding also fits with what we know about ageing and mental health: although physical health is lower in later life, mental health tends to improve (Barry 2020; Public Health England, 2019). This is often attributed to reduced stress in the period after retirement and before health deteriorates significantly, but might also be related to greater emotional maturity. This relationship between age and masculinity is observable in the findings of many papers by different authors over the course of several years (see SPOTLIGHT box 12.2; SPOTLIGHT box 11.4; Section 11.5.1), so has been widely observed, but insufficiently noticed.

(see SPOTLIGHT box 12.2; SPOTLIGHT box 11.4; Section 11.5.1)

SPOTLIGHT BOX 12.2

MASCULINITY RESEARCH: A REVIEW AND CRITIQUE

In 1994 a paper was published that offered some excellent advice to researchers who were using masculinity to investigate men's psychology (Good et al., 1994). The main points of the paper included:

Self-fulfilling definitions of masculinity

Masculine role conflict is the idea that there are detrimental aspects of the traditionally socialised masculine role which may cause stress, strain or conflict. When definitions of masculine role conflict include distress, dysfunction and interpersonal conflict 'then it may not be surprising that studies using such scales may find a relationship between the constructs of masculine role conflict and psychological distress' (Good et al., 1994, pp. 9–10).

In other words, if a questionnaire includes dysfunction in its definition of masculinity, then it will probably correlate with various other questionnaires that measure dysfunction, not because masculinity is dysfunctional, but because the questionnaires ask similar questions about dysfunction. It could be suggested that this problem of 'construct overlap' and lack of 'discriminant validity' leads more to a self-fulfilling prophesy rather than a genuine research finding.

Sample bias

Attention to sampling is 'especially critical in the study of characteristics as culturally defined as masculinity ideology' (Good et al., 1994, p. 10). This is because the findings are likely to vary widely depending on the demographics of the participants. For example, Good et al. cite research from the early 1990s which had already shown that the relationship between masculinity and psychological problems was greater in US undergraduates than in successful businessmen.

Similar research produces similar findings

Even in 1994, 'the vast majority of studies' on masculinity were questionnaire surveys which were analysed using correlational methods (bivariate or multiple regression). Although such a research design is useful in the early exploration of a phenomenon, 'they do not provide information about causality'. Thus, even though 'it has been repeatedly observed that there is a relationship between men's experience of masculine role conflict and depression ... it is unknown whether masculine role conflict causes depression, depression causes men's masculine role conflict, or some other as yet unknown factors account for this observed relationship. Hence, greater methodological diversity is needed to help correct the "research paradigm fixation" (Gelso, 1979) that is becoming characteristic of the research in this area' (Good et al., 1994, p. 10).

In other words, although the findings of these designs are reliable (they always find the same thing), they are not necessarily valid (what they find is not necessarily what they think they have found). This advice is reminiscent of the words attributed to Henry Ford: 'if you always do what you have always done, you always get what you've always got'. Good et al. suggest using other research designs, such as longitudinal studies, which have the potential to identify whether masculinity causes mental health problems or not.

Nearly three decades later, the weaknesses in research in this field remain. If masculinity research is to make any meaningful contribution to psychology, it needs to correct the three fundamental errors identified here.

12.3.3 *Cross-Cultural Studies of Masculinity*

Findings from cross-cultural studies of masculinity show a lot of variation, e.g. a review of cross-national studies found that male and female college students in China, Russia and Japan endorsed traditional masculinity ideology (using the Total Traditional scale of the Male Role Norms Inventory (MRNI)) to a higher degree than male college students in the US (Levant & Richmond, 2007). The authors suggest these cultural differences prove that 'gender roles are not to be regarded as "given," neither psychologically nor biologically, but rather as socially constructed' (Levant & Richmond, 2007, p. 141). However, we know that masculinity appears worldwide (see Section 3.7.2; Ellis et al., 2008), and Levent & Richmond found men scored higher than women on the MRNI in each country, which is hard to explain if gender is purely a social construct. Furthermore, almost all studies were of college-age students (see Section 12.3.2) and doctoral dissertation research, defining masculinity in negative terms (e.g. being homophobic), thus the findings can't reasonably be generalised to more mature men.

12.3.4 *Are Homophobia and Misogyny Aspects of Masculinity?*

Homophobia is sometimes attached to definitions of masculinity as if it were predominantly a characteristic of men and not women. Although it is true that in most Western countries women are less homophobic than men are, the difference is often fairly small e.g. in a survey of 1416 particpants in France the sex difference in homophobia was 1.41 vs 1.62 (d = 0.18) (Vecho et al., 2019). In many non-Western countries women are more homophobic than men, e.g. Brazil (Proulx, 1997) and Vietnam, China and Taiwan (Ng et al., 2012). This raises the question of why homophobia is seen by some researchers as an aspect of masculinity rather than an aspect of social cognition.

A similar error occurs regarding constructs that include misogyny, or a sense of bias against femininity, as an aspect of masculinity. It is normal for men and women, especially in the process of identity formation during childhood, to develop a sense of boundaries between what is appropriately male and female, as it is for the development of other boundaries (Briggs, 2019). This type of group identity is a normal social process, even in adulthood, and is associated with a normal sense of ingroup favouritism and outgroup bias among the sexes – though interestingly there is less ingroup favouritism among males (Rudman & Goodwin, 2004). This means that men favour women relatively more than they favour other men, which undermines the idea that misogyny is a core part of masculinity. Similarly, to say that evidence that domestic violence against women is evidence that misogyny is an aspect of masculinity is very muddled thinking, especially as the rates of domestic violence by women against men are relatively high (28.7% of men are victims of DV by women compared to 32.3% of women who are victims of DV by men), and higher still for women against women (40.4% of lesbians are victims of female partners); (Brown & Herman, 2015).

12.3.5 *Toxic Masculinity*

Toxic masculinity is described as 'the constellation of socially regressive male traits that serve to foster domination, the devaluation of women, homophobia, and wanton violence' (Kupers, 2005, p. 714) (see Section 4.6).

It is sometimes suggested that toxic masculinity is the result of boys learning dysfunctional behaviours from their culture, but the reality today is that the culture that many boys experience is predominantly female, e.g. almost half of boys are raised by single mothers and have female school teachers. When 'dad-deprived' boys 'go off the rails', we should not blame the influence of masculinity, but the lack of influence of masculinity.

The term 'toxic masculinity' was coined around the 1980s or 1990s in the Jung-inspired men's mythopoetic movement, and was used to describe the masculinity of immature males who had not yet learned – usually because they have not taken part in traditional masculine rites of passage – to connect with their deeper, mature masculinity (Schwalbe, 1996). However, taken out of its original context, the term has been used in the media as a generic way to refer to bad behaviour by men, especially violence or sex crimes. It is interesting that the mythopoetic movement recognised the importance of immaturity being an important aspect of 'toxic masculinity', because this is the key to understanding the findings of many studies of masculinity, which find problems predominantly with college-age men.

There are several ways in which the term, as used today, is problematic. Firstly, it is difficult to use a compound term like this without implying that toxicity is part of masculinity. This point is clear if the term 'toxic' is attached to any other demographic or immutable characteristic ('toxic Blackness', 'toxic femininity' etc). In a rare survey on this topic, most people found the term 'toxic masculinity' insulting, unlikely to improve men's behaviour and possibly damaging to boys (Barry, Walker et al., 2020). Secondly, the term tends to focus the cause of bad behaviour in the wrong place; indeed it could be said it confuses cause and effect, because the cause of antisocial behaviour can often be traced back to problems in childhood, such as deprivation, neglect or abuse (see Figure 8.1). Girls might express trauma differently, but their delinquency often has the same root as boys (see Section 8.3.3). Trying to reduce criminality by stamping out 'toxic masculinity' is like trying to cure measles by surgically removing the spots. Thirdly, research based on definitions of masculinity that include negative stereotypes of men will suffer from the problem of 'construct overlap' described by Good et al., 1994 (SPOTLIGHT box 12.2), who pointed out that definitions of masculinity containing negative traits will correlate with other measures of negative traits which amounts to a type of circular reasoning, or – in less kindly terminology invented by pioneering information technologists – 'garbage in, garbage out' (or GIGO) (The Times, 1957).

12.3.5.1 *Toxic masculinity or intoxication?*

The popularly negative view of masculinity is not only a social construct, but one where the evidence is supported largely by a relatively narrow sample: college-age men, mostly in the US. Supporting evidence is sometimes drawn from examples of behaviour that are from specific groups that don't necessarily generalise to other men. For example, the movie *The Mask You Live In* gave examples of masculinity from drunken frat house parties and men in the US prison system (Barry, 2016b). Trying to prove that masculinity is toxic by showing prisoners espousing hypermasculine values is a bit like saying that aspirin is toxic, and using as evidence cases where people have overdosed on aspirin. There are more parsimonious ways of explaining some men's criminal behaviour. For example, in many parts of the world, around 40% to 60% of violent crimes are committed while the offender has been drinking (White, 2016). Some drunk men might behave in ways that are toxic when drunk, but this is because they are intoxicated, not because of their masculinity. Women too can behave badly after drinking, but nobody calls this behaviour 'toxic masculinity', or indeed 'toxic femininity'.

BOYS WILL BE BOYS?

The phrase 'boys will be boys' is 'said to emphasize that people should not be surprised when boys or men act in a rough or noisy way because this is part of the male character' (Cambridge English Dictionary, 2020). The colloquial use of the term usually implies that certain aspects of male-typical behaviour are innate.

Guideline 1 of the APA Guidelines on therapy for boys and men states that 'masculinities are constructed based on social, cultural, and contextual norms' (APA 2018, p. 6). This view has been criticised, because this guideline neglects to say that biological factors also influence male-typical behaviour, such as play behaviour (see Section 4.2.2), ADHD (see Section 4.3.2), interest in competitive sports (see Section 6.3.1), and masculinity in general (SPOTLIGHT box 3.1).

One problem with ignoring biology is that it is then presumed that gender-typical behaviour is something that is merely learned, which implies that it can be unlearned, or learned differently, without any real difficulty. Thus boys being competitive or aggressive or risk-taking could be seen as socially undesirable and therefore to be unlearned, whereas research indicates that the roots of many behaviours run deeper than that (see also the comparison with 'conversion therapy' in Section 11.4.5).

Does the influence of biology mean that, *inevitably*, 'boys will be boys'? Taken as a rigid rule, this sentiment is biological determinism, and as one-sided as social determinism. On the other hand, if the phrase is meant in the sense that 'on average boys are more competitive etc than girls', then most people will see the common sense in the statement.

The narrative around 'boys will be boys' tends to be negative these days. For example, in the *'We believe'* advert for Gillette razors, the phrase was presented as if people use it as a tacit endorsement of violent and sexist behaviour by boys and men (Gillette, 2019). Although the message of the advert might have been well-intentioned, the advert was unpopular and lost the company billions of dollars (Ernst, 2019). This public reaction might reflect the finding that most people don't like the term 'toxic masculinity' and believe that it might be damaging to boys (Barry, Walker et al., 2020). Also, research suggests that shaming tactics are unlikely to be an effective way of reducing problem behaviour by men and boys (see SPOTLIGHT box 11.2).

12.3.6 *Masculinity as an Evolved Part of Human Nature*

There is a huge amount of research suggesting that masculinity, or component aspects of masculinity, are influenced by biological or other innate factors. For example, a review of 18,000 studies found 65 sex differences, many of which map directly onto traditional masculinity (Ellis et al., 2008; Ellis, 2011; see Section 3.7.2.1). However, evidence of this kind is often overlooked by people who are seen as experts in masculinity, who tend to share the social constructionist views promoted in sociology and gender studies. This isn't just a difference of opinion among academics, but has real-world consequences because the social constructionist view predominates in many institutions outside academia, such as the World Health Organisation (WHO), the United Nations (UN) and the media in general.

12.3.7 *Masculinity: The Social Construction of a Stereotype*

Until some time in the 1980s, psychology defined men with adjectives such as 'active', 'dominant', 'self-contained' or 'aggressive' (Barry, Walker et al, 2020, p. 9). However, the New Psychology of Men constructed maleness in a new way, attaching attitudes such as misogyny and homophobia to masculinity (Mahalik et al., 2003; see Section 12.3.4). This blurring of the normative with the deviant (Ferguson, 2018) meant that masculinity was now being declared to be somewhat pathological, and something that everyone should be wary of.

But should we take this version of masculinity at face value? Indeed, does this construct have any face validity, beyond resembling a stereotype of nasty men? Another way of looking at the New Psychology of Men version of masculinity is as a 'straw man argument', constructed to contain defects, with the specific purpose of pointing out those defects in order to discredit it. This is like making an umbrella out of paper, taking it out on a rainy day and saying 'I told you umbrellas are useless'. If psychology is a science, it needs to define and categorise phenomena in a more credible way.

12.4 WHAT DOES GOVERNMENT SAY?

Masculinity is not a topic discussed much by politicians, but it is in the background of discussions on issues such as health, domestic violence and even terrorism (Idris, 2019). However, equating masculinity with violent extremism is a gross misrepresentation of the male role, and overlooks a myriad of other reasons that men become involved in violence (see Figure 8.1).

12.4.1 *Political Bias*

There is evidence of a political bias in the view of masculinity, with left-wing parties being more in favour of women's issues and less in favour of masculinity (Winter, 2010). A left-wing former UK Labour shadow home secretary described the 'masculinity crisis' as men 'caught between the "stiff-upper lip" approach of previous generations and today's cultural tornado of male cosmetics, white collar industry, and modernised workplaces' (Abbott, 2013, p. 6). Suggested solutions, such as strengthening the bond between fathers and children, sound good, but lack credibility in the context of government policies such as family law processes that limit - to a distressing degree - contact between the father and his children after family breakdown (Barry & LIddon, 2020).

Generally speaking, psychologists and others in the social sciences in the US, UK and probably other Western countries lean to the left in terms of their sociopolitical views (Langbert, 2020). This is good news for clients with left-wing views, because clients feel more comfortable and have a better therapeutic alliance if they think their therapist's political views align with their own (Solomonov & Barber, 2018). However, this has serious implications for people whose politics are not left-wing, and who might feel that the profession of psychology is out of touch with their needs. This is not a hypothetical issue, because around two thirds of 504 therapy clients from across the US said they discussed politics with their therapist (Langbert, 2020). Overall, politics could be another potential barrier to men seeking therapy, unless the male client has left-wing views. The current political climate on campus might impact men's willingness to study psychology too, because it is possible that extreme left-wing views, held mainly by professors, are harming the social sciences and driving moderate students away (Magness, 2019).

A large database study examined how people's political views have changed over the years, measured in three cohorts (in the 1980s, 1990s and early 2000s) of people in 13 countries (Western Europe and Canada) born between 1925 and 1985 (aged 18 to 75+ at the time of completing the survey) (Shorrocks, 2018). It was found that men born around 1925 were more left-wing than women in that cohort (men scored 27 and women 26 on a scale of intending to vote left), but in contrast women born around 1985 were more left-wing than men in that cohort (women scored 31 and men 28). Taking into account the tendency for people to become more conservative with age (Tilley & Evans, 2014), and the relevance to politics to the therapeutic alliance (Solomonov & Barber, 2018), these findings have implications for taking age and sex into consideration when matching clients to therapists.

12.4.2 *The United Nations*

The UN celebrates women on nine days per year, most notably International Women's Day. There is no specific day for men. Since 2013, 19 November has been the UN's World Toilet Day, even though by 2013, 19 November had been celebrated as International Men's Day in an increasing number of countries for at least a decade, and is at present celebrated in at least 44 (Wikipedia, 2020). The UN favours women over men in other ways too e.g. their sustainable development goal on 'gender equality' is exclusive to women (Nuzzo, 2020).

The WHO and UN tend to have a negative view of masculinity, in line with the ideas of hegemonic masculinity (see SPOTLIGHT box 10.2). The UN recently produced a report claiming that 'no country in the world – rich or poor – has achieved gender equality. All too often, women and girls are discriminated against in health, in education, at home and in the labour market' (UNDP, 2020, p. 1). Proclamations like these are generally believed, because they come from apparently credible sources. However, the next section shows that sometimes the information from these sources is not reliable.

12.4.3 *Measuring Gender Equality*

Gender equality worldwide is often measured using scales like the Global Gender Gap Index (GGGI; WEF, 2016). Scores on this scale represent gender inequality in health, political empowerment, education and participation in the workforce. This scale yields a score between 0 and 1, indicating how much equality women have, but doesn't indicate how much equality men have. For example, on the GGGI, a score of 1 indicates that women have reached parity with men. In theory, scores higher than 1 would indicate increasing disadvantage to men, but the scoring is capped at 1, which means that any disadvantage to men is not shown.

To overcome this issue, a new scoring system was developed – the Basic Indicator of Gender Inequality (BIGI) – where scores below zero indicate disadvantage to men, and scores above zero indicate disadvantage to women (Stoet & Geary, 2019). Using the BIGI to assess children's education, life satisfaction and healthy lifespan in 134 countries between 2012 and 2016, it was found that countries with low levels of human development tended to show disadvantages for women and girls, and countries with the very highest levels of human development were the most equal for men and women (with a slight advantage to women). Interestingly, countries with medium or high levels of human development tended to show disadvantages for boys and men, generally due to underinvestment in preventative healthcare impacting males.

The very highly developed countries that BIGI scores showed slightly favoured women included the US, Australia, Sweden and the UK. Countries such as Chad, Ethiopia and Pakistan had low levels of development and favoured men.

The scoring of the GGGI is an example of gamma bias (see Section 2.5.5.1): women's inequality is carefully measured, but men's inequality is invisible. As with previous chapters, we can see that claims about gender equality from apparently credible sources such as the UN are very much debatable because of the terminology used to define equality, the methods used to measure it and the gamma bias of the findings.

12.4.4 *What Does the Healthcare Industry Say?*

The COVID-19 pandemic has in many ways confirmed the gamma bias at the heart of the institutions that are supposed to protect men and women (see SPOTLIGHT box 10.2). Although they have recently taken the positive step forward of analysing health data by gender, the WHO continue to promote negative ideas about masculinity, e.g. the statement that masculine risk-taking not only decreases condom use and help-seeking for HIV but also increases substance abuse, and 'can also impact on the health of girls and women, for example through violence, sexually transmitted infections and unwanted pregnancies' (Manandhar et al., 2018, p. 645). This lack of balance in how the health of men and women is viewed is of concern.

12.5 WHAT DOES WESTERN MEDIA AND POPULAR CULTURE SAY?

12.5.1 *Masculinity and the Media*

The media can be extremely powerful in shaping attitudes to men, often in a negative way (Nathanson & Young, 2001). A concrete example is how attitudes to men in Spain changed overnight from being relatively sanguine on gender issues to very distrustful of men, because of the tragic news of the violent death of a woman who was a widely respected advocate for female victims of domestic violence by men (Berganza-Conde, 2003). In some countries the view of men varies by choice of TV channel. For example, in the US, the TV network CNN favours progressive issues and left-leaning politics, whereas Fox is more populist and promotes conservative politics (Groeling, 2008). In the UK there are no populist terrestrial channels, but the BBC has developed a reputation for promoting progressive views and left-leaning politics (Bourne et al., 2016). There are exceptions to this, e.g. a dramatic story about a male victim of domestic violence has seen a thawing in attitude to male victims of domestic violence in the UK (BBC, 2019, p. 2). However, much output from the BBC remains progressive (e.g. the unrelenting references to the supposed sexist nature of the gender pay gap – see Section 7.5.4).

Although much of what is said in the media is not taken seriously by everyone, we know that the media can have an influence on the public (see Section 9.2.3), and indeed advertisers and opinion leaders rely on the strength of the power of media influence. Celebrities and media 'experts' on gender might be especially influential on younger people who have not yet had the life experiences that suggest that biological forces have a role in shaping gender (e.g. realising the relevance of traditional gender roles only after becoming a parent; see Section 4.4.6).

12.5.2 *Masculinity and Popular Culture*

Modern Western culture celebrates every aspect of masculinity, except, it seems, traditional masculinity. Popular culture often appeals to young people but can distract them away from seeing the role of fatherhood as positive at a time when they might otherwise be starting a family (Barry, 2020b). Negative depictions of masculinity can be seen in virtually all aspects of popular culture in the West, with negative stereotypes of men as evil or inadequate in the cinema, television and news media (Nathanson & Young, 2001). This negative attitude to traditional masculinity can be seen in the legal system, especially in relation to domestic violence, sexual offences and family separation (Nathanson & Young, 2006). With this ongoing erosion of respect for traditional gender roles, it is probably not a coincidence that in some European counties, population growth is below replacement levels and has been for years (Kreyenfeld & Konietzka, 2017). On the other hand, in the US, people and states where religion, and by association family values, are taken more seriously have higher birth rates than other people and states (Hayford & Morgan, 2008).

Pop culture views of men and masculinity are much less positive than they were a few generations ago (see SPOTLIGHT box 12.4). We might speculate that the result of decades of erosion of the family may have very serious damage transgenerationally. For example, growing up in a culture where the family is devalued and easily subject to dissolution might cause children to develop a devalued opinion of the family, perceiving the family unit as an outmoded and disharmonious tradition always vulnerable to collapse, not realising this situation is the result of continuous attacks on the family rather than being the natural state of the family. A survey of 2000 men in the UK found that one of the predictors of wellbeing for men 'was being like my father' (Barry 2020), which implies that if there is a masculinity crisis, it is a crisis facing those men who don't feel good about masculinity, and don't want to be like their father (see SPOTLIGHT box 4.2).

12.6 IS MASCULINITY USEFUL?

In what must have seemed like a good idea at the time, in the year 1233, Pope Gregory IX issued a papal decree that Satan was half-cat and sometimes took the form of a cat. The violent result of this decree was a diminished population of feral cats in Europe. A century later, mice and rats spread the bubonic plague throughout Europe with ease, due to the depletion of their natural predator, the cat (Lawrence, 2003; *Theme: 'unintended consequences'*, in Section 13.2.1).

The current trend for defining masculinity in negative ways masks the possibility that the traditional male role is based on self-sacrifice to family and community (Brown, 2019). Masculinity tells a man to suppress his feelings in order to best provide and protect, fight and win, and to do so even at the expense of his own physical and emotional health (Seager et al., 2014a).

Does society still need men with such qualities? Perhaps the value of this role only becomes clear when there is a crisis where strength and stoicism under pressure are needed, such as protecting people from attack, or carrying unconscious people from burning buildings etc. It could be argued that although masculinity is a benign force, it undoubtedly has a dark side, and can be experienced or expressed in a negative way, especially by people with psychopathologies (see Figure 8.1). However, we should no more want to eradicate it than we would want to eradicate other useful aspects of our evolved nature, such as the fight-or-flight response, just because some people experience it as a negative, e.g. people with anxiety disorders who might have panic attacks or phobias (Barry, 2016a). Some people argue that the traditional male role doesn't fit the modern world (e.g. Abbott, 2013), but this is based on a narrow view of modern life as safe and masculinity as dangerous, and doesn't justify the notion that the male role should be abandoned or reshaped.

12.6.1 *Barriers/Obstacles to Help-Seeking*

Traditional masculinity, and aspects of it such as stoicism, has been blamed for men's lack of help-seeking so often that it is more or less taken for granted (Mansfield et al., 2005). Much of the evidence for this has been correlational (i.e. masculinity scores are compared to scores on help-seeking), but correlations are sometimes interpreted incorrectly and do not necessarily prove causation (see SPOTLIGHT box 12.2).

This section looks at the reasons men have given for seeking help – or not – for psychological issues. From the evidence, recurring issues have been identified, and Figure 12.1 shows the most common obstacles. These are usually described as 'barriers', but the terms 'hurdles' or 'obstacles' are probably more suitable because they imply that the issues are surmountable.

The hurdles depicted here are presented in roughly chronological order of the stages of contemplating help-seeking, rather than being a statistical calculation of the magnitude of each hurdle, although it is possible that each hurdle might seem successively higher to the individual. The final barrier is of more concrete issues, such as not being able to afford therapy, get time off work etc.

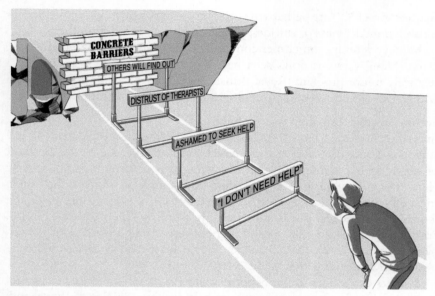

FIGURE 12.1 *Psychological hurdles to psychological therapy for men.*

First hurdle: 'I don't need help'

There are two aspects to this obstacle: refusing to admit needing help, and genuinely not realising that one needs help. Men are both less likely than women to recognise having a problem (30% men; 41% of women) and less likely to admit it (33% of men; 19% women; Liddon et al., 2017).

Men can be under a lot of stress without fully realising it. For example, a man might be drinking more and being irritable, and not recognise these as being symptoms associated with male depression (see Section 11.2.1.1). Or sometimes men with mental health problems might notice physical rather than emotional symptoms (Brown et al., 2019). Problems can be less noticed when they are perceived as gender-atypical, e.g. a man might not recognise that he has an eating disorder because he thinks this disorder only impacts women (Räisänen & Hunt, 2014). This is analogous to help-seeking for physical health conditions, e.g. men are sometimes admonished for seeking help relatively late for prostate cancer, though this can be due to it being asymptomatic (Gannon, 2019; Section 10.2.5).

Symptoms of trauma or depression (e.g. aggression) are sometimes not detected by standard tests of depression, so might not be recognised as such by healthcare professionals either, and might end up being dealt with by the criminal justices system as criminal offences. Some men put off therapy until they have exhausted all other options, and some men don't seek therapy at all, even if it is offered to them (Bilsker et al., 2018). The 'hard to reach' men (see Section 11.5.7) are perhaps the group most at risk of tragic consequences (prison, homelessness or suicide), yet we know very little about them.

Military veterans sometimes don't realise they need help (Fikretoglu et al., 2008). Many veterans don't seek help for their hearing as it is seen as a relatively minor problem (Royal British Legion, 2018). Often men will deal with stress without seeking psychological help, e.g. through exercise.

Second hurdle: Ashamed to seek help

In total, 31% of men and 30% of women in an online survey said that cultural stigma was the main barrier to help-seeking (Liddon et al., 2017). This lack of sex difference is interesting because it suggests that stigma is not specific to men or masculinity. A review found that stigma was ranked the fourth most difficult barrier to seeking help, cited by 21% of participants (male and female combined), and was influenced by ethnicity (Clement et al., 2015). Social judgement was the second highest barrier, cited by 22% of participants (Clement et al., 2015). Younger people are less likely to seek help due to stigma (Steinfeldt & Steinfeldt, 2010).

Soldiers are trained to be hypermasculine warriors who are strong and stoic, which reduces their capacity for help-seeking (Shields & Westwood, 2019). However, the prevalence of help-seeking in the UK armed forces is similar to that in the general population of the UK (~3.4%; Ministry of Defence, 2018).

Third hurdle: Distrust of therapists

Men often have a general distrust of doctors and healthcare workers (Mansfield et al., 2005) in a variety of contexts. For example, a review of qualitative studies of help-seeking for mental health issues found that five studies of men were more likely than 13 studies of women to report more difficulty talking to professionals (80% vs 15% of studies) and issues with judgemental / disrespectful professionals (40% vs 23%) (Clement et al, 2015). For example, an Australian man said: 'It sort of stopped me [utilizing mental health services], like I said, if they have a bad opinion of me I might as well keep it the same' (Aisbett 2007, p. 7). A lack of understanding from civilian clinicians of the veterans' experiences can be off-putting, especially at first contact (Ministry of Defence, 2018). Male victims of domestic violence tend to find the usual sources of help – including helplines and domestic violence agencies – are not always helpful. Almost all men in one survey said that domestic violence agencies were biased against them, with around 15% meeting hostility or ridicule, and others being accused of being the perpetrator rather than victim (Douglas & Hines, 2011). Male victims over the years have tended to rely on friends, family and neighbours where possible, and if no such help was available, men were at increased risk of mental health problems (Powney & Graham-Kevan, 2019; Bates, 2020). The TV series *The Sopranos* has been suggested as a good model for men to seek therapy, but the therapy was ultimately unsuccessful, and when Tony Soprano described two examples where he was the victim of domestic violence, these were totally ignored by his therapist (Barry & Seager, 2014). In cases of 'forced-to-penetrate' rape (where a man has penetrative sex with a woman against his will), being disbelieved is a barrier (Anderson et al., 2020).

Political views can be an impediment to the development of a therapeutic alliance, and it can be speculated that it could be a potential barrier to men seeking therapy, because men tend to have more right leaning views than women but many therapists have left-leaning views (Solomonov & Barber, 2018; Cusack et al., 2006; Johnson et al., 2012; Langbert, 2020). Gender politics might be offputting too. Although not asked in relation to therapy, around 86% of men said they would be unhappy if their job or relationship stress was attributed to their masculinity (Barry, Walker et al., 2020).

There is some evidence that, in the long term, brief counselling might not work as well for men as for women (Wright & McLeod, 2016), and UK military veterans can be put off from seeking psychological help if they have found it to be ineffective (Ministry of Defence, 2018). A lack of male-friendly options was cited by 16% of men as a barrier to seeking help for mental health issues, a figure that might be higher if more men knew that such options exist (Liddon et al., 2018). In addition to these obstacles, Black men in the UK are less likely than White men to seek help, often because of mistrust related to beliefs about discrimination (Keating & Robertson, 2004).

Fourth hurdle: Others will find out

Some men have negative experiences of opening up (Section 11.5.5). Research sometimes finds that confidentiality is the concern most cited by men regarding help-seeking (e.g. 35% of men; 39% of women; Liddon et al., 2017). A review found that 31% of male and female participants (data were not sex-disaggregated) identified confidentiality as the main concern, and 23% of participants were most concerned about employment-related discrimination (Clement et al., 2015). This is one reason why employees might seek support external to their workplace, e.g. soldiers might seek mental health support outside of the military (Ministry of Defence, 2018). For military personnel, risk of damaging reputation with colleagues and leaders can also be a barrier to help-seeking (Eldridge & Fraser, 2019).

Fifth hurdle: Concrete barriers

There is also sometimes acknowledgement of 'concrete barriers', such as lack of finances or insurance, lack of transportation or lack of information about the help available, any of which can prevent help-seeking (Mansfield et al., 2005). Other barriers can be that men might find it more difficult to take time off work, due to concerns over being considered work-shy or malingering (Ashfield & Gouws, 2019). Ex-services personnel in the UK, who are used to a relatively quick response to their health needs within the armed forces, may find external provision in the National Health Service difficult, due to the process of registering with a doctor and going on an indeterminate – possibly long – waiting list (Eldridge & Fraser, 2019). These issues may compound the tendency to avoid asking for help, which anecdotally can take a decade or more (Kingerlee, 2019).

The nature of these obstacles shows that men's help-seeking is much more complex than simply 'hegemonic masculinity' or fear of appearing weak.

12.6.2 *Should we be More Positive About Masculinity?*

We live in a society which sometimes seems to view male behaviour as only one or two steps from descending into savagery. The 'Lord of the Flies' is sometimes cited to make this point, but in fact the true story that inspired this novel told of how a group of boys stranded on an island coped with great intelligence, bravery and compassion to one another (Bregman, 2020).

The positive psychology approach to masculinity suggests that therapy is improved by focusing on the potential strengths of masculinity rather than the potential weaknesses (Kiselica & Englar-Carlson, 2010; Seager & Barry, 2019b).

Two surveys consisting of 2000 men in the UK (mean ± SD age 41.9 ± 15.2) and 5000 men in the US (mean + SD age 33.23 ± 17.2) both found that from a list of values, the core values most aspired to were being honest, reliable and dependable. The two core values least aspired to were being adventurous and athletic (Barry 2020). The key predictor of mental positivity in both countries was job satisfaction, and relationship stability was in the top five predictors in both countries. Taken together, these findings don't suggest at all that men in the US and UK are afflicted by toxic masculinity, and in fact the opposite was true. A strength of these surveys is that masculinity was not predefined by the researchers, but was defined by the responses of the participants to a variety of questions.

There are many positive things about male-typical traits and masculinity that should be valued. Here are just a few examples taken from the topic chapters in this book that are true of men and boys in general:

- Developmental – the high energy typical of boys is naturally positive if channelled appropriately
- Education – boys excel in STEM and sport
- Sports – watching top athletes provides enjoyment for others
- Workplace: men excel in various fields (STEM etc), and also do dangerous and dirty jobs without complaining
- Military – the armed forces channel male potential in a positive way. During war men make huge sacrifices to protect others

- Forensic/crime – research suggests that unless they are damaged in some way (deprivation, trauma etc), men typically are valuable as citizens, especially as fathers
- Physical health: men have pioneered the science of medicine, and risk their health in dangerous Phase I trials
- Mental health – male ways of coping with stress are effective, e.g. stoicism/REBT (rational emotive behaviour therapy)

One of the themes shown by this list is that men and boys are a great asset to society, but if their strengths are overlooked (such as STEM skills) or even seen as weakness (risk-taking, competition, stoicism, energy etc), this is not going to bring the best out of them.

12.6.3 *Rethinking Stoicism*

The male-typical tendency to control their emotions is well-recognised. Some scales observe it non-judgementally as a trait (Seager et al., 2014a); others see it more negatively, e.g. the 'Restrictive Emotionality' subscale of the MRNI (Levant et al., 2010). It is easy to get the impression that not talking about feelings is something done only by men, but it is important to realise that sometimes women are reluctant to talk about their feelings, especially when the problem is related to feminine identity (see Section 11.3.5).

Therapeutic value of stoicism
Rational Emotive Behaviour Therapy (REBT) is a widely used type of CBT. A meta-analysis of 50 years of research concluded that 'REBT appeared to be superior to other psychological interventions' (David et al., 2018, p. 316). The difference between REBT and other interventions on outcomes was a medium effect size ($d = 0.58$). So what makes REBT so successful? Perhaps it is because it includes, as one of the core components, stoicism.

REBT is about learning to control feelings by changing one's views about things. The creator of REBT (or RET as it was known until the 1990s), psychologist Albert Ellis, said that it 'mainly endorses one of the main Stoic tenets, that of (Epictetus, 1865): "Men are disturbed not by things, but by the view which they take of them"' (Ellis 1979, p. 89). The views of Epictetus and other Greek and Roman Stoic philosophers such as Epicurus and Marcus Aurelius, and their philosophical view that psychological disturbance was caused not by events but by a person's beliefs about events, became the foundation of REBT (Ellis, 2007).

Ellis explicitly rejected versions of stoicism that saw emotion as unimportant or bad, such as the views of Zeno (Ellis, 1979). So REBT rejects suppression of feelings, but is about mastering feelings. This sense of mastery and control of feelings is captured by Seager's conception of masculinity (Seager, 2019).

The idea that psychotherapists should consider that, for men in particular, emotional inexpressiveness can be a strength, and useful in helping them deal with their problems, has been suggested by other psychologists (Heesacker & Prichard, 1992). Stoicism is probably an evolved part of men's role as being the providers and protectors, thus the people expected to deal with situations of threat and danger, in which mastering feelings would be a valuable ability. It is unfortunate that this view has generally been overlooked, because an REBT approach might be especially useful for men who don't feel comfortable exploring their feelings, and who feel better about engaging in rational problem solving. However, overlooking stoicism is perhaps inevitable in a culture of therapy that is heavily invested in the idea of the therapeutic necessity of emotional disclosure (Holloway et al., 2018).

It is often said these days that masculinity is bad for help-seeking, and that stoicism is one of the main barriers. However, the success of REBT is very much an elephant in the room of this issue. It seems likely that harnessing men's tendency to stoicism, and formulating it using something like REBT, could be a major step forward in making therapy more appealing for men.

We hypothesise that in relation to masculinity, trying too hard to be masculine – or being too rigid – can backfire. With regards the male gender script about having *mastery and control over one's feelings* (Seager et al, 2014), Figure 12.2 shows that not trying to control feelings at all will result in 'emotional incontinence', trying to hard will lead to extreme stress, but there is a happy medium – perhaps with the help of REBT – where moderate effort gives maximum reward. This concept is based on the Yerkes-Dodson law (see Section 6.5.3), and in theory applies to being too rigid about any aspects of masculinity.

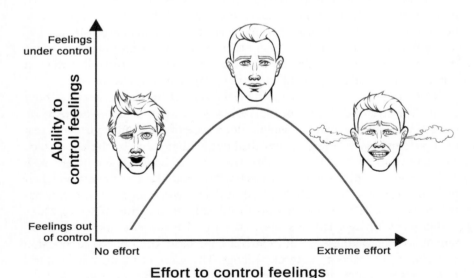

FIGURE 12.2 *An illustration of the hypothesis that there is an optimum level of effort for successfully controlling one's feelings.*

TRADITIONAL MASCULINITY AND RUDYARD KIPLING'S *IF—*

If— was written around 1895 by English author Rudyard Kipling (1865–1936). It has been described as, and voted as, the UK's favourite poem (BBC, 1998). Compared to some poetry, where the meaning is hidden in layers of metaphor, *If—* is a fairly straightforward tribute to stoicism, also known as the British 'stiff upper lip'.

If you can keep your head when all about you
Are losing theirs and blaming it on you;
If you can trust yourself when all men doubt you,
But make allowance for their doubting too;
If you can wait and not be tired by waiting,
Or, being lied about, don't deal in lies,
Or, being hated, don't give way to hating,
And yet don't look too good, nor talk too wise;
If you can dream – and not make dreams
your master;
If you can think – and not make thoughts your aim;
If you can meet with triumph and disaster
And treat those two impostors just the same;
If you can bear to hear the truth you've spoken
Twisted by knaves to make a trap for fools,
Or watch the things you gave your life to broken,
And stoop and build 'em up with worn-out tools;
If you can make one heap of all your winnings
And risk it on one turn of pitch-and-toss,
And lose, and start again at your beginnings
And never breathe a word about your loss;
If you can force your heart and nerve and sinew
To serve your turn long after they are gone,
And so hold on when there is nothing in you
Except the Will which says to them: 'Hold on';
If you can talk with crowds and keep your virtue,
Or walk with kings – nor lose the common touch;
If neither foes nor loving friends can hurt you;
If all men count with you, but none too much;
If you can fill the unforgiving minute
With sixty seconds' worth of distance run –
Yours is the Earth and everything that's in it,
And – which is more – you'll be a Man, my son!

Besides stoicism, the poem contains other themes related to masculinity: the value of hard work ('build 'em up', 'hold on'), risk-taking ('on one turn of pitch-and-toss'), and being a fighter and – ultimately – a winner ('yours is the Earth').

Other virtues are extolled, such as patience ('not be tired of waiting') and modesty ('don't look too good').

These ideals are not usually valued in the same way these days but nonetheless still strike a chord with many people, possibly because they ring true as a resilient approach to life, in contrast to a 'victim mentality' which is unlikely to be good for mental health.

12.6.4   *Masculinity in Men Who Commit Crime*

Previously we have seen that ideas about masculinity have been generalised from young men to men in general, with the result that all men are seen as having a relatively immature attitude. Antisocial attitudes, such as homophobia and misogyny, have also been tagged onto some recent definitions of masculinity, with the result that all men are under suspicion of having antisocial attitudes, and by extension committing criminal acts. This raises the question: what is masculinity like in men who commit crime? One way to explore this is by looking at masculinity in prison.

BEING A MAN... IN PRISON

In even the harshest situations men can be compassionate and caring to each other, but prison is a place where masculinity and hierarchy are distilled to – arguably – the most potently destructive levels.

In the UK, although hypermasculine identities are seen in young offender institutes where hierarchy is often achieved through violence, in adult prisons position in the hierarchy depends on criminal history, masculine conduct in prison and previous reputation (Maguire, 2019). Adult prisoners lose respect if engaging in youth-offender levels of violence, which is seen as immature and a sign of not coping with prison life.

For men in the UK, prison masculinity is demonstrated in stoicism, not having a history of crime against vulnerable people, being able to use controlled aggression or violence to stand up for oneself, giving and receiving respect to fellow prisoners and staff, not relying overly on others, high personal and cell hygiene and demonstrating that you can 'do the time' (i.e. complete the prison sentence without undue distress).

Conversely, the lowest in the hierarchy are informers, serial rapists and paedophiles, and others who may need to go onto the 'vulnerable prisoners unit' for their own protection for other reasons (Maguire, 2019).

Masculinity and age in prison

The difference between what it means to be a man in prison as an adolescent and what it means as a mature man is very clear – violence is much more common in young offenders. This reinforces the idea that age is an important variable when trying to understand masculinity.

'Young male syndrome' is a term given to the increase in atypically competitive, risk-taking and violent behaviour that is not uncommon in young men, rising in the teenage years, peaking around 20 years old, then trailing off (Wilson & Daly, 1985). Many men pass into this phase and grow out of it, and although foolhardy and life-changing actions might be taken during this time, the most challenging aspects of the person usually diminish over time (Moffitt & Caspi, 2001).

12.6.5   *Is Masculinity a Useful Concept in Psychology?*

Until recently the concept of masculinity barely appeared in psychology at all, but the past few decades have seen a steady increase in interest, to the point where guidelines are now being developed for psychologists in various parts of the world. Unfortunately, these are often based on flawed ideas about masculinity borrowed from sociology and gender studies. At the time of writing this book, the negative view of masculinity is not yet part of the core curriculum of undergraduate psychology, but the fact that guidelines have appeared recently in the US, UK and Australia means it is likely that before long therapists will be trained to adopt the views of these guidelines, and most likely undergraduate psychology programmes will teach the same views too.

Some parts of these guidelines are no doubt benign. For example, the APA guidelines contain some good advice on male-friendly therapy (Guideline 9). However, even with the best of intentions towards male clients, it is difficult to imagine how men are going to be helped by an approach founded on the assumption that men's problems are caused by a sinister worldwide system called patriarchy and a social construction called hegemonic masculinity (Guidelines 1 and 3; see Section 11.4.4). No doubt it's much easier to blame masculinity for men's behaviour rather than social deprivation, drugs, or trauma (Figure 8.1). For example, if you attribute male violence to trauma and social deprivation, then you have the tricky and expensive job of treating these issues and preventing them from happening to others, which will mean investing in long-term solutions to issues such as poverty, fatherless homes, child abuse etc.

12.6.5.1   *Can we address masculinity ethically in psychology?*

Psychologists are under ethical obligation to 'take care to do no harm' (APA, 2002, p. 1062), and not to use therapy to change an individual's gender identity, which is called 'conversion therapy': '"Conversion therapy" is the term for therapy that assumes certain sexual orientations or gender identities are inferior to others and seeks to change or suppress them. It is unethical, potentially harmful and is not based on any reputable evidence' (BPS, 2019, p. 3).

12.7 CONCLUDING REMARKS

Given our current state of knowledge, psychologists should be cautious about following any guidelines that are based on negative views of masculinity that could be damaging for some male clients, or have unintended consequences that are worse than the presenting problem (*Theme: 'unintended consequences', in Section 13.2.1*). The risk doesn't seem justified when we already have other therapies (e.g. REBT) that have got a good record of safety and efficacy and seem much more likely to be attractive to male clients.

So far the introduction of masculinity to psychology has not been a success, largely because masculinity has been defined unrealistically. The mischaracterisation of masculinity hasn't been much use in explaining men's mental health, or help-seeking, or other crucial issues in psychology. Perhaps most importantly, it hasn't learned from its own shortcomings, despite these being highlighted decades ago (Good et al., 1994). Its value as applied to therapy remains to be proved, and it seems unlikely that men will flock to a therapy based on hegemonic masculinity and patriarchy theory in order to solve their psychological problems.

Is it possible to redeem masculinity in psychology, e.g. by focusing on a more realistic construction (e.g. Seager et al., 2014a) and with a more humanistic approach (e.g. Kiselica & Englar-Carlson, 2010)? If we are optimistic, we might hope that 'the past should not limit the future of research' (Pardue & Wizemann, 2001).

12.8 SUMMARY

- This chapter considered the relevance of masculinity research to psychology and culture
- Highlighted the problems with how 'masculinity' is defined
- Recognised that masculinity is seen negatively by many institutions, though there is evidence that the general public reject terms like 'toxic masculinity'
- Some psychologists have replaced biology with patriarchy to explain masculinity, but relying solely on a cultural explanation for masculinity is not sufficient and doesn't appear to inspire the development of male-friendly therapies

- Showed that the obstacles to male help-seeking are not explained by masculinity
- Recognised that masculinity changes dramatically over the lifespan
- Recognised that the potential value of the concept of masculinity in psychology has fallen far short of being achieved

Part 4

Concluding Remarks and Final Thoughts

13 Conclusion

CHAPTER OUTLINE

13.1 INTRODUCTION

The chapters in this book have reviewed a large body of research related to the psychology of men and boys. This concluding chapter will bring together some of the main findings and suggest how we can advance these and develop practical applications of male psychology. It will start by bringing together and reviewing some of the overarching and recurring themes. Next, the idea of social-ecological models will be introduced as a way to identify male psychology research needs and interventions. Seven recommendations are then made regarding future directions in male psychology, and the chapter concludes with some thoughts on the journey the readers of this book have been on.

Perspectives in Male Psychology: An Introduction, First Edition.
Louise Liddon and John A. Barry.
© 2021 John Wiley & Sons, Ltd. Published 2021 by John Wiley & Sons, Ltd.

13.2 KEY THEMES IN MALE PSYCHOLOGY

Various themes have emerged in this book. Figure 13.1 shows an overview of these themes. Each theme is described below, followed by an example.

13.2.1   *Theme: Unintended Consequences*

In the 1970s conservation biologists became concerned about the turtle population size because of the huge numbers of newly hatched turtles that were eaten by predators in the rush to the sea. The biologists – sometimes with the assistance of schoolchildren volunteers – would pre-empt the rush by digging up the eggs before they hatched, incubating them under laboratory conditions until they hatched and had grown enough to be more able to survive, and then releasing them directly into the sea. This seemed like a good solution, but the biologists did not realise that the temperature at which the eggs are incubated influences the sex of the turtle, and that colder conditions favour the birth of males. It takes about 20 years for the sex of turtles to become apparent, and in this time the conservationists realised that their incubators were slightly too cool, so they had flooded the turtle ecosystem with males. This reduced breeding opportunities, and negatively impacted the size of the turtle population. So despite their well-meaning efforts, the conservation biologists were working counter to their goal of helping the turtle population (Mank, 2016). This demonstrates not only how an apparently sensible idea can be badly flawed, but also how apparently trivial aspects of the environment – slight variations in temperature at a sensitive period of development – can have an unexpectedly significant negative impact decades later.

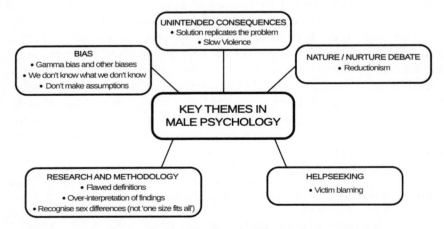

FIGURE 13.1 *Themes around research and methodology in the present book.*

It could that 'turning up the heat' on traditional masculinity will have unintended consequences, such as creating boys who completely lose interest in starting a family, or embrace the idea of 'toxic masculinity' as an ideal to live up to (see Section 4.6). An example that could relate to unintended consequences in this book is that more gender-equal countries show greater sex differences in maths and that mental health is worse for girls in more gender-equal countries, possibly due to greater expectations on them (see Section 5.7).

Subtheme: The solution replicates the problem

Sometimes gender equality schemes seem to replace one type of inequality with another. A better solution is to listen to all voices, which is probably key to a harmonious society. Examples of 'the solution replicating the problem' are replacing the old boys' network with an old girls' network (Section 7.7): the movement of feminist criminologists to bring more focus to the causes of women's criminality appears to have led to a reduced focus on the causes of criminality in men (Section 8.4.3.1).

Subtheme: Slow violence

'Slow violence' is a term coined to explain the destructive consequences of actions which only show up years or decades later (Nixon, 2011). This has not been applied to psychology very much, but examples can be seen e.g., aggression (see Section 8.2.4), such as false allegations (SPOTLIGHT box 8.2), coercive control or criticism in relationships, might not have immediate effects, but can harm mental and physical health in the long term (see Section 8.2.4).

13.2.2   Theme: Nature vs Nurture Debate

A classic problem is when explanations get stuck in the black and white thinking of a nature vs nurture debate. The APA guidelines on therapy for men and boys falls into the 'nurture' side of the trap in asserting that masculinity is wholly a social construct (APA, 2018).

Subtheme: Reductionism

It is tempting to find simple explanations for complex issues, but oversimplification to one explanatory factor is known as reductionism. Human nature is inevitably more complex than can be described in one dimension, and some combination of nature and nurture normally occurs, and issues are best thought of in terms of reciprocal determinism, epigenetics etc (Plomin et al., 2012). An example of this is the APA's view of masculinity, being explained simply as a result of socialisation, and not sufficiently taking other relevant explanatory variables into account.

13.2.3   *Theme: Help-Seeking*

This was a common theme in several chapters (military, crime, clinical, health, education etc) and a key issue in most cases. Not seeking help for mental health issues has potentially catastrophic effects, often leading to the problem getting worse and degenerating into acting out in violence, or suicide (see Figure 12.1).

Subtheme: Victim-blaming
Related to help-seeking, sometimes men are blamed for not seeking help, usually because the barriers to help-seeking (Figure 12.1) have not been taken into consideration. One of the reasons for this is that men tend to be seen as having more agency than women, so are more likely to be blamed when it appears that they have failed to help themselves (Reynolds et al., 2020). Another type of victim-blaming is not seeing how sometimes delinquency is related to being the victim of trauma or deprivation (see Figure 8.1). As long as the victim is being blamed, policy makers fail to investigate how to improve services for men.

13.2.4   *Theme: Research and Methodology*

Several issues around research methodology need to be addressed (Figure 13.1). One of the main issues was seen in masculinity research, where there is a tendency for studies in this field to incorporate the same shortcomings in their research design, thus all coming to similar – but flawed – conclusions (see Section 12.2). The key flaws are definitions of masculinity based on a negative stereotype of men; samples tending to be mostly college-aged men; and data analysis being correlational.

Subtheme: Flawed definitions
There are many examples in this book, but possibly the main one is the redefinition of masculinity (see SPOTLIGHT box 12.2). Research based on flawed definitions will yield flawed conclusions. Masculinity has only recently been a topic in psychology, having been imported from sociology. It can be argued that the contribution of discussions of masculinity to psychology has been minimally beneficial. For example, the term masculinity has been expanded to include behaviours (e.g. homophobia and gender-based violence) that are normally considered somewhat pathological, and not confined to men. Also, aspects of masculinity that were previously respected have been pathologised (e.g. stoicism and competition). Flawed definitions have been used in an attempt to create a connection between masculinity and mental health problems (see SPOTLIGHT boxes 11.3 and 12.2).

Subtheme: Over-interpretation of findings

Another common problem with methodology is the over-interpretation of findings. Most often this occurs in relation to correlational analysis, where the adage 'correlation does not prove causation' is not taken into account. This issue is seen mainly in the correlation between masculinity and mental health problems, which is too often taken at face value, without due consideration of the possible presence of a crucial 'third variable' which would explain the correlation e.g. trauma influences scoring on both 'masculinity' scores and mental health scores, so the causal connection is not between masculinity and mental health problems (see Section 12.2).

Subtheme: The whole is greater than the sum of its parts, and 'the difference that makes the difference'.

The reductionist tendency is to simplify explanations to their smallest component part. However, lots of phenomena are more complex than that, and we can only get a true picture by putting together lots of pieces of evidence, like building up a mosaic or jigsaw puzzle. Even if by themselves the individual piece of evidence is not particularly strong, if it is consistently found, or fits as part of a larger pattern, then we should take notice. This is the case with some of the evidence regarding masculinity, where the individual pieces of evidence might have only a moderate effect size by themselves (measured by Cohen's d), but if pooled with other evidence the combined effect size (Mahalanobi's D) might be much larger (see SPOTLIGHT box 3.3).

Subtheme: Recognising sex/gender differences

Although sex differences are obvious to many people, in some circles pointing them out is virtually taboo. This appears to be in part due to the success of the spread of a rigid interpretation of the maxim that 'there are more similarities than differences between the sexes' (Hyde, 2005) (see Section 7.2). Although this maxim is undoubtedly true, it is only part of the whole truth, and like any partial truth it can be misleading or even harmful if treated as if the whole truth. Many academic journals continue to show reluctance to publish research on sex differences if they reach conclusions that are unpopular in academia (Geary & Stoet, 2020). The consequence is that many people, in academia and the mass media, don't realise that although there are fewer differences than similarities, (a) some differences have implications for lifestyle etc, and (b) when lots of small differences are taken together, they can add up to obvious sex differences.

Subtheme: There are more similarities than differences/'one-size-fits-all'

This is the idea that men and women are so similar that they can be treated as if pretty much the same. However there are differences, and some of these are important e.g. preferences for therapy (see Section 11.6). Beta bias occurs when differences between men and women are overlooked.

Subtheme: Yin and yang (balance of opposites is needed)

Ancient Chinese Taoism sees *yin* and *yang* as a complementary balance of opposite forces, such as femininity and masculinity. According to this philosophy, every man is mostly masculine but also has a small amount of femininity, and every woman is mostly feminine but also has a small amount of masculinity. This theme echoes across many topics in psychology, e.g. Carl Jung's concept of *anima* and *animus*, homeostasis, the ratio of testosterone to oestrogen in men and women, X and Y chromosomes (Barry & Owens, 2019) and subjective/qualitative research vs objective/quantitative research. Yin is associated with feelings and yang with analysis (Slote, 2020), so we could also hypothesise a yin and yang of coping with stress, such as talking about feelings versus fixing the problem see Section 11.4.1).

13.2.5 *Theme: Cognitive Bias and Research Bias*

'Nothing is right or wrong, but thinking makes it so' (Shakespeare's *Hamlet*). In other words, in one sense, anything can be viewed as bad. One way to do this is by highlighting only the negative aspects of something and ignoring any positives.

This book has encountered examples of issues where opinions and feelings seem to count more than facts. This is no doubt an inevitable part of human subjectivity, but it seems to apply especially to issues around sex and gender, perhaps because everyone has their own experiences on this topic, and therefore feelings that are subjectively valid. But increasingly peoples' 'lived experience' is being cited not only as if it is more important than objective truth, but that some scientific facts should not be discussed. How do we achieve a more balanced discourse? Perhaps freedom of speech is the way, but this has been limited on the subject of gender in recent years.

Examples of biases around gender are: alpha bias (Section 2.5.5.1) where sex differences are emphasised, beta bias (Section 2.5.5.1) where sex differences are obscured, gamma bias (Section 2.5.5.1) where sex differences are emphasised for one sex but obscured for the other, delta bias (Section 2.5.5.2) where traits that are more common in one sex are encouraged in the other sex, sample bias and population bias (SPOTLIGHT 12.2) where findings from research with a sample from a specific group of people (e.g. university students) are treated as if they apply to all people.

Subtheme: Unknown unknowns, or 'we don't know what we don't know'

Our knowledge is based on a finite number of possibly fallible sources, e.g. our experiences, the media, education etc. But what if our knowledge includes large gaps, or is significantly distorted by cognitive biases? We need to allow for the possibility that we are wrong about what we think we know, so we should always strive to be flexible in our thinking (see Section 11.5.7).

Subtheme: Don't make assumptions – do the research

There are examples in research into gender where assumptions have been unhelpful, e.g. that the presence of male teachers improves boys' grades (Section 5.3.4), or that men's violence is caused by testosterone (SPOTLIGHT box 3.1). Hypothesis testing should be applied even to – or in some cases especially to – phenomena that we take for granted. Also it is necessary that research findings are not just ignored, as has been the case with evidence that gender is partly innate (Section 3.7.2.1).

13.3 MALE PSYCHOLOGY: A SYSTEMS APPROACH

The male psychology approach is interested in men in various contexts (such as the workplace, in school), the relevance of different demographics (such as age, educational level) and aspects of the culture (such as narratives about masculinity). Other aspects of male psychology include practical applications (e.g. designing mental health interventions). All activities take a scientific and humanistic approach, and can be seen as holistic. Taking a holistic and evidence-based approach means being aware of a sufficient number of relevant variables so as to be able to understand the causes of problems and their likely solutions. We have seen that some approaches have proved too narrow (SPOTLIGHT box 12.2) or incorrect (e.g. Duluth model), leading to inadequate interventions (Section 8.6.5).

One way to take a holistic and evidence-based approach is to view the individual and their environment as an interconnected system, in which all parts of the system can interact, directly and indirectly. The following section will introduce a *systems approach* that can be used as a starting point for planning male psychology research. Firstly, a basic social-ecological model will be outlined, followed by a more complex model which emphasises the study of relationships within and between different systems. The models discussed have been simplified to benefit those not familiar with such theories, and research professionals might find more elaborate models useful, e.g. Bronfenbrenner's ecological model (Bronfenbrenner, 1979).

This section is not essential for researching male psychology, but is a way of helping researchers to think flexibly about research design and avoid 'paradigm fixation'. This section also provides some context to many of the areas of discussion already provided within the previous chapters of this book.

13.3.1 *Social-Ecological Model of Male Psychology*

Generic social-ecological models can act as useful conceptual tools for recognising that individuals are embedded within multiple and larger social systems. They are also useful aids to theorising, researching and identifying factors that might be of importance to understanding a person's experiences and outcomes. Figure 13.2 and corresponding Table 13.1 draw upon examples from this book.

Changes over time, and changes between levels of the system

It should be noted that the various factors will change over time. For example, cultural attitudes to masculinity have, and will, change over time. Also, there are often interactions between the levels of the system, and sometimes the solution to a problem on one level can be found in another level. For example, a man may struggle to connect with a therapist who sees his male-typical communication style as a sign they are not ready to undertake therapy. Changes in the discourse around men's mental health might improve understanding and empathy for men, and an appreciation of male-typical communication. This might in turn increase funding for research, influence improvements on a policy level, which improves the training of therapists in helping male clients.

FIGURE 13.2 *An ecological model of male psychology.*

TABLE 13.1 *Examples of male psychology within different levels of the ecological system.*

Level	Model description	Topic	Example
Individual	Characteristics of men such as age, social class, personality, experience, biology etc	Male-typical traits	Younger men are more inclined to risky behaviours
Interpersonal	Men's personal relationships, social networks and support systems	Male-typical communication styles	Men's banter
Organisational	Characteristics of institutions and organisations impacting men such as rules and regulations	Career development	Gender equality programmes
Community	Social and environmental contexts including cultural norms impacting men	Cultural attitudes to masculinity	Media narrative on men & masculinity
Public policy	Polices and laws that govern men and society	Family courts	Separation of men from children after family breakdown

13.4   RECOMMENDATIONS

Perhaps, like men in general, male psychology is interested not just in exploring problems but finding practical solutions (Figure 11.3). This following section, while not being an exhaustive list, builds on some of the key material in this book to provide seven recommendations for the advancement of knowledge and practice of male psychology.

Recommendations

1. Do no harm
2. Be creative in finding solutions
3. Research masculinity
4. Uphold the standards of science
5. Engage in healthy debate
6. Reduce the influence of gamma bias
7. Encourage empathy for men

Recommendation 1: *Do no harm*
This is an important basic requirement of psychology.

a) **Ethics.** Codes of ethics usually prioritise not doing harm, and the BPS suggests we should respect gender differences (Section 11.4.5). This has implications for ideas based on beta bias (e.g. gender similarities hypothesis) stifling gender differences research (Section 3.6.2.1).

b) Interventions that prove inadequate (e.g. the Duluth model – see Section 8.6.5) should be improved or replaced.

c) Interventions in clinics, and workshops in schools, should be tested for safety and efficacy. It is unethical to apply a theory to people if there is a risk they will be harmed. This applies to hegemonic masculinity, patriarchy and other ideas that cast men in an unreasonably negative light.

d) Be mindful of the effects of language, e.g. 'toxic masculinity' (Section 4.6.1).

Recommendation 2: *Be creative in finding solutions*

Decades of research into masculinity shows the consequences of falling into set ways of thinking.

a) One way forward is to abandon deficit models of masculinity altogether and use tried and tested models of clinical psychology (see Section 12.6.3).

b) Another way forward is to create shifts in thinking by using social-ecological models. These can help identify solutions in unexpected places, e.g. looking at possible solutions to mental health issues (in the individual level) on other levels (e.g. the community level; Section 11.6.3).

c) Another way of looking at this is to look for solutions to problems in one topic area in another. For example, sport as a solution to mental health problems (Section 6.6.3.1); or helping to create more stability in families (Section 8.6.5). This way of thinking also demonstrates advantages of using male psychology as an axis connecting different topic areas.

Recommendation 3: *Research masculinity*

For those who want to continue to research masculinity, on the basis that past mistakes 'should not limit the future of research' (Pardue & Wizemann, 2001, p. 10), then we need to break out of the 'research paradigm fixation' in this field. The following are essential:

a) Evolutionary/archetype-based measures of masculinity (e.g. Seager et al., 2014a) should be used in tandem with constructs of masculinity based on hegemonic masculinity, and the findings compared. On review of several such comparisons, only measures that demonstrate value should be used thereafter.

b) Include older men in research on masculinity, not just college-aged men, and also men from a variety of social backgrounds and cultures.

c) Include all relevant variables: e.g. in studies of masculinity and mental health, especially measure trauma (e.g. ACEs, military combat, or other sources of PTSD), as these might account for a large degree of 'toxic masculinity' behaviour (see Section 4.4.3).

Recommendation 4: *Uphold the standards of science*

It is important that standards of science are upheld in male psychology (SPOTLIGHT box 12.2).

a) **Unscientific/unfalsifiable ideas**. According to Karl Popper, a theory is not scientific unless it has the potential to be proved wrong (aka fallibility). This is the basis for hypothesis testing. If a study finds good evidence against a theory, the theory needs to be modified accordingly, rather than dismiss the evidence or subsume the evidence into the theory in a way that suggests that the theory is fundamentally intact. Patriarchy theory is undermined by even a single instance of where women have power over men. There are many such instances (family courts, reproductive rights etc) but these are minimised by proponents of patriarchy theory. By the same token, new theories such as gamma bias should be tested and refined.

b) **Objectivity**. Although in some ways it is a goal that might never be reached, objectivity should always be strived for in good faith. Researcher bias (e.g. beta bias and alpha bias) is always something to be on guard against. Sometimes researchers bring with them their preconceived notions of the world, as is widely recognised in cross-cultural research, where people are sensitive to ethnocentrism, which occurs when a researcher assumes that their own culturally specific practices or ideas are 'natural' or 'right', and makes judgements about other individuals from other ethnic groups. It can be argued that a similar situation has occurred regarding the study of men's psychology, and that the solution is to recognise that a more 'culturally informed' approach is needed. It might be useful to think of men having a different culture to women in certain respects (e.g. banter in the workplace, sports and the military) that is hard to understand when other cultural standards are imposed on them.

c) **Multidimensional approach**. Unidimensional research that is based only the sociocultural/social constructionist perspective has proved itself to be less than useful. A triangulation of perspectives, or a least a reasonable incorporation of the biological/evolutionary perspective, is needed.

d) Anecdotal evidence. Also popularly known as 'lived experience', anecdotal evidence may be useful and emotionally powerful, but is not a replacement for, or equivalent to, properly conducted scientific evidence, based on repeated systematic observation, measurement and experimentation.

Recommendation 5: *Engage in healthy debate; be reflective and open to new ideas*

Healthy debate is part of science. It is something that should be welcomed by anyone who is genuinely interested in sharing, testing and developing ideas. We have seen that debate is not enthusiastically embraced in gender studies (Section 5.5.1; Stewart-Williams, 2018) and this trend is unhealthy for science. One outcome of debate is to keep ideas from stagnating in silos and echo chambers where 'research paradigm fixation' can run unchecked. Proponents of the critical perspective, postmodernism and other views must be prepared to debate and rationally defend their views as a condition of being an equal part of the science of psychology. Preventing others from discussing or debating issues, should not be an option. Methods designed to avoid healthy discussion such as cancelling and no-platforming, have no place in academia (Pluckrose & Lindsay, 2020). The media should represent issues in a genuinely balanced way.

Recommendation 6: *Reduce the influence of gamma bias*

Gamma bias distorts our ability to clearly see gender issues. It is probably impossible to eradicate this, given that it is probably part of our evolved way of seeing the world. However, we need to (a) be aware that it exists and (b) be able to limit its influence, especially in professionals (e.g. policy makers) who influence the lives of others. One way to limit the influence of gamma bias is to imagine for a moment that the sexes were reversed for some of the issues raised in this book:

> *What if you heard that a cultural anthropologist had found a previously undiscovered village in a very remote part of the world. The anthropologist reported that the dirty and dangerous jobs were almost always done by women, almost all of the people in prison were women, women were forced to fight each other in wars with neighbouring villages, many women came home from the wars traumatised by killing and seeing others killed, women often developed mental health problems - becoming aggressive or even violent - but these signs of trauma went unrecognised; women often treated their mental health problems themselves, numbing their feelings with alcohol or drugs, and many eventually ended their lives through suicide. The men in the village didn't seem to notice these problems, so the anthropologist decided to take action: in order to get the men to recognise the problems facing women, he presented the facts as if they were problems being faced by men.*

Recommendation 7: *Encourage empathy for men*
Perhaps the most important recommendation of this book is that researchers, therapists and everybody else take serious steps to develop their capacity for empathy for men. This might involve reading books, taking workshops, and attending conferences that incorporate a balanced, male-friendly view of men and masculinity (see Section 11.6). Empathy for men should be considered a key part of any therapeutic interaction with men.

13.5   FINAL THOUGHTS

Article 1 of the United Nations' *Universal Declaration of Human Rights* states: 'All human beings are born free and equal in dignity and rights. They are endowed with reason and conscience and should act towards one another in a spirit of brotherhood' (UN, 1948, p. 2). Most people would agree with this, but gamma bias prevents many of us from having an accurate perception of equality, so that we mistakenly see sexism as implicated in some inequalities (e.g. STEM), but don't see it as implicated in other inequalities (e.g. male suicide). Little wonder that we live in a world of intractable problems such as the mysterious 'leaky pipeline' in STEM, and the perennial problem of male suicide. Until we focus on sex/gender issues clearly we will live in a world where we are unable to solve problems that are related to sex/gender. We hope that this introductory book, and the future books in this series, will help to improve this situation for everyone, men and women alike.

References

Abbott, D. (2013). *Britain's Crisis of Masculinity*. http://www.demos.co.uk/files/Diane-Abbottspeech16May2013.pdf

Abram, K. M., Washburn, J. J., Teplin, L. A., Emanuel, K. M., Romero, E. G., & McClelland, G. M. (2007). Posttraumatic stress disorder and psychiatric comorbidity among detained youths. *Psychiatric Services, 58*(10), 1311–1316.

Abotsie, G., Kingerlee, R., Fisk, A., Watts, S., Cooke, R., Woodley, L., Collins, D., & Teague, B. (2020). The men's wellbeing project: promoting the well-being and mental health of men. *Journal of Public Mental Health, Ahead-of-print*, (ahead-of-print). https://doi.org/10.1108/JPMH-03-2020-0014

Adams, Z. W., McCart, M. R., Zajac, K., Danielson, C. K., Sawyer, G. K., Saunders, B. E., & Kilpatrick, D. G. (2013). Psychiatric problems and trauma exposure in nondetained delinquent and nondelinquent adolescents. *Journal of Clinical Child & Adolescent Psychology, 42*(3), 323–331.

Addis, M. E. (2010). Response to commentaries on the problem of masculinity. *Psychology of Men & Masculinity, 11*(2), 109–112. https://doi.org/10.1037/a0019314

Adegbesan, O. A. (2007). Indices of choking under pressure among athletes during competition. *Perceptual and Motor Skills, 105*(3_suppl), 1093–1098. https://doi.org/10.2466/pms.105.4.1093-1098

Affleck, W., Carmichael, V., & Whitley, R. (2018). Men's mental health: social determinants and implications for services. *The Canadian Journal of Psychiatry, 63*(9), 581–589. https://doi.org/10.1177/0706743718762388

Aggarwal, N. K., Pieh, M. C., Dixon, L., Guarnaccia, P., Alegria, M., & Lewis-Fernandez, R. (2016). Clinician descriptions of communication strategies to improve treatment engagement by racial/ethnic minorities in mental health services: a systematic review. *Patient Education and Counseling, 99*(2), 198–209.

Aisbett, D. L., Boyd, C. P., Francis, K. J., & Newnham, K. (2007). Understanding barriers to mental health service utilization for adolescents in rural Australia. *Rural and Remote Health, 7*, 624.

Alamgir, H., Turner, C. A., Wong, N. J., Cooper, S. P., Betancourt, J. A., Henry, J., Senchak, A. J., Hammill, T. L., & Packer, M. D. (2016). The impact of hearing impairment and noise-induced hearing injury on quality of life in the active-duty military population: challenges to the study of this issue. *Military Medical Research, 3*. https://doi.org/10.1186/s40779-016-0082-5

Allen, M. S., & Walter, E. E. (2019). Erectile dysfunction: an umbrella review of meta-analyses of risk-factors, treatment, and prevalence outcomes. *The Journal of Sexual Medicine, 16*(4), 531–541. https://doi.org/10.1016/j.jsxm.2019.01.314

Almås, I., Cappelen, A. W., Salvanes, K. G., Sørensen, E. Ø., & Tungodden, B. (2016). What explains the gender gap in college track dropout? Experimental and administrative evidence. *American Economic Review, 106*(5), 296–302. https://doi.org/10.1257/aer.p20161075

American Psychological Association, Boys and Men Guidelines Group. (2018). *APA Guidelines for Psychological Practice with Boys and Men. 36.*

American Society for Reproductive Medicine. (2019). *Infertility. Infertility.* https://www.asrm.org/topics/topics-index/infertility/

Amodia-Bidakowska, A., Laverty, C., & Ramchandani, P. G. (2020). Father-child play: a systematic review of its frequency, characteristics and potential impact on children's development. *Developmental Review, 57*, 100924. https://doi.org/10.1016/j.dr.2020.100924

Anda, R. F., Porter, L. E., & Brown, D. W. (2020). Inside the adverse childhood experience score: strengths, limitations, and misapplications. *American Journal of Preventive Medicine.* https://doi.org/10.1016/j.amepre.2020.01.009

Anderson, P. B., Struckman-Johnson, C., & Smeaton, G. L. (2020). Generation by gender differences in use of sexual aggression: a replication of the millennial shift. *The Journal of Sex Research*, 1–13. https://doi.org/10.1080/00224499.2020.1733457

Andersson, A. M., Jensen, T. K., Juul, A., Petersen, J. H., Jørgensen, T., & Skakkebæk, N. E. (2007). Secular decline in male testosterone and sex hormone binding globulin serum levels in Danish population surveys. *The Journal of Clinical Endocrinology & Metabolism, 92*(12), 4696–4705. https://doi.org/10.1210/jc.2006-2633

Angst, J., Gamma, A., Gastpar, M., Lépine, J.-P., Mendlewicz, J., & Tylee, A. (2002). Gender differences in depression. *European Archives of Psychiatry and Clinical Neuroscience, 252*(5), 201–209.

APA. (2002). Ethical principles of psychologists and code of conduct. *American Psychologist, 57*(12), 1060–1073. https://doi.org/10.1037/0003-066X.57.12.1060

APA. (2015). *Resolution on Violent Video Games.* https://www.apa.org/about/policy/violent-video-games

APA. (2018). *APA Guidelines for Psychological Practice with Boys and Men: (505472019-001)* [Data set]. American Psychological Association. https://doi.org/10.1037/e505472019-001

APS. (2017). *Men and Boys: Ethical Guidelines | APS.* https://www.psychology.org.au/for-members/resource-finder/resources/ethics/Ethical-guidelines-for-psychological-practice-with

Arnocky, S., & Vaillancourt, T. (2014). Sex differences in response to victimization by an intimate partner: more stigmatization and less help-seeking among males. *Journal of Aggression, Maltreatment & Trauma, 23*(7), 705–724.

Assari, S., Caldwell, C. H., & Zimmerman, M. A. (2014). Sex differences in the association between testosterone and violent behaviors. *Trauma Monthly, 19*(3). https://doi.org/10.5812/traumamon.18040

Ashfield, J. A. & Gouws, D. S. (2019). *Dignifying Psychotherapy with Men: Developing Empathic – Google Scholar.* https://scholar.google.co.uk/scholar?hl=en≈sdt=1%2C5&q=Dignifying+Psychotherapy+with+Men%3A+Developing+Empathic&btnG=

Asztalos, M., De Bourdeaudhuij, I., & Cardon, G. (2010). The relationship between physical activity and mental health varies across activity intensity levels and dimensions of mental health among women and men. *Public Health Nutrition, 13*(8), 1207–1214. https://doi.org/10.1017/S1368980009992825

Athow, J. (2019). *Decoding the gender pay gap: how a Bletchley Park codebreaker helped explain a strange paradox | National Statistical.* https://blog.ons.gov.uk/2019/04/16/decoding-the-gender-pay-gap-how-a-bletchley-park-codebreaker-helped-explain-a-strange-paradox/

Autor, D. H., & Wasserman, M. (2013). *Wayward Sons: The Emerging Gender Gap in Labor Markets and Education | VOCEDplus, the International Tertiary Education and Research Database.* https://www.voced.edu.au/content/ngv:73400

Azmat, G., Cuñat, V., & Henry, E. (2020). Gender promotion gaps: career aspirations and workplace discrimination. *SSRN Electronic Journal.* https://doi.org/10.2139/ssrn.3518420

Babcock, J. C., Green, C. E., & Robie, C. (2004). Does batterers' treatment work? A meta-analytic review of domestic violence treatment. *Clinical Psychology Review, 23*(8), 1023–1053. https://doi.org/10.1016/j.cpr.2002.07.001

Bacon, C. G., Giovannucci, E., Testa, M., & Kawachi, I. (2001). The impact of cancer treatment on quality of life outcomes for patients with localized prostate cancer. *The Journal of Urology, 166*(5), 1804–1810.

Baker, A. J. L. (2005). The long-term effects of parental alienation on adult children: a qualitative research study. *The American Journal of Family Therapy, 33*(4), 289–302. https://doi.org/10.1080/01926180590962129

Bandura, A. (2003). Social Cognitive Theory for Personal and Social Change by Enabling Media. In A. Singhal, M. J. Cody, E. M. Rogers, & M. Sabido (Eds.), *Entertainment-Education and Social Change* (pp. 97–118). Routledge.

Bandura, A., Ross, D., & Ross, S. A. (1961). Transmission of aggression through imitation of aggressive models. *The Journal of Abnormal and Social Psychology, 63*(3), 575–582. https://doi.org/10.1037/h0045925

Banyard, P. (2002). *Psychology in Practice: Health: Health.* Hachette UK.

Baratedi, W. M., Tshiamo, W. B., Mogobe, K. D., & McFarland, D. M. (2020). Barriers to prostate cancer screening by men in sub-Saharan Africa: an integrated review. *Journal of Nursing Scholarship, 52*(1), 85–94. https://doi.org/10.1111/jnu.12529

Barker, D. J. (1990). The fetal and infant origins of adult disease. *BMJ, 301*(6761), 1111–1111. https://doi.org/10.1136/bmj.301.6761.1111

Barlett, C., & Coyne, S. M. (2014). A meta-analysis of sex differences in cyber-bullying behavior: the moderating role of age: sex differences in cyber-bullying. *Aggressive Behavior, 40*(5), 474–488. https://doi.org/10.1002/ab.21555

Baron-Cohen, S., Auyeung, B., Ashwin, E., Knickmeyer, R., Lombardo, M., & Chakrabarti, B. (2011). The extreme male brain theory of autism: the role of fetal androgens. In D. Amaral, D. Geschwind, & G. Dawson (Eds.), *Autism Spectrum Disorders* (pp. 991–998). Oxford University Press. https://doi.org/10.1093/med/9780195371826.003.0062

Barr, P. (2004). *Guilt-and shame-proneness and the grief of perinatal bereavement. Psychology and psychotherapy: Theory, research and practice,* 77(4), 493–510.

Barry, J. A. (2016a, Winter). Can psychology bridge the gender empathy gap? *South West Review 4,* 31–38.

Barry, J. A. (2016b). *Review of 'The Mask You Live In' – Male Psychology Network.* https://malepsychology.org.uk/2016/08/25/review-of-the-mask-you-wear/

Barry, J. A. (2019). *Psychological Aspects of Polycystic Ovary Syndrome.* Cham: Palgrave Macmillan.

Barry, J. A. (2020a). *Bold Claims in Need of the Softer Side | The Psychologist.* https://thepsychologist.bps.org.uk/bold-claims-need-softer-side

Barry, J. A. (2020b, April 22). COVID-19's gender gap. *Quillette.* https://quillette.com/2020/04/22/covid-19s-gender-gap/

Barry, J. A. (2020). Job satisfaction, relationship, stability, and valuing one's health are the strongest predictors of men's mental well-being. *Psychreg Journal of Psychology, 4*(3), 4–27.

Barry, J. A., & Liddon, L. (2020). Child contact problems and family court issues are related to chronic mental health problems for men following family breakdown. *Psychreg Journal of Psychology, 4*(3), 57–66.

Barry, J. A., Liddon, L., Kingerlee, R., & Seager, M. J. (2016). More male psychologists? | *The Psychologist.* https://thepsychologist.bps.org.uk/volume-29/june-2016/more-male-psychologists

Barry, J. A., Liddon, L., Walker, R., & Seager, M. J. (in press). How therapists work with men is related to their views on masculinity, patriarchy and politics. *Psychreg Journal of Psychology, 5*, 1.

Barry, J. A., & Seager, M. J. (2014, July 8). *What Can Tony Soprano Teach Men about Therapy?* https://www.menshealthforum.org.uk/what-can-tony-soprano-teach-men-about-therapy

Barry, J. A., & Todd, B. K. (2021). Children Spend Less Time Playing with Gender-Typical Toys These Days, 50, 2, 1-1.

Barry, J. A., Mollan, S., Burdon, M. A., Jenkins, M., & Denniston, A. K. (2017). Development and validation of a questionnaire assessing the quality of life impact of Colour Blindness (CBQoL). *BMC Ophthalmology, 17*(1), 179. https://doi.org/10.1186/s12886-017-0579-z

Barry, J. A., & Owens, R. (2019). From fetuses to boys to men: the impact of testosterone on male lifespan development. In J. A. Barry, R. Kingerlee, M. Seager, & L. Sullivan (Eds.), *The Palgrave Handbook of Male Psychology and Mental Health* (pp. 3–24). Springer International Publishing. https://doi.org/10.1007/978-3-030-04384-1_1

Barry, J. A., & Roper, T. (2016). The developmental and initial validation of the Wellbeing Benefits of Everyday Activities Scale (WBEAS) and the Hairstylist Visit Questionnaire (HVQ): a short report. *New Male Studies, 5*(2), 76–87.

Barry, J. A., Seager, M. J., Liddon, L., Holbrook, J., & Morison, L. (2020). Adults are expected to take responsibility for their problems, especially when those problems are congruent with traditional gender role expectations. *Psychreg Journal of Psychology, 4*(3), 100–119.

Barry, J. A., Walker, R., Liddon, L., & Seager, M. J. (2020). Reactions to contemporary narratives about masculinity: a pilot study. *Psychreg Journal of Psychology, 4*(2), 8–21.

Bassiouni, D. H., Hackley, C., & Meshreki, H. (2019). The integration of video games in family-life dynamics: an adapted technology acceptance model of family intention to consume video games. *Information Technology & People, 32*(6), 1376–1396. https://doi.org/10.1108/ITP-11-2017-0375

Basterrechea, B. B. (2016). Report on promoting gender equality in mental health and clinical research. Committee on Women's Rights and gender Equality, 2016/2096 (INI). https://www.europarl.europa.eu/doceo/document/A-8-2016-0380_EN.pdf

Bates, E. A. (2020). "No one would ever believe me": an exploration of the impact of intimate partner violence victimization on men. *Psychology of Men & Masculinities, 21*(4), 497–507.

Bates, E. A., & Taylor, J. C. (2019). *Intimate Partner Violence: New Perspectives in Research and Practice*. Routledge.

Batten, J., Ripley, M., Anderson, E., Batey, J., & White, A. (2020). Still an occupational hazard? The relationship between homophobia, heteronormativity, student learning and performance, and an openly gay university lecturer. *Teaching in Higher Education, 25*(2), 189–204. https://doi.org/10.1080/13562517.2018.1553031

Bavelier, D., Green, C. S., Han, D. H., Renshaw, P. F., Merzenich, M. M., & Gentile, D. A. (2011). *Brains on Video Games | Nature Reviews Neuroscience*. https://www.nature.com/articles/nrn3135

BBC. (1998). *The Nation's Favourite Poems* (Unabridged edition). BBC Physical Audio.

BBC News. (2019, August 13). Generation X "peak" for deaths by drugs and suicide. *BBC News*. https://www.bbc.com/news/health-49329595

BBC News. (2020, January 27). Football banter at work "excludes women". *BBC News*. https://www.bbc.com/news/business-51261999

Beck, A. T. (1967). *Depression: Clinical, Experimental, and Theoretical Aspects*. Hoeber Medical Division.

Begle, A. M., Hanson, R. F., Danielson, C. K., McCart, M. R., Ruggiero, K. J., Amstadter, A. B., Resnick, H. S., Saunders, B. E., & Kilpatrick, D. G. (2011). Longitudinal pathways of victimization, substance use, and delinquency: findings from the national survey of adolescents. *Addictive Behaviors, 36*(7), 682–689. https://doi.org/10.1016/j.addbeh.2010.12.026

Bell, L., Burtless, G., Gornick, J., & Smeeding, T. M. (2007). *Failure to Launch: Cross-National Trends in the Transition to Economic Independence* (Working Paper No. 456). LIS Working Paper Series. https://www.econstor.eu/handle/10419/95476

Berganza-Conde, M. R. (2003). La construcción mediática de la violencia contra las mujeres desde la Teoría del Enfoque. *Communication & Society, 16*(2), 9–32. https://doi.org/10.15581/003.16.2.9-32

Berger, J. M., Levant, R., McMillan, K. K., Kelleher, W., & Sellers, A. (2005). Impact of gender role conflict, traditional masculinity ideology, alexithymia, and age on men's attitudes toward psychological help seeking. *Psychology of Men & Masculinity, 6*(1), 73.

Berne, E. (1968). *Games People Play: The Psychology of Human Relationships*. Penguin UK.

Berni, T. R., Morgan, C. L., Berni, E. R., & Rees, D. A. (2018). Polycystic ovary syndrome is associated with adverse mental health and neurodevelopmental outcomes. *The Journal of Clinical Endocrinology & Metabolism, 103*(6), 2116–2125. https://doi.org/10.1210/jc.2017-02667

Bertrand, M., & Pan, J. (2013). The trouble with boys: social influences and the gender gap in disruptive behavior. *American Economic Journal: Applied Economics, 5*(1), 32–64.

Bilsker, D., Goldenberg, L., & Davison, J. (2010). *A Roadmap to Men's Health: Current Status, Research, Policy & Practice.*

Bilsker, D., Fogarty, A. S., & Wakefield, M. A. (2018). Critical issues in men's mental health. *The Canadian Journal of Psychiatry, 63*(9), 590–596. https://doi.org/10.1177/0706743718766052

Birger, J. (2015). *Date-onomics: How Dating Became a Lopsided Numbers Game.* Workman Publishing.

Bjerke, T. A., & Rones, N. (2017). The fine line between funny and offensive humour in a total institution. *Res Militaris, 7*(2), 1–23. https://ffi-publikasjoner.archive.knowledgearc.net/bitstream/handle/20.500.12242/857/1534462.pdf?sequence=1

Blanton, H., Jaccard, J., Klick, J., Mellers, B., Mitchell, G., & Tetlock, P. E. (2009). Strong claims and weak evidence: reassessing the predictive validity of the IAT. *Journal of Applied Psychology, 94*(3), 567–582. https://doi.org/10.1037/a0014665

BliegeBird, R., & Smith, E. A. (2005). Signaling Theory, Strategic Interaction, and Symbolic Capital. *Current Anthropology, 46*(2), 221–248. https://doi.org/10.1086/427115

Block, K., Croft, A., De Souza, L., & Schmader, T. (2019). Do people care if men don't care about caring? The asymmetry in support for changing gender roles. *Journal of Experimental Social Psychology, 83*, 112–131. https://doi.org/10.1016/j.jesp.2019.03.013

Blyler, N. (1998). Taking a political turn: the critical perspective and research in professional communication. *Technical Communication Quarterly, 7*(1), 33–52. https://doi.org/10.1080/10572259809364616

Bolster, A., & Berzengi, A. (2019). Hope in the face of despair: an acceptance and commitment therapy approach to working with suicidal ideation in men. In J. A. Barry, R. Kingerlee, M. Seager, & L. Sullivan (Eds.), *The Palgrave Handbook of Male Psychology and Mental Health* (pp. 439–459). Springer International Publishing. https://doi.org/10.1007/978-3-030-04384-1_22

Book, A. S., Starzyk, K. B., & Quinsey, V. L. (2001). The relationship between testosterone and aggression: a meta-analysis. *Aggression and Violent Behavior, 6*(6), 579–599. https://doi.org/10.1016/S1359-1789(00)00032-X

Bookwala, J., & Gaugler, T. (2020). Relationship quality and 5-year mortality risk. *Health Psychology.* https://doi.org/10.1037/hea0000883

Bourne, R., Congdon, T., Davies, S., & Veljanovski, C. (2016). *In focus: The case for privatising the BBC.* Do Sustainability.

BPS. (2019). *A Psychological Manifesto.* https://www.bps.org.uk/news-and-policy/psychological-manifesto

Bramley, T., & Rodeiro, C. V. (2014). *Using Statistical Equating for Standard Maintaining in GCSEs and A levels* (p. 32). Cambridge: Cambridge Assessment Research Report, Cambridge Assessment. https://www.cambridgeassessment.org.uk/Images/182461-using-statistical-equating-for-standard-maintaining-in-gcses-and-a-levels.pdf.

Braithwaite, I., Zhang, S., Kirkbride, J. B., Osborn D. P. J., & Hayes, J. F. (2020). Air pollution (particulate matter) exposure and associations with depression, anxiety, bipolar, psychosis and suicide risk: a systematic review and meta-analysis. *Environmental Health Perspectives, 127*(12), 126002. https://doi.org/10.1289/EHP4595

Braun Joe, M., Kahn Robert, S., Tanya, F., Peggy, A., & Lanphear Bruce, P. (2006). Exposures to environmental toxicants and attention deficit hyperactivity disorder in U.S. children. *Environmental Health Perspectives, 114*(12), 1904–1909. https://doi.org/10.1289/ehp.9478

Brazzoli, M. S. (2007). Future prospects of information warfare and particularly psychological operations. In L. Le Roux (Ed.), *South African Army Vision 2020: Security Challenges Shaping the Future South African Army*. Pretoria/Tshwane: Institute for Security Studies.

Breda, T., & Hillion, M. (2016). Teaching accreditation exams reveal grading biases favor women in male-dominated disciplines in France. *Science, 353*(6298), 474–478. https://doi.org/10.1126/science.aaf4372

Bregman, R. (2020, May 9). The real Lord of the Flies: what happened when six boys were shipwrecked for 15 months. *The Guardian*. https://www.theguardian.com/books/2020/may/09/the-real-lord-of-the-flies-what-happened-when-six-boys-were-shipwrecked-for-15-months

Briggs, A. (2019). The impact of father absence on child mental health: three possible outcomes. In J. A. Barry, R. Kingerlee, M. Seager, & L. Sullivan (Eds.), *The Palgrave Handbook of Male Psychology and Mental Health* (pp. 67–85). Springer International Publishing. https://doi.org/10.1007/978-3-030-04384-1_4

British Psychological Society, Ethics Committee, & British Psychological Society. (2018). Code of ethics and conduct. Leicester: The British Psychological Society. https://www.bps.org.uk/sites/www.bps.org.uk/files/Policy/Policy%20-%20Files/BPS%20Code%20of%20Ethics%20and%20Conduct%20%28Updated%20July%202018%29.pdf

Bronfenbrenner, U. (1979). *The Ecology of Human Development*. Harvard University Press.

Brooks, G. R. (2001). Masculinity and men's mental health. *Journal of American College Health, 49*(6), 285–297. https://doi.org/10.1080/07448480109596315

Brogden, M., & Nijhar, S. K. (2004). *Abuse of Adult Males in Intimate Partner Relationships in Northern Ireland*. Citeseer.

Brower, M. C. (2001). Advances in neuropsychiatry: neuropsychiatry of frontal lobe dysfunction in violent and criminal behaviour: a critical review. *Journal of Neurology, Neurosurgery & Psychiatry, 71*(6), 720–726. https://doi.org/10.1136/jnnp.71.6.720

Brown, B. (2016). From boys to men: the place of the provider role in male development. *An International Journal, 5*(2), 22.

Brown, B. (2019). From hegemonic to responsive masculinity: the transformative power of the provider role. In J. A. Barry, R. Kingerlee, M. Seager, & L. Sullivan (Eds.), *The Palgrave Handbook of Male Psychology and Mental Health* (pp. 183–204). Springer International Publishing. https://doi.org/10.1007/978-3-030-04384-1_10

Brown, J., Long-McGie, J., Wartnik, J. A., Oberoi, P., Wresh, J., Weinkauf, E., Falconer, G., & Kerr, A. (2014). Fetal alcohol spectrum disorders in the criminal justice system: a review. *The Journal of Law Enforcement, 3*(6), 10.

Brown, J. S. L., Sagar-Ouriaghli, I., & Sullivan, L. (2019). Help-seeking among men for mental health problems. In J. A. Barry, R. Kingerlee, M. Seager, & L. Sullivan (Eds.), *The Palgrave Handbook of Male Psychology and Mental Health* (pp. 397–415). Springer International Publishing. https://doi.org/10.1007/978-3-030-04384-1_20

Brown, M. J., & Cody, M. J. (1991). Effects of a prosocial television soap opera in promoting women's status. *Human Communication Research, 18*(1), 114–144. https://doi.org/10.1111/j.1468-2958.1991.tb00531.x

Brown, T. N. T., & Herman, J. L., (2015). Intimate partner violence and sexual abuse among LGBT people. eScholarship, University of California.

Brownhill, S., Wilhelm, K., Barclay, L., & Schmied, V. (2005). 'Big build': hidden depression in men. *Australian and New Zealand Journal of Psychiatry, 39*(10), 921–931.

Brown, D., Barry, J. A., & Todd, B. K. (2020). Barriers to academic help-seeking: The relationship with gender-typed attitudes. *Journal of Further and Higher Education, 44,* 1–16. https://iris.ucl.ac.uk/iris/publication/1737790/1

Brugha, T. S., Spiers, N., Bankart, J., Cooper, S.-A., McManus, S., Scott, F. J., Smith, J., & Tyrer, F. (2016). Epidemiology of autism in adults across age groups and ability levels. *British Journal of Psychiatry, 209*(6), 498–503. https://doi.org/10.1192/bjp.bp.115.174649

Bryan, C. J., Cukrowicz, K. C., West, C. L., & Morrow, C. E. (2010). Combat experience and the acquired capability for suicide. *Journal of Clinical Psychology, 66*(10), 1044–1056. https://doi.org/10.1002/jclp.20703

Buhrich, N., Hodder, T., & Teesson, M. (2000). Lifetime prevalence of trauma among homeless people in Sydney. *Australian & New Zealand Journal of Psychiatry, 34*(6), 963–966.

Bulbeck, C. (2010). Unpopularising feminism: 'blaming feminism' in the generation debate and the mother wars. *Sociology Compass, 4*(1), 21–37. https://doi.org/10.1111/j.1751-9020.2009.00257.x

Burger, C., Strohmeier, D., Spröber, N., Bauman, S., & Rigby, K. (2015). How teachers respond to school bullying: an examination of self-reported intervention strategy use, moderator effects, and concurrent use of multiple strategies. *Teaching and Teacher Education, 51,* 191–202. https://doi.org/10.1016/j.tate.2015.07.004

Burkley, M., Wong, Y. J., & Bell, A. C. (2016). The Masculinity Contingency Scale (MCS): scale development and psychometric properties. *Psychology of Men & Masculinity, 17*(2), 113–125. https://doi.org/10.1037/a0039211

Butchart, A., Mikton, C., & Organization, W. H. (2014). United Nations Office on Drugs and Crime, United Nations Development Programme. *Global Status Report on Violence Prevention, 2014.*

Butwicka, A., L\aangström, N., Larsson, H., Lundström, S., Serlachius, E., Almqvist, C., Frisén, L., & Lichtenstein, P. (2017). Increased risk for substance use-related problems in autism spectrum disorders: a population-based cohort study. *Journal of Autism and Developmental Disorders, 47*(1), 80–89.

Cain, M. (1989). *Growing Up Good: Policing the Behaviour of Girls in Europe.* Sage London.

Cahill, L . (2019, March 29). Denying the neuroscience of sex differences. *Quillette.* https://quillette.com/2019/03/29/denying-the-neuroscience-of-sex-differences/

Cahill, L. (2014). Equal ≠ the same: Sex differences in the human brain. *Cerebrum: The Dana Forum on Brain Science, 2014.* https://www.ncbi.nlm.nih.gov/pmc/articles/PMC4087190/

Cairns, P., & Howells, L. (2019). Angry young men: interpersonal formulation of anger to effect change. In J. A. Barry, R. Kingerlee, M. Seager, & L. Sullivan (Eds.), *The Palgrave Handbook of Male Psychology and Mental Health* (pp. 351–368). Springer International Publishing. https://doi.org/10.1007/978-3-030-04384-1_18

Callanan, V. J., & Davis, M. S. (2009). A comparison of suicide note writers with suicides who did not leave notes. *Suicide and Life-Threatening Behavior, 39*(5), 558–568. https://doi.org/10.1521/suli.2009.39.5.558

Calsyn, R. J., & Winter, J. P. (2002). Social support, psychiatric symptoms, and housing: a causal analysis. *Journal of Community Psychology, 30*(3), 247–259.

Cambridge English Dictionary. (2020). *BOYS WILL BE BOYS | Meaning in the Cambridge English Dictionary.* https://dictionary.cambridge.org/dictionary/english/boys-will-be-boys

Campbell, M., & Brauer, M. (2020). *Is Discrimination Widespread? Testing Assumptions about Bias on a University Campus.* https://doi.org/10.31234/osf.io/evp8b

Campbell, O., Bann, D., & Patalay, P. (2020). The gender gap in adolescent mental health: a cross-national investigation of 566,827 adolescents across 73 countries. *MedRxiv,* 2020.06.12.20129312. https://doi.org/10.1101/2020.06.12.20129312

Cancer Research UK. (2014, October 21). *Phases of Clinical Trials. Cancer Research UK.* https://www.cancerresearchuk.org/about-cancer/find-a-clinical-trial/what-clinical-trials-are/phases-of-clinical-trials

Cancer Research UK. (2020). *Breast Cancer Statistics. Cancer Research UK.* https://www.cancerresearchuk.org/health-professional/cancer-statistics/statistics-by-cancer-type/breast-cancer

Cancer Research UK. (2020). *Prostate Cancer Mortality Statistics. Cancer Research UK.* https://www.cancerresearchuk.org/health-professional/cancer-statistics/statistics-by-cancer-type/prostate-cancer/mortality

Capraro, R. L. (2004). Men's studies as a foundation for student development work with college men. *New Directions for Student Services, 2004*(107), 23–34.

Careersmart. (2020). *Which Jobs Do Men and Women Do? Occupational Breakdown by Gender | Careersmart.* https://careersmart.org.uk/occupations/equality/which-jobs-do-men-and-women-do-occupational-breakdown-gender

Carlson, M. J. (2006). Family structure, father involvement, and adolescent behavioral outcomes. *Journal of Marriage and Family, 68*(1), 137–154. https://doi.org/10.1111/j.1741-3737.2006.00239.x

Carrington, B., & McPhee, A. (2008). Boys' 'underachievement' and the feminization of teaching. *Journal of Education for Teaching, 34*(2), 109–120. https://doi.org/10.1080/02607470801979558

Carter, G. L., Campbell, A. C., & Muncer, S. (2014). The Dark Triad personality: attractiveness to women. *Personality and Individual Differences, 56*, 57–61. https://doi.org/10.1016/j.paid.2013.08.021

Cassady, D., Jetter, K. M., & Culp, J. (2007). Is price a barrier to eating more fruits and vegetables for low-income families? *Journal of the American Dietetic Association, 107*(11), 1909–1915. https://doi.org/10.1016/j.jada.2007.08.015

CDCMMWR. (2020). QuickStats: percentage of children and adolescents aged 4–17 years with serious emotional or behavioral difficulties, by sex and urbanization level – National health interview survey, 2016–2018. *MMWR. Morbidity and Mortality Weekly Report, 69*. https://doi.org/10.15585/mmwr.mm6910a6

Ceci, S. J., Ginther, D. K., Kahn, S., & Williams, W. M. (2014). Women in academic science: a changing landscape. *Psychological Science in the Public Interest, 15*(3), 75–141. https://doi.org/10.1177/1529100614541236

Chan, X. B. V., Goh, S. M. S., & Tan, N. C. (2014). Subjects with colour vision deficiency in the community: what do primary care physicians need to know? *Asia Pacific Family Medicine, 13*(1), 10. https://doi.org/10.1186/s12930-014-0010-3

Charen, M. (2018). *Sex Matters: How Modern Feminism Lost Touch with Science, Love, and Common Sense.* Crown Publishing Group.

Chen, X., Chughtai, A. A., Dyda, A., & MacIntyre, C. R. (2017). Comparative epidemiology of Middle East respiratory syndrome coronavirus (MERS-CoV) in Saudi Arabia and South Korea. *Emerging Microbes & Infections, 6*(1), 1–6.

Chen, L. P., Murad, M. H., Paras, M. L., Colbenson, K. M., Sattler, A. L., Goranson, E. N., Elamin, M. B., Seime, R. J., Shinozaki, G., Prokop, L. J., & Zirakzadeh, A. (2010). Sexual abuse and lifetime diagnosis of psychiatric disorders: systematic review and meta-analysis. *Mayo Clinic Proceedings, 85*(7), 618–629. https://doi.org/10.4065/mcp.2009.0583

Chheda-Varma, B. (2019). Attention Deficit Hyperactivity Disorder (ADHD): a case study and exploration of causes and interventions. In J. A. Barry, R. Kingerlee, M. Seager, & L. Sullivan (Eds.), *The Palgrave Handbook of Male Psychology and Mental Health* (pp. 291–307). Cham: Palgrave Macmillan.

Christopher, S. (2015). An introduction to black humour as a coping mechanism for student paramedics. *Journal of Paramedic Practice, 7*(12), 610–617. https://doi.org/10.12968/jpar.2015.7.12.610

Churchard, A., Ryder, M., Greenhill, A., & Mandy, W. (2019). The prevalence of autistic traits in a homeless population. *Autism, 23*(3), 665–676. https://doi.org/10.1177/1362361318768484

Cislaghi, B., Weber, A. M., Gupta, G. R., & Darmstadt, G. L. (2020). Gender equality and global health: intersecting political challenges. *Journal of Global Health, 10*(1), 010701. https://doi.org/10.7189/jogh.10.010701

The City of London Corporation's Suicide Prevention Work – Nov 2019 Update. (2019, November 27). National Suicide Prevention Alliance. https://www.nspa.org.uk/the-city-of-london-corporations-suicide-prevention-work-nov-2019-update/

Clark, A. (2018). "I found that joking back actually made me not on edge, and I didn't feel threatened": women's embodied experiences of sexist humour (banter) in a UK gym. *International Journal of Gender and Women's Studies, 6*(1), 15–29.

Clark, D. (2019a). *Apprenticeship starts by gender 2011–2018 Statistic. Statista.* https://www.statista.com/statistics/376781/apprenticeship-starts-gender-england-timeline/

Clark, D. (2019b). *Quarterly youth unemployment rate by gender in the UK 2019. Statista.* https://www.statista.com/statistics/280292/youth-unemployment-rate-uk-quarter/

Clark, K., & Fallon, A. C. (2019). *Enhancing Therapy for Men in Prison. Dr Kerry Clark & Dr Ashley-Christopher Fallon, Birmingham MHFT. – YouTube.* Male Psychology Youtube Channel. https://www.youtube.com/watch?v=3eJ9MEfc7fg&t=9s

Clarke, P., Sheffield, D., & Akehurst, S. (2020). Personality predictors of yips and choking susceptibility. *Frontiers in Psychology, 10.* https://doi.org/10.3389/fpsyg.2019.02784

Clement, S., Schauman, O., Graham, T., Maggioni, F., Evans-Lacko, S., Bezborodovs, N., Morgan, C., Rüsch, N., Brown, J. S. L., & Thornicroft, G. (2015). What is the impact of mental health-related stigma on help-seeking? A systematic review of quantitative and qualitative studies. *Psychological Medicine, 45*(1), 11–27. https://doi.org/10.1017/S0033291714000129

Cofnas, N., Parvini, N., Arden, R., Sesardic, N., & Anomaly, J. (2018, October 1). The grievance studies scandal: five academics respond. *Quillette*. https://quillette.com/2018/10/01/the-grievance-studies-scandal-five-academics-respond/

Colbert, R. (2011). Discrimination needed: the over-inclusive definition of who is a sex offender. *Journal of Criminal Psychology, 1*(1), 43–50. https://doi.org/10.1108/20093829201100005

Connell, R.W. (1987). *Gender and Power: Society, the Person and Sexual Politics*. John Wiley & Sons.

Connell, R.W. (2005). *Masculinities*. Polity.

Connolly, R. M., Carducci, M. A., & Antonarakis, E. S. (2012). Use of androgen deprivation therapy in prostate cancer: indications and prevalence. *Asian Journal of Andrology, 14*(2), 177.

Coleman, D. L., Joyner, M. J., & Lopiano, D. (2020). *Re-Affirming the Value of the Sports Exception to Title IX's General Non-Discrimination Rule* (SSRN Scholarly Paper ID 3523305). Social Science Research Network. https://papers.ssrn.com/abstract=3523305

Collin, L., Reisner, S. L., Tangpricha, V., & Goodman, M. (2016). Prevalence of transgender depends on the "case" definition: a systematic review. *The Journal of Sexual Medicine, 13*(4), 613–626. https://doi.org/10.1016/j.jsxm.2016.02.001

Collins, W. (2019). *The Empathy Gap: Male Disadvantages and the Mechanisms of Their Neglect*. LPS Publishing.

Cooke, L. J., & Wardle, J. (2005). Age and gender differences in children's food preferences. *British Journal of Nutrition, 93*(5), 741–746. https://doi.org/10.1079/BJN20051389

Cooper-Patrick, L., Gallo, J. J., Gonzales, J. J., Vu, H. T., Powe, N. R., Nelson, C., & Ford, D. E. (1999). Race, gender, and partnership in the patient-physician relationship. *Jama, 282*(6), 583–589.

Corry, C. E., Fiebert, M. S., & Pizzey, E. (2002). *Controlling Domestic Violence Against Men*. http://www.familytx.org/research/Control_DV_against_men.pdf

Cornell, M., Horton, K., Colvin, C., Medina-Marino, A., & Dovel, K. (2020). Perpetuating gender inequity through uneven reporting. *The Lancet, 395*(10232), 1258. https://doi.org/10.1016/S0140-6736(20)30216-6

Corston, J. (2007). *The Corston Report: the need for a distinct, radically different, visibly-led, strategic, proportionate, holistic, woman-centred, integrated approach*. Home Office.

Costa, P. T., Terracciano, A., & McCrae, R. R. (2011). Gender Differences in Personality Traits Across Cultures: Robust and Surprising Findings. *Journal of Personality and Social Psychology, 81*(2), 322–331.

Coulter, A., Roberts, S., & Dixon, A. (2013). *Delivering Better Services for People with Long-term Conditions. Building the House of Care* (pp. 1–28). London: The King's Fund.

Courtenay, W. H. (2000). Constructions of masculinity and their influence on men's well-being: a theory of gender and health. *Social Science & Medicine, 50*(10), 1385–1401. https://doi.org/10.1016/S0277-9536(99)00390-1

Crawford, R. (1980). Healthism and the medicalization of everyday life. *International Journal of Health Services: Planning, Administration, Evaluation, 10*(3), 365–388. https://doi.org/10.2190/3H2H-3XJN-3KAY-G9NY

Crepaldi, M., Colombo, V., Mottura, S., Baldassini, D., Sacco, M., Cancer, A., & Antonietti, A. (2020). Antonyms: a computer game to improve inhibitory control of impulsivity in children with Attention Deficit/Hyperactivity Disorder (ADHD). *Information, 11*(4), 230. https://doi.org/10.3390/info11040230

Cripps, B. (2012). Performance enhancement. In L. Brann, J. Owens, & A. Williamson (Eds.), *The Handbook of Contemporary Clinical Hypnosis* (pp. 547–566). John Wiley & Sons, Ltd. https://doi.org/10.1002/9781119950905.ch37

Croft, A., Schmader, T., & Block, K. (2015). An underexamined inequality: cultural and psychological barriers to men's engagement with communal roles. *Personality and Social Psychology Review, 19*(4), 343–370.

CRUK. (2020). *Male Breast Cancer | Cancer Research UK.* https://www.cancerresearchuk.org/about-cancer/breast-cancer/stages-types-grades/types/male-breast-cancer

Csordas, T. (1994). Embodiment and experience: the existential ground of culture and self. *American Ethnologist, 24*(4), 940–941. https://doi.org/10.1525/ae.1997.24.4.940

Cummings-Knight, J. (2019). The gaze: the male need to look vs the female need to be seen – an evolutionary perspective. In J. A. Barry, R. Kingerlee, M. Seager, & L. Sullivan (Eds.), *The Palgrave Handbook of Male Psychology and Mental Health* (pp. 249–265). Springer International Publishing. https://doi.org/10.1007/978-3-030-04384-1_13

Curtis, P., & editor, education. (2007, November 22). Under-sevens "too young to learn to read". *The Guardian.* https://www.theguardian.com/uk/2007/nov/22/earlyyearseducation.schools

Cusack, J., Deane, F. P., Wilson, C. J., & Ciarrochi, J. (2006). Emotional expression, perceptions of therapy, and help-seeking intentions in men attending therapy services. *Psychology of Men & Masculinity, 7*(2), 69–82. https://doi.org/10.1037/1524-9220.7.2.69

Dale, J. (2016). The scale of online misogyny. https://demosuk.wpengine.com/wp-content/uploads/2016/05/Misogyny-online.pdf

Daly, K., & Chesney-Lind, M. (1988). Feminism and criminology. *Justice Quarterly, 5*(4), 497–538.

Daly, M. (2014, May 1). *Evolutionary Perspectives on Sex, Gender, and Crime.* The Oxford Handbook of Gender, Sex, and Crime. https://doi.org/10.1093/oxfordhb/9780199838707.013.0014

Danese, A., & Widom, C. S. (2020). Objective and subjective experiences of child maltreatment and their relationships with psychopathology. *Nature Human Behaviour,* 1–8. https://doi.org/10.1038/s41562-020-0880-3

Daubney. (2015). *Meet the men giving up on women | The sunday times.* https://www.thetimes.co.uk/article/meet-the-men-giving-up-on-women-zqmmthbvjrr

David, D., Cotet, C., Matu, S., Mogoase, C., & Stefan, S. (2018). 50 years of rational-emotive and cognitive-behavioral therapy: a systematic review and meta-analysis. *Journal of Clinical Psychology, 74*(3), 304–318. https://doi.org/10.1002/jclp.22514

Davidson, N. (1990). Life without father: America's great EST social catastrophe. *Policy Review.*

Davis, J. T. M., & Hines, M. (2020). How large are gender differences in toy preferences? A systematic review and meta-analysis of toy preference research. *Archives of Sexual Behavior, 49*(2), 373–394. https://doi.org/10.1007/s10508-019-01624-7

Davis, R. (2010). Domestic violence-related deaths. *Journal of Aggression, Conflict and Peace(Lowe & Balfour, 2015) Research, 2*(2), 44–52. https://doi.org/10.5042/jacpr.2010.0141

De Fraine, B., Van Damme, J., & Onghena, P. (2007). A longitudinal analysis of gender differences in academic self-concept and language achievement: a multivariate multilevel latent growth approach. *Contemporary Educational Psychology, 32*(1), 132–150.

DeLisi, M., & Vaughn, M. G. (2016). Correlates of crime. *The Handbook of Criminological Theory*, 18–36.

de Salis, C. A., Rowley, A., Stokell, K., & Brundrett, M. (2019). Do we need more male primary teachers? Tensions and contradictions in the perspectives of male and female trainees. *Education 3-13*, 47(4), 475–489. https://doi.org/10.1080/03004279.2018.1498997

de Visser, R. O., & McDonnell, E. J. (2013). "Man points": masculine capital and young men's health. *Health Psychology*, 32(1), 5–14. https://doi.org/10.1037/a0029045

Deaner, R. O., Addona, V., & Mead, M. P. (2014). U.S. masters track participation reveals a stable sex difference in competitiveness. *Evolutionary Psychology*, 12(5), 147470491401200. https://doi.org/10.1177/147470491401200501

Deaner, R. O., Balish, S. M., & Lombardo, M. P. (2016). Sex differences in sports interest and motivation: an evolutionary perspective. *Evolutionary Behavioral Sciences*, 10(2), 73–97. https://doi.org/10.1037/ebs0000049

Deaner, R. O., Carter, R. E., Joyner, M. J., & Hunter, S. K. (2015). Men are more likely than women to slow in the marathon. *Medicine and Science in Sports and Exercise*, 47(3), 607–616. https://doi.org/10.1249/MSS.0000000000000432

Del Giudice, M. (2008). Sex-biased ratio of avoidant/ambivalent attachment in middle childhood. *British Journal of Developmental Psychology*, 26(3), 369–379. https://doi.org/10.1348/026151007X243289

Del Giudice, M. (2021). Ideological bias in the psychology of sex and gender. In C. L. Frisby, W. T. O'Donohue, R. E. Redding, & S. O. Lilienfeld (Eds.), *Political Bias in Psychology: Nature, Scope, and Solutions*. Springer.

Del Re, A. C., Flückiger, C., Horvath, A. O., Symonds, D., & Wampold, B. E. (2012). Therapist effects in the therapeutic alliance–outcome relationship: a restricted-maximum likelihood meta-analysis. *Clinical Psychology Review*, 32(7), 642–649. https://doi.org/10.1016/j.cpr.2012.07.002

Demyan, A. L., & Anderson, T. (2012). Effects of a brief media intervention on expectations, attitudes, and intentions of mental health help seeking. *Journal of Counseling Psychology*, 59(2), 222–229. https://doi.org/10.1037/a0026541

Dench, G. (Ed.). (1998). *Transforming Men: Changing Patterns of Dependency and Dominance in Gender Relations* (1st edition). Transaction Publishers.

Department for Education. (2017). *Special Educational Needs in England*.

DeVine, M. (2013). *Failure to Launch: Guiding Clinicians to Successfully Motivate the Long-Dependent Young Adult*. Jason Aronson, Incorporated.

Digest of Education Statistics, 2018. *National center for education statistics*. Retrieved April 5, 2020, from https://nces.ed.gov/programs/digest/2018menu_tables.asp

Ding, G. L., Liu, Y., Liu, M. E., Pan, J. X., Guo, M. X., Sheng, J. Z., & Huang, H. F. (2015). The effects of diabetes on male fertility and epigenetic regulation during spermatogenesis. *Asian Journal of Andrology*, 17(6), 948–953. https://doi.org/10.4103/1008-682X.150844

Dobbin, F., & Kalev, A. (2018). Why doesn't diversity training work? The challenge for industry and academia. *Anthropology Now*, 10(2), 48–55.

Dobersek, U., Wy, G., Adkins, J., Altmeyer, S., Krout, K., Lavie, C. J., & Archer, E. (2020). Meat and mental health: a systematic review of meat abstention and depression, anxiety, and related phenomena. *Critical Reviews in Food Science and Nutrition*, 1–14. https://doi.org/10.1080/10408398.2020.1741505

Doyle, I., & Doyle, D. (2018). *The Conference 2018, UCL, 22–23 June – Male Psychology Network.* https://malepsychology.org.uk/the-conference-2018/

Douglas, E. M., & Hines, D. A. (2011). The reported availability of us domestic violence services to victims who vary by immigration status, primary language, and disability. *Partner Abuse, 2*(4), 427–451.

Duffy, J., & Hutchison, A. (2019). Working with homeless men in London: a mental health service perspective. In *The Palgrave Handbook of Male Psychology and Mental Health* (pp. 533–556). Springer.

Dunbar, R. I. M., Launay, J., Wlodarski, R., Robertson, C., Pearce, E., Carney, J., & MacCarron,P. (2017). Functional benefits of (modest) alcohol consumption. *Adaptive Human Behavior and Physiology, 3*(2), 118–133. https://doi.org/10.1007/s40750-016-0058-4

D'Unger, A. V., Land, K. C., & McCall, P. L. (2002). Sex differences in age patterns of delinquent/criminal careers: results from Poisson latent class analyses of the Philadelphia cohort study. *Journal of Quantitative Criminology, 18*(4), 349–375.

Dunne, E. M., Burrell, L. E., Diggins, A. D., Whitehead, N. E., & Latimer, W. W. (2015). Increased risk for substance use and health-related problems among homeless veterans. *The American Journal on Addictions, 24*(7), 676–680. https://doi.org/10.1111/ajad.12289

Dunphy, L. (2018, January 18). *Lesbian mum who viciously beat bride tells court she has 'male hormones'. Mirror.* https://www.mirror.co.uk/news/uk-news/lesbian-mum-who-viciously-beat-11872183

DuPaul, G. J., & Stoner, G. (2014). *ADHD in the Schools, Third Edition: Assessment and Intervention Strategies.* Guilford Publications.

Durrant, R. (2019). Evolutionary approaches to understanding crime: explaining the gender gap in offending. *Psychology, Crime & Law, 25*(6), 589–608. https://doi.org/10.1080/1068316X.2018.1558224

Durkheim, E. (1897). *On Suicide.* Penguin UK.

Dutton, D. G., & Corvo, K. (2006). Transforming a flawed policy: a call to revive psychology and science in domestic violence research and practice. *Aggression and Violent Behavior, 11*(5), 457–483.

Eagly, A. H. (2018). The shaping of science by ideology: how feminism inspired, led, and constrained scientific understanding of sex and gender. *Journal of Social Issues, 74*(4), 871–888. https://doi.org/10.1111/josi.12291

Easterbrook, J. A. (1959). The effect of emotion on cue utilization and the organization of behavior. *Psychological Review, 66*(3), 183–201. https://doi.org/10.1037/h0047707

Eckert, P., & McConnell-Ginet, S. (2013). *Language and Gender.* Cambridge University Press.

Edwards, S., Tinning, L., Brown, J. S. L., Boardman, J., & Weinman, J. (2007). Reluctance to seek help and the perception of anxiety and depression in the United Kingdom: a pilot vignette study. *The Journal of Nervous and Mental Disease, 195*(3), 258–261. https://doi.org/10.1097/01.nmd.0000253781.49079.53

Eisenegger, C., Naef, M., Snozzi, R., Heinrichs, M., & Fehr, E. (2010). Prejudice and truth about the effect of testosterone on human bargaining behaviour. *Nature, 463*(7279), 356–359. https://doi.org/10.1038/nature08711

Eldridge, R., & Fraser, E. (2019). We are warriors: the psychology of men at war. In J. A. Barry, R. Kingerlee, M. Seager, & L. Sullivan (Eds.), *The Palgrave Handbook of Male Psychology and Mental Health* (pp. 267–288). Springer.

El-Emadi, A. A., Said, Z., & Friesen, H. L. (2019). Teaching style differences between male and female science teachers in Qatari schools: possible impact on student achievement. *EURASIA Journal of Mathematics, Science and Technology Education, 15,* 12. https://doi.org/10.29333/ejmste/109236

Ellis, A. (1979). Is rational-emotive therapy stoical, humanistic, or spiritual? *Journal of Humanistic Psychology, 19*(3), 89–92. https://doi.org/10.1177/002216787901900314

Ellis, A., & Dryden, W. (2007). *The Practice of Rational Emotive Behavior Therapy.* Springer Publishing Company.

Ellis, B. J., & Del Giudice, M. (2019). Developmental adaptation to stress: an evolutionary perspective. *Annual Review of Psychology, 70,* 111–139.

Ellis, L. (2011). Identifying and explaining apparent universal sex differences in cognition and behavior. *Personality and Individual Differences, 51*(5), 552–561. https://doi.org/10.1016/j.paid.2011.04.004

Ellis, B. J., Del Giudice, M., Dishion, T. J., Figueredo, A. J., Gray, P., Griskevicius, V., Hawley, P. H., Jacobs, W. J., James, J., Volk, A. A., & Wilson, D. S. (2012). The evolutionary basis of risky adolescent behavior: implications for science, policy, and practice. *Developmental Psychology, 48*(3), 598–623. https://doi.org/10.1037/a0026220

Ellis, L., Hershberger, S., Field, E., Wersinger, S., Pellis, S., Geary, D., Palmer, C., Hoyenga, K., Hetsroni, A., & Karadi, K. (2013). *Sex Differences: Summarizing More than a Century of Scientific Research.* Psychology Press.

Ellis, L., Hershberger, S., Pellis, S., Field, E., & Wersinger, S. (2008). *Sex Differences: Summarizing More than a Century of Scientific Research.* Taylor & Francis.

Elson, M., & Ferguson, C. J. (2014). Twenty-five years of research on violence in digital games and aggression. *European Psychologist, 19*(1), 33–46. https://doi.org/10.1027/1016-9040/a000147

Eme, R. (2015). Sex difference in attention-deficit/hyperactivity disorder contributes to the sex difference in crime and antisocial behavior. *Violence and Gender, 2*(2), 101–106. https://doi.org/10.1089/vio.2014.0025

Emslie, C., Hunt, K., & Lyons, A. (2013). The role of alcohol in forging and maintaining friendships amongst Scottish men in midlife. *Health Psychology, 32*(1), 33–41. https://doi.org/10.1037/a0029874

Emslie, C., Ridge, D., Ziebland, S., & Hunt, K. (2006). Men's accounts of depression: reconstructing or resisting hegemonic masculinity? *Social Science & Medicine, 62*(9), 2246–2257. https://doi.org/10.1016/j.socscimed.2005.10.017

Enayati, J., Grann, M., Lubbe, S., & Fazel, S. (2008). Psychiatric morbidity in arsonists referred for forensic psychiatric assessment in Sweden. *The Journal of Forensic Psychiatry & Psychology, 19*(2), 139–147.

Englar-Carlson, M . (2019). *Foreword to The Palgrave Handbook of Male Psychology and Mental Health.* J. A. Barry, R. Kingerlee, M. Seager, & L. Sullivan (Eds.). Springer International Publishing. https://doi.org/10.1007/978-3-030-04384-1

Englar-Carlson, M. (2006). Masculine norms and the therapy process. In M. Englar-Carlson & M. A. Stevens (Eds.), *In the Room with Men: A Casebook of Therapeutic Change* (pp. 13–47). American Psychological Association. https://doi.org/10.1037/11411-002

Epictetus. (1865). *The Works of Epictetus: Consisting of His Discourses, in Four Books, the Enchiridion, and Fragments.* Little, Brown.

Equality Challenge Unit. (2013). *Unconscious Bias and Higher Education*. http://www.ecu. ac.uk/wp-content/uploads/2014/07/unconscious-bias-and-higher-education.pdf

Erdem, H., Wilson, G., Limbrick, H., & Swainston, K. (2020). An interpretive phenomenological exploration of the barriers, facilitators and benefits to male mental health help-seeking. *BPS North of England Bulletin, 1*.

Ernst, D. (2019). *Gillette's "Toxic Masculinity" Ad Haunts P&G as Shaving Giant Takes $8B Writedown – Washington Times*. https://m.washingtontimes.com/news/2019/jul/31/gillettes-toxic-masculinity-ad-haunts-pg-as-shavin/

Evening Standard. (2015). *Rush for Gender Equality with Judges "Could Be Appalling for Justice." Evening Standard*. http://www.standard.co.uk/news/uk/rush-for-gender-equality-with-top-judges-could-have-appalling-consequences-for-justice-a2952331.html

Fahs, B., & Karger, M. (2016). Women's studies as virus: institutional feminism, affect, and the projection of danger. *Multidisciplinary Journal of Gender Studies, 5*(1), 929–957.

Fahy, G. E., Richards, M., Riedel, J., Hublin, J. J., & Boesch, C. (2013). Stable isotope evidence of meat eating and hunting specialization in adult male chimpanzees. *Proceedings of the National Academy of Sciences, 110*(15), 5829–5833. https://doi.org/10.1073/pnas.1221991110

Falk, Ö., Wallinius, M., Lundström, S., Frisell, T., Anckarsäter, H., & Kerekes, N. (2014). The 1 % of the population accountable for 63 % of all violent crime convictions. *Social Psychiatry and Psychiatric Epidemiology, 49*(4), 559–571. https://doi.org/10.1007/s00127-013-0783-y

Farrell, W., & Grey, J. (2019). *The Boy Crisis: Why Our Boys Are Struggling and What We Can Do About It* (Reprint edition). BenBella Books.

Farrell, W. (2001). *Myth of Male Power*. Berkley Trade.

Farrington, D. P. (1995). The Twelfth Jack Tizard memorial lecture*. *Journal of Child Psychology and Psychiatry, 36*(6), 929–964. https://doi.org/10.1111/j.1469-7610.1995.tb01342.x

Farrington, D. P. (2010). Family influences on delinquency. *Juvenile Justice and Delinquency, 10*, 203–222.

Fazio, R. L. (2018). Toward a neurodevelopmental understanding of pedophilia. *The Journal of Sexual Medicine, 15*(9), 1205–1207. https://doi.org/10.1016/j.jsxm.2018.04.631

Fear, N. T., Jones, M., Murphy, D., Hull, L., Iversen, A. C., Coker, B., Machell, L., Sundin, J., Woodhead, C., Jones, N., Greenberg, N., Landau, S., Dandeker, C., Rona, R. J., Hotopf, M., & Wessely, S. (2010). What are the consequences of deployment to Iraq and Afghanistan on the mental health of the UK armed forces? A cohort study. *The Lancet, 375*(9728), 1783–1797. https://doi.org/10.1016/S0140-6736(10)60672-1

Felix, D. S., Robinson, W. D., & Jarzynka, K. J. (2013). The influence of divorce on men's health. *Journal of Men's Health, 10*(1), 3–7. https://doi.org/10.1016/j.jomh.2012.09.002

Feng, Y., Lou, C., Gao, E., Tu, X., Cheng, Y., Emerson, M. R., & Zabin, L. S. (2012). Adolescents' and young adults' perception of homosexuality and related factors in three Asian cities. *The Journal of Adolescent Health: Official Publication of the Society for Adolescent Medicine, 50*(30), S52–S60. https://doi.org/10.1016/j.jadohealth.2011.12.008

Ferguson. (2020a, April 11). Are gamer stereotypes accurate? *Quillette*. https://quillette. com/2020/04/11/are-gamer-stereotypes-accurate/

Ferguson, C. J. (2010). Genetic contributions to antisocial personality and behavior: a meta-analytic review from an evolutionary perspective. *The Journal of Social Psychology, 150*(2), 160–180. https://doi.org/10.1080/00224540903366503

Ferguson, C. (2018, March 26). *How "Toxic Masculinity" Is Hurting Boys [Opinion]*. HoustonChronicle.Com. https://www.houstonchronicle.com/local/gray-matters/ article/toxic-masculinity-gender-norms-harmful-boys-12782202.php

Ferguson, C. J. (2020b, March 3). *The American Psychological Association Keeps Getting the Science of Video Games Wrong*. *Medium*. https://arcdigital.media/the-american-psychological-association-keeps-getting-the-science-of-video-games-wrong-b1539971fbd

Fernald, D. (2007). *Psychology: Six Perspectives*. SAGE Publications.

Fikretoglu, D., Guay, S., Pedlar, D., & Brunet, A. (2008). Twelve month use of mental health services in a nationally representative, active military sample. *Medical Care, 46*(2), 217–223. https://doi.org/10.1097/MLR.0b013e31815b979a

Fink, D. S., Santaella-Tenorio, J., & Keyes, K. M. (2018). Increase in suicides the months after the death of Robin Williams in the US. *PLoS ONE, 13*(2). https://doi.org/10.1371/ journal.pone.0191405

Fisher, J., & Hammarberg, K. (2017). Psychological aspects if infertility among men. *Endocrinology of the Testis and Male Reproduction*, 1–31. https://doi. org/10.1007/978-3-319-29456-8_46-1

Fisher, W. A., & Kohut, T. (2017). Pornography viewing: keep calm and carry on. *The Journal of Sexual Medicine, 14*(3), 320–322. https://doi.org/10.1016/j.jsxm.2017.01.003

Fletcher, R. (2013). *Science, Ideology, and the Media: The Cyril Burt Scandal*. Transaction Publishers.

Flore, P. C., & Wicherts, J. M. (2015). Does stereotype threat influence performance of girls in stereotyped domains? A meta-analysis. *Journal of School Psychology, 53*(1), 25–44. https://doi.org/10.1016/j.jsp.2014.10.002

Fonseka, T. M., McKinley, G. P., & Kennedy, S. H. (2017). Is tetraethyl lead poison affecting contemporary indigenous suicides in Ontario, Canada? *Psychiatry Research, 251*, 253–254. https://doi.org/10.1016/j.psychres.2017.01.003

Forscher, P. S., Lai, C. K., Axt, J. R., Ebersole, C. R., Herman, M., Devine, P. G., & Nosek, B. A. (2019). A meta-analysis of procedures to change implicit measures. *Journal of Personality and Social Psychology, 117*(3), 522–559.

Fox, B. H., Perez, N., Cass, E., Baglivio, M. T., & Epps, N. (2015). Trauma changes everything: examining the relationship between adverse childhood experiences and serious, violent and chronic juvenile offenders. *Child Abuse & Neglect, 46*, 163–173. https://doi.org/10.1016/j.chiabu.2015.01.011

Fox, I. (1996). *Soap Operas and Social Marketing: The PCI Strategy* (pp. 115–117). Pennsylvania: Almanac (National Academy of Television Arts and Sciences (U.S.). International Council).

Fradera, A. (2017, February 28). There's a psychological case for paying female managers more than male managers, or giving them more holiday. *Research Digest*. https:// digest.bps.org.uk/2017/02/28/theres-a-psychological-case-for-paying-female-managers-more-than-male-managers-or-giving-them-more-holiday/

Francis, B., Skelton, C., Carrington, B., Hutchings, M., Read, B., & Hall, I. (2008). A perfect match? Pupils' and teachers' views of the impact of matching educators and learners by gender. *Research Papers in Education*, *23*(1), 21–36. https://doi.org/10.1080/02671520701692510

Frankl, V. E. (1985). *Man's Search for Meaning*. Simon and Schuster.

Freeth, P. (2008). *NLP in Business: A Practical Handbook for Using NLP, Easily and Professionally*. Communications in Action.

Frisén, L., Nordenström, A., Falhammar, H., Filipsson, H., Holmdahl, G., Janson, P. O., Thorén, M., Hagenfeldt, K., Möller, A., & Nordenskjöld, A. (2009). Gender role behavior, sexuality, and psychosocial adaptation in women with congenital adrenal hyperplasia due to CYP21A2 deficiency. *The Journal of Clinical Endocrinology & Metabolism*, *94*(9), 3432–3439. https://doi.org/10.1210/jc.2009-0636

Funk, C., & Parker, K. (2018, January 9). Women and men in STEM often at odds over workplace equity. *Pew Research Center's Social & Demographic Trends Project*. https://www.pewsocialtrends.org/2018/01/09/women-and-men-in-stem-often-at-odds-over-workplace-equity/

Furlong, A. (2008). The Japanese Hikikomori phenomenon: acute social withdrawal among young people. *The Sociological Review*, *56*(2), 309–325. https://doi.org/10.1111/j.1467-954X.2008.00790.x

Furst, D. M., & Tenenbaum, G. (1986). The relationship between worry, emotionality and sport performance. In D. M. Landers (Ed.), Sport and Elite Performers (pp. 89–96).

Gabay, R., Hameiri, B., Rubel-Lifschitz, T., & Nadler, A. (2020). The tendency for interpersonal victimhood: the personality construct and its consequences. *Personality and Individual Differences*, *165*, 110134.

Galambos, N. L., Almeida, D. M., & Petersen, A. C. (1990). Masculinity, femininity, and sex role attitudes in early adolescence: exploring gender intensification. *Child Development*, *61*(6), 1905–1914. https://doi.org/10.1111/j.1467-8624.1990.tb03574.x

Galdas, P., Fell, J., Bower, P., Kidd, L., Blickem, C., McPherson, K., Hunt, K., Gilbody, S., & Richardson, G. (2015). The effectiveness of self-management support interventions for men with long-term conditions: a systematic review and meta-analysis. *BMJ Open*, *5*(3), e006620–e006620. https://doi.org/10.1136/bmjopen-2014-006620

Gale. (2017). *President's letter, May 2017 | The Psychologist*. https://thepsychologist.bps.org.uk/volume-30/may-2017/presidents-letter-may-2017

Ganley, C. M., Mingle, L. A., Ryan, A. M., Ryan, K., Vasilyeva, M., & Perry, M. (2013). An examination of stereotype threat effects on girls' mathematics performance. *Developmental Psychology*, *49*(10), 1886–1897. https://doi.org/10.1037/a0031412

Gannon, K. (2019). Men's Health and Cancer – The Case of Prostate Cancer. In J. A. Barry, R. Kingerlee, M. Seager, & L. Sullivan (Eds.), *The Palgrave Handbook of Male Psychology and Mental Health* (pp. 145–163). Springer International Publishing. https://doi.org/10.1007/978-3-030-04384-1_8

Geary, D. (2021). *Male, Female: The Evolution of Human Sex Differences, Third Edition*. Https://Www.Apa.Org.https://www.apa.org/pubs/books/male-female-third-edition

Geary, D. C., & Stoet, G. (2020). Ideological Blinders in the Study of Sex Differences in Participation in Science, Technology, Engineering, and Mathematics Fields. In D. M. Allen & J. W. Howell (Eds.), *Groupthink in Science* (pp. 175–183). Springer.

Gebhard, C., Regitz-Zagrosek, V., Neuhauser, H. K., Morgan, R., & Klein, S. L. (2020). Impact of sex and gender on COVID-19 outcomes in Europe. *Biology of Sex Differences, 11*(1), 29. https://doi.org/10.1186/s13293-020-00304-9

Gee, D. (2007). Informed choice? *Armed Forces Recruitment Practice in the Britain Joseph Rountree Charitable Trust Www. Informcedchoice. Org. Uk [Accessed October 3rd 2009].*

Gelso, C. J. (1979). Research in counseling: methodological and professional issues. *The Counseling Psychologist, 8*(3), 7–35. https://doi.org/10.1177/001100007900800303

Geniole, S. N., Bird, B. M., Ruddick, E. L., & Carré, J. M. (2017). Effects of competition outcome on testosterone concentrations in humans: an updated meta-analysis. *Hormones and Behavior, 92,* 37–50. https://doi.org/10.1016/j.yhbeh.2016.10.002

Gentile, A., Boca, S., & Giammusso, I. (2018). 'You play like a woman!' Effects of gender stereotype threat on women's performance in physical and sport activities: a meta-analysis. *Psychology of Sport and Exercise, 39,* 95–103. https://doi.org/10.1016/j.psychsport.2018.07.013

Gerken, T. (2020, February 28). Teen girl beats boys to win wrestling trophy. *BBC News.* https://www.bbc.com/news/world-us-canada-51666728

Gesch, B. (2013). Adolescence: does good nutrition = good behaviour? *Nutrition and Health, 22*(1), 55–65. https://doi.org/10.1177/0260106013519552

Gesch, C. B., Hammond, S. M., Hampson, S. E., Eves, A., & Crowder, M. J. (2002). Influence of supplementary vitamins, minerals and essential fatty acids on the antisocial behaviour of young adult prisoners: randomised, placebo-controlled trial. *British Journal of Psychiatry, 181*(1), 22–28. https://doi.org/10.1192/bjp.181.1.22

GHO. (2017). *GHO | By Category | Suicide Rate Estimates, Age-Standardized – Estimates by Country. WHO; World Health Organization.* https://apps.who.int/gho/data/node.main.MHSUICIDEASDR?lang=en

Gil-Gonzalez, D., Vives-Cases, C., Ruiz, M. T., Carrasco-Portino, M., & Alvarez-Dardet, C. (2008). Childhood experiences of violence in perpetrators as a risk factor of intimate partner violence: a systematic review. *Journal of Public Health, 30*(1), 14–22. https://doi.org/10.1093/pubmed/fdm071

Gillette. (2019). *We Believe: The Best Men Can Be | Gillette (Short Film).* https://www.youtube.com/watch?v=koPmuEyP3a0

Gilligan, C. (1977). In a different voice: women's conceptions of self and of morality. *Harvard Educational Review, 47*(4), 481–517. https://doi.org/10.17763/haer.47.4.g6167429416hg5l0

Gizer, I. R., Ficks, C., & Waldman, I. D. (2009). Candidate gene studies of ADHD: a meta-analytic review. *Human Genetics, 126*(1), 51–90. https://doi.org/10.1007/s00439-009-0694-x

Godfrey, R. (2016). Soldiering on: exploring the role of humour as a disciplinary technology in the military. *Organization, 23*(2), 164–183. https://doi.org/10.1177/1350508414533164

Gomes, C. M., & Boesch, C. (2009). Wild chimpanzees exchange meat for sex on a long-term basis. *PLoS ONE, 4,* 4. https://doi.org/10.1371/journal.pone.0005116

Gonzalez, M., & Jones, L. A. (n.d.). Our struggle is my struggle: solidarity feminism as an intersectional reply to neoliberal and choice feminism. *ournal of Women and Social Work,* 17.

Good, G. E., Borst, T. S., & Wallace, D. L. (1994). Masculinity research: a review and critique. *Applied and Preventive Psychology, 3*(1), 3–14. https://doi.org/10.1016/S0962-1849(05)80104-0

Goodman, J. H. (2004). Paternal postpartum depression, its relationship to maternal postpartum depression, and implications for family health. *Journal of Advanced Nursing, 45*(1), 26–35. https://doi.org/10.1046/j.1365-2648.2003.02857.x

Goodwin, L., Wessely, S., Hotopf, M., Jones, M., Greenberg, N., Rona, R. J., Hull, L., & Fear, N. T. (2015). Are common mental disorders more prevalent in the UK serving military compared to the general working population? *Psychological Medicine, 45*(9), 1881–1891. https://doi.org/10.1017/S0033291714002980

Gottfredson, M. R., & Hirschi, T. (1990). *A general theory of crime.* Stanford University Press.

Gough, B. (2013). The psychology of men's health: maximizing masculine capital. *Health Psychology, 32*(1), 1–4. https://doi.org/10.1037/a0030424

GOV.UK. (2018). *Prison population figures: 2018.* GOV.UK. https://www.gov.uk/government/statistics/prison-population-figures-2018

Gradus, J. L., Rosellini, A. J., Horváth-Puhó, E., Street, A. E., Galatzer-Levy, I., Jiang, T., Lash, T. L., & Sørensen, H. T. (2020). Prediction of sex-specific suicide risk using machine learning and single-payer health care registry data from Denmark. *JAMA Psychiatry, 77*(1), 25–34. https://doi.org/10.1001/jamapsychiatry.2019.2905

Gräff, J., & Mansuy, I. M. (2008). Epigenetic codes in cognition and behaviour. *Behavioural Brain Research, 192*(1), 70–87. https://doi.org/10.1016/j.bbr.2008.01.021

Gramsci. (1971). *Selections from the Prison Notebooks.* http://www.normadiconline.com/selections/selections-from-the-prison-notebooks.pdf

Gray, J. (1982). The effect of the doctor's sex on the doctor-patient relationship. *The Journal of the Royal College of General Practitioners, 32*(236), 167–169.

Great Britain, & Department for Work and Pensions. (2018). Female offender strategy. https://assets.publishing.service.gov.uk/government/uploads/system/uploads/attachment_data/file/719819/female-offender-strategy.pdf

Greening, L., & Stoppelbein, L. (2002). Religiosity, attributional style, and social support as psychosocial buffers for African American and white adolescents'perceived risk for suicide. *Suicide and Life-Threatening Behavior, 32*(4), 404–417. https://doi.org/10.1521/suli.32.4.404.22333

Griffiths, S., Mond, J. M., Murray, S. B., & Touyz, S. (2015). Positive beliefs about anorexia nervosa and muscle dysmorphia are associated with eating disorder symptomatology. *Australian & New Zealand Journal of Psychiatry, 49*(9), 812–820. https://doi.org/10.1177/0004867415572412

Grinza, E., Devicienti, F., Rossi, M., & Vannoni, D. (2017). *How Entry into Parenthood Shapes Gender Role Attitudes: New Evidence from Longitudinal UK Data* (p. 28). https://www.econstor.eu/bitstream/10419/173998/1/dp11088.pdf

Groeling, T. (2008). Who's the fairest of them all? An empirical test for partisan bias on ABC, CBS, NBC, and Fox News. *Presidential Studies Quarterly, 38*(4), 631–657. https://doi.org/10.1111/j.1741-5705.2008.02668.x

Groening. (1997). *The Simpsons – Matt Groening – Paperback.* https://www.harpercollins.com/9780060952525/the-simpsons/

Grönlund, A., & Magnusson, C. (2018). Do atypical individuals make atypical choices? Examining how gender patterns in personality relate to occupational choice and wages among five professions in Sweden. *Gender Issues, 35*(2), 153–178. https://doi.org/10.1007/s12147-017-9194-9

Gross, G. M., Bastian, L. A., Smith, N. B., Harpaz-Rotem, I., & Hoff, R. (2020). Sex differences in associations between depression and posttraumatic stress disorder symptoms and tobacco use among Veterans of recent conflicts. *Journal of Women's Health.* https://doi.org/10.1089/jwh.2019.8082

Grossman. (1997). Underdiagnosis of PTSD and substance use disorders in hospitalized female veterans. *Psychiatric Services, 48*(3), 393–395. https://doi.org/10.1176/ps.48.3.393

Grossmann, M. (2011). Low testosterone in men with type 2 diabetes: significance and treatment. *The Journal of Clinical Endocrinology & Metabolism, 96*(8), 2341–2353. https://doi.org/10.1210/jc.2011-0118

Groth, M. (2019). Working with adolescent males: special considerations from an existential perspective. In J. A. Barry, R. Kingerlee, M. Seager, & L. Sullivan (Eds.), *The Palgrave Handbook of Male Psychology and Mental Health* (pp. 331–349). Springer International Publishing. https://doi.org/10.1007/978-3-030-04384-1_17

Grunseit, A., Richards, J., & Merom, D. (2018). Running on a high: parkrun and personal well-being. *BMC Public Health, 18*(1), 59. https://doi.org/10.1186/s12889-017-4620-1

Guardian. (2020). *UK Women Bear Emotional Brunt of Covid-19 Turmoil – Poll.* MSN. https://www.msn.com/en-gb/news/world/uk-women-bear-emotional-brunt-of-covid-19-turmoil-%E2%80%93-poll/ar-BB14kR3y

Haag, K., Fraser, A., Hiller, R., Seedat, S., Zimmerman, A., & Halligan, S. L. (2019). The emergence of sex differences in PTSD symptoms across development: evidence from the ALSPAC cohort. *Psychological Medicine, 1–6.* https://doi.org/10.1017/S0033291719001971

Hacker-Hughes, J. (2017). *Military Veteran Psychological Health and Social Care: Contemporary Issues.* Taylor & Francis.

Hadley, R. (2019). Deconstructing Dad. In J. A. Barry, R. Kingerlee, M. Seager, & L. Sullivan (Eds.), *The Palgrave Handbook of Male Psychology and Mental Health* (pp. 47–66). Springer International Publishing. https://doi.org/10.1007/978-3-030-04384-1_3

Hadley, R., Newby, C., & Barry, J. (2019). Anxious childhood attachment predicts childlessness in later life. *Psychreg Journal of Psychology, 3*(3), 7–27.

Halpern, D. F. (2013). *Sex Differences in Cognitive Abilities.* Psychology Press.

Hamilton, P. L., & Jones, L. (2016). Illuminating the 'boy problem' from children's and teachers' perspectives: a pilot study. *Education 3-13, 44*(3), 241–254. https://doi.org/10.1080/03004279.2014.903987

Hammond, M. D., & Cimpian, A. (2020). 'Wonderful but weak': Children's ambivalent attitudes toward women. *Sex Roles.* https://doi.org/10.1007/s11199-020-01150-0

Hare-Mustin, R. T., & Marecek, J. (1988). The meaning of difference: gender theory, postmodernism, and psychology. *American Psychologist, 43*(6), 455–464. https://doi.org/10.1037/0003-066X.43.6.455

Harman, J. J., Leder-Elder, S., & Biringen, Z. (2019). Prevalence of adults who are the targets of parental alienating behaviors and their impact. *Children and Youth Services Review, 106,* 104471. https://doi.org/10.1016/j.childyouth.2019.104471

Harris, M. G., Diminic, S., Reavley, N., Baxter, A., Pirkis, J., & Whiteford, H. A. (2015). Males' mental health disadvantage: an estimation of gender-specific changes in service utilisation for mental and substance use disorders in Australia. *Australian & New Zealand Journal of Psychiatry, 49*(9), 821–832. https://doi.org/10.1177/0004867415577434

Harrower, J. (2001). *Psychology in Practice: Crime.* Hachette UK.

Hashi, M . (2019). *We Need to Listen to Young Men, Even When We Don't Like What They Are Saying – Male Psychology Network.* https://malepsychology.org.uk/2019/01/20/we-need-to-listen-to-young-men-even-when-we-dont-like-what-they-are-saying/

Haskell, S. G., Gordon, K. S., Mattocks, K., Duggal, M., Erdos, J., Justice, A., & Brandt, C. A. (2010). Gender differences in rates of depression, PTSD, pain, obesity, and military sexual trauma among Connecticut war Veterans of Iraq and Afghanistan. *Journal of Women's Health, 19*(2), 267–271. https://doi.org/10.1089/jwh.2008.1262

Hawkins, K., Bottone, F. G., Ozminkowski, R. J., Musich, S., Bai, M., Migliori, R. J., & Yeh, C. S. (2012). The prevalence of hearing impairment and its burden on the quality of life among adults with Medicare Supplement Insurance. *Quality of Life Research, 21*(7), 1135–1147. https://doi.org/10.1007/s11136-011-0028-z

Hayford, S. R., & Morgan, S. P. (2008). Religiosity and fertility in the United States: The role of fertility intentions. *Social Forces; a Scientific Medium of Social Study and Interpretation, 86*(3), 1163–1188. https://doi.org/10.1353/sof.0.0000

Heesacker, M., & Prichard, S. (1992). In a different voice, revisited: men, women, and emotion. *Journal of Mental Health Counseling, 14*(3), 274–290.

Heilman, B., Barker, G., & Harrison, A. (2017). *The Man Box: A Study on Being a Young Man in the US, UK, and Mexico: Key Findings.* https://promundoglobal.org/wp-content/uploads/2017/03/TheManBox-KeyFindings-EN-Final-29.03.2017-POSTPRINT.v3-web.pdf

Hermann, Z., & Diallo, A. (2017). Does teacher gender matter in Europe? Evidence from TIMSS data (No. BWP-2017/2). Budapest Working Papers on the Labour Market.

Heyman, G. D. (2001). Children's interpretation of ambiguous behavior: evidence for a 'boys are bad' bias. *Social Development, 10*(2), 230–247. https://doi.org/10.1111/1467-9507.00161

Hemelt, S. (2018). *Why Is Math Cheaper than English? Understanding Cost Differences in Higher Education* (p. 77). https://www.nber.org/system/files/working_papers/w25314/w25314.pdf

HESA. (2018). *Table 9 – HE Student Enrolments by Subject of Study 2014/15 to 2018/19 | HESA.* https://www.hesa.ac.uk/data-and-analysis/students/table-9

Hines, M. (2005). *Brain Gender.* Oxford University Press.

Hines, M. (2017). 5.11 – Gonadal hormones and sexual differentiation of human brain and behavior. In D. W. Pfaff & M. Joëls (Eds.), *Hormones, Brain and Behavior (Third Edition)* (pp. 247–278). Academic Press. https://doi.org/10.1016/B978-0-12-803592-4.00103-6

Hine, B., & Arrindell, O. (2015). *"Yeah but, it's funny if she does it to him": Comparing ratings of acceptability, humour, and perpetrator and victim blame in female-to-male versus male-to-female domestic violence scenarios.*

Hines, D. A., & Douglas, E. M. (2009). Women's use of intimate partner violence against men: prevalence, implications, and consequences. *Journal of Aggression, Maltreatment & Trauma, 18*(6), 572–586.

Hines, M., Ahmed, S. F., & Hughes, I. A. (2003). Psychological Outcomes and Gender-Related Development in Complete Androgen Insensitivity Syndrome. *Archives of Sexual Behavior, 32*(2), 93–101. https://doi.org/10.1023/A:1022492106974

Hirschi, T. (1969). *Causes of delinquency.* New Brunswick. *NJ: Transaction Publishers. Hoffmann, JP, & Johnson, RA (1998). A National Portrait of Family Structure and Adolescent Drug Use. Journal of Marriage & Family, 60,* 633–646.

Hirnstein, M., Andrews, L. C., & Hausmann, M. (2014). Gender-stereotyping and cognitive sex differences in mixed-and same-sex groups. *Archives of Sexual Behavior, 43*(8), 1663–1673.

Hoelterhoff, M., & Chung, M. C. (2020). Self-efficacy as an agentic protective factor against death anxiety in PTSD and psychiatric co-morbidity. *Psychiatric Quarterly, 91*(1), 165–181. https://doi.org/10.1007/s11126-019-09694-5

Hoeve, M., Stams, G. J. J. M., van der Put, C. E., Dubas, J. S., van der Laan, P. H., & Gerris, J. R. M. (2012). A meta-analysis of attachment to parents and delinquency. *Journal of Abnormal Child Psychology, 40*(5), 771–785. https://doi.org/10.1007/s10802-011-9608-1

Hofmann, J., Platt, T., Lau, C., & Torres-Marín, J. (2020). Gender differences in humor-related traits, humor appreciation, production, comprehension, (neural) responses, use, and correlates: a systematic review. *Current Psychology,* 1–14. https://doi.org/10.1007/s12144-020-00724-1

Holloway, K., Seager, M., & Barry, J. A. (2018). *Are Clinical Psychologists, Psychotherapists and Counsellors Overlooking the Needs of Their Male Clients? Clinical Psychology Forum, 307,* 15–21.

Hom, M. A., Stanley, I. H., & Joiner, T. E. (2015). Evaluating factors and interventions that influence help-seeking and mental health service utilization among suicidal individuals: a review of the literature. *Clinical Psychology Review, 40,* 28–39. https://doi.org/10.1016/j.cpr.2015.05.006

Homeless Link. (2015). Autism and homelessness: briefing for frontline staff. https://www.homeless.org.uk/sites/default/files/site-attachments/Autism%20&%20HomelessnesOct%202015.pdf

Hoogeveen, S., Sarafoglou, A., & Wagenmakers, E. J. (2020). Laypeople can predict which social-science studies will be replicated successfully. *Advances in Methods and Practices in Psychological Science, 3*(3), 267–285.

Houston, J. M., Carter, D., & Smither, R. D. (1997). Competitiveness in elite professional athletes. *Perceptual and Motor Skills, 84*(3_suppl), 1447–1454. https://doi.org/10.2466/pms.1997.84.3c.1447

HSE. (2019). *Statistics – Fatal Injuries in Great Britain.* https://www.hse.gov.uk/Statistics/fatals.htm

Huang, H. (2015). Propaganda as signaling. *Comparative Politics, 47*(4), 419–444. https://doi.org/10.5129/001041515816103220

Hughes, J. H., Cameron, F., Eldridge, R., Devon, M., Wessely, S., & Greenberg, N. (2005). Going to war does not have to hurt: preliminary findings from the British deployment to Iraq. *The British Journal of Psychiatry, 186*(6), 536–537.

Hughes, K., Bellis, M. A., Hardcastle, K. A., Sethi, D., Butchart, A., Mikton, C., Jones, L., & Dunne, M. P. (2017). The effect of multiple adverse childhood experiences on health: a systematic review and meta-analysis. *The Lancet Public Health, 2*(8), e356–e366. https://doi.org/10.1016/S2468-2667(17)30118-4

Hunt, T., Wilson, C. J., Caputi, P., Woodward, A., & Wilson, I. (2017). Signs of current suicidality in men: a systematic review. *Plos One, 12*(3), e0174675. https://doi.org/10.1371/journal.pone.0174675

Hyde, J. S. (2005). The gender similarities hypothesis. *American Psychologist, 60*(6), 581–592. https://doi.org/10.1037/0003-066X.60.6.581

Hyde, J. S., Bigler, R. S., Joel, D., Tate, C. C., & van Anders, S. M. (2019). The future of sex and gender in psychology: five challenges to the gender binary. *American Psychologist, 74*(2), 171–193. https://doi.org/10.1037/amp0000307

Hyde, J. S., Fennema, E., & Lamon, S. J. (1990). Gender differences in mathematics performance: a meta-analysis. *Psychological Bulletin, 107*(2), 139.

Idris, I. (2019). Preventing/Countering violent extremism programming on men, women, boys and girls. GSDRC, University of Birmingham. https://opendocs.ids.ac.uk/opendocs/bitstream/handle/20.500.12413/14748/671_P-CVE_Programming_on_Men_Women_Boys_and_Girls.pdf?sequence=1

Innamorati, M., Pompili, M., Gonda, X., Amore, M., Serafini, G., Niolu, C., Lester, D., Rutz, W., Rihmer, Z., & Girardi, P. (2011). Psychometric properties of the Gotland scale for depression in Italian psychiatric inpatients and its utility in the prediction of suicide risk. *Journal of Affective Disorders, 132*(1–2), 99–103. https://doi.org/10.1016/j.jad.2011.02.003

Ismael, Z. K., AL-Anbari, L. A., & Mossa, H. A. (2017). Relationship of FSH, LH, DHEA and testosterone levels in serum with sperm function parameters in infertile men. *Journal of Pharmaceutical Sciences and Research, 9*(11), 2056–2061.

ISNA. (2008). *How Common Is Intersex? | Intersex Society of North America.* https://isna.org/faq/frequency/

Jacobson, J., & Prison Reform Trust (Great Britain). (2010). Punishing disadvantage: a profile of children in custody. Project Report. Prison Reform Trust, London, UK. https://eprints.bbk.ac.uk/id/eprint/3771/1/3771.pdf

Jaggar, A. M. (1987). Sex inequality and bias in sex differences research. *Canadian Journal of Philosophy Supplementary Volume, 13*, 24–39. https://doi.org/10.1080/00455091.1987.10715927

Jennings, W. G., Maldonado-Molina, M. M., Piquero, A. R., Odgers, C. L., Bird, H., & Canino, G. (2010). Sex differences in trajectories of offending among Puerto Rican youth. *Crime & Delinquency, 56*(3), 327–357.

Jennings, W. G., & Reingle, J. M. (2012). On the number and shape of developmental/life-course violence, aggression, and delinquency trajectories: a state-of-the-art review. *Journal of Criminal Justice, 40*(6), 472–489. https://doi.org/10.1016/j.jcrimjus.2012.07.001

Jespersen, A. F., Lalumière, M. L., & Seto, M. C. (2009). Sexual abuse history among adult sex offenders and non-sex offenders: a meta-analysis. *Child Abuse & Neglect, 33*(3), 179–192. https://doi.org/10.1016/j.chiabu.2008.07.004

Jóhannesson, I. Á., Lingard, B., & Mills, M. (2009). Possibilities in the boy turn? Comparative lessons from Australia and Iceland. *Scandinavian Journal of Educational Research, 53*(4), 309–325.

John, A., & Mansfield, L. (2018). *StreetGames: Safe, Fit and Well-case Study Research.* London: Brunel University. https://network.streetgames.org/sites/default/files/Brunel_University_London_Safe_Fit_and_Well_Case%20Study%20Research%20Report_Aug2018_0.pdf

Johnson, J. L., Oliffe, J. L., Kelly, M. T., Galdas, P., & Ogrodniczuk, J. S. (2012). Men's discourses of help-seeking in the context of depression. *Sociology of Health & Illness, 34*(3), 345–361. https://doi.org/10.1111/j.1467-9566.2011.01372.x

Johnson, R. R. (2017). Examining the facts on implicit bias. Dolan Consulting Group - Research Brief. https://www.dolanconsultinggroup.com/wp-content/uploads/2019/02/Examining-the-Facts-on-Implicit-Bias.pdf

Johnstone, L., & Boyle, M. (2018). The power threat meaning framework: towards the identification of patterns in emotional distress, unusual experiences and troubled or troubling behaviour, as an alternative to functional psychiatric diagnosis. https://www.bps.org.uk/sites/bps.org.uk/files/Policy%20-%20Files/PTM%20Framework%20%28January%202018%29_0.pdf

Johnstone, L., & Dallos, R. (Eds.). (2014). *Formulation in Psychology and Psychotherapy: Making Sense of People's Problems* (2nd edition). Oxfordshire: Routledge.

Jones, M. D. (2015). *Sequalae of Combat Trauma in Male and Female Veterans* [Psy.D., Alliant International University]. http://search.proquest.com/docview/1738947475/abstract/8E9CD23834A6470APQ/1

Jones, N., Campion, B., Keeling, M., & Greenberg, N. (2018). Cohesion, leadership, mental health stigmatisation and perceived barriers to care in UK military personnel. *Journal of Mental Health, 27*(1), 10–18. https://doi.org/10.3109/09638237.2016.1139063

Jung, C. G. (1969). *Psychology of the Transference: (From Vol. 16 Collected Works).* Princeton University Press.

Kahlenberg, S. M., & Wrangham, R. W. (2010). Sex differences in chimpanzees' use of sticks as play objects resemble those of children. *Current Biology, 20*(24), R1067–R1068. https://doi.org/10.1016/j.cub.2010.11.024

Kalish, R., & Kimmel, M. (2010). Suicide by mass murder: masculinity, aggrieved entitlement, and rampage school shootings. *Health Sociology Review, 19*(4), 451–464. https://doi.org/10.5172/hesr.2010.19.4.451

Kandel, E., & Mednick, S. A. (1991). Perinatal Complications Predict Violent Offending. *Criminology, 29*(3), 519–529. https://doi.org/10.1111/j.1745-9125.1991.tb01077.x

Kaufman, S. B. (2019). *Taking Sex Differences in Personality Seriously. Scientific American Blog Network.* https://blogs.scientificamerican.com/beautiful-minds/taking-sex-differences-in-personality-seriously/

KCMHR. (2018). *The Mental Health of The UK Armed Forces (September 2018 version).* https://www.kcl.ac.uk/kcmhr/publications/assetfiles/2018/kcmhr-admmh-factsheet-sept2018.pdf

Kealy, D., Rice, S. M., Ferlatte, O., Ogrodniczuk, J. S., & Oliffe, J. L. (2019). Better doctor-patient relationships are associated with men choosing more active depression treatment. *The Journal of the American Board of Family Medicine, 32*(1), 13–19. https://doi.org/10.3122/jabfm.2019.01.170430

Keating, F., & Robertson, D. (2004). Fear, black people and mental illness: a vicious circle? *Health & Social Care in the Community, 12*(5), 439–447.

Keenan, K. G., Senefeld, J. W., & Hunter, S. K. (2018). Girls in the boat: sex differences in rowing performance and participation. *Plos One, 13*(1), e0191504. https://doi.org/10.1371/journal.pone.0191504

Kelly, D., Steiner, A., Mason, H., & Teasdale, S. (2019). Men's Sheds: a conceptual exploration of the causal pathways for health and well-being. *Health & Social Care in the Community, 27*(5), 1147–1157. https://doi.org/10.1111/hsc.12765

Kerig, P. K., Becker, S. P., & Egan, S. (2010). From internalizing to externalizing: theoretical models of the processes linking PTSD to juvenile delinquency. *Posttraumatic Stress Disorder (PTSD): Causes, Symptoms and Treatment, 33*, 78.

Kessels, U., & Steinmayr, R. (2013). Macho-man in school: toward the role of gender role self-concepts and help seeking in school performance. *Learning and Individual Differences, 23*, 234–240.

Kessler, A., Sollie, S., Challacombe, B., Briggs, K., & Van Hemelrijck, M. (2019). The global prevalence of erectile dysfunction: a review. *BJU International, 124*(4), 587–599. https://doi.org/10.1111/bju.14813

Kimmel, M. S. (1987). *Changing Men: New Directions in Research on Men and Masculinity* (p. 320). Sage Publications, Inc.

Kimmel, M. S. (1994). Masculinity as homophobia. Fear, shame, and silence in the construction of gender identity. *Theorizing Masculinities, 5*, 213–219.

King, C., & Murphy, G. H. (2014). A Systematic Review of People with Autism Spectrum Disorder and the Criminal Justice System. *Journal of Autism and Developmental Disorders, 44*(11), 2717–2733. https://doi.org/10.1007/s10803-014-2046-5

King, D. W., King, L. A., Gudanowski, D. M., & Vreven, D. L. (1995). Alternative representations of war zone stressors: relationships to posttraumatic stress disorder in male and female Vietnam veterans. *Journal of Abnormal Psychology, 104*(1), 184.

Kingerlee, R. (2019). Practising eye movement desensitisation and reprocessing (EMDR) with male civilians and male veterans. In J. A. Barry, R. Kingerlee, M. Seager, & L. Sullivan (Eds.), *The Palgrave Handbook of Male Psychology and Mental Health* (pp. 461–482). Springer International Publishing. https://doi.org/10.1007/978-3-030-04384-1_23

Kingerlee, R., Abotsie, G., Fisk, A., & Woodley, L. (2019a). Reconnection: designing interventions and services with men in mind. In J. A. Barry, R. Kingerlee, M. Seager, & L. Sullivan (Eds.), *The Palgrave Handbook of Male Psychology and Mental Health* (pp. 647–669). Springer International Publishing. https://doi.org/10.1007/978-3-030-04384-1_31

Kingerlee, R., Cawdron, J., & Barnard, C. (2019b). Opening a dialogue: using cognitive analytic therapy with depressed men. In J. A. Barry, R. Kingerlee, M. Seager, & L. Sullivan (Eds.), *The Palgrave Handbook of Male Psychology and Mental Health* (pp. 509–531). Springer International Publishing. https://doi.org/10.1007/978-3-030-04384-1_25

Kiselica, M. S. (2008). *When Boys Become Parents: Adolescent Fatherhood in America*. Rutgers University Press.

Kiselica, M. S., & Englar-Carlson, M. (2010). Identifying, affirming, and building upon male strengths: the positive psychology/positive masculinity model of psychotherapy with boys and men. *Psychotherapy: Theory, Research, Practice, Training, 47*(3), 276–287. https://doi.org/10.1037/a0021159

Kitzinger, C. (1994). *Should Psychologists Study Sex Differences? – Celia Kitzinger, 1994. Feminism & Psychology.* https://journals.sagepub.com/doi/10.1177/0959353594044003

Klämpfl, M. K., Lobinger, B. H., & Raab, M. (2013). Reinvestment – the cause of the yips? *PLoS ONE, 8,* 12. https://doi.org/10.1371/journal.pone.0082470

Klotz, L., Derya, T., Neil, F., Gregory, D. A., & Martin, T. (2020). Mp75-14   analysis of small non-coding RNAs in urinary exosomes accurately classifies prostate cancer into low grade and higher grade disease. *Journal of Urology, 203*(Supplement4), e1147–e1147. https://doi.org/10.1097/JU.0000000000000961.014

Kolliakou, A., Bakolis, I., Chandran, D., Derczynski, L., Werbeloff, N., Osborn, D. P. J., Bontcheva, K., & Stewart, R. (2020). Mental health-related conversations on social media and crisis episodes: a time-series regression analysis. *Scientific Reports, 10*(1), 1–7. https://doi.org/10.1038/s41598-020-57835-9

Koppes, C. R., & Black, G. D. (1990). *Hollywood Goes to War: How Politics, Profits and Propaganda Shaped World War II Movies.* University of California Press.

Koss, M. P. (1993). Detecting the scope of rape: a review of prevalence research methods. *Journal of Interpersonal Violence, 8*(2), 198–222.

Kposowa, A. J. (2003). Divorce and suicide risk. *Journal of Epidemiology & Community Health, 57*(12), 993–993. https://doi.org/10.1136/jech.57.12.993

Kreyenfeld, M., & Konietzka, D. (2017). *Childlessness in Europe: Contexts, Causes, and Consequences.* Springer.

Krischer, M. K., & Sevecke, K. (2008). Early traumatization and psychopathy in female and male juvenile offenders. *International Journal of Law and Psychiatry, 31*(3), 253–262.

Krumm, S., Checchia, C., Koesters, M., Kilian, R., & Becker, T. (2017). Men's views on depression: a systematic review and metasynthesis of qualitative research. *Psychopathology, 50*(2), 107–124. https://doi.org/10.1159/000455256

Kruttschnitt, C. (2013). Gender and crime. *Annual Review of Sociology, 39*(1), 291–308. https://doi.org/10.1146/annurev-soc-071312-145605

Kung, H. C., Pearson, J. L., & Liu, X. (2003). Risk factors for male and female suicide decedents ages 15–64 in the United States: results from the 1993 national mortality followback survey. *Social Psychiatry and Psychiatric Epidemiology, 38*(8), 419–426. https://doi.org/10.1007/s00127-003-0656-x

Kupers, T. A. (2005). Toxic masculinity as a barrier to mental health treatment in prison. *Journal of Clinical Psychology, 61*(6), 713–724. https://doi.org/10.1002/jclp.20105

Kurosawa, A. (1954, April 26). *Shichinin No Samurai* [Action, Adventure, Drama]. Toho Company.

Kwiek, M., Florek, S., & Piotrowski, P. (2016). The theory of life history and criminal behavior. *Resocjalizacja Polska, 12*(2), 9–25.

Labots, G., Jones, A., de Visser, S. J., Rissmann, R., & Burggraaf, J. (2018). Gender differences in clinical registration trials: is there a real problem? *British Journal of Clinical Pharmacology, 84*(4), 700–707. https://doi.org/10.1111/bcp.13497

Lamb, M. E. (2004). *The Role of the Father in Child Development.* John Wiley & Sons.

Lamm, B., Gernhardt, A., & Rübeling, H. (2019). How societal changes have influenced German children's gender representations as expressed in human figure drawings in 1977 and 2015. *Sex Roles, 81*(1), 118–125. https://doi.org/10.1007/s11199-018-0978-5

Lancet, T. (2020). The gendered dimensions of COVID-19. *The Lancet, 395*(10231), 1168. https://doi.org/10.1016/S0140-6736(20)30823-0

Lane, J. M., & Addis, M. E. (2005). Male gender role conflict and patterns of help seeking in Costa Rica and the United States. *Psychology of Men & Masculinity, 6*(3), 155.

Lang, J. C., & Lee, C. H. (2010). Workplace humor and organizational creativity. *The International Journal of Human Resource Management, 21*(1), 46–60. https://doi.org/10.1080/09585190903466855

Langbert, M., & Stevens, S . (2020). *National Association of Scholars – Partisan Registration and Contributions of Faculty in Flagship Colleges by Sean Stevens*. https://www.nas.org/blogs/article/partisan-registration-and-contributions-of-faculty-in-flagship-colleges

Laqueur, T. W. (1992). *The Facts of Fatherhood in Rethinking the Family: Some Feminist Questions* (Eds. B. Thorne & M. Yalom, pp. 155–175). Boston, MA: Northeastern University Press.

Lavy, V. (2004). *Do Gender Stereotypes Reduce Girls' Human Capital Outcomes? Evidence from a Natural Experiment* (No. w10678; p. w10678). National Bureau of Economic Research. https://doi.org/10.3386/w10678

Lawrence E. A. (2003). *Feline fortunes: contrasting views of cats in popular culture - ProQuest*. https://search.proquest.com/openview/03f8cc6c8f207c9d8c787dce2c9b3a6e/1?pq-origsite=gscholar&cbl=34704

Lea, G. W., Belliveau, G., & Westwood, M. (2020). Staging Therapeutic Enactment with Veterans in Contact!Unload. *Qualitative Research in Psychology, 17*(4), 521–540. https://doi.org/10.1080/14780887.2018.1442776

Leach, C., Stewart, A., & Smallbone, S. (2016). Testing the sexually abused–sexual abuser hypothesis: a prospective longitudinal birth cohort study. *Child Abuse & Neglect, 51*, 144–153. https://doi.org/10.1016/j.chiabu.2015.10.024

Lee, D. H., Porta, M., Jacobs, D. R., & Vandenberg, L. N. (2014). Chlorinated persistent organic pollutants, obesity, and type 2 diabetes. *Endocrine Reviews, 35*(4), 557–601. https://doi.org/10.1210/er.2013-1084

Leggett, V., Jacobs, P., Nation, K., Scerif, G., & Bishop, D. V. M. (2010). Neurocognitive outcomes of individuals with a sex chromosome trisomy: XXX, XYY, or XXY: a systematic review*. *Developmental Medicine & Child Neurology, 52*(2), 119–129. https://doi.org/10.1111/j.1469-8749.2009.03545.x

Leiblum, S. R. (2006). *Principles and Practice of Sex Therapy, Fourth Edition*. Guilford Press.

Lemkey, L. E., Brown, B., & Barry, J. A. (2015). Gender distinctions: Should we be more sensitive to the different therapeutic needs of men and women in clinical hypnosis? Findings from a pilot interview study. *Australian Journal of Clinical Hypnotherapy and Hypnosis, 37*(2), 10–20.

Lemmens, J. S., Valkenburg, P. M., & Peter, J. (2011). The effects of pathological gaming on aggressive behavior. *Journal of Youth and Adolescence, 40*(1), 38–47.

Lemkey, L. E., Fletcher, C., & Barry, J. A. (2016). How much do job satisfaction and relationship quality predict intention to engage in health behaviours in men and women? A Pilot Study. *New Male Studies, 5*(1), 31–47.

Lemos, G. C., Abad, F. J., Almeida, L. S., & Colom, R. (2013). Sex differences on g and non-g intellectual performance reveal potential sources of STEM discrepancies. *Intelligence, 41*(1), 11–18. https://doi.org/10.1016/j.intell.2012.10.009

Leong, J. Y., Blachman-Braun, R., Patel, A., Patel, P., & Ramasamy, R. (2020). 181 association between polychlorinated biphenyl (PCB) 153 exposure and serum testosterone levels: analysis of the national health and nutrition examination survey. *The Journal of Sexual Medicine*, *17*(1), S60–S61. https://doi.org/10.1016/j.jsxm.2019.11.127

Levant, R., & Richmond, K. (2007). A review of research on masculinity ideologies using the male role norms inventory. *The Journal of Men's Studies*, *15*(2), 130–146. https://doi.org/10.3149/jms.1502.130

Levant, R. F., Jadaszewski, S., Alto, K., Richmond, K., Pardo, S., Keo-Meier, C., & Gerdes, Z. (2019). Moderation and mediation of the relationships between masculinity ideology and health status. *Health Psychology*, *38*(2), 162–171. https://doi.org/10.1037/hea0000709

Levant, R. F., & Pollack, W. S. (Eds.). (1995). *New Psychology of Men*. Basic Books.

Levant, R. F., Rankin, T. J., Williams, C. M., Hasan, N. T., & Smalley, K. B. (2010). Evaluation of the factor structure and construct validity of scores on the Male Role Norms Inventory – Revised (MRNI-R). *Psychology of Men & Masculinity*, *11*(1), 25–37. https://doi.org/10.1037/a0017637

Lewis, H. (2020, March 19). *The Coronavirus Is a Disaster for Feminism*. The Atlantic. https://www.theatlantic.com/international/archive/2020/03/feminism-womens-rights-coronavirus-covid19/608302/

Liddon, L., Kingerlee, R., & Barry, J. A. (2017). Gender differences in preferences for psychological treatment, coping strategies, and triggers to help-seeking. *British Journal of Clinical Psychology*, *57*(1), 42–58.

Liddon, L., Kingerlee, R., Seager, M., & Barry, J. A. (2019). What are the factors that make a male-friendly therapy? In J. A. Barry, R. Kingerlee, M. Seager, & L. Sullivan (Eds.), *The Palgrave Handbook of Male Psychology and Mental Health* (pp. 671–694). Springer International Publishing. https://doi.org/10.1007/978-3-030-04384-1_32

Liem, J. H., Lustig, K., & Dillon, C. (2010). Depressive symptoms and life satisfaction among emerging adults: a comparison of high school dropouts and graduates. *Journal of Adult Development*, *17*(1), 33–43. https://doi.org/10.1007/s10804-009-9076-9

Lindsay, J., & Boyle, P. (2017). The conceptual penis as a social construct. *Cogent Social Sciences*, *3*, 1. https://doi.org/10.1080/23311886.2017.1330439

Lippa, R. A. (2006). The gender reality hypothesis. *American Psychologist*, *61*(6), 639–640. https://doi.org/10.1037/0003-066X.61.6.639

Lippa, R. A., Preston, K., & Penner, J. (2014). Women's representation in 60 occupations from 1972 to 2010: more women in high-status jobs, few women in things-oriented jobs. *Plos One*, *9*(5), e95960. https://doi.org/10.1371/journal.pone.0095960

Lisak, D. (2005). *Male Survivors of Trauma*.

Liu, W. M. (2005). The study of men and masculinity as an important multicultural competency consideration. *Journal of Clinical Psychology*, *61*(6), 685–697. https://doi.org/10.1002/jclp.20103

Liu, K. A., & DiPietro Mager, N. A. (2016). Women's involvement in clinical trials: historical perspective and future implications. *Pharmacy Practice*, *14*(1), 708–708. https://doi.org/10.18549/PharmPract.2016.01.708

Lombardo, M. P. (2012). On the Evolution of Sport. *Evolutionary Psychology*, *10*(1), 147470491201000. https://doi.org/10.1177/147470491201000101

Lombardo, M. P., & Deaner, R. O. (2018). On the evolution of the sex differences in throwing: throwing is a male adaptation in humans. *The Quarterly Review of Biology, 93*(2), 91–119. https://doi.org/10.1086/698225

Loosemore, M., Knowles, C. H., & Whyte, G. P. (2007). Amateur boxing and risk of chronic traumatic brain injury: systematic review of observational studies. *BMJ, 335*(7624), 809. https://doi.org/10.1136/bmj.39342.690220.55

Lopez, J. (2020). *Unconscious Bias Training. Statement made on 15 December 2020. UK Parliament.* https://questions-statements.parliament.uk/written-statements/detail/2020-12-15/hcws652

Lowe, M., & Balfour, B. (2015). The unheard victims. *The Psychologist, 28,* 118–121.

Löwe, B., Wahl, I., Rose, M., Spitzer, C., Glaesmer, H., Wingenfeld, K., Schneider, A., & Brähler, E. (2010). A 4-item measure of depression and anxiety: validation and standardization of the Patient Health Questionnaire-4 (PHQ-4) in the general population. *Journal of Affective Disorders, 122*(1–2), 86–95.

Lovett, C. C. (1997). *Olympic Marathon: A Centennial History of the Games' Most Storied Race.* Praeger Publishers.

Lundahl, B. W., Tollefson, D., Risser, H., & Lovejoy, M. C. (2008). A Meta-Analysis of Father Involvement in Parent Training. *Research on Social Work Practice, 18*(2), 97–106. https://doi.org/10.1177/1049731507309828

Maccoby, E. E. (1988). Gender as a social category. *Developmental Psychology, 24*(6), 755–765. https://doi.org/10.1037/0012-1649.24.6.755

Mack, K. Y., Leiber, M. J., Featherstone, R. A., & Monserud, M. A. (2007). Reassessing the family-delinquency association: do family type, family processes, and economic factors make a difference? *Journal of Criminal Justice, 35*(1), 51–67. https://doi.org/10.1016/j.jcrimjus.2006.11.015

Ma, G. L., & Sandlow, J. I. (2020). Causes of Male Infertility. In S. J. Parekattil, S. C. Esteves, & A. Agarwal (Eds.), *Male Infertility: Contemporary Clinical Approaches, Andrology, ART and Antioxidants* (pp. 3–14). Springer International Publishing. https://doi.org/10.1007/978-3-030-32300-4_1

Machin, A. J. (2015). Mind the gap: the expectation and reality of involved fatherhood. *Fathering: A Journal of Theory, Research & Practice about Men as Fathers, 13*(1), 36–60. https://www.fatherhood.gov/sites/default/files/resource_files/e000003349.pdf

MacQueen, R., & Fisher, P. (2019). Masculine Identity and Traumatic Brain Injury. In J. A. Barry, R. Kingerlee, M. Seager, & L. Sullivan (Eds.), *The Palgrave Handbook of Male Psychology and Mental Health* (pp. 601–622). Springer International Publishing. https://doi.org/10.1007/978-3-030-04384-1_29

MacQueen, R., Fisher, P., & Williams, D. (2020). A qualitative investigation of masculine identity after traumatic brain injury. *Neuropsychological Rehabilitation, 30*(2), 298–314. https://doi.org/10.1080/09602011.2018.1466714

Madison, G., & Fahlman, P. (2020). Sex differences in the number of scientific publications and citations when attaining the rank of professor in Sweden. *Studies in Higher Education,* 1–22. https://doi.org/10.1080/03075079.2020.1723533

Madison, G., & Söderlund, T. (2018). Comparisons of content and scientific quality indicators across peer-reviewed journal articles with more or less gender perspective: gender studies can do better. *Scientometrics, 115*(3), 1161–1183. https://doi.org/10.1007/s11192-018-2729-3

Madsen, S. A. (2019). Men and perinatal depression. *Trends in Urology & Men's Health*, *10*(2), 7–9. https://doi.org/10.1002/tre.681

Magaard, J. L., Seeralan, T., Schulz, H., & Brütt, A. L. (2017). Factors associated with help-seeking behaviour among individuals with major depression: a systematic review. *Plos One*, *12*(5), e0176730. https://doi.org/10.1371/journal.pone.0176730

Magness, P. (2019, May 16). *Why Students Are Fleeing the Humanities. AIER*. https://www.aier.org/article/why-students-are-fleeing-the-humanities

Magrath, R. (2018). 'To try and gain an advantage for my team': homophobic and homosexually themed chanting among English football fans. *Sociology*, *52*(4), 709–726. https://doi.org/10.1177/0038038517702600

Magrath, R. (2019). Inclusive masculinities of working-class university footballers in the South of England. *Sport in Society*, *0*(0), 1–18. https://doi.org/10.1080/17430437.2019.1672157

Magrath, R., & Stott, P. (2019). 'Impossible to implement?': the effectiveness of anti-homophobia policy in English professional football. *International Journal of Sport Policy and Politics*, *11*(1), 19–38. https://doi.org/10.1080/19406940.2018.1479284

Maguire, D. (2019) Vulnerable prisoner masculinities in an English prison. *Men and Masculinities*, https://doi.org/10.1177/1097184X19888966

Mahalik, J. R., Burns, S. M., & Syzdek, M. (2007). Masculinity and perceived normative health behaviors as predictors of men's health behaviors. *Social Science & Medicine*, *64*(11), 2201–2209. https://doi.org/10.1016/j.socscimed.2007.02.035

Mahalik, J. R., Good, G. E., Tager, D., Levant, R. F., & Mackowiak, C. (2012). Developing a taxonomy of helpful and harmful practices for clinical work with boys and men. *Journal of Counseling Psychology*, *59*(4), 591–603. https://doi.org/10.1037/a0030130

Mahalik, J. R., Locke, B. D., Ludlow, L. H., Diemer, M. A., Scott, R. P. J., Gottfried, M., & Freitas, G. (2003). Development of the Conformity to Masculine Norms Inventory. *Psychology of Men & Masculinity*, *4*(1), 3–25. https://doi.org/10.1037/1524-9220.4.1.3

Manandhar, M., Hawkes, S., Buse, K., Nosrati, E., & Magar, V. (2018). Gender, health and the 2030 agenda for sustainable development. *Bulletin of the World Health Organization*, *96*(9), 644–653. https://doi.org/10.2471/BLT.18.211607

Mank, J. (2016, April 27). *The Evolution of Males and Females – With Judith Mank*. https://www.youtube.com/watch?v=En26p6GvtHw

ManKind Initiative. (2015). *#ViolenceIsViolence: Domestic Abuse Advert Mankind*. https://www.youtube.com/watch?v=u3PgH86OyEM

Mansdotter, A., Lundin, A., Falkstedt, D., & Hemmingsson, T. (2009). The association between masculinity rank and mortality patterns: a prospective study based on the Swedish 1969 conscript cohort. *Journal of Epidemiology & Community Health*, *63*(5), 408–413. https://doi.org/10.1136/jech.2008.082628

Mansfield, A. K., Addis, M. E., & Courtenay, W. (2005). Measurement of men's help seeking: development and evaluation of the barriers to help seeking scale. *Psychology of Men & Masculinity*, *6*(2), 95–108. https://doi.org/10.1037/1524-9220.6.2.95

Mariani, E., Özcan, B., & Goisis, A. (2017). Family trajectories and well-being of children born to lone mothers in the UK. *European Journal of Population*, *33*(2), 185–215. https://doi.org/10.1007/s10680-017-9420-x

Marino, M., Masella, R., Bulzomi, P., Campesi, I., Malorni, W., & Franconi, F. (2011). Nutrition and human health from a sex–gender perspective. *Molecular Aspects of Medicine, 32*(1), 1–70. https://doi.org/10.1016/j.mam.2011.02.001

Martin, L. A., Neighbors, H. W., & Griffith, D. M. (2013). The experience of symptoms of depression in men vs women: analysis of the national comorbidity survey replication. *JAMA Psychiatry, 70*(10), 1100. https://doi.org/10.1001/jamapsychiatry.2013.1985

Maruna, S., & Mann, R. E. (2006). A fundamental attribution error? Rethinking cognitive distortions. *Legal and Criminological Psychology, 11*(2), 155–177.

Mastroianni, A. C., Faden R., & Federman, D. (1994). *Women and Health Research: Ethical and Legal Issues of Including Women in Clinical Studies, Volume 1*. National Academies Press.

Mastroianni, A. C., Faden, R., & Federman, D. (Eds.). (1994). *Women and Health Research: Ethical and Legal Issues of Including Women in Clinical Studies*, volume 2, workshop and commissioned papers (Vol. 1). National Academies Press.

Matthews, M. D . (2018). *Moral Injury. Psychology Today*. https://www.psychologytoday.com/blog/head-strong/201803/moral-injury

Matthews, C. R., & Channon, A. (2019). The 'Male Preserve' thesis, sporting culture, and men's power. In L. Gottzén, U. Mellström, & T. Shefer (Eds.), *Routledge International Handbook of Masculinity Studies* (1st edition, pp. 373–383). Routledge. https://doi.org/10.4324/9781315165165-37

Matthews, M. (2014). Stress among UAV operators – post-traumatic stress disorder, existential crisis, or moral injury? *Ethics and Armed Forces*.

Matthews, M. D. (2013). *Head Strong: How Psychology Is Revolutionizing War*. Oxford University Press, Incorporated. http://ebookcentral.proquest.com/lib/ucl/detail.action?docID=1573137

Matthews, M. D. (2020). *Head Strong: How Psychology Is Revolutionizing War, Revised and Expanded Edition*. Oxford University Press.

May, T. (1993). *Between Genealogy and Epistemology: Psychology, Politics, and Knowledge in the Thought of Michel Foucault*. Penn State Press.

McCormack, M., & Anderson, E. (2010). 'It's just not acceptable any more': the erosion of homophobia and the softening of masculinity at an English sixth form. *Sociology, 44*(5), 843–859. https://doi.org/10.1177/0038038510375734

McCormack, M., Wignall, L., & Morris, M. (2016). Gay guys using gay language: friendship, shared values and the intent-context-effect matrix: gay guys using gay language. *The British Journal of Sociology, 67*(4), 747–767. https://doi.org/10.1111/1468-4446.12203

McDermott, J. (2020). 'It's like therapy but more fun': armed forces and veterans' breakfast clubs: a study of their emergence as veterans' self-help communities. *Sociological Research Online*, 1360780420905845. https://doi.org/10.1177/1360780420905845

McNeely, R. L., Cook, P. W., & Torres, J. B. (2001). Is domestic violence a gender issue, or a human issue? *Journal of Human Behavior in the Social Environment, 4*(4), 227–251. https://doi.org/10.1300/J137v04n04_02

Meinert, R., & Hatkevich, B. (2019). The effect of community-based therapeutic boxing on the speech, social interaction skills, and mental health of individuals with Parkinson's disease. *American Journal of Occupational Therapy, 73*(4_Supplement_1), 7311515312p1-7311515312p1. https://doi.org/10.5014/ajot.2019.73S1-PO5059

Men & Boys Coalition. (2020). *A More Inclusive Decade: Ten Policy Measures to Better Support the Well-being of Men and Boys in the UK | Men & Boys Coalition*. http://www.menandboyscoalition.org.uk/newsevents/the-top-ten-policy-measures-to-boost-the-well-being-of-men-and-boys/

Metcalf, H. (2010). Stuck in the pipeline: a critical review of STEM workforce literature. *InterActions: UCLA Journal of Education and Information Studies, 6*(2). https://escholarship.org/uc/item/6zf09176

Metropolitan Police. (2014). *Bullying – get the facts.* https://safe.met.police.uk/bullying/get_the_facts.html

Mildorf, J. (2007). *Storying Domestic Violence: Constructions and Stereotypes of Abuse in the Discourse of General Practitioners.* U of Nebraska Press.

Millett, K. (1970). *Sexual Politics.* Columbia University Press.

Millett, K. (2008, July 22). "Freedom from Torture or Cruel, Inhuman and Degrading Treatment or Punishment" – MFIPortal. *MindFreedom International (MFI).* https://mindfreedom.org/kb/millett-freedom-from-torture/

Ministry of Defence. (2017). Defence People Mental Health and Wellbeing Strategy 2017-2022. London: Crown. https://assets.publishing.service.gov.uk/government/uploads/system/uploads/attachment_data/file/689978/20170713-MHW_Strategy_SCREEN.pdf

Ministry of Defence, L. (2018). *Written Evidence Submitted by the Ministry of Defence. House of Commons Inquiry.* http://data.parliament.uk/writtenevidence/committeeevidence.svc/evidencedocument/defence-committee/armed-forces-and-veterans-mental-health/written/79961.pdf

Ministry of Justice. (2019a). *10,000 Extra Prison Places to Keep the Public Safe.* GOV.UK. https://www.gov.uk/government/news/10-000-extra-prison-places-to-keep-the-public-safe

Ministry of Justice. (2019b). *Justice Secretary Announces New Female Offender Funding at Women's Aid speech.* GOV.UK. https://www.gov.uk/government/news/justice-secretary-announces-new-female-offender-funding-at-womens-aid-speech

Mitchell, J. L., & Lashewicz, B. (2019). Generative fathering: a framework for enriching understandings of fathers raising children who have disability diagnoses. *Journal of Family Studies, 25*(2), 184–198. https://doi.org/10.1080/13229400.2016.1212727

Moffitt, T. E., & Caspi, A. (2001). Childhood predictors differentiate life-course persistent and adolescence-limited antisocial pathways among males and females. *Development and Psychopathology, 13*(2), 355–375. https://doi.org/10.1017/S0954579401002097

Moller-Leimkuhler, A. M. (2003). The gender gap in suicide and premature death or: why are men so vulnerable? *European Archives of Psychiatry and Clinical Neuroscience, 253*(1), 1–8. https://doi.org/10.1007/s00406-003-0397-6

Möller-Leimkühler, A. M. (2002). Barriers to help-seeking by men: a review of sociocultural and clinical literature with particular reference to depression. *Journal of Affective Disorders, 71*(1–3), 1–9. https://doi.org/10.1016/S0165-0327(01)00379-2

Möller-Leimkühler, A. M., & Yücel, M. (2010). Male depression in females? *Journal of Affective Disorders, 121*(1–2), 22–29. https://doi.org/10.1016/j.jad.2009.05.007

Molnar, C., & Gair, J. (2019). 24.4. Hormonal control of human reproduction. *Concepts of Biology – 1st Canadian Edition.* BC campus. https://opentextbc.ca/biology/chapter/24-4-hormonal-control-of-human-reproduction/

Moreau, M.-P., & Brownhill, S. (2017). Teachers and educational policies: negotiating discourses of male role modelling. *Teaching and Teacher Education, 67*, 370–377. https://doi.org/10.1016/j.tate.2017.07.001

Moreira, C. A., Marinho, M., Oliveira, J., Sobreira, G., & Aleixo, A. (2015). Suicide attempts and alcohol use disorder. *European Psychiatry, 30*, 521. https://doi.org/10.1016/S0924-9338(15)30409-0

Moss-Racusin, C. A., Dovidio, J. F., Brescoll, V. L., Graham, M. J., & Handelsman, J. (2012). Science faculty's subtle gender biases favor male students. *Proceedings of the National Academy of Sciences, 109*(41), 16474–16479. https://doi.org/10.1073/pnas.1211286109

Moss-Racusin, C. A., Sanzari, C., Caluori, N., & Rabasco, H. (2018). Gender bias produces gender gaps in STEM engagement. *Sex Roles, 79*(11), 651–670. https://doi.org/10.1007/s11199-018-0902-z

Movember. (2019). Perceptions of masculinity & the challenges of opening up. Retrieved May 11, 2020, from https://d3n8a8pro7vhmx.cloudfront.net/amhf/pages/722/attachments/original/1572840692/Movember_Masculinity_Report_%281%29.pdf?1572840692

Msiza, V. (2019). 'You are a male teacher but you have a woman's heart'. *Foundation Phase Teachers Negotiating Identities in South Africa. Education, 3-13*, 1–10. https://doi.org/10.1080/03004279.2019.1638957

Murray, C. (2008). *Real Education: Four Simple Truths for Bringing America's Schools Back to Reality*. New York: Crown Forum.

Murray, T. (2009). *The Oppressed Women of Afghanistan: Fact, Fiction, or Distortion. Middle East Institute*. https://www.mei.edu/publications/oppressed-women-afghanistan-fact-fiction-or-distortion

Mwangangi, R. K. (2019). The role of family in dealing with Juvenile delinquency. *Open Journal of Social Sciences, 7*(3), 52–63. https://doi.org/10.4236/jss.2019.73004

Mykyta, L. (2012). Economic downturns and the failure to launch: the living arrangements of young adults in the US 1995-2011. US Census Bureau Social, Economic and Housing Statistics Division (SEHSD) Working Paper, 24.

Nathanson, P., & Young, K. K. (2001). *Spreading Misandry: The Teaching of Contempt for Men in Popular Culture*. McGill-Queen's Press-MQUP.

Nathanson, P., & Young, K. K. (2006). *Legalizing Misandry: From Public Shame to Systemic Discrimination against Men*. McGill-Queen's Press-MQUP.

Nathanson, P., & Young, K. K. (2009). Coming of age as a villain: what every boy needs to know in a misandric world. *Boyhood Studies, 3*(2), 155–177. https://doi.org/10.3149/thy.0301.155

National Audit Office. (2017). *Mental Health in Prisons*. London: National Audit Office.

National Science Foundation. (2017). *Women, Minorities, and Persons with Disabilities in Science and Engineering: 2013: (558442013-001)* [Data set]. American Psychological Association. https://doi.org/10.1037/e558442013-001

Nelson, A. (2005). Children's toy collections in Sweden – a less gender-typed country? *Sex Roles, 52*(1), 93–102. https://doi.org/10.1007/s11199-005-1196-5

Neuberg, S. L., Williams, K. E. G., Sng, O., Pick, C. M., Neel, R., Krems, J. A., & Pirlott, A. G. (2020). Chapter Five – Toward capturing the functional and nuanced nature of social stereotypes: an affordance management approach. In B. Gawronski (Ed.),

Advances in Experimental Social Psychology (Vol. 62, pp. 245–304). Academic Press. https://doi.org/10.1016/bs.aesp.2020.04.004

Neugebauer. (1999). *Prenatal exposure to wartime famine and development of antisocial personality disorder in early adulthood | Global Health | JAMA | JAMA Network*. https://jamanetwork-com.libproxy.ucl.ac.uk/journals/jama/article-abstract/190990

Nevin, R. (2007). Understanding international crime trends: the legacy of preschool lead exposure. *Environmental Research, 104*(3), 315–336. https://doi.org/10.1016/j.envres.2007.02.008

New York Times. (2020). *Alcohol Deaths Have Risen Sharply, Particularly Among Women – The New York Times*. https://www.nytimes.com/2020/01/10/health/alcohol-deaths-women.html

Newsome, J. L. (2008). The chemistry PhD: the impact on women's retention. *A Report for the UK Resource Centre for Women in SET and the Royal Society of Chemistry*, 1–38.

NHS Inform. (2020). *Erectile dysfunction*. https://www.nhsinform.scot/illnesses-and-conditions/sexual-and-reproductive/erectile-dysfunction-impotence

Nielsen, M. W. (2015). Make academic job advertisements fair to all. *Nature News, 525*(7570), 427. https://doi.org/10.1038/525427a

Nielsen, M. W., Andersen, J. P., Schiebinger, L., & Schneider, J. W. (2017). One and a half million medical papers reveal a link between author gender and attention to gender and sex analysis. *Nature Human Behaviour, 1*(11), 791–796. https://doi.org/10.1038/s41562-017-0235-x

Nierengarten, M. B. (2019). Fathers' influence on development and wellbeing of children. *Contemporary Pediatrics, 36*(6), 1–3.

NIH. (2015). *NOT-OD-15-102: Consideration of Sex as a Biological Variable in NIH-funded Research*. https://grants.nih.gov/grants/guide/notice-files/not-od-15-102.html

Nixon, R. (2011, June 26). *Slow Violence. The Chronicle of Higher Education*. https://www.chronicle.com/article/Slow-Violence/127968

Nordenström, A., Servin, A., Bohlin, G., Larsson, A., & Wedell, A. (2002). Sex-typed toy play behavior correlates with the degree of prenatal androgen exposure assessed by *CYP21* genotype in girls with congenital adrenal hyperplasia. *The Journal of Clinical Endocrinology & Metabolism, 87*(11), 5119–5124. https://doi.org/10.1210/jc.2001-011531

Nosek, B. A., Banaji, M. R., & Greenwald, A. G. (2002). Harvesting implicit group attitudes and beliefs from a demonstration web site. *Group Dynamics: Theory, Research, and Practice, 6*(1), 101–115. https://doi.org/10.1037/1089-2699.6.1.101

Nuzzo, J. (2020). Bias against men's issues within the United Nations and the World Health Organization: a content analysis. *Psychreg Journal of Psychology, 4*(3), 120–150.

Nuzzo, J. L. (2020a). Men's health in the United States: a national health paradox. *The Aging Male, 23*(1), 42–52. https://doi.org/10.1080/13685538.2019.1645109

Nuzzo, J. L. (2020b). Large sex difference despite equal opportunity: authorship of over 3000 letters in exercise science and physical therapy journals over 56 years. *Scientometrics*. https://doi.org/10.1007/s11192-020-03427-3

Nyante, S. J., Graubard, B. I., Li, Y., McQuillan, G. M., Platz, E. A., Rohrmann, S., Bradwin, G., & McGlynn, K. A. (2012). Trends in sex hormone concentrations in US males: 1988–1991 to 1999–2004. *International Journal of Andrology, 35*(3), 456–466. https://doi.org/10.1111/j.1365-2605.2011.01230.x

O'Brien, R., Hunt, K., & Hart, G. (2005). 'It's caveman stuff, but that is to a certain extent how guys still operate': men's accounts of masculinity and help seeking. *Social Science & Medicine, 61*(3), 503–516.

O'Connor, R. C., & Kirtley, O. J. (2018). The integrated motivational–volitional model of suicidal behaviour. *Philosophical Transactions of the Royal Society B: Biological Sciences, 373*, 1754. https://doi.org/10.1098/rstb.2017.0268

OED. (2020). *Patriarchy. Oxford Reference.* https://doi.org/10.1093/oi/authority. 20110803100310604

Ogas, O., & Gaddam, S. (2011). *A Billion Wicked Thoughts: What the World's Largest Experiment Reveals about Human Desire* (pp. xii, 394). Dutton/Penguin Books.

Ogrodniczuk, J., Oliffe, J., Kuhl, D., & Gross, P. A. (2016). Men's mental health: spaces and places that work for men. *Canadian Family Physician, 62*(6), 463–464.

Oliffe, J. L., Rossnagel, E., Bottorff, J. L., Chambers, S. K., Caperchione, C., & Rice, S. M. (2019). Community-based men's health promotion programs: eight lessons learnt and their caveats. *Health Promotion International*, daz101. https://doi.org/10.1093/heapro/daz101

ONS. (2016). *Why Are More Young People Living with Their Parents? Office for National Statistics.* https://www.ons.gov.uk/peoplepopulationandcommunity/birthsdeathsandmarriages/families/articles/whyaremoreyoungpeoplelivingwiththeirparents/2016-02-22

ONS. (2019a). *Gender Pay Gap in the UK – Office for National Statistics.* https://www.ons.gov.uk/employmentandlabourmarket/peopleinwork/earningsandworkinghours/bulletins/genderpaygapintheuk/2019

ONS. (2019b). *Milestones: Journeying into Adulthood – Office for National Statistics.* https://www.ons.gov.uk/peoplepopulationandcommunity/populationandmigration/populationestimates/articles/milestonesjourneyingintoadulthood/2019-02-18

ONS. (2019c). *Suicides in the UK – Office for National Statistics.* https://www.ons.gov.uk/peoplepopulationandcommunity/birthsdeathsandmarriages/deaths/bulletins/suicidesintheunitedkingdom/2018registrations

ONS. (2019d). *What Is the Difference Between Sex and Gender? Office for National Statistics.* https://www.ons.gov.uk/economy/environmentalaccounts/articles/whatisthe differencebetweensexandgender/2019-02-21

ONS. (2020a). *Coronavirus (COVID-19) related deaths by ethnic group, England and Wales—Office for National Statistics. [Table 4 shows sex differences].* https://tinyurl.com/y6d6yjj4

ONS. (2020). *Deaths Involving COVID-19, UK – Office for National Statistics.* https://www.ons.gov.uk/peoplepopulationandcommunity/birthsdeathsandmarriages/deaths/bulletins/deathsinvolvingcovid19uk/deathsoccurringbetween1marchand30april2020

Opazo, R. M. (2008). *Latino youth and machismo: working towards a more complex understanding of marginalized masculinities.* Retrieved from Ryerson University Digital Commons Thesis Dissertation Paper, 108.

Opondo, C., Redshaw, M., Savage-McGlynn, E., & Quigley, M. A. (2016). Father involvement in early child-rearing and behavioural outcomes in their pre-adolescent children: evidence from the ALSPAC UK birth cohort. *BMJ Open, 6*(11), e012034. https://doi.org/10.1136/bmjopen-2016-012034

Orwell, G. (1945). *George Orwell: Notes on Nationalism.* https://orwell.ru/library/essays/nationalism/english/e_nat

Oxford Research & Policy | Resources for Athena SWAN and Juno. (2017). https://www.oxfordresearchandpolicy.co.uk/supporting-athena-swan/resourses-for-athena-swan/

Page, A., Liu, S., Gunnell, D., Astell-Burt, T., Feng, X., Wang, L., & Zhou, M. (2017). Suicide by pesticide poisoning remains a priority for suicide prevention in China: analysis of national mortality trends 2006–2013. *Journal of Affective Disorders, 208,* 418–423. https://doi.org/10.1016/j.jad.2016.10.047

Paolacci, G., Chandler, J., & Ipeirotis, P. G. (2010). *Running Experiments on Amazon Mechanical Turk* (SSRN Scholarly Paper ID 1626226). Social Science Research Network. https://papers.ssrn.com/abstract=1626226

Pape, M. (2020). Gender segregation and trajectories of organizational change: the under-representation of women in sports leadership. *Gender & Society, 34*(1), 81–105. https://doi.org/10.1177/0891243219867914

Pardue, M. L., & Wizemann, T. M. (Eds.). (2001). *Exploring the Biological Contributions to Human Health: Does Sex Matter?* National Academies Press.

Paul, K. I., & Moser, K. (2009). Unemployment impairs mental health: meta-analyses. *Journal of Vocational Behavior, 74*(3), 264–282. https://doi.org/10.1016/j.jvb.2009.01.001

Paulson, J. F., & Bazemore, S. D. (2010). Prenatal and postpartum depression in fathers and its association with maternal depression: a meta-analysis. *JAMA, 303*(19), 1961. https://doi.org/10.1001/jama.2010.605

Pecora, P. J., Whittaker, J. K., Barth, R. P., Borja, S., & Vesneski, W. (2018). *The Child Welfare Challenge: Policy, Practice, and Research.* Oxfordshire: Routledge.

Pelletier, R., Khan, N. A., Cox, J., Daskalopoulou, S. S., Eisenberg, M. J., Bacon, S. L., Lavoie, K. L., Daskupta, K., Rabi, D., Humphries, K. H., Norris, C. M., Thanassoulis, G., Behlouli, H., & Pilote, L. (2016). Sex versus gender-related characteristics. *Journal of the American College of Cardiology, 67*(2), 127–135. https://doi.org/10.1016/j.jacc.2015.10.067

Perheentupa, A., Mäkinen, J., Laatikainen, T., Vierula, M., Skakkebaek, N. E., Andersson, A. M., & Toppari, J. (2013). A cohort effect on serum testosterone levels in Finnish men. *European Journal of Endocrinology, 168*(2), 227–233. https://doi.org/10.1530/EJE-12-0288

Peterson, B., Boivin, J., Norré, J., Smith, C., Thorn, P., & Wischmann, T. (2012). An introduction to infertility counseling: a guide for mental health and medical professionals. *Journal of Assisted Reproduction and Genetics, 29*(3), 243–248. https://doi.org/10.1007/s10815-011-9701-y

Pew. (2013). Breadwinner Moms. *Pew Research Center's Social & Demographic Trends Project.* https://www.pewsocialtrends.org/2013/05/29/breadwinner-moms/

Phillips, J. (2001). Cultural construction of manhood in prison. *Psychology of Men & Masculinity, 2*(1), 13.

Phipps, C., Seager, M., Murphy, L., & Barker, C. (2017). Psychologically informed environments for homeless people: resident and staff experiences. *Housing, Care and Support, 20*(1), 29–42. https://doi.org/10.1108/HCS-10-2016-0012

Pietri, E. S., Hennes, E. P., Dovidio, J. F., Brescoll, V. L., Bailey, A. H., Moss-Racusin, C. A., & Handelsman, J. (2019). Addressing unintended consequences of gender diversity interventions on women's sense of belonging in STEM. *Sex Roles, 80*(9), 527–547. https://doi.org/10.1007/s11199-018-0952-2

Player, M. J., Proudfoot, J., Fogarty, A., Whittle, E., Spurrier, M., Shand, F., Christensen, H., Hadzi-Pavlovic, D., & Wilhelm, K. (2015). What interrupts suicide attempts in men: a qualitative study. *PLoS ONE, 10*, 6. https://doi.org/10.1371/journal.pone.0128180

Plester, B. A., & Sayers, J. (2007). "Taking the piss": functions of banter in the IT industry. *Humor – International Journal of Humor Research, 20*, 2. https://doi.org/10.1515/HUMOR.2007.008

Plomin, R., DeFries, J., & Knopik, V. (2012). *Behavioral Genetics* (6th edition). New York: Worth Publishers.

Pluckrose, H., & Lindsay, J. (2020). *Cynical Theories: How Activist Scholarship Made Everything about Race, Gender, and Identity – And Why This Harms Everybody.* Pitchstone Publishing.

Pollard, J. (2016). Early and effective intervention in male mental health. *Perspectives in Public Health.* https://doi.org/10.1177/1757913916666219

Ponton, H., Osborne, A., Thompson, N., & Greenwood, D. (2020). The power of humour to unite and divide: a case study of design coordination meetings in construction. *Construction Management and Economics, 38*(1), 32–54. https://doi.org/10.1080/01446193.2019.1656339

Pop, D. (2017). *?Major-effects-of-psyops-on-military-actions_Content File-PDF.pd.* https://www-ceeol-com.libproxy.ucl.ac.uk/search/viewpdf?id=609095

Popper, K. R. (1959). *The Logic of Scientific Discovery.* University Press.

Portela-Pino, I., López-Castedo, A., Martínez-Patiño, M. J., Valverde-Esteve, T., & Domínguez-Alonso, J. (2020). Gender differences in motivation and barriers for the practice of physical exercise in adolescence. *International Journal of Environmental Research and Public Health, 17*(1), 168. https://doi.org/10.3390/ijerph17010168

Powney, D., & Graham-Kevan, N. (2019). Male victims of intimate partner violence: a challenge to the gendered paradigm. In J. A. Barry, R. Kingerlee, M. Seager, & L. Sullivan (Eds.), *The Palgrave Handbook of Male Psychology and Mental Health* (pp. 123–143). Springer International Publishing. https://doi.org/10.1007/978-3-030-04384-1_7

Prättälä, R., Paalanen, L., Grinberga, D., Helasoja, V., Kasmel, A., & Petkeviciene, J. (2007). Gender differences in the consumption of meat, fruit and vegetables are similar in Finland and the Baltic countries. *European Journal of Public Health, 17*(5), 520–525. https://doi.org/10.1093/eurpub/ckl265

Prediger, D. J. (1982). Dimensions underlying Holland's hexagon: missing link between interests and occupations? *Journal of Vocational Behavior, 21*(3), 259–287. https://doi.org/10.1016/0001-8791(82)90036-7

Priest, R. F., & Swain, J. E. (2002). Humor and its implications for leadership effectiveness. *HUMOR, 15*(2), 169–189. https://doi.org/10.1515/humr.2002.010

Proulx. (1997). Homophobia in Northeastern Brazilian university students. *Journal of Homosexuality, 34*(1), 47–56. https://doi.org/10.1300/J082v34n01_04

Public Health England. (2018). *Drug misuse deaths fall but still remain too high – public health matters.* https://publichealthmatters.blog.gov.uk/2018/08/08/drug-misuse-deaths-fall-but-still-remain-too-high/

Public Health England. (2019). *Health Profile for England 2019 by Public Health England on Exposure. Exposure.* https://publichealthengland.exposure.co/health-profile-for-england-2019

Public Health England. (2020). COVID-19: mental health and wellbeing surveillance report. https://www.gov.uk/government/publications/covid-19-mental-health-and-wellbeing-surveillance-report

Quillette. (2018, October 1). The grievance studies scandal: five academics respond. *Quillette.* https://quillette.com/2018/10/01/the-grievance-studies-scandal-five-academics-respond/

Raglin, J. S. (1992). 9: Anxiety and Sport Performance. *Exercise and Sport Sciences Reviews, 20*(1), 243–274. https://doi.org/10.1249/00003677-199200200-00009

Raine, A., Yang, Y., Narr, K. L., & Toga, A. W. (2011). Sex differences in orbitofrontal gray as a partial explanation for sex differences in antisocial personality. *Molecular Psychiatry, 16*(2), 227–236. https://doi.org/10.1038/mp.2009.136

Räisänen, U., & Hunt, K. (2014). The role of gendered constructions of eating disorders in delayed help-seeking in men: a qualitative interview study: Table 1. *BMJ Open, 4*(4), e004342. https://doi.org/10.1136/bmjopen-2013-004342

Ramos. (2020, June 20). Exploring "Other Ways of Knowing": the new religious threat to science education. *Quillette.* https://quillette.com/2020/06/20/exploring-other-ways-of-knowing-the-new-religious-threat-to-science-education/

Reddy, P., Dutke, S., Papageorgi, I., & Bakker, H. (2014). Educating Europe. *Psychologist, 27*(12), 928–931.

Reddy, P., Dias, I., Holland, C., Campbell, N., Nagar, I., Connolly, L., Krustrup, P., & Hubball, H. (2017). Walking football as sustainable exercise for older adults – A pilot investigation. *European Journal of Sport Science, 17*(5), 638–645. https://doi.org/10.1080/17461391.2017.1298671

Regitz-Zagrosek, V. (2012). Sex and gender differences in health. *EMBO Reports, 13*(7), 596–603. https://doi.org/10.1038/embor.2012.87

Rehm, J., Mathers, C., Popova, S., Thavorncharoensap, M., Teerawattananon, Y., & Patra, J. (2009). Global burden of disease and injury and economic cost attributable to alcohol use and alcohol-use disorders. *The Lancet, 373*(9682), 2223–2233. https://doi.org/10.1016/S0140-6736(09)60746-7

Reidy, D. E., Smith-Darden, J. P., Cortina, K. S., Kernsmith, R. M., & Kernsmith, P. D. (2015). Masculine discrepancy stress, teen dating violence, and sexual violence perpetration among adolescent boys. *The Journal of Adolescent Health: Official Publication of the Society for Adolescent Medicine, 56*(6), 619–624. https://doi.org/10.1016/j.jadohealth.2015.02.009

Reiner, A. (2020). *Better Boys, Better Men – Andrew Reiner – Hardcover.* https://www.harpercollins.com/9780062854940/better-boys-better-men/

Reivich, K. J., Seligman, M. E. P., & McBride, S. (2011). Master resilience training in the U.S. Army. *American Psychologist, 66*(1), 25–34. https://doi.org/10.1037/a0021897

Reynolds, T., Howard, C., Sjåstad, H., Zhu, L., Okimoto, T. G., Baumeister, R. F., Aquino, K., & Kim, J. (2020). Man up and take it: gender bias in moral typecasting. *Organizational Behavior and Human Decision Processes, 161*, 120–141. https://doi.org/10.1016/j.obhdp.2020.05.002

Rhee, S. H., & Waldman, I. D. (2002). Genetic and environmental influences on antisocial behavior: a meta-analysis of twin and adoption studies. *Psychological Bulletin, 128*(3), 490–529. https://doi.org/10.1037/0033-2909.128.3.490

Rice, S., Fallon, B., & Bambling, M. (2011). Men and depression: the impact of masculine role norms throughout the lifespan. *The Australian Educational and Developmental Psychologist, 28*(2), 133–144. https://doi.org/10.1375/aedp.28.2.133

Rice, S. M., Ogrodniczuk, J. S., Kealy, D., Seidler, Z. E., Dhillon, H. M., & Oliffe, J. L. (2019). Validity of the male depression risk scale in a representative Canadian sample: sensitivity and specificity in identifying men with recent suicide attempt. *Journal of Mental Health, 28*(2), 132–140. https://doi.org/10.1080/09638237.2017.1417565

Richerson, P. J., & Boyd, R. (2008). *Not By Genes Alone: How Culture Transformed Human Evolution.* University of Chicago Press.

Ridge, D. (2019). Games people play: the collapse of "masculinities" and the rise of masculinity as spectacle. In J. A. Barry, R. Kingerlee, M. Seager, & L. Sullivan (Eds.), *The Palgrave Handbook of Male Psychology and Mental Health* (pp. 205–225). Springer International Publishing. https://doi.org/10.1007/978-3-030-04384-1_12

Rippon, G. (2019). *The Gendered Brain: The New Neuroscience that Shatters the Myth of the Female Brain.* Random House.

Risberg, G., Johansson, E. E., & Hamberg, K. (2011). 'Important... but of low status': male education leaders' views on gender in medicine. *Medical Education, 45*(6), 613–624. https://doi.org/10.1111/j.1365-2923.2010.03920.x

Roberts, S. E., Jaremin, B., & Lloyd, K. (2013). High-risk occupations for suicide. *Psychological Medicine, 43*(6), 1231–1240. https://doi.org/10.1017/S0033291712002024

Robertson, I. T., Cooper, C. L., Sarkar, M., & Curran, T. (2015). Resilience training in the workplace from 2003 to 2014: a systematic review. *Journal of Occupational and Organizational Psychology, 88*(3), 533–562. https://doi.org/10.1111/joop.12120

Robertson, S., Gough, B., Hanna, E., Raine, G., Robinson, M., Seims, A., & White, A. (2018). Successful mental health promotion with men: the evidence from 'tacit knowledge'. *Health Promotion International, 33*(2), 334–344. https://doi.org/10.1093/heapro/daw067

Romano, E., Babchishin, L., Marquis, R., & Fréchette, S. (2015). Childhood maltreatment and educational outcomes. *Trauma, Violence, & Abuse, 16*(4), 418–437. https://doi.org/10.1177/1524838014537908

Rona, R. J., Jones, M., Sundin, J., Goodwin, L., Hull, L., Wessely, S., & Fear, N. T. (2012). Predicting persistent posttraumatic stress disorder (PTSD) in UK military personnel who served in Iraq: a longitudinal study. *Journal of Psychiatric Research, 46*(9), 1191–1198. https://doi.org/10.1016/j.jpsychires.2012.05.009

Roos, G., Prättälä, R., & Koski, K. (2001). Men, masculinity and food: interviews with Finnish carpenters and engineers. *Appetite, 37*(1), 47–56. https://doi.org/10.1006/appe.2001.0409

Roper, T., & Barry, J. A. (2016). Is having a haircut good for your mental health? *New Male Studies, 5*(2), 18.

Roter, D., & Hall, J. A. (2006). *Doctors Talking with Patients/Patients Talking with Doctors: Improving Communication in Medical Visits.* Greenwood Publishing Group.

Roter, D., Lipkin, M., & Korsgaard, A. (1991). Sex differences in patients?? And physicians?? Communication during primary care medical visits. *Medical Care, 29*(11), 1083–1093. https://doi.org/10.1097/00005650-199111000-00002

Rotermann, M. (2007). Marital breakdown. *Health Reports, 18*(2), 33–44.

Roy, P., Tremblay, G., & Robertson, S. (2014). Help-seeking among male farmers: connecting masculinities and mental health. *Sociologia Ruralis, 54*(4), 460–476.

Royal British Legion. (2018, May 14). *300,000 Veterans living with hearing loss in the UK – Legion urges veterans to seek help during deaf awareness week. Cobseo.* https://www.cobseo.org.uk/300000-veterans-living-hearing-loss-uk-legion-urges-veterans-seek-help-deaf-awareness-week/

Rubinstein, N. (2010, May 28). *Should We Feel Sympathy for Sociopaths?* GoodTherapy. Org Therapy Blog. https://www.goodtherapy.org/blog/empathy-for-sociopathy/

Rudman, L. A., & Goodwin, S. A. (2004). Gender differences in automatic in-group bias: why do women like women more than men like men? *Journal of Personality and Social Psychology, 87*(4), 494–509. https://doi.org/10.1037/0022-3514.87.4.494

Rumney, P. N. S., & Fenton, R. A. (2013). Rape, defendant anonymity and evidence-based policy making: rape, defendant anonymity and evidence-based policy making. *The Modern Law Review, 76*(1), 109–133. https://doi.org/10.1111/1468-2230.12004

Russ, S., Ellam-Dyson, V., Seager, M., & Barry, J. (2015). Coaches' views on differences in treatment style for male and female clients. *New Male Studies, 4*(3), 18.

Ruth, K. S., Day, F. R., Tyrrell, J., Thompson, D. J., Wood, A. R., Mahajan, A., Beaumont, R. N., Wittemans, L., Martin, S., Busch, A. S., Erzurumluoglu, A. M., Hollis, B., O'Mara, T. A., McCarthy, M. I., Langenberg, C., Easton, D. F., Wareham, N. J., Burgess, S., Murray, A., & Perry, J. R. B. (2020). Using human genetics to understand the disease impacts of testosterone in men and women. *Nature Medicine*, 1–7. https://doi.org/10.1038/s41591-020-0751-5

Sagar-Ouriaghli, I., Godfrey, E., Bridge, L., Meade, L., & Brown, J. S. L. (2019). Improving mental health service utilization among men: a systematic review and synthesis of behavior change techniques within interventions targeting help-seeking. *American Journal of Men's Health, 13*(3), 155798831985700. https://doi.org/10.1177/1557988319857009

Saleh, R. A., Ranga, G. M., Raina, R., Nelson, D. R., & Agarwal, A. (2003). Sexual dysfunction in men undergoing infertility evaluation: a cohort observational study. *Fertility and Sterility, 79*(4), 909–912. https://doi.org/10.1016/S0015-0282(02)04921-X

Salisbury, E. J., & Van Voorhis, P. (2009). Gendered pathways: a quantitative investigation of women probationers' paths to incarceration. *Criminal Justice and Behavior, 36*(6), 541–566.

Sample, C., Justice, C., & Darraj, E. (2019). A model for evaluating fake news. *The Cyber Defense Review, 171–192*(JSTOR). https://doi.org/10.2307/26846127

Samuels, J. (2003). *Reviewing the Play: How Faulty Premises Affected the Work of the Commission on Opportunity in Athletics and Why Title IX Protections Are Still Needed to Ensure Equal Opportunity in Athletics. 3*, 25.

Sanday, P. R. (1980). Margaret mead's view of sex roles in her own and other societies. *American Anthropologist, 82*(2), 340–348. https://doi.org/10.1525/aa.1980.82.2.02a00060

Sanders, R. (1987). The Pareto Principle: its use and abuse. *Journal of Services Marketing, 1*(2), 37–40. https://doi.org/10.1108/eb024706

Sandilands, G. P., Wilson, M., Huser, C., Jolly, L., Sands, W. A., & McSharry, C. (2010). Were monocytes responsible for initiating the cytokine storm in the TGN1412 clinical trial tragedy? *Clinical & Experimental Immunology, 162*(3), 516–527. https://doi.org/10.1111/j.1365-2249.2010.04264.x

Sarkadi, A., Kristiansson, R., Oberklaid, F., & Bremberg, S. (2008). Fathers' involvement and children's developmental outcomes: a systematic review of longitudinal studies. *Acta Paediatrica, 97*(2), 153–158. https://doi.org/10.1111/j.1651-2227.2007.00572.x

Sax, L. (2009). *Boys Adrift: The Five Factors Driving the Growing Epidemic of Unmotivated Boys and Underachieving Young Men: Amazon.co.uk: Sax, Leonard: 9780465072101: Books.* https://www.amazon.co.uk/Boys-Adrift-Epidemic-Unmotivated-Underachieving/dp/0465072100

Schiffer, B., Müller, B. W., Scherbaum, N., Hodgins, S., Forsting, M., Wiltfang, J., Gizewski, E. R., & Leygraf, N. (2011). Disentangling structural brain alterations associated with violent behavior from those associated with substance use disorders. *Archives of General Psychiatry, 68*(10), 1039–1049. https://doi.org/10.1001/archgenpsychiatry.2011.61

Schiltz, K., Witzel, J. G., Bausch-Hölterhoff, J., & Bogerts, B. (2013). High prevalence of brain pathology in violent prisoners: a qualitative CT and MRI scan study. *European Archives of Psychiatry and Clinical Neuroscience, 263*(7), 607–616. https://doi.org/10.1007/s00406-013-0403-6

Schimmack, U. (2019). The implicit association test: a method in search of a construct. *Perspectives on Psychological Science,* 1745691619863798. https://doi.org/10.1177/1745691619863798

Schlichthorst, M., King, K., Turnure, J., Phelps, A., & Pirkis, J. (2019). Engaging Australian men in masculinity and suicide-a concept test of social media materials and a website. *Health Promotion Journal of Australia: Official Journal of Australian Association of Health Promotion Professionals, 30*(3), 390.

Schoenbaum, M., Kessler, R. C., Gilman, S. E., Colpe, L. J., Heeringa, S. G., Stein, M. B., Ursano, R. J., & Cox, K. L. (2014). Predictors of suicide and accident death in the army study to assess risk and resilience in service members (army STARRS): results from the army study to assess risk and resilience in service members (army STARRS). *JAMA Psychiatry, 71*(5), 493–503. https://doi.org/10.1001/jamapsychiatry.2013.4417

Schwalbe, M. (1996). *Unlocking the Iron Cage: Men's Movement, Gender Politics and American Culture.* Oxford University Press Inc.

Scorza, P., Duarte, C. S., Hipwell, A. E., Posner, J., Ortin, A., Canino, G., & Monk, C. (2019). Research Review: intergenerational transmission of disadvantage: epigenetics and parents' childhoods as the first exposure. *Journal of Child Psychology and Psychiatry, and Allied Disciplines, 60*(2), 119–132. https://doi.org/10.1111/jcpp.12877

Seager, M. (2011). Homelessness is more than houselessness: a psychologically-minded approach to inclusion and rough sleeping. *Mental Health and Social Inclusion, 15*(4), 183–189. https://doi.org/10.1108/20428301111186822

Seager, M. (2013, October 8). *Using Attachment Theory to Inform Psychologically Minded Care Services, Systems and Environments. Attachment Theory in Adult Mental Health;* Routledge. https://doi.org/10.4324/9781315883496-29

Seager, M. (2019). From stereotypes to archetypes: an evolutionary perspective on male help-seeking and suicide. In J. A. Barry, R. Kingerlee, M. Seager, & L. Sullivan (Eds.), *The Palgrave Handbook of Male Psychology and Mental Health* (pp. 227–248). Springer International Publishing. https://doi.org/10.1007/978-3-030-04384-1_12

Seager, M., & Barry, J. A. (2019a). Cognitive distortion in thinking about gender issues: gamma bias and the gender distortion matrix. In J. A. Barry, R. Kingerlee, M. Seager, & L. Sullivan (Eds.), *The Palgrave Handbook of Male Psychology and Mental Health* (pp. 417–438). Springer International Publishing. https://doi.org/10.1007/978-3-030-04384-1_21

Seager, M., & Barry, J. A. (2019b). Positive masculinity: including masculinity as a valued aspect of humanity. In J. A. Barry, R. Kingerlee, M. Seager, & L. Sullivan (Eds.), *The Palgrave Handbook of Male Psychology and Mental Health* (pp. 105–122). Springer International Publishing. https://doi.org/10.1007/978-3-030-04384-1_21

Seager, M. J., & Barry, J. A. (2020). Delta bias in how we celebrate gender-typical traits and behaviours. *Psychreg Journal of Psychology, 4*(3), 166–169.

Seager, M., Sullivan, L., & Barry, J. (2014a). Gender-related schemas and suicidality: validation of the male and female traditional gender scripts questionnaires. *New Male Studies, 3*(3), 34–54.

Seager, M., Sullivan, L., & Barry, J. (2014b). The Male Psychology Conference, University College London, June 2014. *New Male Studies, 3*(2), 28.

Seager, M., & Thümmel, U. (2009). 'Chocolates and flowers? You must be joking!' of men and tenderness in group therapy. *Group Analysis.* https://doi.org/10.1177/0533316409341335

Sell, A., Hone, L. S. E., & Pound, N. (2012). The importance of physical strength to human males. *Human Nature, 23*(1), 30–44. https://doi.org/10.1007/s12110-012-9131-2

Servin, A., Bohlin, G., & Berlin, L. (1999). Sex differences in 1-, 3-, and 5-year-olds' toy-choice in a structured play-session. *Scandinavian Journal of Psychology, 40*(1), 43–48. https://doi.org/10.1111/1467-9450.00096

Shand, F. L., Proudfoot, J., Player, M. J., Fogarty, A., Whittle, E., Wilhelm, K., Hadzi-Pavlovic, D., McTigue, I., Spurrier, M., & Christensen, H. (2015). What might interrupt men's suicide? Results from an online survey of men. *BMJ Open, 5*(10), e008172. https://doi.org/10.1136/bmjopen-2015-008172

Sharpe, R. M. (2017). Environmental causes of testicular dysfunction. In S. J. Winters & I. T. Huhtaniemi (Eds.), *Male Hypogonadism: Basic, Clinical and Therapeutic Principles* (pp. 281–304). Springer International Publishing. https://doi.org/10.1007/978-3-319-53298-1_14

Sharma, N., & Sharma, K. (2015). Self-fulfilling prophecy: a literature review. *International Journal of Interdisciplinary and Multidisciplinary Studies, 2*(3), 41–42.

Shenfeld, T. (2019). What are the telltale signs that you need to change therapists? *Child Psychology Resources.* https://www.psy-ed.com/wpblog/change-therapist

Shermer, M. (2005). *Rumsfeld's Wisdom. Scientific American.* https://doi.org/10.1038/scientificamerican0905-38

Shields, D., & Westwood, M. (2019). Counselling male military personnel and veterans: addressing challenges and enhancing engagement. In J. A. Barry, R.

Kingerlee, M. Seager, & L. Sullivan (Eds.), *The Palgrave Handbook of Male Psychology and Mental Health* (pp. 417–438). Springer International Publishing. https://doi.org/10.1007/978-3-030-04384-1_21

Shiner, M., Scourfield, J., Fincham, B., & Langer, S. (2009). When things fall apart: gender and suicide across the life-course. *Social Science & Medicine, 69*(5), 738–746.

Shirani, F., Henwood, K., & Coltart, C. (2012). "Why Aren't You at Work?": negotiating economic models of fathering identity. *Fathering: A Journal of Theory, Research, and Practice about Men as Fathers, 10*(3), 274–290. https://doi.org/10.3149/fth.1003.274

Shorrocks, R. (2018). Cohort change in political gender gaps in Europe and Canada: the role of modernization. *Politics & Society, 46*(2), 135–175. https://doi.org/10.1177/0032329217751688

Shpancer. (2018). Stereotype accuracy: a displeasing truth. *Psychology Today.* https://www.psychologytoday.com/blog/insight-therapy/201809/stereotype-accuracy-displeasing-truth

Shum-Pearce, A. (2016). *Young Men Talk about Partner Abuse: Experiences, Beliefs, and Help-Seeking After Partner Abuse from Women* [PhD Thesis]. ResearchSpace@ Auckland.

Siegel, J. A., & Williams, L. M. (2003). The relationship between child sexual abuse and female delinquency and crime: a prospective study. *Journal of Research in Crime and Delinquency, 40*(1), 71–94. https://doi.org/10.1177/0022427802239254

Sierra Hernandez, C. A., Han, C., Oliffe, J. L., & Ogrodniczuk, J. S. (2014). Understanding help-seeking among depressed men. *Psychology of Men & Masculinity, 15*(3), 346–354. https://doi.org/10.1037/a0034052

Signorella, M. L., Bigler, R. S., & Liben, L. S. (1993). Developmental differences in children's gender schemata about others: a meta-analytic review. *Developmental Review, 13*(2), 147–183. https://doi.org/10.1006/drev.1993.1007

Simpson, T. L., & Miller, W. R. (2002). Concomitance between childhood sexual and physical abuse and substance use problems: a review. *Clinical Psychology Review, 22*(1), 27–77.

Sinkeviciute, V. (2017). 'It's just a bit of cultural [...] lost in translation': Australian and British intracultural and intercultural metapragmatic evaluations of jocularity. *Lingua, 197*, 50–67. https://doi.org/10.1016/j.lingua.2017.03.004

Sisask, M., Värnik, A., K[otilde]lves, K., Bertolote, J. M., Bolhari, J., Botega, N. J., Fleischmann, A., Vijayakumar, L., & Wasserman, D. (2010). Is religiosity a protective factor against attempted suicide: a cross-cultural case-control study. *Archives of Suicide Research, 14*(1), 44–55. https://doi.org/10.1080/13811110903479052

Skärsäter, I., Dencker, K., Häggström, L., & Fridlund, B. (2003). A salutogenetic perspective on how men cope with major depression in daily life, with the help of professional and lay support. *International Journal of Nursing Studies, 40*(2), 153–162. https://doi.org/10.1016/S0020-7489(02)00044-5

Sloan, C., Gough, B., & Conner, M. (2010). Healthy masculinities? How ostensibly healthy men talk about lifestyle, health and gender. *Psychology & Health, 25*(7), 783–803. https://doi.org/10.1080/08870440902883204

Slote, M. (2020). Yin-yang, mind, and heart-mind. In M. Slote (Ed.), *Between Psychology and Philosophy: East-West Themes and Beyond* (pp. 5–26). Springer International Publishing. https://doi.org/10.1007/978-3-030-22503-2_2

Smiler, A. P. (2006). Conforming to masculine norms: evidence for validity among adult men and women. *Sex Roles, 54*(11–12), 767–775. https://doi.org/10.1007/s11199-006-9045-8

Smith, J., Lad, S., & Hiskey, S. (2019). Of compassion and men: using compassion focused therapy in working with men. In J. A. Barry, R. Kingerlee, M. Seager, & L. Sullivan (Eds.), *The Palgrave Handbook of Male Psychology and Mental Health* (pp. 483–507). Springer International Publishing. https://doi.org/10.1007/978-3-030-04384-1_24

Smith, K. L., Matheson, F. I., Moineddin, R., Dunn, J. R., Lu, H., Cairney, J., & Glazier, R. H. (2013). Gender differences in mental health service utilization among respondents reporting depression in a national health survey. *Health*, 2013.

Söderlund, T., & Madison, G. (2015). Characteristics of gender studies publications: a bibliometric analysis based on a Swedish population database. *Scientometrics, 105*(3), 1347–1387. https://doi.org/10.1007/s11192-015-1702-7

Solal, I., & Snellman, K. (2019). Women don't mean business? Gender penalty in board composition. *Organization Science, 30*(6), 1270–1288. https://doi.org/10.1287/orsc.2019.1301

Solomonov, N., & Barber, J. P. (2018). Patients' perspectives on political self-disclosure, the therapeutic alliance, and the infiltration of politics into the therapy room in the Trump era. *Journal of Clinical Psychology, 74*(5), 779–787. https://doi.org/10.1002/jclp.22609

Sommers, C. H. (1995). *Who Stole Feminism? How Women Have Betrayed Women*. Simon and Schuster.

Spörrle, M., & Försterling, F. (2007). Which thoughts can kill a boxer? Naïve theories about cognitive and emotional antecedents of suicide. *Psychology and Psychotherapy: Theory, Research and Practice, 80*(4), 497–512.

Stack, S. (2016). Suicide and Divorce. In *Encyclopedia of Family Studies* (pp. 1–5). American Cancer Society. https://doi.org/10.1002/9781119085621.wbefs084

Stearns, E., & Glennie, E. J. (2006). When and Why Dropouts Leave High School. *Youth & Society, 38*(1), 29–57. https://doi.org/10.1177/0044118X05282764

Steenkamp, M. M., Litz, B. T., & Marmar, C. R. (2020). First-line psychotherapies for military-related PTSD. *JAMA, 323*(7), 656–657. https://doi.org/10.1001/jama.2019.20825

Steinfeldt, J. A., & Steinfeldt, M. C. (2010). Gender role conflict, athletic identity, and help-seeking among high school football players. *Journal of Applied Sport Psychology, 22*(3), 262–273. https://doi.org/10.1080/10413201003691650

Stevinson, C., & Hickson, M. (2014). Exploring the public health potential of a mass community participation event. *Journal of Public Health, 36*(2), 268–274. https://doi.org/10.1093/pubmed/fdt082

Stewart-Williams, S. (2018). *The Ape that Understood the Universe: How the Mind and Culture Evolve*. Cambridge University Press.

Stewart-Williams, S., & Halsey, L. G. (2018). *Men, Women, and Science: Why the Differences and What Should Be Done?* https://doi.org/10.31234/osf.io/ms524

Stoet, G., & Yang, J. (2016). The boy problem in education and a 10-point proposal to do something about it. *New Male Studies, 5*(2), 17–35.

Stoet, G. (2017). *It's a myth that boys have beaten girls in A-level results – Male Psychology Network*. https://malepsychology.org.uk/2017/08/29/its-a-myth-that-boys-have-beaten-girls-in-a-level-results/

Stoet, G. (2019). The challenges for boys and men in twenty-first-century education. In J. A. Barry, R. Kingerlee, M. Seager, & L. Sullivan (Eds.), *The Palgrave Handbook of Male Psychology and Mental Health* (pp. 25–45). Springer International Publishing. https://doi.org/10.1007/978-3-030-04384-1_2

Stoet, G., Bailey, D. H., Moore, A. M., & Geary, D. C. (2016). Countries with higher levels of gender equality show larger national sex differences in mathematics anxiety and relatively lower parental mathematics valuation for girls. *Plos One, 11*(4), e0153857. https://doi.org/10.1371/journal.pone.0153857

Stoet, G., & Geary, D. C. (2012). Can stereotype threat explain the gender gap in mathematics performance and achievement? *Review of General Psychology, 16*(1), 93–102. https://doi.org/10.1037/a0026617

Stoet, G., & Geary, D. C. (2013). Sex differences in mathematics and reading achievement are inversely related: within- and across-nation assessment of 10 years of PISA data. *PLoS ONE, 8*, 3. https://doi.org/10.1371/journal.pone.0057988

Stoet, G., & Geary, D. C. (2018). The gender-equality paradox in science, technology, engineering, and mathematics education. *Psychological Science, 29*(4), 581–593. https://doi.org/10.1177/0956797617741719

Stoet, G., & Geary, D. C. (2019). A simplified approach to measuring national gender inequality. *Plos One, 14*(1), e0205349. https://doi.org/10.1371/journal.pone.0205349

Stoet, G., & Geary, D. C. (2020a). Gender differences in the pathways to higher education. *Proceedings of the National Academy of Sciences*. https://doi.org/10.1073/pnas.2002861117

Stoet, G., & Geary, D. C. (2020b). Sex-specific academic ability and attitude patterns in students across developed countries. *Intelligence, 81*, 101453. https://doi.org/10.1016/j.intell.2020.101453

Stokes, E. K. (2020). Coronavirus disease 2019 case surveillance – United States, January 22–May 30, 2020. *MMWR. Morbidity and Mortality Weekly Report, 69*. https://doi.org/10.15585/mmwr.mm6924e2

Strand, S., Cadwallader, S. & Firth, D (2011). Using statistical regression methods in educational research: 3.7 Adding Nominal Variables with More than Two Categories (Model 3). National Centre for Research Methods, University of Warwick. https://www.restore.ac.uk/srme/www/fac/soc/wie/research-new/srme/authors/index.html

Strömberg, R., Backlund, L. G., & Löfvander, M. (2010). A comparison between the Beck's Depression Inventory and the Gotland Male Depression Scale in detecting depression among men visiting a drop-in clinic in primary care. *Nordic Journal of Psychiatry, 64*(4), 258–264. https://doi.org/10.3109/08039480903511407

Su, R., Rounds, J., & Armstrong, P. I. (2009). Men and things, women and people: a meta-analysis of sex differences in interests. *Psychological Bulletin, 135*(6), 859–884. https://doi.org/10.1037/a0017364

Sullivan, G. (2019). Divorce is a risk factor for suicide, especially for men. *Psychology Today.* https://www.psychologytoday.com/blog/acquainted-the-night/201906/divorce-is-risk-factor-suicide-especially-men

Sullivan, A. (2020). Sex and the census: why surveys should not conflate sex and gender identity. *International Journal of Social Research Methodology, 0*(0), 1–8. https://doi.org/10.1080/13645579.2020.1768346

Sullivan, A., Joshi, H., & Leonard, D. (2010). Single-sex schooling and academic attainment at school and through the lifecourse. *American Educational Research Journal, 47*(1), 6–36. https://doi.org/10.3102/0002831209350106

Swanson, J. M., & Castellanos, F. X. (2002). Biological bases of ADHD – neuroanatomy, genetics, and pathophysiology. In P. S. Jensen & J. R. Cooper (Eds.), *Attention Deficit Hyperactivity Disorder: State of the Science-Best Practices* (pp. 7-1–7-20). Civic Research Institute.

Tajfel, H., & Turner, J. C. (1979). *An Integrative Theory of Intergroup Conflict.* Oxford University Press.

Talarowska, M. E., Gromniak-Haniecka, E., Rawska, J., & Gałecki, P. (2018). Male depression – causes, symptoms, and diagnosis. *Neuropsychiatria I Neuropsychologia; Poznan, 13*(3), 98–103. http://dx.doi.org.libproxy.ucl.ac.uk/10.5114/nan.2018.81250

Tannenbaum, C., Ellis, R. P., Eyssel, F., Zou, J., & Schiebinger, L. (2019). Sex and gender analysis improves science and engineering. *Nature, 575*(7781), 137–146. https://doi.org/10.1038/s41586-019-1657-6

Tanturri, M. L., Mills, M., Rotkirch, A., Sobotka, T., Takács, J., Miettinen, A., Faludi, C., Kantsa, V., & Nasiri, D. (2015). State-of-the-art report: childlessness in Europe. *Families and Societies, 32*, 1–53.

The Times. (1957, November 10). Work with New Electronic "Brains" Opens Field for Army Math Experts. *The Times*, 65.

Thelwall, M., Bailey, C., Tobin, C., & Bradshaw, N.-A. (2019). Gender differences in research areas, methods and topics: can people and thing orientations explain the results? *Journal of Informetrics, 13*(1), 149–169. https://doi.org/10.1016/j.joi.2018.12.002

Tilley, J., & Evans, G. (2014). Ageing and generational effects on vote choice: combining cross-sectional and panel data to estimate APC effects. *Electoral Studies, 33*, 19–27.

Todd, B. K. (2018, April 26). *Children's Colour Blindness Is Not a Black and White Issue. BPS Developmental Psychology Section.* https://www1.bps.org.uk/networks-and-communities/member-microsite/developmental-psychology-section/blog/children%E2%80%99s-colour-blindness-not-black-and-white-issue

Todd, B. K., Fischer, R. A., Di Costa, S., Roestorf, A., Harbour, K., Hardiman, P., & Barry, J. A. (2018). Sex differences in children's toy preferences: a systematic review, meta-regression, and meta-analysis. *Infant and Child Development, 27*(2), e2064.

Torchalla, I., Strehlau, V., Li, K., Schuetz, C., & Krausz, M. (2012). The association between childhood maltreatment subtypes and current suicide risk among homeless men and women. *Child Maltreatment, 17*(2), 132–143.

Travison, T. G., Araujo, A. B., Kupelian, V., O'Donnell, A. B., & McKinlay, J. B. (2007). The relative contributions of aging, health, and lifestyle factors to serum testosterone decline in men. *The Journal of Clinical Endocrinology & Metabolism, 92*(2), 549–555. https://doi.org/10.1210/jc.2006-1859

Tsai, J., & Rosenheck, R. A. (2015). Risk factors for homelessness among US veterans. *Epidemiologic Reviews, 37*(1), 177–195. https://doi.org/10.1093/epirev/mxu004

Tsui, V. (2014). Male victims of intimate partner abuse: Use and helpfulness of services. *Social Work, 59*(2), 121–130.

Tsui, V., Cheung, M., & Leung, P. (2010). Help-seeking among male victims of partner abuse: men's hard times. *Journal of Community Psychology, 38*(6), 769–780.

Tsipursky, G. (2020). *Why You Should Hire Women Over Men, According to Science. Psychology Today.* https://www.psychologytoday.com/blog/intentional-insights/202003/why-you-should-hire-women-over-men-according-science

Tzanakou, C. (2019). Unintended consequences of gender-equality plans. *Nature, 570*(7761), 277–277. https://doi.org/10.1038/d41586-019-01904-1

Tzu, S. (2003). *The Art of War: The Denma Translation.* Shambhala Publications.

Uchida, A., Bribiescas, R. G., Ellison, P. T., Kanamori, M., Ando, J., Hirose, N., & Ono, Y. (2006). Age related variation of salivary testosterone values in healthy Japanese males. *The Aging Male, 9*(4), 207–213. https://doi.org/10.1080/13685530601060461

UN. (1948). *Universal Declaration of Human Rights.* https://www.ohchr.org/EN/UDHR/Documents/UDHR_Translations/eng.pdf

UNDP. (2020). *Tackling Social Norms. A Game Changer for Gender Inequalities.* http://hdr.undp.org/sites/default/files/hd_perspectives_gsni.pdf

UNESCO. (2018). *Achieving Gender Equality in Education: Don't Forget the Boys – UNESCO Digital Library.* https://unesdoc.unesco.org/ark:/48223/pf0000262714

US Dept of Education. (2020a). *Secretary DeVos Takes Historic Action to Strengthen Title IX Protections for All Students.* U.S. Department of Education. https://www.ed.gov/news/press-releases/secretary-devos-takes-historic-action-strengthen-title-ix-protections-all-students

US Dept of Education. (2020b). *The Condition of Education – Postsecondary Education – Postsecondary Students – College Enrollment Rates – Indicator May (2020).* https://nces.ed.gov/programs/coe/indicator_cpb.asp

Valji, N., & Castillo, P. (2018). The importance of gender parity in the UN's efforts on international peace and security. *Whitehead Journal of Diplomacy and International Relations, 20*, 4.

Valkonen, J., & Hänninen, V. (2013). Narratives of masculinity and depression. *Men and Masculinities, 16*(2), 160–180. https://doi.org/10.1177/1097184X12464377

van Creveld, M. (2013). *The Privileged Sex.* CreateSpace Independent Publishing Platform.

van IJzendoorn, M. H., Moran, G., Belsky, J., Pederson, D., Bakermans-Kranenburg, M. J., & Kneppers, K. (2000). The similarity of siblings' attachments to their mother. *Child Development, 71*(4), 1086–1098. https://doi.org/10.1111/1467-8624.00211

van Wijngaarden-Cremers, P. (2019). Autism in Boys and Girls, Women and Men Throughout the Lifespan. In J. A. Barry, R. Kingerlee, M. Seager, & L. Sullivan (Eds.), *The Palgrave Handbook of Male Psychology and Mental Health* (pp. 309–330). Springer International Publishing. https://doi.org/10.1007/978-3-030-04384-1_16

Vandell, D. L., Belsky, J., Burchinal, M., Vandergrift, N., & Steinberg, L. (2010). Do effects of early child care extend to age 15 years? Results from the NICHD study of early child care and youth development. *Child Development, 81*(3), 737–756. https://doi.org/10.1111/j.1467-8624.2010.01431.x

Vecho, O., Gross, M., Gratton, E., D'Amore, S., & Green, R. J. (2019). Attitudes toward same-sex marriage and parenting, ideologies, and social contacts: the mediation role of sexual prejudice moderated by gender. *Sexuality Research and Social Policy, 16*(1), 44–57. https://doi.org/10.1007/s13178-018-0331-3

Venker, S., & Schlafly, P. (2011). *The Flipside of Feminism: What Conservative Women Know – And Men Can't Say.* WND Books.

Verdonk, P. (2007). Gender matters in medical education: integrating a gender perspective in medical curricula. Radboud University Repository. https://repository.ubn.ru.nl/handle/2066/57009

Villanueva. (2019). *Clearing House Numbers. Google Data Studio.* http://datastudio.google.com/reporting/45fd4dc2-11f2-4f71-a883-181676f7879a/page/LOKMB?feature=opengraph

Vollset, S. E., Goren, E., Yuan, C. W., Cao, J., Smith, A. E., Hsiao, T., Bisignano, C., Azhar, G. S., Castro, E., Chalek, J., Dolgert, A. J., Frank, T., Fukutaki, K., Hay, S. I., Lozano, R., Mokdad, A. H., Nandakumar, V., Pierce, M., Pletcher, M., & Murray, C. J. L. (2020). Fertility, mortality, migration, and population scenarios for 195 countries and territories from 2017 to 2100: a forecasting analysis for the Global Burden of Disease Study. *The Lancet, 0,* 0. https://doi.org/10.1016/S0140-6736(20)30677-2

Walby, S. (1989). THEORISING PATRIARCHY. *Sociology, 23*(2), 213–234.

Walby, S. (1990). *Theorizing Patriarchy | Wiley.* Wiley.Com.https://www.wiley.com/en-gb/Theorizing+Patriarchy-p-9780631147695

Wald, A. (1980). A method of estimating plane vulnerability based on damage of survivors, CRC 432, July 1980. *Center for Naval Analyses.*

Waling, A., & Fildes, D. (2017). 'Don't fix what ain't broke': evaluating the effectiveness of a Men's Shed in inner-regional Australia. *Health & Social Care in the Community, 25*(2), 758–768. https://doi.org/10.1111/hsc.12365

Wallach, J. D., Sullivan, P. G., Trepanowski, J. F., Steyerberg, E. W., & Ioannidis, J. P. A. (2016). Sex based subgroup differences in randomized controlled trials: empirical evidence from Cochrane meta-analyses. *BMJ, 355.* https://doi.org/10.1136/bmj.i5826

Walther, A., Breidenstein, J., & Miller, R. (2019). Association of testosterone treatment with alleviation of depressive symptoms in men: a systematic review and meta-analysis. *JAMA Psychiatry, 76*(1), 31–40. https://doi.org/10.1001/jamapsychiatry.2018.2734

Wang, J. (2002). Developing and testing an integrated model of choking in sport. Doctoral dissertation, Victoria University. http://vuir.vu.edu.au/230/1/02whole.pdf

Wann, D. L., & Weaver, S. (2009). Understanding the relationship between sport team identification and dimensions of social well-being. *North American Journal of Psychology, 11*(2), 219–230.

Wang, B., Xu, Y., Wu, Z., Xu, H., & Wang, D. (2015). Effect of wushu boxing teaching on college students' physical and mental health. *Education of Chinese Medicine, 1,* 9.

Wardle, J., Haase, A. M., Steptoe, A., Nillapun, M., Jonwutiwes, K., & Bellisie, F. (2004). Gender differences in food choice: the contribution of health beliefs and dieting. *Annals of Behavioral Medicine, 27*(2), 107–116.

Watson, R. J., Snapp, S., & Wang, S. (2017). What we know and where we go from here: a review of lesbian, gay, and bisexual youth hookup literature. *Sex Roles, 77*(11–12), 801–811. https://doi.org/10.1007/s11199-017-0831-2

Watt, L., & Elliot, M. (2019). Homonegativity in Britain: changing attitudes towards same-sex relationships. *The Journal of Sex Research, 56*(9), 1101–1114. https://doi.org/10.1080/00224499.2019.1623160

Weare, S. (2018). From coercion to physical force: aggressive strategies used by women against men in "forced-to-penetrate" cases in the UK. *Archives of Sexual Behavior, 47*(8), 2191–2205. https://doi.org/10.1007/s10508-018-1232-5

WEF. (2016). *The Global Gender Gap Report 2016. World Economic Forum.* https://www.weforum.org/reports/the-global-gender-gap-report-2016

Wertz, J., Caspi, A., Belsky, D. W., Beckley, A. L., Arseneault, L., Barnes, J. C., Corcoran, D. L., Hogan, S., Houts, R. M., Morgan, N., Odgers, C. L., Prinz, J. A., Sugden, K., Williams, B. S., Poulton, R., & Moffitt, T. E. (2018). Genetics and crime: integrating new genomic discoveries into psychological research about antisocial behavior. *Psychological Science, 29*(5), 791–803. https://doi.org/10.1177/0956797617744542

West, D. J., & Farrington, D. P. (1973). *Who Becomes Delinquent? Second Report of the Cambridge Study in Delinquent Development.* Crane: Russak.

West, C., & Zimmerman, D. H. (1987). Doing gender. *Gender & Society, 1*(2), 125–151.

Westwood, M. J., McLean, H., Cave, D., Borgen, W., & Slakov, P. (2010). Coming home: a group-based approach for assisting military veterans in transition. *The Journal for Specialists in Group Work, 35*(1), 44–68. https://doi.org/10.1080/01933920903466059

Whitcombe, S. (2013). Psychopathology and the conceptualisation of mental disorder: the debate around the inclusion of Parental Alienation in DSM-5. *Counselling Psychology Review, 28*(3), 13.

White, C. (2007). Mixed martial arts and boxing should be banned, says BMA. *BMJ: British Medical Journal, 335*(7618), 469. https://doi.org/10.1136/bmj.39328.674711.DB

White, H. R. (2016). Substance Abuse and Crime. In K. J. Sher (Eds.), *The Oxford Handbook of Substance Use and Substance Use Disorders: Volume 2.* Oxford University Press.

Whitley, R. (2018). Men's mental health: beyond victim-blaming. *The Canadian Journal of Psychiatry, 63*(9), 577–580. https://doi.org/10.1177/0706743718758041

Whitley, R., & Zhou, J. (2020). Clueless: an ethnographic study of young men who participate in the seduction community with a focus on their psychosocial well-being and mental health. *Plos One, 15*(2), e0229719. https://doi.org/10.1371/journal.pone.0229719

WHO. (2020). *WHO | Gender and Genetics. WHO; World Health Organization.* https://www.who.int/genomics/gender/en/

WHO | Promoting Fruit and Vegetable Consumption Around the World. (2004). WHO; World Health Organization. https://www.who.int/dietphysicalactivity/fruit/en/

Whyte, J. (2010). *Bad Thoughts: A Guide to Clear Thinking.* Penguin.

Widom, C. S., Schuck, A. M., & White, H. R. (2006). An examination of pathways from childhood victimization to violence: the role of early aggression and problematic alcohol use. *Violence and Victims, 21*(6), 675–690.

Wiepjes, C. M., den Heijer, M., Bremmer, M. A., Nota, N. M., de Blok, C. J. M., Coumou, B. J. G., & Steensma, T. D. (2020). Trends in suicide death risk in transgender people: results from the Amsterdam Cohort of Gender Dysphoria study (1972-2017). *Acta Psychiatrica Scandinavica.* https://doi.org/10.1111/acps.13164

Wierenga, L. M., Doucet, G. E., Dima, D., Agartz, I., Aghajani, M., Akudjedu, T. N., Albajes-Eizagirre, A., Alnæs, D., Alpert, K. I., Andreassen, O. A., Anticevic, A., Asherson, P., Banaschewski, T., Bargallo, N., Baumeister, S., Baur-Streubel, R., Bertolino, A., Bonvino, A., Boomsma, D. I., & Tamnes, C. K. (2020). Greater male than female variability in regional brain structure across the lifespan [Preprint]. *Neuroscience.* https://doi.org/10.1101/2020.02.17.952010

Wikipedia. (2020). International Men's Day. *Wikipedia.* https://en.wikipedia.org/w/index.php?title=International_Men%27s_Day&oldid=967569962

Wille, B., Wiernik, B. M., Vergauwe, J., Vrijdags, A., & Trbovic, N. (2018). Personality characteristics of male and female executives: distinct pathways to success? *Journal of Vocational Behavior, 106,* 220–235. https://doi.org/10.1016/j.jvb.2018.02.005

Williams, C. L. (2013). The glass escalator, revisited: gender inequality in neoliberal times, SWS feminist lecturer. *Gender & Society, 27*(5), 609–629. https://doi.org/10.1177/0891243213490232

Williams, W. H., Chitsabesan, P., Fazel, S., McMillan, T., Hughes, N., Parsonage, M., & Tonks, J. (2018). Traumatic brain injury: a potential cause of violent crime? *The Lancet. Psychiatry, 5*(10), 836–844. https://doi.org/10.1016/S2215-0366(18)30062-2

Williams, W. M., & Ceci, S. J. (2012). When scientists choose motherhood. *American Scientist, 100*(2), 138–145. https://doi.org/10.1511/2012.95.138

Williams, W. M., & Ceci, S. J. (2015). National hiring experiments reveal 2:1 faculty preference for women on STEM tenure track. *Proceedings of the National Academy of Sciences, 112*(17), 5360–5365. https://doi.org/10.1073/pnas.1418878112

Willoughby, E. A., Love, A. C., McGue, M., Iacono, W. G., Quigley, J., & Lee, J. J. (2019). Free will, determinism, and intuitive judgments about the heritability of *behavior. Behavior Genetics, 49*(2), 136–153.

Wilson, H . (2018). Statement of retraction: human reactions to rape culture and queer performativity at urban dog parks in Portland, Oregon. *Gender, Place & Culture, 27*(2), (307)-(326). https://doi.org/10.1080/0966369X.2018.1475346

Wilson, M., & Daly, M. (1985). Competitiveness, risk taking, and violence: the young male syndrome. *Ethology and Sociobiology, 6*(1), 59–73. https://doi.org/10.1016/0162-3095(85)90041-X

Winter, N. J. G. (2010). Masculine republicans and feminine democrats: gender and Americans' explicit and implicit images of the political parties. *Political Behavior, 32*(4), 587–618. https://doi.org/10.1007/s11109-010-9131-z

Wise, A. (2016). Convivial labour and the 'joking relationship': humour and everyday multiculturalism at work. *Journal of Intercultural Studies, 37*(5), 481–500. https://doi.org/10.1080/07256868.2016.1211628

Wise, A., & Velayutham, S. (2020). Humour at work: conviviality through language play in Singapore's multicultural workplaces. *Ethnic and Racial Studies, 43*(5), 911–929. https://doi.org/10.1080/01419870.2019.1588341

Wolensky, M. E. (2018). Gender differences among professional football fans: serious leisure, emotional expressivity, and cognitive distortions. Philadelphia College of Osteopathic Medicine, Dissertations Repository. https://digitalcommons.pcom.edu/cgi/viewcontent.cgi?article=1456&context=psychology_dissertations

Wolfe, N. (1991). *The Beauty Myth: How Images of Beauty Are Used Against Women*. New York: William Morrow.

Wong, Y. J., Ho, M. H. R., Wang, S. Y., & Miller, I. S. K. (2017). Meta-analyses of the relationship between conformity to masculine norms and mental health-related outcomes. *Journal of Counseling Psychology, 64*(1), 80–93. https://doi.org/10.1037/cou0000176

World Economic Forum. (2017). *Global Gender Gap Report 2020. World Economic Forum*. https://www.weforum.org/reports/gender-gap-2020-report-100-years-pay-equality/

Wright, K., & McLeod, J. (2016). Gender difference in the long-term outcome of brief therapy for employees. *New Male Studies, 5*(2), 88–110.

Xirocostas, Z. A., Everingham, S. E., & Moles, A. T. (2020). The sex with the reduced sex chromosome dies earlier: a comparison across the tree of life. *Biology Letters, 16*(3), 20190867. https://doi.org/10.1098/rsbl.2019.0867

Yang, A., Li, X., & Salmivalli, C. (2016). Maladjustment of bully-victims: validation with three identification methods. *Educational Psychology, 36*(8), 1390–1407. https://doi.org/10.1080/01443410.2015.1015492

Yang, E. Y., Lee, D. K., & Yang, J. H. (2018). Environmental endocrine disruptors and neurological disorders. *Journal of the Korean Neurological Association, 36*(3), 139–144. https://doi.org/10.2018.36.3.139

Yarrow, A. L. (2018). *Man Out: The Marginalization of Millions of Men from American Life*. Brookings Institution.

Yavorsky, J. E., & Dill, J. (2020). Unemployment and men's entrance into female-dominated jobs. *Social Science Research, 85*, 102373. https://doi.org/10.1016/j.ssresearch.2019.102373

Yousaf, O., Grunfeld, E. A., & Hunter, M. S. (2015). A systematic review of the factors associated with delays in medical and psychological help-seeking among men. *Health Psychology Review, 9*(2), 264–276. https://doi.org/10.1080/17437199.2013.840954

Zaalberg, A., Nijman, H., Bulten, E., Stroosma, L., & van der Staak, C. (2010). Effects of nutritional supplements on aggression, rule-breaking, and psychopathology among young adult prisoners. *Aggressive Behavior, 36*(2), 117–126. https://doi.org/10.1002/ab.20335

Zahn, M. A. (2008). The girls study group: charting the way to delinquency prevention for girls. US Department of Justice, Office of Justice Programs, Office of Juvenile Justice and Delinquency Prevention.

Zambrana, I. M., Ystrom, E., & Pons, F. (2012). Impact of gender, maternal education, and birth order on the development of language comprehension: a longitudinal study from 18 to 36 months of age. *Journal of Developmental & Behavioral Pediatrics, 33*(2), 146–155.

Zapf, D., Einarsen, S., Hoel, H., & Vartia, M. (2003). Empirical findings on bullying in the workplace. In S. Einarsen, H. Hoel, & C. Cooper (Eds.), *Bullying and Emotional Abuse in the Workplace: International Perspectives in Research and Practice*. CRC Press.

Zavlek, S., & Maniglia, R. (2007). Developing correctional facilities for female juvenile offenders: design and programmatic considerations. *Corrections Today, 69*(4), 58.

Zhu, K., Ou Yang, T. H., Dorie, V., Zheng, T., & Anastassiou, D. (2019). Meta-analysis of expression and methylation signatures indicates a stress-related epigenetic mechanism in multiple neuropsychiatric disorders. *Translational Psychiatry, 9*(1), 1–12. https://doi.org/10.1038/s41398-018-0358-5

Zierau, F., Bille, A., Rutz, W., & Bech, P. (2002). The Gotland male depression scale: a validity study in patients with alcohol use disorder. *Nordic Journal of Psychiatry, 56*(4), 265–271. https://doi.org/10.1080/08039480260242750

Zortea, T. C., Gray, C. M., & O'Connor, R. C. (2019). The relationship between adult attachment and suicidal thoughts and behaviors: a systematic review. *Archives of Suicide Research*, 1–36. https://doi.org/10.1080/13811118.2019.1661893

Zortea, T. C., Gray, C. M., & O'Connor, R. C. (2020). Perceptions of past parenting and adult attachment as vulnerability factors for suicidal ideation in the context of the integrated motivational–volitional model of suicidal behavior. *Suicide and Life-Threatening Behavior, 50*(2), 515–533. https://doi.org/10.1111/sltb.12606

Index

Perspectives in Male Psychology: An Introduction, First Edition.
Louise Liddon and John A. Barry.
© 2021 John Wiley & Sons, Ltd. Published 2021 by John Wiley & Sons, Ltd.